No.1 Songs In Heaven

The Sparks Story

Dave Thompson

CHERRY RED BOOKS

CONTENTS

INTRODUCTION

'There wasn't a lot to get excited about in 1974-75.' Thus spake Siouxsie Sioux in 1994, as she and I discussed the state of the British music scene 20 years earlier.

'There was Roxy Music, but Bowie was past it, Lou Reed was...losing it. And there was Sparks, and thank goodness for them, because it was really important to see them on television. They were one of the few bands you'd see and say "Thank God there's something good on in amongst all this idiocy." But that was it.'

She was right, too. Bowie and Reed had both declined mightily from the lofty musical peaks they once scaled and, while Roxy Music were certainly still in the ball park, they were scarcely the band that burst forth two years earlier, all retro-futurist spangles and death rays, *Rocky Horror* with stranger songs.

Abba's 'Waterloo' was at the top of the charts the week most people heard Sparks for the first time, and Terry Jacks' 'Seasons In The Sun' had been there the week before. Little Jimmy Osmond was still scoring regular hits, country and western was making massive chart inroads, and the best of the rest of the glam-rock explosion was either desperately in search of a new direction (ballads from Gary Glitter and Slade) or simply churning out reruns on the off-chance that inspiration might somehow be reborn (Wizzard, Alvin Stardust and Mud).

And then you switched on the radio one afternoon in late April 1974...it was just after four o'clock and it may have been a Tuesday. School was out for the day and some friends and I had retired to the common room to change. The wonderful Radio 1 was our constant companion in those days – what else was there to listen to? But that particular afternoon, the Beeb pushed its luck a little too far. For, fading in over the DJ's half-heard introduction, rushing pell-mell through a frenetic landscape strewn with spaghetti-hoop keyboards, echoing gunshots and anguished howls, and driven by a voice so high that it made the notoriously falsetto-led Stylistics sound growlingly ferocious, came the most discomforting... not to mention *annoying...* record any of us had ever heard in our lives. And that's our *entire* lives, and not just the few blessed minutes it was since the Wombles last asked us to remember what they were.

The record ended and we stood in disbelieving silence. Finally, somebody spoke; 'That was horrible...' – and then we went back to whatever we'd been doing beforehand, in the sincere belief that we'd never hear that woman again. Because that's what we thought had been singing. But we were wrong. It wasn't horrible, it wasn't discomforting, it wasn't a woman, and it certainly wasn't weird. It was Sparks.

The truth dawned swiftly. The following morning, with breakfast just a distant smell and the bedclothes still beckoning seductively, that same record came on the radio again. Tony Blackburn played it and, in my mind's eye, I could picture him grinning callously as he placed the needle on the vinyl, knowing the nightmare he was unleashing upon an early-morning nation. '*Still having trouble getting dressed, sleepyheads? Well, this'll get you moving...*'

Only this time it wasn't so frenetic, it wasn't so quirky, the gunshots made sense and even the howling fell into place. So did a few other details. The singer was a man, the song was called 'This Town Ain't Big Enough For Both Of Us' and, by the time I descended upon my local branch of WH Smith that weekend, having just executed one of the most colossal U-turns of my entire musical life, it was to discover that I was not the only person in Boscombe, Dorset, who had devoted their Saturday to procuring a copy.

I wound up walking miles and stopping by every record shop in town before I finally discovered one that still had a copy in stock and, back beside my record player that evening, I'd already played the A-side six times before I even thought of flipping the disc over – to discover that the B-side, 'Barbecutie,' was just as good. By the time Sparks made it onto *Top*

Of The Pops a fortnight or so later, they were so firmly enshrined among my all-time favourite bands that it would have taken an absolute earthquake to dislodge them.

Thirty-five years later, there have been a lot of earthquakes. Famously, May 2008 – the 34th anniversary of that maiden chart entry – saw Sparks take over Islington's Carling Academy to present more or less their entire recorded *oeuvre* in concert, 21 albums over 21 nights. And that includes the ones that we didn't think we liked at the time, and the ones that even they admit were greeted with little more than sigh of resignation; 'Oh, another Sparks album. I can't believe they're still going.'

It was a reasonable response, after all. No other band with such a history, having weathered the firestorms of the preceding decades, was still making records I felt I should listen to – when was the last time, for example, that I bought a new Slade album? A new Sweet record? Or Genesis? Why should I expect Sparks to be any different?

Because Sparks *were* different. That was why I hated them the first time I heard them, that's why I loved them so unstintingly thereafter. For, even at their worst, in those moments when the quirk-o-meter shot into the red, the lyrics fell over themselves trying to be clever, and the entire show sounded like the novelty house band in a *Carry On* movie, there was always that last thread of dignity for your ears to cling onto, one final reminder that underneath it all Sparks continued to matter. It could be 'Goofing Off' spinning out of 'Introducing', which was otherwise the first Sparks LP I never played, or 'Shopping Mall Of Love' a full decade later. It could be any one of a dozen songs that had kept me smiling when all hope seemed lost. But it was always there and all you had to do was look for it.

So I never stopped buying them, never stopped listening and the funny thing is, digging through the pile of albums that have laid unplayed since I bought them and hearing them again as I wrote this book, I discovered I kind of like them after all. Which is something I never expected to happen.

There again, that's more or less *de rigueur* with Sparks; the knowledge that whatever you're expecting from them is probably the very last thing they'll deliver. They warned us of that back in 1974, when 'Something For The Girl With Everything' ricocheted out as a single. The longer the song went on, the more astonishing were the gifts that they'd lined up for the woman of their dreams – a lot of girls, let's be truthful, would be content with chocolates, shoes and a handbag. The Maels were delivering a crate of Frank Sinatra.

But my favourite tale of the Maels' capacity to surprise...shock...stun...comes courtesy of John Lennon and a quote that, were it not for the fact that it would be commercially unmarketable (not to mention politically incorrect) on so many levels, very nearly became the title of this book.

Lennon was living in New York City at the time, and nobody seems certain which television show he was watching when he saw Sparks for the first time. It certainly wasn't the *Top Of The Pops* appearance that sundry Internet sites suggest, because no New York television station carried it. Maybe *Don Kirshner's Rock Concert*, then, or *Midnight Special* or *ABC In Concert*. It doesn't really matter which it was, Lennon was sitting there and probably not paying much attention. He'd seen so groups many come and go over the years that very little could still shock him. Until the camera zoomed in on Ron Mael at the keyboards, and then John was leaping up and down in his seat, and shouting as loud as he could....

The story is hearsay, so his exact words are unrecorded. One source has him turning to son Julian and asking 'Have you seen Sparks? They've got Hitler on the piano.' Another has him simply musing, aloud, something a little less restrained. But my favourite, the one I prefer to believe, has him leaping out of his seat and shouting, 'Fuck me, it's Hitler!'

Fuck Me, It's Hitler. Even I'd go out and buy a book with a title like that, and I wrote the thing.

Dave Thompson

8

CHAPTER ONE

WHAT'S IT GONNA BE, SOD OR CELEBRITY?

They live, like the Monkees (or the Beatles in *A Hard Day's Night*) in a sprawling California hacienda with personalised front doors. Inside, all is pristine white, the sparse Scandinavian-style furniture selected for its aesthetic values as much as its purpose. Life-sized prints of European street scenes alternate as windows with the mansion's actual views of the Pacific Ocean. But the sky is always blue, and the sea is always calm, with just enough breakers to ensure that surfing is forever in season.

It is the Palace of Versailles transplanted to Pacific Palisades. In a corner of the dining room, a bewigged and costumed string quartet plays selections from Handel and Bach, interspersed with the occasional Beach Boys song. Smart, penguin-suited staff lurk with unobtrusive military bearing in the corners, silver platters laden with canapés forever at the ready. A delicate china tea set stands on a white occasional table, the pot always steaming and filling the room with the gentle aroma of the latest choice blend.

The brothers, too, are dressed in white, moving languidly around the rooms, repositioning a magazine here, a portrait there. Occasionally one might make a gentle observation, or give instructions to the butler, in a soft-spoken voice betraying just a hint of a European accent. When they do seat themselves in the luxuriously upholstered armchairs that are so exquisitely positioned to afford maximum vantage, their limbs fold rather than bend, so that their suits never crease and their joints never crack.

Occasionally, your eye falls upon a curious nick-nack that appears totally out of place with the rest of the décor. Russell, the younger of the brothers, is an avid collector of Russian Matryoshka dolls and autographed cereal boxes; Ron, the elder, of sports figurines and snow globes. Those are his old Beatles trading cards that are framed on the walls, and his antique automobile catalogues that are displayed on the coffee tables. 'It's like a disease, collecting things,' he smiles when you catch his eye to query them, but it is a disease that has no cure, even if he wanted one. Besides, in a world where no alcohol, drugs or cigarettes have ever passed the brothers' lips, spending money on the things they love is scarcely a headline-grabbing vice.

It is a lifestyle that few of us could even imagine, much less adopt as our own. But for the brothers, it is home. They have neither known, nor demanded, anything else. Except once, a long time ago. Once, life was very different to this and, if you close your eyes to the imagery that their music so magically insinuates, it still is.

They don't really live in the same house, you know. They're not even in the same part of town. And, although they did spend some of their childhood in Pacific Palisades, they actually grew up in the lower-class Culver City, the offspring of Pennsylvania-born Meyer Mael, a graphic designer, and Miriam Moskowitz, a librarian. Her father in turn had been a school teacher, a career that Miriam herself once considered following. In the end she opted not to, but their background ensured the boys would be raised in a household that both valued and encouraged art and education.

Meyer Mael worked at the *Hollywood Citizen-News*, a left-wing daily that referred to itself as 'the Home Newspaper of Northwest Los Angeles, California', and which was once described by *Time* magazine, as 'a lonely liberal voice in the midst of [the] die-hard desert' ruled at that time by the right-wing publishing tycoons William Randolph Hearst and Harry Chandler. But while its offices, in a grandiose Wilcox Avenue edifice designed by Francis D Rutherford, may have looked a million dollars, the *Citizen-News* was a notoriously poor payer.

No matter. Mael's salary afforded his family a tidy home in Culver City, at 5263 West Adams Boulevard, and it was there that their first son, Ronald David Mael, was born on Sunday, 12th August 1945 – the same day that the United States announced it would accept the surrender of the Japanese, and bring to an end the Second World War.

A second son, Russell Craig Mael, arrived three years later on Tuesday, 5th October 1948, with the family now living at 1121 Washington Boulevard, one of the major thoroughfares through Culver City. It was in this neighbourhood that the local *Star News Vanguard* newspaper captured the two brothers' smiling faces in 1954, at the Fiesta La Ballona Kiddies Parade, an annual celebration of the first Spanish families to settle in the area. People would attend the parade – and even go into work – in costume that day; there would be floats and street vendors and a Fiesta Queen, and even a fancy-dress competition for the children. Nine year-old Ronnie and five year old Russell were winners of the Early Americans contest, and sat cross-legged and smiling for the photographer, heavily feathered and delightfully clothed. And yes, Ron already had a moustache. Either that, or it was a prophetic splash of war paint.

Sitting around in England in the early- to mid-Seventies, desperately trying to think of new things to tell the journalists who came parading into their presence, each demanding his or her own personal hot scoop on Sparks' genesis, the Maels fabricated an idyllic childhood.

Their parents' occupations singled the boys out for at least an interest in the arts, fascinations which Mr and Mrs Mael inevitably encouraged. Initially, the brothers kept the stories small and manageable. 'Every parent in Los Angeles sees their child as a potential movie star,' Ron admitted, and he and his sibling were no exception, 'then, when success eluded us in that field, piano lessons for me and violin lessons for Russell followed.' Russell even sang in the school choir, although he was adamant 'that was simply because you had to do something extra-curricular.'

Small stories, little lies. But, as time went by, and the demand for information kept building, Russell confessed that he and his brother indulged in ever more grandiose invention. 'We had done so many interviews, all asking the same thing, so we thought we ought to spice it up a little. So we were child actors, catalogue models and all that. We didn't have that background, to be honest,' he admitted, but it would not have been surprising if they had. Most parents in Los Angeles have pursued modelling as they searched for Junior's lucky break, and there are still fans who gladly take Russell at his 1974 word, scouring through the pages of vintage Fifties catalogues in search of two familiar faces. They even know where they should be looking. 'We did really well,' Russell fibbed back then, 'posing for all these different adverts. We appeared in the Roebucks' Catalogue, also Montgomery Ward's...'

There were other, more outrageous fabrications. 'We were Doris Day's sons for a long time,' Russell smirked and, in some peoples' minds, they still are. As recently as 2003, *Record Collector* magazine was repeating the fictions of a 30-year-old press release, and introducing the duo to its readers as 'brothers J Donald and Dwight Russell Day', who 'rechristened themselves Mael in a country that viewed masculinity strictly as John Wayne and the Marlboro Man'. On another occasion, whilst visiting Sweden, the Maels were astonished to receive a call from Doris Day's music publisher asking if they would visit his office in Stockholm to pick up some overdue Swedish royalties!

'There seemed to be no reason why we started doing the music,' Ron shrugged, 'so we started making up these...lies.'

The music lessons were not a fiction and, of course, they did pay off. But neither child appeared more gifted than the other, and neither won the lion's share of their parents' approval.

Three decades later, video director Sophie Muller would portray the two as prodigious sibling rivals in her video for the song 'When Do I Get To Sing "My Way"?', little Ronnie already a moustachioed and sullen-looking boy, bitterly pounding the piano, while the handsome cherubic

Russ steals their mother's heart with his singing and dancing.

In truth, however, their early childhood was happy and unscarred by any but the most mundane of boyish squabbles, a blissful state of affairs that their parents engineered by making sure that both boys were treated with absolute equality. Even gifts were offered to the pair as a joint present, and it was only the difference in age that saw Ron pick up a handful of memories that Russell would not share.

One treat that was reserved for Ron alone (at least until Russell was old enough to join him) was a regular trip to the cinema with his parents to catch whatever big movie was playing. The early- to mid-Fifties, of course, were the heyday of post-war Hollywood, and there was never any shortage of new releases, new stars or new ideas to latch on to. And so, the promise of a trip to see *The Blackboard Jungle* during the spring of 1955 probably didn't excite him any more than any of the other movies they'd witnessed over the past few weeks. Neither did Meyer and Miriam give too much thought to the movie's potential impact upon the boy. Why would they? He wasn't even ten years old.

But *The Blackboard Jungle* was no ordinary movie. Taken from a best-selling novel by a former schoolteacher, Evan Hunter, *The Blackboard Jungle* was a no-holds-barred account of life at a 'typical' American High School, Bronx Vocational High School in New York City. The portrait it painted, however, was a nightmare, a saga of feral youth at its most literal, while the headmaster turns a blind eye to everything, refusing to acknowledge that his school has a disciplinary problem.

It was a well-timed work. The problems of juvenile delinquency had been growing ever more pronounced over the previous few years, and there was no shortage of suggestions as to how the cancer could be cured. Comic books were banned for fear of the effect they might be having on impressionable young minds (there was little TV and no video games to blame in those days), and the entertainment industry at large trembled to think that it, too, might be turned upon next. Even the period's most virile celebrations of turbulent youth each had a salutary lesson somewhere within, and as screenwriter Richard Brooks worked to bring *The Blackboard Jungle* to the big screen he doubtless believed that his brutal portrayal of life on the wrong side of the tracks might itself help deter future troublemakers.

He was wrong. He was wrong from the moment the producers set about compiling the movie's soundtrack, and chose to open it with a piece of music by a raucous country and western band named Bill Haley and the Comets. It was called 'Rock Around The Clock' and, although sundry learned musicologists have since pinpointed any number of prior recordings that share the Comets' musical bearing, it single-handedly created rock'n'roll.

The nine-year-old Ron Mael sat staring at the screen in astonishment, unable to believe what he was hearing. Even once the movie started, that opening theme music played on in his mind and, when he got home that afternoon, his little brother would hear it all over again.

Ron tries to explain the impact today, but the very concepts are no longer a part of our language. It is impossible to imagine a time when rock music, pop music, the blaring radio and the big beat were not a part of our lives, to be absorbed from every avenue where we can find them. In 1955, however, that is exactly how it was. Rock music did not exist.

'Every movie, every cultural thing, even the start of television, it was all polka music and really traditional values,' he declared. The day *The Blackboard Jungle* premiered in New York City, 19th March 1955, the sweetly singing McGuire Sisters were finally approaching the end of their ten-week reign at the top of the American hit parade, and there could hardly been a soul in the country who could not now sing along with 'Sincerely'. By the end of the month, Bill Hayes' 'The Ballad Of Davy Crockett' had taken over at the top; a month later, Perez Prado's 'Cherry Pink and Apple Blossom White' would begin its own ten-week stay at Number 1. It was still there when *The Blackboard Jungle* opened in Los Angeles; it was probably still there when Ron and his parents went to see the film.

Compare that to the sound of Bill Haley. 'Rock Around The Clock,' Ron admits, sounds 'a little twee' today. Even compared to the earliest hits by Elvis Presley, Little Richard and Jerry Lee Lewis, it has a politeness that makes it the unlikeliest of all standard-bearers. But Presley had yet to make any impact on a national scale, and neither Little Richard nor Jerry Lee Lewis had yet set foot inside a recording studio. To a generation of teenagers who had *never* heard such wild sounds before, 'Rock Around The Clock' wasn't simply a call to rock'n'rolling arms, remembers Ron, 'it was like a complete jolt to your nervous system. And it obviously had the same effect on a lot of other people, because there were riots in the movie theatres!'

The opening credits had only to begin rolling, Haley needed only to count the song in – 'one two three o'clock, four o'clock rock' – and every teen in the house would rise up in response to celebrate the liberation that was bound up in that single song. 'It was so diametrically opposed to the cultural sense of things,' Ron continued and, although such thoughts were far from his mind at that tender age, even he knew that life, or at least that part of his life that was already wrapping itself in music, would never be the same again. 'It didn't make me want to be in a band,' he admitted, 'but it made me realise that that kind of music, rebelling against all the bland, awful, family-style music, was something that had to happen.' And he would rebel with it.

His parents appear to have been willing conspirators. A year later, in the summer of 1956, the boys' father came home with a couple of records that he'd bought for them, 'Hound Dog', the latest hit single by the hottest newcomer of the year, Elvis Presley, and 'Long Tall Sally' the second smash by Little Richard. And, looking back, Ron cannot contain his astonishment. Bill Haley was in the cultural dumper by then; now it was Presley who was the arch-fiend of American society, a hip-swivelling, word-slurring, long-haired ruffian whose effect on the nation's youth was one of incalculable carnage. And Little Richard, flamboyant in a manner that was open code for homosexual, wild and shrieking like a lorry-load of devils, was even worse.

'I don't know what his inspiration was for doing that,' Ron shuddered. 'They weren't the kind of records you usually bought as educational tools for your child!'

Ron was eleven and Russell 8 when their father died on 5th February 1957 and, for much of the next four years, they were raised by their mother. Understandably, it is a period they do not speak about. Times were hard, as the old cliché goes, with Miriam, a widow in her mid-thirties, struggling to bring up two growing boys. But she did it, alone at first but not forever. In August 1961, four years after Meyer's death, Miriam married Oscar Roganson – 'Rogie' to his friends and family.

They now lived on Galloway Street in Pacific Palisades, three blocks off West Sunset Boulevard. It was a modest home in a wealthy neighbourhood and, visitors swiftly discovered, an eccentric one, packed full of intriguing kitsch. There were lava lamps and statues of hula dancers with bobble heads. Magazines and newspapers were stacked wherever they looked best. Later in the decade, with Miriam and Rogie now running their own head shop, the delightfully named Gilded Prune, in Pacific Palisades, further remarkable merchandise made its way into the house – black light posters, hiply worded badges and so on.

The Maels' house was within walking distance of so many local attractions, including Wil Wright's ice cream store, where the traditional metal chairs were bent into the shape of hearts and the penny candy really did cost only a penny. There was the Bay Theatre, with the double feature Saturday matinée, and Art Poole's coffee shop, home to the best cinnamon rolls in town, as well as the Hot Dog Show, Colvey's Men's Store and the takeaway Chicken Delight – slogan 'Don't cook tonight, call Chicken Delight'. Finally, not far from all of that, was their High School.

Perched between Sunset and Bowdoin Road, Palisades High, nicknamed 'Pali,' was opened in 1961, a $7,000,000 red brick campus that catered to the educational needs of 2,100 students... 'upper-middle class students,' as *Time* magazine put it when they profiled the school in a January 1965 article entitled *On The Fringe Of A Golden Era*.

Two fellow Pali students, future film critic Michael Medved and author David Wallechinsky, later wrote a book about the article and their findings were depressing, to say the least. At the time, however, there was plenty of reason for optimism. The Vietnam War had barely begun to cast its shadow over the youth of the day, and life stretched ahead in an endless sequence of girls, cars, sun and surf.

Erase the problems that all teenagers, no matter how well-off their parents might be, are convinced ensure that their life is simply one calamitous disaster after another, and it was a Beach Boys record come to life; High School, cheerleading girls, lounging on the shore and getting evenly tanned to a golden brown, playing beach volleyball and going to the teenage fair – where, Ron bemoaned, 'these cheap-looking girl models would be vying for the title of 'Miss Teenage America', and the Beach Boys would always be advertised, but they never would show…someone like Dick Dale and the Del-Tones would come on instead.'

The *Time* piece certainly left less privileged readers with no doubt as to how perfect life for the average Pali student must have been; '"These are the students' cars," says English teacher Jeanne Hernandez, pointing to a fast collection of 'wheels' ranging up to Jags, "and there are the teachers' cars," pointing to a sedate group of compacts and the like. "It's so lush here that it's unreal," she says. "After a while you feel like a missionary in the tropics. If you don't get out, you go native."'

Like schools everywhere, the Pali campus was fiercely clique-ridden. According to *Time*, there were 'the squares who really believe in student government', the Saracens, who included 'a small motorcycling hood element', the intellectuals, 'who lounge on the steps of the administration building as the rest of the student body speculates over whether the long-haired girls among them are professional virgins or real swingers, and an amorphous crowd that defies classification by declaring unanimously: "I'm myself".' And there were the clowns, 'a group of practical jokers who wear Mickey Mouse shirts to signify that all human existence is fraudulent.'

The Mael boys slipped into another sub-section of student life, the jocks. Both were handy at baseball, while Russell – Russ, as his friends knew him – would soon be established as a quarterback for the football team, coaches Dick North and Merritt Stanfield's Dolphins.

He was not an NFL star in the making. 'I was good, but I knew my limitations. I was really too small to think of it professionally. My calling card was "He's small, but he's quick!" That justified the fact that I was a little wimp; I could run fast. In college, of course, all the athletes were six times bigger than I was.'

Away from sport and the artistic tendencies they had inherited from their father, music remained a consuming passion, even through those years at the dawn of the Sixties when the American music scene seemingly devoted itself to High School-themed balladeering that wasn't so far from the blandness that rock'n'roll had supposedly exorcised.

Slowly, however, the tide began to turn. Jan and Dean were already pushing their woodies out into the Pacific Ocean, igniting the surf-music craze that would overwhelm first Los Angeles and California, and then the entire country, as the Beach Boys set the lifestyle to music. The Shangri-Las slipped moodily onto the scene, releasing record after record filled with bad boys, worse girls, and more teenage angst than a single heart could bear. One day in school, Russell got up in front of his classmates and lip-synched his way through the Dovells' sweetly harmonic 'You Can't Sit Down'. He won a standing ovation.

But it was the Beatles who blew the Maels away; the Beatles, and then the battalion of British Invaders who followed them into the heartland of America.

'It was like Martians – in a good way,' Russell enthused. 'Musically, lyrically and even physically, English bands were so alien. It was a naïve time. The Beatles had the same haircuts as each other, but Americans just thought that was an amazing coincidence. The English accents, the manners, and the idea of thinking about an image at all, it was utterly different to what we knew.'

In August 1964, mother Miriam drove her sons to Las Vegas to see the Beatles in concert. A year later, they were at the Hollywood Bowl to see them again. But it wasn't only the Beatles. Every big British band of the day passed through Los Angeles at some point, and the Maels set out to see as many of them as they could. The Rolling Stones and the Yardbirds were particular favourites, as well as the Who, even though it would be 1967 before they got the chance to see them in person.

Russell recalled the Yardbirds' 'Happenings Ten Years Time Ago' as the first single he ever bought with his own money. Ron, however, 'was absolutely mad about the Who. I was an absolute fan of guitarist Pete Townshend.' He bought their second album, 'A Quick One While He's Away' as a British import long before it was given an American release (as 'Happy Jack'), a mark of devotion that allowed him to consider the band his own exclusive 'property'.

'I would have given anything to have been the young Pete Townshend with his Rickenbacker guitar doing the windmill thing with his arm... We were buying all the English imports when they came out – the floppy albums with the bendable covers that you couldn't get here.'

America's attempts to compete with the Brits, on the other hand, left the pair cold. They adored Motown, of course. KHJ and Boss Radio aired the Hitsville sound constantly, and when, 40 years later, the brothers were approached to compile their own 'best of Motown', fully half of their selections dated back to the early years of the label's American chart dominance.

Move away from Motor City, however, and their homeland's attempts to compete with the Fab Four were doomed to disappoint. 'The Beach Boys were the only kind of American thing we really liked... We detested folk music because it was cerebral and sedate and we had no time for that,' Ron sniffed. 'Gene Clark and the Byrds were okay, because they had electric guitars and English hairstyles...' But the rest of the pack? Forget it.

It was to see the Byrds and to catch a glimpse of Donovan, an English folkie, that Ron and Russell picked up tickets for one of the biggest local concerts of 1965, an all-star spectacular taking place at the Moulin Rouge Theatre in Hollywood on 29th November. To be truthful, the bulk of the bill really didn't interest them. Joan Baez, Ray Charles, Petula Clark, Bo Diddley, the Lovin' Spoonful, Roger Miller, the Modern Folk Quartet, the Ronettes and Ike and Tina Turner were also scheduled to perform. The evening's biggest attraction, however, was the knowledge that the entire event was to be filmed for release as the follow-up to *The TAMI Show*, a rocking spectacular that had featured both the Beach Boys and the Stones. Position themselves correctly and, who knows? The Mael boys might make it onto the big screen as well.

Which they did. The Maels' moment on screen is just that, a moment – friends of theirs, they knew, enjoyed as much, if not more, exposure as the cameras panned across the crowd. But they were there all the same.

Nevertheless, time was slipping by, and with it their teenage years. Ron celebrated his twentieth birthday in 1965, while Russell was closing in on 17, and really, if you're going to make it in California, you should be halfway to doing it by the time you reach that age. But the Maels didn't know what they wanted to do. They chased girls, they bought records, they went to gigs and they took odd little jobs to bring in the money that might make them more successful at those other pursuits.

Once, Ron tried his hand working as an ice-cream man. 'I always thought it would just be incredible driving around the neighbourhood selling ice-cream like Mr Whippy.' It seemed like a good job when he first thought about it, 'going around in a little van with music playing.' Instead, he was just a couple of hours into his first day of work and 'was going nuts with the same song going round and round my head. And it was in one of the most dangerous areas of Los Angeles, too, so it was like imagining getting gunned down with that same song still playing in the background. The chimes repeating over and over again, plus the fact that my life was in danger – I kept reading about people who were killed doing it – meant I lasted one day.'

He enrolled in university, the UCLA. Ever a chip off the old block, Ron intended following directly in his father's footsteps by studying graphic design. But his heart wasn't in it, even though he had the talent. Some 30 years later, he admitted, 'I sometimes wonder what I'd be doing if I weren't a musician. Anything else would require such an effort. This comes as second nature, it doesn't require decisions. When I was growing up in Pacific Palisades, I was a nut about cars, and wanted to be a car designer, or a professional baseball player. I think I got more of my wish of being a ball player by being in a band; I see a strong connection between major-league sports and rock performances.'

Russell joined him at university, taking a course in theatre arts and film-making. Again, like Ron, he viewed it more as a stop-gap than anything else, but it offered a career if all else should fail, and he enjoyed it. Taking the helm of one class project, he wrote and performed a paean to the summertime, sensibly titled 'Summer Days', for the benefit of the cameras. Having enjoyed that, and eventually convinced Ron that they really ought to try and make something move, the pair finally formed their first band sometime around 1966...although it probably wasn't really a band.

'We did a lot of lip-synching, but we were never actually in bands that played. If you *actually* played in a band, everyone would ask you to play all their favourite songs, whereas if you just lip-synched you could do anything you wanted.'

It was only gradually, over a period of weeks, or even months, that they began to pick up instruments and plug them in. Russell would sing and play bass, while Ron settled behind his keyboard – and he hated it. 'My brother liked flamboyant, outgoing rock stars like Pete Townshend,' Russell reflected, 'but he couldn't emulate them on the keyboard.'

It would take him a lot longer than the handful of rehearsals that each of these embryonic bands undertook to actually figure out how to get around his distaste, but the seeds were already being sown. If he couldn't go completely mad, then he would go completely sane instead, realising that by doing so he would appear even madder.

'We've always been interested in the media,' Russell mused, but the problem with a lot of the areas into which they could have moved, be it art or design or even film, was that 'you don't get an instant reaction from that sort of thing. We were really interested in the pop field because you *do* get an immediate response from people, even if they're only throwing things at you.'

Their first 'real' band, as in a group that played its instruments and made some kind of noise with them, was the Bel Air Blues Project – named, Russell insisted, without a hint of irony. 'We always thought...and so did a lot of bands at that time...that it was the easiest form of music to play, a 1-4-5 blues song, because it's the first thing you learn to play. So we were a blues band obviously, or we thought we were a blues band. I played harmonica, so we had to be a blues band. It was an absurd name.'

Another group was formed with Harrold Zellman, one of Ron's fellows in the design class and today a well-respected author and historian of modernist architecture and communitarian movements. The group came very close to being christened the Three Minute Earwash, but wound up remaining unnamed.

Another UCLA student, Larry Dupont, witnessed these early manoeuvrings. He is usually described in band retrospectives simply as their photographer. In fact, he was as much a part of the combo as any of the musicians.

'We were good friends, we hung out a lot, and we would use my old Sony equipment to make their demo tapes. They asked me to pretend to be their manager for their first Whisky-A-Go-Go gig, where I actually had to do the job. From that point forward, I was in very deep. When they were recording or on tour, I was with them days or weeks on end. Except for one instantly deleted studio session where they forced me to do some percussion, I was involved in most every other way than musician.'

He initially met Ron when they found themselves in the same design area at UCLA, 'or I may have known him casually before that. Harrold was a good friend of mine and, when he joined the band, my relationship with Ron skyrocketed. We were all design majors, Ron was graphic design, while Harrold and I were industrial design, but it was a tiny department and we were all in there together. And Russ was a film major in the building next door.' Many times when the band had a rehearsal scheduled, Dupont would be invited round to listen or maybe even bring his portable tape recorder along so they could tape the day's proceedings.

'Ron was an interesting guy to be around,' Dupont said. 'He also had a part-time job at the Student Union – I think there was a specialty record area which I frequented, so he was just a part of my social world. We had a lot of common interests, and Ron and Russ and I went to a whole gaggle of Japanese films of the period and earlier that were being shown at a little Japanese theatre in the central Los Angeles area, and both Ron and Russ and I, and whoever the heck else, were very much into European cinema.'

The Harrold Zellman incarnation of the band didn't work out, and the Maels moved on. 'They were very determined,' said Dupont,' and that describes them in a lot of ways. There really was nothing that would prevent them from pursuing their desire to become rock stars.'

A Mael-led new band, Moonbaker Abbey, took its name in vague emulation of sundry British psychedelic bands that featured in the London music papers that sporadically made their way to LA. Another of their early incarnations, Farmers Market, was named for a local landmark, a vacant lot on Third and Fairfax where local farmers used to unload their excess produce to Depression-era Los Angelinos but which had now expanded into a miniature paradise of restaurants, coffee bars and even circus acts and a petting zoo.

Their repertoire was no more challenging than any other bottom-feeding band of the age, and included a handful of well-chosen covers – 'My White Bicycle', an underground hit for the British psychedelic band Tomorrow, was an early favourite that survived in the brothers' repertoire for much of the next five years. For the most part, though, they played whatever caught their ear on the day of the rehearsal – or, at least, they tried their best to play it and, if it didn't work out, they'd move on to something else.

The Maels' musical history, like that of many other performers, tends to overlook these earliest strivings as being somehow inconsequential. In fact, Russell insisted, their only failings were those that the musicians' own inexperience brought into play.

'They were bands, they were really bands. But you didn't know, because you're so young and naive and green, you don't know what the goals are, what the rules are. So you're just doing it and you meet up once a week to rehearse. But you don't know what you're even attempting to achieve, so you're in a band, but then you're also going to school or university and all that kind of stuff, so it's all kinda hazy what the end game is.'

Neither is that a situation that is necessarily remedied by experience. Three years later, with the brothers now performing as Halfnelson, 'it was still being gone at with that kind of attitude and mindset. You don't even think about it; you're doing it, but then you're going to school as well, so whatever kicks in first – if you get your teacher's degree before you get a record contract, then you're an English teacher. We were passionate about it, but we didn't know we were *that* passionate until we were signed by a label, and even then you don't know that anything will come of it.'

In fact, the Maels understood very early on what makes the biggest difference between a band that makes it, and one that doesn't. It was a lesson they'd learned from watching the Beatles, and which they'd seen put into practise on innumerable occasions ever since. Image, packaging, visibility. If a band wanted to be noticed, then it needed to make people notice it. It was as simple as that. It was not a band's talent or musicality that initially raised them above the crowd. It was their ability to be seen.

Which is why, as Ron prepared for one of their first ever public appearances a few years later, he didn't even blink as he watched Russell patiently construct a miniature ocean liner from papier-mâché and an old set of pram wheels, and then climb aboard wearing a blue sailor's suit. All those years watching old movies were paying off; everybody who saw the band recognised Ron's resemblance to Charlie Chaplin. But few realised Russell was paying homage to an equally significant icon, Tadzio in the movie *Death In Venice*.

Nightly, Russell would make his entrance on stage aboard his little boat, and he wasn't at all fazed when he rolled up to the microphone and discovered that there was no more than half a dozen people in the crowd. He waved hello to them anyway.

'That's when we realised that maybe we were not going to be the Who,' Ron smiled sadly.

CHAPTER TWO

IN FIFTY YEARS,
YOU MAY OUTGROW IT

On 23rd June 1967, Ron, Russell, Larry Dupont and a bunch of other friends headed over to Century City to attend one of the largest anti-war demonstrations yet staged in Los Angeles. President Lyndon B Johnson was in town that day, attending a $1,000-a-dish Democratic Party fundraiser at the Century Plaza Hotel. Outside, some 25,000 protesters were determined to take the anti-war movement to the President's dining table, but he never even saw them. The marchers were held at bay by 1,500 police officers, and the demonstration moved on to an afternoon 'Peace In' held in a nearby park. Muhammad Ali and Dr Benjamin Spock were among the speakers and, when it was over, the crowds began to disperse, passing the still heavily guarded hotel as they did so...and the law attacked.

'We were chased down an embankment on to a major street by club-wielding police,' recalled Larry Dupont. 'Ah, the good old days...'

With both Ron and Russell now writing their own songs, summer 1967 saw the duo form a new band named, with at least half an eye on the volatile state of national politics, Urban Renewal Project. Riots were both shaking and shaping America, and would continue to do so as Newark, Detroit and Milwaukee all went up in flames that summer. Even if the Maels' songs did not carry any true political intent, their band name was still a rallying call for change.

Musically, their influences remained firmly rooted in the English stylings that had already pegged them as Anglophiles among their friends and acquaintances. Pressed to compare their own sounds with those of any other acts, the brothers would patiently reel off a list of favourite groups and artists, and then affect amazement when they were informed they sounded nothing like them. But none of this would change their tastes one bit.

Little known in America at that time, but firm favourites on the import racks, the likes of Tyrannosaurus Rex, featuring a young and still hungry Marc Bolan, and the Incredible String Band were both to lay heavy hands on the Maels' songwriting, although not in terms of lyrical content or even delivery. Both acts were far too acoustic and folk-oriented for the brothers' tastes, but each had a disregard for conventional songwriting, and their ability to weave strange beauty from what might otherwise have appeared discordant and tuneless was a trick that the Maels instinctively understood.

Fed through whichever electric instrumentation they could lay their hands on, the brothers' love of the first Pink Floyd album, the Syd Barrett-led 'The Piper At The Gates Of Dawn', shone through, and they were already hatching a sound that was quite unique. (A quarter of a century later, the Maels were seriously considering contributing a version of Barrett's 'Bike' to the Floyd tribute album, 'A Saucerful Of Pink').

Unfortunately, it was all still a long way from fruition. Songs like 'The Windmill', 'Computer Girl', 'As You Like It' and 'A Quick Thought' would never develop beyond the rehearsal room and the handful of gigs that Urban Renewal Project were able to play. Indeed, the promising connotations of its name notwithstanding, Urban Renewal Project was a ramshackle affair, to say the least.

'There were all sorts of people in that band,' Larry Dupont recalled. A friend named Dean was a member for a time, before Russell recruited another friend, Fred Frank, to play guitar. Frank, in turn, suggested adding his wife, Ronna, on drums. Costuming, such as it was, would focus on Ron's newly-acquired penchant for ten-gallon hats. They then looked around for a suitable arena in which to debut, and entered a Battle of the Bands being hosted by the Los Angeles Sports Centre. A venue better known (as its name suggests) for hosting major sporting events, it was home at that time to the Los Angeles Stars basketball team.

The Battle of the Bands was a regular feature of the American music scene in the Sixties, encompassing talent contests that ranged from the most impromptu gathering of neighbourhood hopefuls to vast city- (or even state- or country-) wide competitions, with all manner of fabulous riches for the victors. Record companies frequently used these contests as a means of finding new talent, as did local promoters. This particular Battle was a distinctly local affair, despite its grandiose setting and the presence on the bill of Massachusetts-born bluesman Taj Mahal, still fresh from the demise of his band the Rising Sons. Within the year, Taj Mahal would be signing with CBS, and, while nobody seems to recall who else was on the battlefield that day, the Maels were well aware that their little band didn't have a hope of victory.

All they wanted was to be noticed, and even the patent inadequacy of their instruments - the drum kit which consisted of a single snare drum and nothing else, the $20 guitar on which bassist Russell would pick out the low notes, and the solitary amplifier which the entire band would be using simultaneously - couldn't dampen their enthusiasm. When Urban Renewal Project failed even to reach the final stages of the competition, the Maels took solace in the fact that neither did Taj Mahal.

A second Battle of the Bands contest, this time at a local YMCA, saw their hopes take another battering as the quartet suddenly realised that they were all playing in different keys - something which went a long way towards explaining why the other band (the competition had attracted only two entrants) kept pulling the plugs on them. Small wonder, then, that the rest of the Los Angeles music community, or at least that tiny part of it that had heard of them, already considered the Maels to be little more than a joke, and not a particularly funny one either.

A third and, as it transpired, final show followed, when Larry Dupont pulled some strings at UCLA and landed the group a booking to provide entertainment at an industrial design conference. In the minds of Urban Renewal Project the booking was a masterstroke, their answer to Andy Warhol landing the nascent Velvet Underground a gig performing for a psychiatry convention. In years to come, they imagined, rock historians would marvel at the incongruity of it all.

Of course it didn't work out that way. Whatever the group thought they might have the potential to become, accompaniment to the evening meal was not it. 'It was a total joke,' Dupont sighs. 'A group of college design majors...there couldn't have been a more boring group of people, and Urban Renewal Project couldn't have been a more inappropriate selection. It was simply a case of "Oh, I know a group, and we need a band..."'

But the Maels, with characteristic perversity, continued on what more and more people were assuring them was a wild goose chase. They recorded 'Computer Girl' and considered using it as a demo to try and spread their name even further, although in the end, they kept it to themselves. (It was finally released in 2006 as a free CD within the Japanese Sparks Guide Book)

It was time to start again. Fred and Ronna Frank dropped away; the Urban Renewal Project was scrapped, and Ron and Russell began rebuilding, pinning a 'Guitarist Wanted' note on the UCLA notice board. It was answered by Earle Mankey, a fellow student who could not only play his instrument but who also had a degree in sound engineering from UCLA and was happy to put his expertise at the band's disposal. With Mankey's arrival, Halfnelson was born.

The name was taken from a wrestling hold, but the passing years would see the Maels, and others, develop any number of possible alternative explanations for its appeal - including its appearance on the introductory page of what was the hot paperback among Anglophile Americans around that time, Hunter Davies' novelisation of the movie Here We Go Round The Mulberry Bush:

I decided I should wet my lips, that might help a bit. Or perhaps I should suck her skin in a love bite, whatever that was. Or a French kiss. A half-Nelson would probably be the most effective.

A year older than Russell, Earle Mankey had grown up steeped in the street culture of East LA. In earlier times he had been a greaser, his immaculately sculpted hair setting off a cool leather jacket. Now he was firmly in the grip of Byrds-mania, his hair and sunglasses modelled devotedly on *Gene Clark's*, and later, when that grew out, he assumed a vague resemblance to Rod Stewart, then singer with the Jeff Beck Group.

His musical ideas, however, had little to do with the strumming Rickenbackers and post-Dylan country wash of his heroes' own records, nor with the Englishness that the Maels espoused. Captain Beefheart was a firm favourite, weird and earthy, and inclined never to take the direct route between the start of a song and its ending when there was a cacophonous detour that could be taken along the way. There was not a note Mankey played, or a word he sang, that he had not twisted and teased beyond all recognition, and the songs that the Maels were now bringing to life were all ripe for further manipulation, the guitarist running Dupont's long-suffering tape machine through every trial that his imagination could devise and transforming each into a miniature symphony of sound effects.

No noise was too *outré* for the Maels to ask whether it had something special to offer, no tape effect was so awful that they did not look to see how it could be improved. Like the Beatles ferreting away to create *Sgt Pepper*, but without the budget, musicianship or George Martin to help them, Halfnelson twisted and tormented the tape into a series of jangling, tinkling collages, and then layered the bones of their songs over the top. One afternoon, rehearsing at a long-forgotten location in one of the canyons around Los Angeles, they were horrified to discover that they could be heard clear across the other side of the canyon – and even more shocked when a voice came echoing back to them from there; 'Turn that goddamned noise down!'

'Computer Girl' was resurrected as was Russell's 'Summer Days'. Mankey contributed a handful of his own, already maddeningly esoteric compositions to the brew – 'Big Rock Candy Mountain' was one of his, and it sounded as enormous as it ought to have. But it was Ron and Russell together who were the dynamo powering Halfnelson's songwriting machine and, if the majority of the songs they wrote were little more than ideas when they started, the magic of the studio would soon whip them into shape: 'Chile Farm Farney', 'Johnny's Adventure', 'Roger', 'Arts And Crafts Spectacular', 'Landlady', 'The Animals At Jason's Bar And Grill', 'Millie', 'Saccharin And The War', 'Join The Firm', 'Jane Church', 'Do The Factory' and so many more. Weeks turned into months, which threatened to become years, and the trio, plus Dupont, simply got together whenever they could, set up around the Maels' living room, and made tapes.

The problem was that there was only so much that could be done with keyboards and guitar, and Russell throwing in a few lines of bass. As Ron cautioned, 'the sound was very thin and reedy, totally unheavy and very naïve. We just made these tapes because we liked 'em. We didn't have a master-plan or anything.' In terms of musical development, there was no question that their work was becoming more and more proficient, and Halfnelson knew that the only limitations they faced were those that they imposed upon themselves. But attempts to convince anybody else to see their efforts in the same light seemed doomed to failure.

Tapes were regularly being mailed out to anyone and everyone who they thought might listen to them, but most of them fell on deaf ears. Of the handful of recipients who did respond, the majority usually mentioned something about the unconventional sound. The remainder, Russell laughed, the few who actually liked what they heard, lost their jobs.

'We didn't do anything live, we just made tapes and elaborate presentations to record companies.' He claims they recorded 12 albums' worth of material, 'but every time we got to the guy just below the one who signs the contracts, he got fired for wanting to sign a group like us.' It was time, Halfnelson decided, to recruit a full-time rhythm section.

In a way, it's strange that they hadn't already thought of that. Asked how they actually saw themselves, Russell still rattled off the British beat bands that he and Ron most enjoyed; 'We thought

Halfnelson was like a British band. I liked British bands and I kind of admired Mick Jagger from the Rolling Stones, and Ron's earliest listening influences were the Kinks, the Move and, above all, the early Who.' (In 2004, Russell was still listing 'The Best Of The Move' among his all-time Top 5 records, alongside the more esoteric pleasures of the Velvet Underground's 'White Light White Heat', the Galliano Septet's 'Paszzolla', a Fifties rock'n'roll compilation called 'Forever Loud Fast And Out Of Control' and Isabelle Adjani's 'Pull Marine'. Ron picked the original radio broadcast of Orson Welles' *War of the Worlds*, alongside titles by NWA, Strauss, Miles Davis and Schoenberg).

Other listeners might have shrugged at the brothers' devotion to all things British, and pinpointed more esoteric influences – among them Frank Zappa and Captain Beefheart, fellow local artistes who, even then, were placing sonic extremity ahead of musical comfort. But they, too, usually had a bassist and drummer. It was time for Halfnelson to get with the programme.

'They went through a long string of disastrous drummers,' recalled Dupont, including one who was already making a name for himself on the other side of the musical fence. John Mendelsohn was the drummer with a jazz-rock trio called the 1930 Four, but he was probably better known for his occasional contributions to the *Los Angeles Times*. Claiming he was lured into Halfnelson's orbit by the bright pink paper upon which the latest ad was written, he then discovered that he and Russell had studied Italian 101 together a couple of years before. The only two long-haired boys in the class, '[we] had sneaked suspicious glances at one another,' as Mendelsohn later put it.

Shortly afterwards, a bassist arrived in the shape of 'Surly' Ralph Oswald. A manager was also procured – another drummer, oddly enough, but more importantly a reasonably wealthy character – named Mike Berns. Together, the team dived back into the sack of songs at Halfnelson's disposal and emerged with what the Maels insisted, and manager Berns agreed, was to become their very first album.

They decided that the traditional path to recorded fame and glory was boring and strewn with too many pitfalls. Playing gigs in the hope that an audience might turn up was pointless – they'd been to too many shows, and seen too many great bands playing in front of a crowd of six and then disappearing back into obscurity. All the record labels were interested in was records – so give them one. Berns was happy to provide any finance they needed; Halfnelson could record the album themselves on Dupont's tape machine, press up a few copies, and then sit back while the offers poured in. It had worked for Phil Spector, it worked for the Rolling Stones, so why shouldn't it work for them? The figure of $100,000 was mentioned and seized upon – Halfnelson would not sign a contract for anything less than that.

The best dozen or so of the songs at their disposal were dusted down and reworked for a full band. Unfortunately, even as the sessions progressed, it became painfully apparent that neither of the new arrivals had much interest in the music that Halfnelson wanted to make.

Mendelsohn placed the blame squarely on differing interpretations of what rock'n'roll music ought to represent. 'They wanted to be precious and adorable, as they wrongly imagined the Kinks to be, while I, a Who fan, wanted to be intimidating.' He succeeded, too. The others found him *very* intimidating.

Years later, asked to expand upon his time with the band, Mendelsohn preferred to contract it. 'I can't bear being defined in anyone's eyes on the basis of three rehearsals with Halfnelson,' he said. A parting of the ways was inevitable and, early that summer of 1969, Mendelsohn was 'asked not to be in the group any more'. Oswald followed him and, shortly after catching the Stooges at the Whisky and deciding Iggy Pop was as viable a future for rock'n'roll as anybody, the pair formed a band that was more to their tastes and called it Christopher Milk. There were clearly no hard feelings, however – Christopher Milk's earliest shows saw Mendelsohn borrowing Mike Berns' drum kit.

CHAPTER THREE

PARADISE WAS HERE,
PARADISE WAS GONE

A trio once again, Halfnelson soldiered on, with Berns now stepping into Mendelsohn's role, while Russell reacquainted himself with the bass. It was a stop-gap line-up. Berns owned one of the most impressive drum kits his band-mates had ever seen, a Rogers double bass set in mother of pearl, festooned with tom-toms. But rehearsals with him behind the kit seemed to give everything that the band was playing a strangely folky vibe, anathema to two as devoutly anti-folk as the Maels. Not that Berns agreed with them, but he was allowed to remain *in situ* until they could find a replacement, which all hoped would be sooner rather than later.

Late in 1969, passing by a local music store, Ace Music in Santa Monica, Russell spotted an ad that had been placed on the notice board just a few days earlier: 'Drummer looking for people to jam with. I'm into rock, blues, jazz, country. 477-6822.' It was placed there by Harley Feinstein, a Los Angeles boy three years Russell's junior but a rock-solid drummer who made up in enthusiasm what he lacked in virtuosity – even if Russell did have to drag him out of the bathtub to discover that.

Feinstein recalled, 'I was still living at home with my parents. I was exhausted from surfing all morning, and had gotten into the bathtub for a soak. The phone started ringing at the other end of the house. After debating whether or not to answer it, I jumped out of the tub, wrapped a towel around my body and ran into the kitchen, dripping. There was a high voice on the other end of the line. Of course, that was Russell – or Russ, as he was then known. Russ told me that he'd seen the card I'd stuck up on the bulletin board.'

Russell explained his group's predicament. 'He said he was in a band called Halfnelson, and they were making an album. This was extraordinary in 1970. Ordinarily a band had to be signed to a record contract to make an album. You had to be big. I had never met anyone that had actually made an album. Russ explained that rather than signing a recording contract, Halfnelson had found someone (Mike Berns) who would independently finance the recording, which they would then sell to a record company.'

Feinstein asked whether they had a drummer. 'Russ said that they didn't need to have a drummer in the band to record. When they recorded, they beat on objects like boxes and frying pans for percussion. But, since they were almost finished with the album, they needed to put together a band to play live. My role, if I joined the band, would be as part of a live show. We had a good rapport over the phone. We agreed that the band would come over to my house so we could check each other out.'

By the time Feinstein finally put the phone down, his bath water was beyond cold. They'd been talking for an hour. Ron, Russell, Mankey and his wife Elisa came over that same afternoon. Instruments were set up in the family living room and, while Feinstein's mother, Blanche, kept up a constant stream of refreshments, the quartet jammed a little ('probably some blues,' declared Feinstein), then sat back while Halfnelson played through a tape of the songs they'd recorded so far. Feinstein wasn't impressed. 'I didn't think too much of the music. But I remember sort of liking "The Animals At Jason's Bar And Grill" and "Factory".'

He liked the Maels as well. All tank-top and muscles, 'Ron was very cool. He had a full on Afro, and a great handlebar moustache. Russ and Earle were good guys. We all got along great.' As they talked, they even found some unexpected common ground; Harrold Zellman, their old band-mate from the abortive Three Minute Earwash, was best friends with Feinstein's brother, Allan.

Musical tastes were compared, and Feinstein was instantly struck by Earle Mankey. 'Earle said he liked the same music Ron and Russ liked – the Move, the Kinks, the Who, the British Invasion bands. But his musical ideas seemed weird. He really got excited by Captain Beefheart. Earle seemed to like music that sounded off, counter-intuitive, odd. He was obviously a talented musician, but his tendency to make music in this way had a profound effect on those early recordings. Most people would agree that the Halfnelson demo, and the first two Sparks albums after it, were strange. It was Earle's influence that made them strange.'

Feinstein had little in common with the others. 'I *wasn't* an Anglophile. I idolised the members of the Southern Californian surfing culture, not skinny English white boys trying to play American blues.' Years later, he was thrilled – and maybe vindicated, too – to discover that Keith Moon felt the same way as he did. 'He even peroxided his hair!' But the meeting went well and the visitors left with the promise that they'd be in touch soon.

A few days later, Russell called and invited Feinstein to the tiny rented studio where they were mixing the Halfnelson album. Mike Berns was there as well, a little perplexed to discover that he was about to be relieved of his drumsticks and not too shy about letting the newcomer know that. Feinstein recalled, 'Mike was okay being the manager. He was okay investing the money to make the album. But he what he really wanted was to be the drummer. He couldn't understand why the boys wanted me to be the drummer instead of him,' and neither could Feinstein.

'I asked the guys why they didn't want Mike to be the drummer. They said he wasn't right, because he played the melody on the snare instead of the back beat. But I heard Mike play and he sounded fine. I didn't know what they were talking about. I think the real reason was that he would have totally taken over the band. Also, he looked like a hippie. He had a beard. There was no way he was going to be the drummer of Halfnelson!'

Not that that was an especially arduous duty. Occasionally Feinstein would ask if the band intended having any rehearsals. He was all too aware that he had been invited to join the group on the strength of just one casual jam session in his parents' living room. Surely, before his involvement went too far, they should make sure the chemistry was as strong across Halfnelson's original material as it was across a handful of blues tunes. It was strange, he thought, being in a band that didn't actually get together and play music. 'But, like I said, I liked these guys.'

In fact, rehearsals were being planned, but not until the Maels had made one final change. Russell was tired, once again, of playing bass. If he was to be the group's front man, he wanted to present as much front as he could, which meant leaping around the stage with his mike stand, doing all the things that his own idols – Mick Jagger, Roger Daltrey, Keith West – were doing. Not standing frozen behind a bass guitar. The search was on.

It wasn't easy. The most obvious choice, all agreed, was Jim Mankey, Earle's younger brother. He was constantly hanging out with the band – the first time Feinstein met him was at the demo mixing sessions – and his own group, a heavy blues act called Three Days Blues, were certainly an effective showcase for his abilities. Earle, however, refused to even ask him. For a start, Jim was a lead guitar player, but more importantly he was a *better* guitarist than Earle. The elder Mankey happily admitted that he couldn't handle the idea of his little brother blowing him away any time he was given the opportunity to pick up the guitar.

Thwarted, the band turned instead to adverts and auditions and seemed to turn up trumps immediately. Skip, a player whose surname has, sadly, been lost to the mists of time, lived in Laurel Canyon and arrived with the additional bonus of a garage that he was willing to turn over to the band for a practice space. For days thereafter, Halfnelson toured the local carpet stores, dumpster-iving for remnants that could be nailed to the garage walls to act as soundproofing.

Unfortunately, they couldn't figure out how to attach more of the material to the ceiling, much to the chagrin of Skip's neighbours. Every time the band started up, the hammering on the door started with it, and, although Halfnelson attempted to persevere, Skip's own strongly-held musical beliefs were taking an equal toll on their nerves. Their music, he told them, was completely wrong. The only way to make it, he was convinced, was to strip everything back to the Fifties and jump aboard the Sha Na Na rock'n'roll revival bandwagon. So Skip was out of the band.

Next in was Neil, another seemingly surname-less musician, who also came equipped with a personal practice space, out in the industrial wastelands around Los Angeles in a factory owned by his uncle. There were no neighbours, therefore no need for soundproofing, and they could just go in and play to their hearts' content. And if anybody needed a nap, that was sorted out too...the factory made dog beds.

Again the group set to work and, again, they quickly discovered that their latest recruit was not what they were looking for. Neil was a great bassist and a great comedian – his party trick was a spot-on impersonation of Allan Sherman of 'Hello Mudduh, Hello Fadduh' fame. Unfortunately, he was also somewhat overweight and, in the Mael's lexicon of rock'n'roll style, fat was almost as bad as beards.

So Neil was out as well, but he very graciously allowed the band to hang on to what Russell had already christened the Doggy Factory. With Earle having equally graciously consented to allow brother Jim finally to pick up Halfnelson's bass guitar, the quintet was, at last, complete – albeit with a few reservations. According to Ron, Jim almost quit during one of his earliest rehearsals with them after he heard his band-mates' version of the Troggs' 'Give It To Me'...and Earle never got over his reluctance to have his playing compared with his brother's.

Occasionally, over the years, a song would require Jim to play lead guitar ('Whippings And Apologies' was one example), and Earle would shift down to rhythm guitar, while Ron supplied the bass via his keyboards. But if Jim ever argued about his role in the band, Earle had that settled as well. Jim, he admitted, was 'a far better guitar player than me, but he's playing bass because I'm bigger than him.'

'It was great having Jim in the band,' Feinstein recalled. 'He didn't have a car, so one of us would have to drive many miles east of Los Angeles to pick Jim up and take him home after rehearsals. But we didn't mind, because Jim finally made us a real band.'

The new boys' first duty as members of Halfnelson, in January 1970, was to co-star in the band's first set of promo photographs, taken in the basement of the Ethnic Arts Department at UCLA, the day-job domain of Larry Dupont. He was engaged at that time in making a visual record of the department's holdings, a bewildering array of ethnic artefacts, African carvings, and so forth, for an upcoming catalogue, but his spare time found him photographing Halfnelson.

'Larry was Woody Allen,' said Feinstein. 'I instantly liked him. He had a strong physical resemblance to Woody, was a horrible dresser, witty, and artistic. We spent days taking pictures. Larry was an absolute perfectionist. The pictures came out great.'

Feinstein, meanwhile, was receiving a fascinating cultural education from both the Maels and Dupont. 'They knew a lot about music and film. I didn't. They told me about Fellini, Bernardo Bertolucci, and Luchino Visconti. When I said I thought that surf music was cool, they talked about how much they liked the Move, the Kinks and the Who.'

Russell spoke about the movie he was making for one of his classes at UCLA, a plot-less epic about a man rowing a boat across the Santa Monica Bay. Earle Mankey, his wife and Russell's girlfriend manned one rowboat, Russell and Larry were in the other, busily getting seasick while trying to load the camera. At the end of the college year, the film would play a major part in his decision whether or not to continue at UCLA. All it had to do was win the

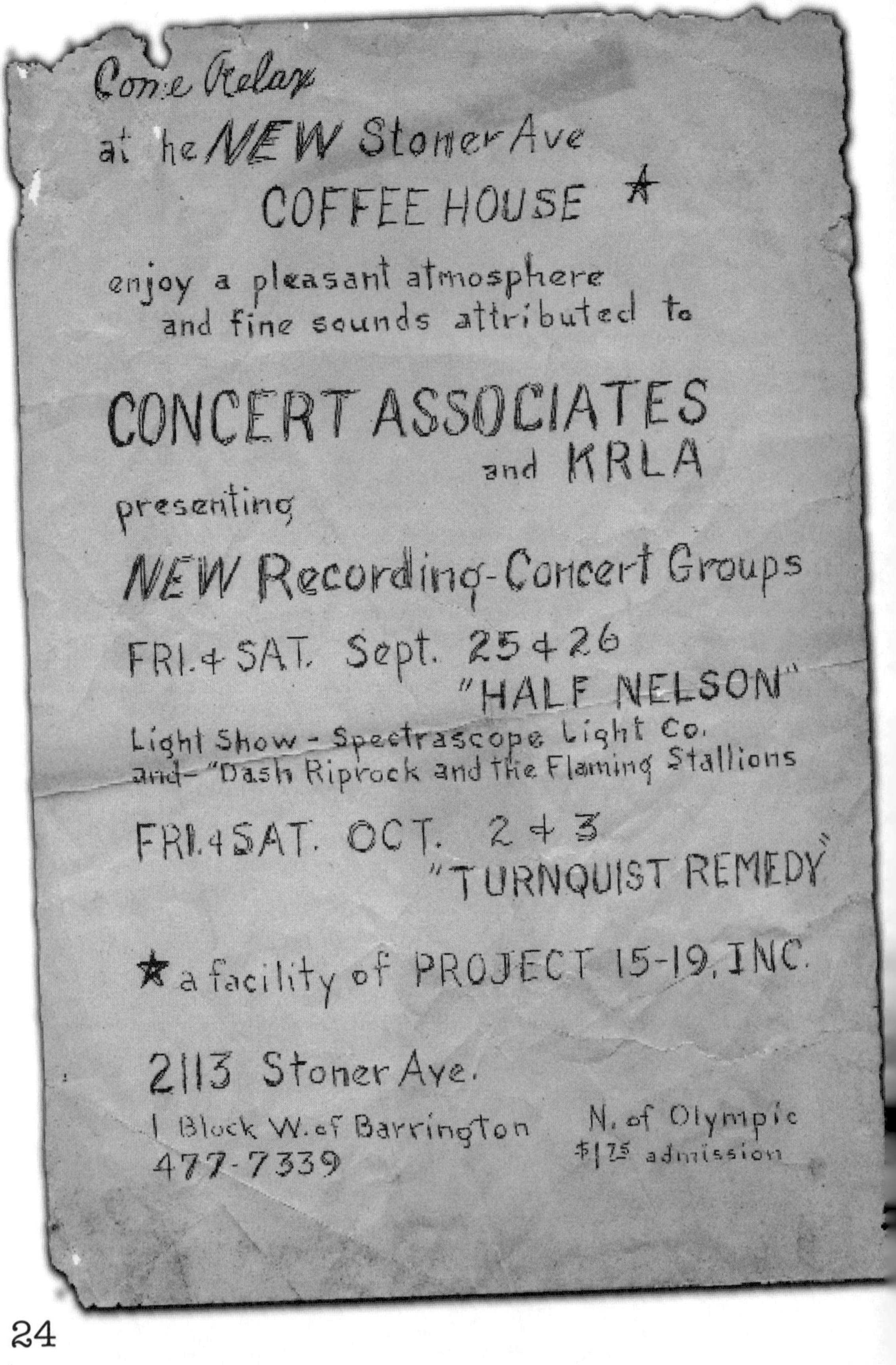

Come Relax

at he *NEW* Stoner Ave

COFFEE HOUSE ✱

enjoy a pleasant atmosphere
and fine sounds attributed to

CONCERT ASSOCIATES
and KRLA

presenting

NEW Recording-Concert Groups

FRI. & SAT. Sept. 25 & 26
"HALF NELSON"

Light Show - Spectrascope Light Co.
and "Dash Riprock and the Flaming Stallions

FRI. & SAT. OCT. 2 & 3
"TURNQUIST REMEDY"

★ a facility of PROJECT 15-19, INC.

2113 Stoner Ave.

1 Block W. of Barrington   N. of Olympic
477-7339 $1.75 admission

24

approval of a 'jury' of his peers, as they sat to watch every student's handiwork, and decide whether or not its maker had what it took to move into film making. Russell was good, and he knew it. There should be no problem.

Larry Dupont chimed in with his cinematic ambitions – his latest opus was about a blimp, and he asked if Halfnelson would be interested in scoring it. They were. Days later, Dupont drove his portable reel-to-reel tape recorder over to the Doggy Factory, and work began on the instrumental theme for a blimp, a drawn-out organ-led instrumental that, periodically, would break into a maddeningly perky Dixieland style break.

'We never finished the film,' Dupont mourned. 'It was just after I got my masters and, by that time, my major had morphed from industrial design to a broader area. But I remember we dumped the Halfnelson soundtrack and used a Saint-Saëns organ concerto. It was pretty cool, though. We got to ride in the blimp!'

All the while, the band were anxiously awaiting delivery of their debut LP from the pressing plant. Ron had already designed the packaging, a box printed to resemble the note pads on which waitresses take orders in a restaurant.

'We always subscribed to the theory that the packaging was an essential part of one's presentation, even at this early stage when we didn't know what the hell we were doing,' said Russell. Open the box and inside was a copy of the record and a handful of photographs. The idea, Feinstein explained, was for prospective suitors to fill out the form on the cover 'and put in an order for one Halfnelson'. The cost of such a treat had already been filled out – $100,000.

One hundred copies of the 12-song acetate disc were pressed. But Feinstein laughingly dismisses the later conviction, perpetuated in every Sparks discography of the past 35 years, that Ron also designed a sleeve depicting a surfboarder riding past the Eiffel Tower – 'There was no surfer or Eiffel Tower.'

Larry Dupont agreed. 'I put the thing together with them, they used my dark room in the ethnographic museum to make the prints to do this thing, and there were never any surfers or Eiffel Towers.'

Neither was the package then gifted with the title 'A Woofer In Tweeter's Clothing', again routinely reported in the discographies. As Feinstein confirms, 'the demo wasn't called 'Woofer...' It didn't have a name. It didn't have a sleeve or even a label on the record itself.' As for where the erroneous story originated, however, that's easy. One or other of the Maels thought it up sometime after the fact, and then dropped it into an interview in an attempt to give the demo a little more traction. As Dupont puts it, 'they had absolutely no compunction about throwing curve balls. As a matter of fact, they relished it.'

Whatever its title (or lack thereof), the demo didn't stand a hope in hell, either way. Los Angeles in 1970 was a strangely conservative place. The great tide of new musical talent that had hallmarked the previous three or four years had ebbed now. The Doors, the city's biggest contribution to popular culture, had long since left their roots behind them. Love, its most revered, were now little more than a heavyweight bar band. Canned Heat, its hardest-working, were still running on the same spot they'd been occupying for five years. New bands were still forming, of course, and the record label guys were still prowling the bars and running up their expense accounts in search of the next big thing. But little of what they found was worth more than a passing sneer. When the most excitement on the streets was to be drawn from second-guessing the latest line-up change in the Flying Burrito Brothers, you know you're in trouble.

Nationwide, too, very little seemed to be happening. The hits of the season were BJ Thomas complaining 'Raindrops Keep Falling On My Head', the Jackson Five's debut 'I Want You Back', and Peter Paul & Mary's 'Leaving On A Jet Plane'. Fleetwood Mac's 'Oh Well' was on the radio a lot, and Jefferson Airplane's 'Volunteers', but they were the old guard. Later in the year, Elton John would break through, and in his wake would come a plethora of earnest singer-songwriters, but even that could only be appreciated with hindsight. Right there, right then, the vista was one of unimaginable despair.

The Beatles were on the verge of splitting up, and the Rolling Stones were still in shock following the nightmare of Altamont. Just six months old, the Manson murders, with their own twisted take on the meaning of rock'n'roll, were still on everybody's lips and the Vietnam War was tearing the country apart. Everybody agreed that music needed a fresh injection of excitement, but it certainly wasn't getting one. In later years, the Maels would pride themselves in having built a reputation for bucking whatever the current musical trends might be. But it was a reputation that could only be established once they had proved their ability to play by the rules. In 1970, when even their friends admired their nerve more than anything else, they were so far out on a limb it was vertiginous.

Greg Shaw, publisher of the San Francisco-based *Who Put The Bomp* fanzine, was among the recipients of the Halfnelson demo. The typewritten, Xeroxed and stapled 'zine was just two issues old at the time, but was already the widely-acclaimed successor to the earlier *Mojo Navigator*, and Shaw admitted, 'I don't remember whether they mailed me a copy hoping that I might be able to do something with them, or if somebody else handed it to me. But I do remember listening to it and thinking they were onto something, even if they didn't seem to know what it was.'

Another early admirer of the band, New Yorker Joseph A (for August) Fleury, later described the disc as 'Psychedelic – Tomorrow meets Syd Barrett meets Frank Zappa,' and recalled hearing that a copy was in fact sent to Zappa, care of his Straight Records label. The problem was that Zappa was being sent tapes by every weirdo in the country at that time; he probably never even listened to most of them. Another copy was allegedly sent to the Beatles' Apple Corps – '...and it would have arrived at probably the same time as the band's break up was announced,' said Fleury.

'So I figured they'd grown up with the same kind of music as I had, and we had a lot of the same reference points,' Greg Shaw continued, 'but I didn't like the sound so much, it was too fussy and too clever. It sounded as though they were trying to disguise the songs with the sound effects, so if you listened really carefully you could hear all their influences buzzing about. But otherwise it got very annoying, very quickly.'

At least Shaw appreciated some of what he heard. All but a handful of copies of the acetate were sent out to every conceivable music industry mogul or mover in the state, and most of them were promptly sent back again, accompanied by terse little notes that described Halfnelson as sounding like a bunch of acid-drenched freaks – and that was if they were lucky. On one of the walls of the Doggy Factory, the band pinned up a roll of wrapping paper on which they wrote the name of every person who turned them down. 'It was an extremely long list,' shuddered Dupont, 'an awful lot of people, and they wore them like a badge of honour.'

Even as the rejection slips mounted up, Halfnelson did not lose faith. New songs were arriving all the time. Inspired by radio's then current love affair with the Beatles' valedictory 'Let It Be' and Simon and Garfunkel's 'Bridge Over Troubled Water', Ron wrote a ballad, 'Slowboat', that was every bit as moving as its illustrious contemporaries. Other songs, 'Wonder Girl', 'Fa La Fa Lee' and 'High C' followed, but another legend, that these were then packaged onto a four-song demo and sent out to people who hadn't heard the acetate, are dismissed by Feinstein. He remembered that they were still waiting for the acetate itself to pay dividends.

'The routine was that Mike Berns would find a music-business executive, give him a copy of the Halfnelson album and invite him to a private concert at the Doggie Factory. Mike knew a lot of people. We played for countless music executives, but none of them liked us.'

There was supposedly a degree of interest in the band at Warner Brothers but unfortunately, it did not extend as far as the A&R department. There was more encouragement from the head of UNI Records, Russ Regan, soon to be riding high on his discovery of Elton John. He described Halfnelson as being 'two years ahead of their time', but he wouldn't even sign them as a long-term investment.

Things were not moving any further on the live front. Rehearsed to what they considered perfection, Halfnelson made their concert debut at the New Stoner Coffee House on Stoner Avenue in West Los Angeles, early in the summer. The band played well, and though the audience was sparse it seemed enthusiastic enough. Word of mouth, however, did not travel far. At least one of Halfnelson's four consecutive nights at the Gregar on Beverly Boulevard, 20th-23rd August 1970, failed to attract a single paying customer, although a series of Larry Dupont photographs shot that evening at least captured Ron's distinctive keyboard decoration for posterity – his instrument was adorned with a picture of the Quaker Oats man.

But the New Stoner invited them back for a two-night stand in September, while more encouraging still was a Paradise Ballroom show, headlining a West Hollywood party whose dress code perfectly summed up the mood of the evening: 'Black Tie or Bizarre'. Close to a thousand people turned up, and few of them wore black ties.

The band's most successful concerts, however, were at High Schools. Feinstein recalled; 'We played at Palisades High. This was the high school that Ron and Russ had attended, so it was probably a very important gig to them. It went great. They loved us.' Soon after, they played Bishop Amant High, a Catholic school in La Puerta, southern California. 'They loved us there too.'

Amid so much activity, Halfnelson did find one possibly influential new fan. Los Angeles-based journalist Kathy Orloff was freelancing for the London music paper *Sounds* when she first encountered Halfnelson, and persuaded her editors to accept a profile of the unknown group. But, no matter how glowing her praise of the band might have been, her opening paragraph set out the band's current status in neon-lit lettering. 'It's not too difficult to "discover" groups who are just beginning long and shiny careers…but how about discovering a group that is a total failure? An accomplishment indeed.'

The interview – which was the first to offer up the erroneous title and description of the band's so-called debut album – was conducted in the early summer, before Halfnelson embarked on their first burst of gigging. Looking ahead to the Stoner Avenue show, the band speculated that they were going to be seriously out of pocket as a result, simply because of the cost of hiring the equipment.

The story would not actually see publication until *Sounds'* 17th October edition, when it was buried away on page 18. But it was worth the wait, even if it was sitting beneath the promise 'Kathy Orloff looks at one of America's weirder bands', and a peculiarly captioned photograph of the short-haired Russell: 'Used to lead a group with brother Ron'. *Used to*?

'Musically… [they are] somewhere between the Kinks and the Bonzo Dog Band,' wrote Orloff, 'closer to the Kinks musically and they are, well, weird. Their sound and manner is very English. They could be an immensely popular performing band.'

With the *Sounds* story to add to their press package, a handful of other live shows did creep into view. Even as they worked towards becoming better known, however, Halfnelson were also acutely aware that at least one of their number needed to remain as anonymous as possible.

In 1969, faced with ever-growing criticism of the manner in which American youth was being harvested for service in the increasingly unpopular Vietnam War, the authorities announced a change in the system. Reverting to a practise that had last been seen in 1942, they announced that, henceforth, drafting would be done by lottery.

The first drawing, on 1st December 1969, was designed for the 850,000 potential inductees who were born between 1st January 1944 and 31st December 1950 – that is, every young man then aged between 18 and 26.

In a widely (if somewhat sadistically) televised event, 366 blue plastic capsules, each containing one birth date, were placed in a glass jar and then drawn by hand. The order in which the capsules were removed from the jar would determine the order in which young men would be called up; the first capsule, for example, contained the date 14th September, so all men born on that day, in any of the years between 1944 and 1950, were assigned lottery number one. The drawing then continued until every day of the year had been matched to a lottery number.

The members of Halfnelson, like everybody else in the country, were glued to the proceedings, and their fortunes were decidedly mixed. Harley Feinstein, born on 10th April, had number 218, while Earle Mankey, born 8th March, was number 213, and brother Jim, born 23rd May, was number 319. They were what would be described as good numbers, nice and high. A lot could happen, including the fulfilment of the army's manpower requirements, between now and whenever their numbers were called. Besides, they all had student deferments, which postponed the day of reckoning even further.

But Ron was in grad school now, which was not protected. His birth date, 12th August, was the 142nd date to be drawn, a bad number which all but guaranteed a call-up before the end of the year. Larry Dupont (8th November) landed number 97, but Russell fared even worse. He wasn't even in school any longer – against all his own predictions, and those of his friends as well, his rowing-boat film had failed.

As Larry Dupont explained, 'The way the jury process worked was that all the art people sat in an auditorium and graded the movies. If you passed, you went on to become a film-maker; if you failed, you became a film historian.'

Among the criticisms aimed at Russell's effort was that it was too heavily influenced by Polish director Roman Polanski, whose *Knife In The Water*, an art-house favourite since the mid-Sixties, also took place on a rowboat. Of course that may have been true but still Dupont insisted, 'They were very harsh in the beginning, and it was only later in the day that they realised if they continued to be this harsh, nobody would get in. So an awful lot of crap did get in, because it was shown later in the day. Russell was in there early, so he was out. And that was the end of his film-making career.'

Now he was too early again. His birth date, 5th October, was drawn 24th. With the military estimating 30 numbers being called up every month, he could be summoned to duty by the end of January 1970.

Drastic measures were required and enacted. For Ron, it was simply a matter of visiting his dentist and, upon display of his less than perfect teeth, being fitted with dental braces. That, incredibly, was sufficient for him to fail the army medical. Larry, too, found a medical get-out. Russell, however, was not so fortunate. His teeth were fine, and his years of football had rendered him a more or less perfect physical specimen. He had no option but to disappear underground, joining a nationwide draft-evasion network in which supporters all over the United States would allow him to claim their address as his official place of residence. These addresses changed just quickly enough to keep him a step or two ahead of the authorities until the danger was past.

CHAPTER FOUR

A SMILE CAME TO MY FACE FOR THE FIRST TIME IN A WHILE

Philadelphia-born Todd Rundgren was an unusual choice of potential saviour, even for a band as defiantly off the wall as Halfnelson. True, he had led his band the Nazz through three albums of increasingly eccentric, but righteously Anglocentric pop-rock, and it was that which initially placed him on the Maels' radar. Likewise, his debut solo album, 'Runt', was being loudly hailed as a minor masterpiece, with Rundgren the self-sufficient technological whiz who threw everything together in the studio.

Albert Grossman, Bob Dylan's former manager, adored Rundgren and had already installed him at Bearsville Studios in Woodstock with a more or less free hand to do whatever he liked. But when Ron was asked which of these claims to fame it was that drew Halfnelson's thoughts towards Rundgren, his answer surprised even Todd; 'He had a pair of satin trousers,' Ron claimed, 'and we thought that that was a sign of sharpness on his part.' And the rest, said the Maels, was history.

Rundgren remembered his recruitment a little differently. It was Mike Berns who made the initial contact, he said, 'the guy who handled their so-called management; he wasn't doing it seriously, I don't think. I think they were interested in me because of my solo album ['Runt']. They got in touch and sent me this tape which was really strange. It had some really strange music on it, and I really liked that. I like stuff which isn't necessarily mainstream, so I became interested in what they were doing and went out to see them.'

Initially, in fact, Rundgren wasn't too certain, either. Russell Mael recalled, 'It was Miss Christine, who was Todd's girlfriend [and a member of Frank Zappa's groupie-girl protégés the GTOs], who was really instrumental. I don't know the chronology of how things worked, but we sent the demo to Todd, not Miss Christine, because we didn't know Miss Christine...we would have sent her one otherwise! But we sent the demo to Todd, and I don't know if she was aware of us before, but she heard the tape and she was the one who was instrumental in helping Todd to make a decision to take us on. He wouldn't have done it unless he liked it, of course, but she was very supportive of what we were doing.'

The first Harley Feinstein heard of these new developments was when Berns announced that Rundgren wanted to come to the Doggy Factory to hear the band, at which point every eye in the room turned to glare at him. The luckless drummer had just broken his arm in a bike-riding accident. There was no way he could perform, particularly in front of such illustrious company. A replacement date was agreed and Halfnelson threw themselves into as much excited rehearsal as they could manage while they waited for Feinstein's arm to mend.

Rundgren would be accompanied on his mission by Thaddeus James Lowe, the San Fernando Valley-based engineer who had been working alongside him since the Nazz days. A founding member of the Electric Prunes in 1965, Lowe quit the band three years later when he realised that his interest was more in the studio than in performance. 'I started engineering and producing records for other people, just to have something to do. At that time there were few musicians working as audio engineers, and I saw that as an opportunity for me when it came to recording. I felt I could contribute because of my past recording experiences with the Electric Prunes, and I

30

just plain loved the studio and all that was possible in that dim light.'

Over the next couple of years, Lowe worked with Van Dyke Parks, Ry Cooder and the Limelighters, then encountered Rundgren for the first time when he was called upon to work with the Nazz. He was present for 'Runt', too, and also joined Rundgren producing the James Cotton Blues Band albums. 'We got along well and I was able to stay awake – his previous engineer had some kind of problem with that!'

Excitedly, Rundgren gave Lowe a taste of what they were about to encounter in the surreal surroundings of the Doggy Factory. 'Todd played me "Roger" at his place, as I recall. It sounded real crazy. He asked me if I would be interested in doing an album with these guys called Halfnelson. A band with the name of a wrestling hold. I remember wondering what else they did. "Roger" sounded like banging on pots and pans – cool banging, but still banging.'

'"Roger" *is* better on the demo than on the first album,' Harley Feinstein insisted. 'For one thing, Russ re-recorded his voice, and it didn't come out as natural-sounding. But more importantly, the music, particularly the percussion, just lost its pizzazz when it was put on the real album. It's ironic that very few people have heard the original "Roger" from the acetate, and yet that original version is what caused Halfnelson to be signed to the recording contract.' He pauses and laughs... 'I didn't play on either version, so I'm objective about this!'

Lowe recalled his first encounter with the band, after he, his wife Pamela, Rundgren and Miss Christine made the journey out to the Doggy Factory. 'It was kind of awkward at first, but I remember they were very gentlemanly and polite and, above everything, I remember their shyness. It wasn't affected, it was real. They were dressed pretty spacey, as I recall, looking like rock stars on vacation. Russ had on something flamboyant. Doing this kind of raw show-and-tell for people can be hard for bands; I always feel a little embarrassed for anyone having to let it out of the cage for three or four people just sitting there looking at them. But the awkward part evaporated as soon as they played. They looked comfortable doing the music, and it sounded like it had potential.

'They were a bit nervous at first,' Lowe continued, 'but when they went into the set they just hit it. There is no way to play Halfnelson music tentatively – you are committed as soon as the first falsetto note comes out of the singer's mouth. This was like a trip to another world. My God! It was *all* as weird as "Roger"! It rocked, but you wanted to hear what the hell this guy was saying in that operatic voice. The band seemed to inhabit this musical landscape collectively, and had obviously agreed that this was "normal". Pamela thought the band looked great.'

The next step was to introduce the band to Albert Grossman. According to Rundgren, Halfnelson 'put on this little show in their rehearsal room. They didn't just play the songs, they put on this show, wearing funny costumes and things like that. I remember when they were about to be signed to Bearsville, we had Albert Grossman go out to their rehearsal rooms in the San Fernando Valley and they actually had tapes of crowd noises in the background, and a little concessions stall selling candy bars and programmes, and they had put on a whole show. They used to go to a lot of trouble, even for the smallest things, and they were charming and quirky, and seemed to have a lot going for them.'

Halfnelson were walking on air. 'These guys were big shots,' Feinstein shivered. 'Albert had been Bob Dylan's manager! The only other band I can remember that also got signed to Bearsville was Foghat. We had no idea what we had to do with Bob Dylan or Foghat.' Personally, he always believed that it was Rundgren, not Grossman, who liked the band, and that the older man simply went along with Rundgren's instincts. 'Todd, like Ron and Russ, was an Anglophile. He had a band called the Nazz which, like Halfnelson, was cute, pale, British-sounding.'

A deal was quickly agreed, but Halfnelson's belief that Bearsville would simply pick up the tapes for the demo album and release that were to be dashed. 'Albert and Todd did not want the Halfnelson album. They wanted us to record a new album with Todd producing!' It was more than the group could ever have dreamed of.

Looking back over the decades, Rundgren never lost his affection for Halfnelson. 'They were a really funny band, and a lot of their stuff was really strange, the words were strange and the whole approach was very left-field. There wasn't enough straight-ahead stuff for it to be a commercial success at the time, and it was always more likely that, although maybe somebody would like it, most people wouldn't.'

Following the audition, he and Lowe retired to a coffee shop to talk over their impressions and, as Lowe puts it, decompress. 'I was very impressed with them. They were doing something really different to my ears. And writing songs about crucifying doctors on a gold cross in a town, trying to lose weight, and setting their sights much lower than they would sing – Christ, it was just too damned interesting.'

Time was booked at ID Sound studios on La Brea, and the sessions kicked off with a new version of 'High C'. 'Wonder Girl' followed, blending an archetypal Rundgren production with a stone cold classic Russell Mael vocal. True, Rundgren's attempts to layer a few harmony vocals across the tapes provoked nothing but a dismissive bellow of 'slick ballads!' from the band, and everybody was getting tired of 'Fletcher Honorama' long before it reached its twentieth and final take.

Lowe continued, 'At that time I hated recording most bands because you would be pressed against the wall with sound coming from the control-room speakers, and every guy in the band claiming they couldn't hear their instrument, for some reason. Halfnelson were not like that. They had their parts together and knew what they were going to play and just sort of let me try to make it sound like something.'

He admitted to having had 'a few issues with Earle Mankey's guitar, as it would sometimes turn to mush with the effects from his amp – but it was all good-natured, and in fact it became a joke between us. My intent was to give the record some tone and less "gnash".'

The sessions seemed to last forever, Ron remembers; 'It took a long time [to record] because we weren't used to having to play on time and in tune. Todd's way of recording was totally different from Earle's way. Earle was a genius at doing home tapes. It's a different thing getting into the studio, where somebody's trying to make what was intended to be a professional record.

'The object for us was to keep as much of that amateur quality as we could, but still have it be a record...keeping it a little slapdash, so that it has some personality and doesn't sound like it's done in a conference room. A lot of bands now seem to be rebelling against a certain kind of slickness; that's always been our aim. Todd was really easy to work with because he was of our age group, he was in a band – so there wasn't that barrier between producer and band – and he screwed about a lot.'

But there were problems, as Russell recalled. 'Todd thought we were groovy. His girlfriend thought we were really, *really* groovy.' At first, Rundgren didn't seem to notice as Miss Christine's attentions slipped further away from him, and closer towards Russell Mael. By the time it did click, it was too late. 'Talk about being naïve,' Russell laughed. 'She used to say she wanted to come home with me and I never knew what for. And all the time I was thinking "Gee she's a GTO"...'

He figured it out eventually – probably around the same time as Rundgren – and the affair was finally consummated. But, he continued, 'It was a funny relationship. Like, we'd spend the day baking bread and taking the results back to show Ron. She really had...umm... interesting...umm...interests. It sure was fun baking things during the day, though.'

Ron, too, acknowledged conflict, and further admitted that working with Rundgren was often a chore, simply because the producer was so creative in his own right that he completely forgot whose record it was.

'Todd Rundgren is extremely nice, but if you had to work with him, you wouldn't have much space for your own ideas.' At the same time, however, Rundgren 'pushed us to be even more strange than we were at that time, which is something that might not happen these days. When you sign to a record label [now], the A&R staff steps in and puts their two cents' worth about how you need the hit, and if you did this it would make it more palatable for such and such a format. Todd just took what we were doing intact, and sonically improved the fidelity of the recordings.'

'We didn't feel Todd's way of producing was suitable for our music... However, he could not be convinced otherwise. We started to behave a bit nasty and aggressive towards him and finally he didn't turn up anymore.'

Lowe, however, remembered things somewhat differently. 'Todd was getting pretty busy at that time, and had other things to do and I would be left in sessions with the band. This was not unusual for me – Terry Melcher and I had done the same thing with a band called Grapefruit. Besides, this was fun stuff, interesting to record, and Halfnelson were not as serious and self-conscious as some bands.'

All four songs from the most recent Halfnelson demo tape would make it onto the album, along with a couple of Russell's contributions to the earlier demo acetate, 'Saccharin And The War', which was completely rerecorded, and 'Roger', which was simply a remix of the original, near-perfect, demo take with a re-recorded vocal. A Ron and Russell co-write, 'Big Bands', meanwhile underwent a complete change of pace before it was consigned to tape. Feinstein explained, 'We played it in an old-fashioned Latin style, like Ricky Ricardo would have done it. I loved it. Russ called it "Herbert Hoover's Latin American Tour".'

'(No More) Mr Nice Guys', penned by Ron and Jim Mankey, followed, while Jim alone offered up the plaintive 'I'm An Old Retired Man', a song that was scheduled for inclusion right up until the very last minute. 'It was recorded, mixed and everything,' said Feinstein, 'but it was left off... Not sure why. It was good.' The sessions were completed with 'Simple Ballet', another Ron and Russell co-write which Rundgren later described as one of Halfnelson's defining moments.

Performing the song at their very first audition for Rundgren, the band suggested that Feinstein play 'minimal drums'. Not at all certain whether it would work, but unable to think of anything else, Feinstein carried his cymbal alone into the Doggy Factory bathroom, and played along from there. Now, counselling the group never to lose the quirkiness that had attracted him in the first place, Rundgren cited Feinstein's trip to the bathroom as the perfect example of what he meant.

Not one of the songs slipped into what could be described as a comfortable musical pigeonhole, then. But for sheer individuality, and proof that, as Los Angeles oddballs went, Halfnelson were probably the oddest, it was Earle Mankey's 'Biology 2' which scooped the honours.

If this hadn't been California, he'd probably have been institutionalised for writing a love song for chromosomes. 'Oh hold me,' the song's composer sang, 'You know you are my one and only phenotype, and together we can have a genotype.' And, perhaps tellingly, 'Biology 2' was the only album cut to receive even a little local airplay, which was great for the band but a sad day for Russell, who'd stepped aside from the microphone to allow Earle to take lead vocal (and wife Elisa to add a line as well – 'Oooh, let's do it!'). 'Yes,' he explained, 'it was the first [Halfnelson] song I ever heard on the radio. How boring. I didn't even get to hear myself singing on the radio!'

'Halfnelson' was released in the United States only, in late 1971, alongside new releases by two of their Bearsville label-mates, Jesse Winchester and Lazarus. Ron designed the sleeve, an enthralling adaptation of an old General Motors advertisement picturing a glamorous woman sitting in the back of a 1969 Oldsmobile, with the band members' heads cut and pasted behind the car's windows.

'That was all Ron's idea,' said Dupont. 'He found the photograph, and I think it was his idea to photograph the band looking in the window, although I don't remember whose idea it was to have me colour tint it. But, ironically, that turned into a very peculiar career for me, because I did the second Sparks album, and then I was called on literally hundreds of times to colour tint LP covers, photographs and, later, movie posters. And that all came from doing those early Sparks covers...'

Russell: We cut our photos into that photo. We actually went to the legal step of asking permission from the auto company before using the photo. Kind of like an early form of sampling.'

To coincide with the album's release, Halfnelson launched into their first spate of truly intensive gigging. Unfortunately, it didn't go well.

It was, Russell shuddered, 'Absolutely terrible. We were playing at High School dances – one time we played at the opening of a Hollywood delicatessen. The other act was a blind piano player! And then we actually found ourselves performing at a Mormon dance, which was a real problem because Mormons aren't supposed to dance, and they don't like suggestive lyrics.'

Reviews of the album failed to materialise; radio play seem to be confined to that single airing of 'Biology 2' – 'Halfnelson' was dying on its feet. Finally, Albert Grossman called them up to his office to tell them exactly what he thought was wrong with them.

The band's relationship with Grossman had always been a little peculiar, as Ron explained. 'He bought us a lot of Chinese meals and, all the time, we kept begging him for a PA! Onetime he actually said: "Fellas, a PA has just rolled into your lives" and we said "A…A…Albert". It wasn't true, of course, but it was still kinda neat to see this Great White Father keep promising you a PA.'

Russell continued, 'Albert… We met him a couple of times in New York,' including one occasion when he did indeed treat them to dinner at a traditional Szechuan restaurant, the first time that any of the band had experienced Chinese food out of anything more glamorous than a grease-proof cardboard box. 'He was musically very supportive of what we were doing; we didn't have much contact with him, he was almost like a God figure. You knew he was there in the background but you didn't really deal with him that much, because things were running well just with us and Todd. He was a ceremonial figure; he'd give us the token dinner.' When the call came to present themselves in his office, Halfnelson could not imagine what his solution to their difficulties might be. Probably more Chinese food…

In fact, 'He said it was the band's name,' said Ron. 'He told us that no-one would go for a band called Halfnelson, and that we ought to change it to something more suitable.' Idly, the band wondered whether Grossman had been taken in by one of Russell's favourite insistences, that 'halfnelson is the name of an obscene Japanese sex act,' but they did agree that they could perhaps benefit from a more accessible name.

Russell took up the story; 'He'd always thought we were really funny, like the Marx Brothers, and his suggestion was that we call ourselves the Sparks Brothers. We just said (raspberry), but rather than ruin the whole situation with him, we took the Sparks bit, which is kind of anonymous, bland, and boring, but it is a band name.' More caustically, he later snapped, '[Grossman] was against our old image and wanted us to change radically. We could not convince him otherwise, so we just had to do it. After all, he's the big boss.'

At the same time, however, he was impressed that Grossman should have even cared about such things. 'My memory of him was that he was always very supportive, even to the point of wanting to know why the album didn't succeed. Even if it was a bad idea about it having to be the name being too obscure and oblique…that was the sole reason the album didn't do well in his eyes, so let's change the name. But even to the point of trying to figure out what we would do, he wasn't saying change your music, he was saying change your name.'

In fact, Grossman's original Sparks Brothers name would see some action, courtesy of a series of trade paper advertisements arranged by Bearsville's parent label and distributor. 'Warner Brothers welcomes…the one and only Sparks Brothers'. By the time the 'Halfnelson' album had been re-pressed with new labels and sleeves in mid-1972, however, the name had been truncated once again – they were now simply Sparks.

A new band, a new look. Ron was nursing a fascination with brickwork at the time, the simple utilitarian red brick building blocks that hold up much of the civilised world. For a while, he was even considering building himself a pair of trousers out of bricks (albeit plastic ones), although the idea never got past the design stage. Now, however, his dreams could take flight, as the old 'Halfnelson' cover art was ditched in favour of a plain red brick wall with the band members arranged somewhat threateningly in front of it. Lowe recalled being especially disappointed; 'I loved the car-interior version.'

But Grossman knew what he was talking about. In July 1972, 'Wonder Girl' was pulled off the album as a single, and the band promptly found themselves vying with the Osmonds' 'Hold Her Tight', Gary Glitter's 'Rock'n'Roll' and local heroes Sailcat's 'Motorcycle Mama' at the top of the WHHY radio charts in Montgomery County, Alabama. Listeners in Fargo, North Dakota, followed suit, pushing 'Wonder Girl' to the top of the chart, from where it gazed down upon all the superstars in the land. Something was happening.

'Sparks make you feel stupid because you can't pin them down at all,' Todd Rungren once declared. 'Their music relates a little to the real world, but their lyrics don't relate at all to anything that's real.' Maybe he was right. You can sell a lot of rubbish to the general public, but would they ever buy a sense of their own stupidity? Sparks were beginning to believe that they would.

American Bandstand came calling. It was America's leading music show of the era, and although an appearance was not the cast-iron guarantee of a hit that Britain's *Top Of The Pops* could generally offer, it was the closest thing the country had to such a programme, and Sparks did not need to be asked twice. Their appearance went out on 29th July 1972, in a show headlined by Australian-born songbird Helen Reddy and, back at Bearsville, all eyes alternately watched with pride and with mounting horror as Sparks set out to win the hearts of America.

Host Dick Clark had already given the watching public some taste of what to expect when he introduced the band as being good 'despite their appearance'. But the sight of Russell in a violently chequered red and white suit, wielding a huge wooden sledgehammer, was enough to catch most viewers' attention, and that was before the cameras zoomed in on Ron, Charlie Chaplin in a Curly Howard mop-top, with a Beatles pendant around his neck.

Nattily attired in suit and quiff, looking for all the world like a disreputable stand-in for one of Bill Haley's Comets, Clark fingered the pendant and stared at the camera. No matter what words he actually said, you could still hear the grand old man of American musical broadcasting wondering what the hell his producers had lumbered him with now, but this meeting ignited Clark's friendship with and admiration for the Maels that would last until well into the Eighties.

But 'Wonder Girl' was a good song and, although *American Bandstand* could ultimately push it no higher than Number 92 on the *Cashbox* magazine chart, at last Sparks were getting noticed.

In Omaha, Nebraska, a 20-year-old drummer named Hilly Michaels was sitting in his car with friends, listening to the radio. Suddenly a song came on that was like nothing he'd ever heard before, by a band he'd never heard of. 'Wonder Girl', by Sparks.

---

1. 2:15
2. 2:54
   Half Music
   ASCAP
3. 2:30
   M.C.B.
   Music

4. 3:03
5. 4:01
6. 3:50
   Half Music
   ASCAP

BEARSVILLE

PROMOTION
Playing Time:
18:33

NOT FOR SALE

HALFNELSON
Produced by Todd Rundgren
Engineered by James Lowe

SIDE 1   STEREO   BV 2048 (31,310)   33⅓ RPM

1. WONDER GIRL (Ron Mael)
2. FA LA FA LEE (Ron Mael)
3. ROGER (Russell Mael)
4. HIGH C (Ron Mael)
5. FLETCHER HONORAMA (Ron Mael)
6. SIMPLE BALLET (Russell Mael and Ron Mael)

DISTRIBUTED BY WARNER BROS RECORDS, INC./A SUBSIDIARY AND LICENSEE OF WARNER BROS. INC./MADE IN U.S.A

'I said "Shush, listen to this you guys! Turn this up!" I became an instant fan. I couldn't believe how understated and cool the production was, and I thought the vocals were great. It had such a fresh and unique sound, even a bit Beatle-ish sounding, which really drew me in. I zeroed into the drum part, which was so underplayed – there was just a single kick-snare hit on the drums, with an echo repeat on the hi-hat and kick drum. That's it! Very, very, clever. I thought it was brilliantly produced, a super great *new* sound and, although I heard it many times while living in Omaha and Iowa, I never tired of it.'

Sparks were in demand. Their first out-of-state concerts materialised, including one memorable trip to Houston, Texas. It was, as Larry Dupont recalled, a nightmare from start to finish.

'We had to split up into two groups because our vehicle wouldn't even hold the entire band, and Jimmy ended up in the truck with the gear. The rental car broke down two or three times, but the first time was in the middle of the Mojave Desert. We were finally picked up by a bunch of Mexicans in a truck, which was a welcome sight, because otherwise we could have died.

'We finally got to the Texas border and Earle told us how you have got to be careful driving along these little roads at night, because people had been killed crashing into deer, and the deer's antlers would go through the windscreen. But our real adventure was on our way into Houston, where an immense thunderstorm broke out. The rain was coming down so heavily that it was sheeting *up* the windshield, lightning and thunder were absolutely all over the place, and my headlights were shining maybe three to five feet ahead of us.

'I knew we couldn't stop, because we'd probably die; you don't want to be parked by the side of the road or under a bridge during a storm like that. At one point we saw lightning silhouette a house and some trees; we drove around the corner and the house was in flames.'

Finally they reached Houston, but their ordeal was not yet over. The storm had passed, but the humidity was merciless, so high that even climbing into the hotel pool to try and cool off was useless. You couldn't even tell whether you were in or out of the water. The only upside to the weather, they discovered, was when they came offstage following their first show in town, and were able to steam the wrinkles out of their stage suits by hanging them out on the hotel balcony over night.

And still Texas conspired against them. Russell was accompanied again by his giant mallet as he performed, but this was the night that he misjudged one particular swing and brought the mallet crashing down on his own head. He continued to perform for a moment, while his band-mates laughed all around him. It was only when they noticed the blood running down the side of his face before disappearing into the black and red check of his jacket that they realised he'd seriously hurt himself. The show was stopped and Russell was rushed off to hospital.

Larry Dupont: 'Of course, the rest of us still thought this thing with Russ was really funny as hell. As long as he didn't have a concussion, and as long as he was still conscious, it was fine. But Ron is extremely protective of his younger brother, and he didn't find it at all funny. He was very perturbed, and he couldn't understand why the rest of us were still laughing. I think even Russ thought it was funny until he saw how upset Ron was.'

CHAPTER FIVE

SKIP THE FOREPLAY,
LET HER RIP

Sparks management had long since passed out of Mike Berns' hands and into those of Roy Silver, a co-owner of the Tetragrammaton group of companies, and a man seemingly well-versed in nurturing the eccentric. Tiny Tim and the all-girl group Fanny (at a time when the notion of an all-girl rock group really did strike most onlookers as bizarre) were already in his stable, and Harley Feinstein recalled, 'Roy was a character. He played the cigar-chomping high-powered manager role perfectly.'

'Roy Silver absolutely made me quake in my boots, the first time I met him,' said Larry Dupont. 'He did everything in his power to be intimidating and oppressive. He was a New York screamer, the open collar with the hairy chest, the gold chains, the lot. He studied intimidation. His office was intimidating. Even the way the chairs were set up was intimidating.'

But he was also a smart judge of character. Quickly realising that Dupont was already working in almost every capacity for the band that he could, Silver deputised him to act as his assistant, and then put the band to work recording radio commercials for some of his other acts. Feinstein recalled, 'We did one for Fanny. This was *a cappella*. I sang the bass part'. They also cut one for Bobby Charles, a veteran Cajun performer (his first single, 'Later Alligator,' had been released by Chess back in 1955) who had recently signed to Bearsville…

'It came out pretty good, I thought,' said Feinstein, 'but it bore no relationship to Bobby Charles. In fact, we never even listened to his music. It sounded like another Sparks song.' It was that same day, incidentally, that Sparks fell into conversation with one of the other guys who was hanging around the studio. 'He was telling us how he had an album, and was going to make it. His name was Warren Zevon.'

Sparks, too, were going to make it – everybody believed that. 'Wonder Girl' might not have been a huge hit, but the groundswell of interest that it had created could only continue to grow. It was time to record a new album.

It was almost two years since they had teased writer Kathy Orloff with the imaginary title of 'A Woofer In Tweeter's Clothing', during which time the band had lost none of their affection for such an excruciating pun (the woofer and tweeter being components within a loudspeaker). Beyond that, however, there were few similarities between the new material and the nearly two-year-old demos that they insisted bore that name, or even the eponymous album that was released in-between.

James Thaddeus Lowe would produce. He had remained in touch with the band in between albums. 'Pamela and I went to the Whisky a couple of times and saw them. Russell was running around swinging a mallet in his checked suit, as I remember. The band was grinding it out and there was that damned "gnash" guitar again. I remember wishing I could just go up and tweak the effects knob a little. The audience seemed to be on the same planet with the band. It was a great show.'

It was Grossman's decision to promote Lowe to producer. 'Todd got another commitment, Badfinger, I think, and Albert called me up and asked if I would be interested in producing the

WARNER BROTHE[RS]
RECORDS

welcomes the

Parad[ise]

and
the one
and only

SPARKS BROTHERS

a new act on the
Bearsville Label
distributed by

second Sparks album. I jumped at the chance, because we had gotten along well and I felt there was mutual respect. One of the nicest bands I had encountered.

'My own band had been a studio-oriented group, so I brought experience from making those records, and I had also produced an album for Ananda Shankar [Ravi's nephew]. Many of the engineering projects I was working on blurred the line between producer and engineer, anyway. This was around the time of the producer/engineer title being born. When you are the only one sitting in the control room, you get used to making decisions. So I got to take "Woofer..." from the gate out. That was inspirational.'

Grossman had just one request. 'He said, "I only have one thing to ask. *Please* get the singer's voice out in front so we can understand the words".' The man who had shepherded Bob

Dylan through his earliest years knew the value of lyrics, but also understood the need for those lyrics to be comprehensible. Sparks' were not, although Lowe insisted that it was not a failing within the recording process.

'Actually, the problem was that Russell was articulating the lyrics in an odd way. It was almost like an accent you had to get used to hearing, rather than a level issue. But Grossman was a smart man; he knew the magic was in the lyrics. He actually called me a few times about this.'

The sessions kicked off at Wally Heider's studio in Hollywood. As before, the song writing was split between the various members – Ron delivered 'Whippings And Apologies', 'The Louvre' and 'Nothing Is Scared', and co-wrote 'Moon Over Kentucky' with Jim Mankey. Earle contributed another of his divisively eccentric visions, 'Underground', and the entire band threw themselves into the maniacal, and largely improvised, chant of 'Beaver O'Lindy'. 'Moon Over Kentucky', incidentally, features the one and only recorded appearance of Larry Dupont – who himself was convinced it had been erased immediately after he recorded it.

Harley Feinstein recalls; 'On some of the floor tom rolls I play, there's a cymbal playing on the upbeat... this beat is also referred to as the "one and two and". It's the beat that years later became popularised by disco, and which Franz Ferdinand has in most of their songs. That's Larry playing it.'

A pair of Ron and Russell compositions, meanwhile, hinted at an unspoken fascination with vintage erotica: 'Angus Desire', with its homo-erotic visions of public school life, and 'Here Comes Bob', a song that might have been wholly inspired by the mid-Twenties stag film, *A Smash-Up Romance*, in which the protagonist, a gentleman named Bob, crashes his car and is then plunged into a seriously erotic scene with one of his nurses. The Sparks song shifted the scenario somewhat to allow Bob to score instead with the victims of his bad driving, but the intention was surely the same.

Two songs, however, leapt out of the demos as prospective monsters, the first a Mach 1 remake of the old Rodgers and Hammerstein special 'Do Re Mi' (because, said Russell, 'It resembles something everyone's heard'), the second another Mael/Mael composition, 'Girl From Germany'. At one of the very first sessions, Lowe recalled, 'they played me a song that sounded

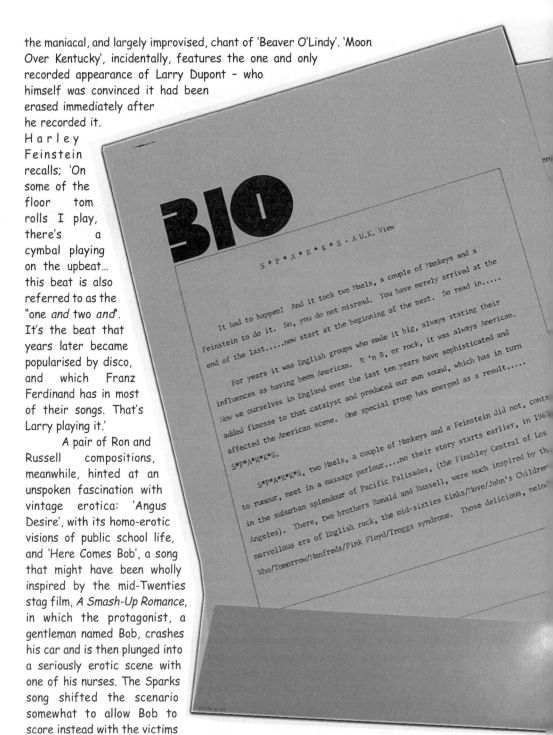

BIO

S * P * A * R * K * S - A U.K. View

It had to happen! And it took two Maels, a couple of Monkeys and a Feinstein to do it. No, you do not misread. You have merely arrived at the end of the last.....now start at the beginning of the next. So read in.....

For years it was English groups who made it big, always stating their influences as having been American. R 'n B, or rock, it was always American. Now we ourselves in England over the last ten years have sophisticated and added finesse to that catalyst and produced our own sound, which has in turn affected the American scene. One special group has emerged as a result.....
S*P*A*R*K*S.

S*P*A*R*K*S, two Maels, a couple of Monkeys and a Feinstein did not, contr to rumour, meet in a massage parlour....no their story starts earlier, in 196 in the suburban splendour of Pacific Palisades, (the Finchley Central of Los Angeles). There, two brothers Ronald and Russell, were much inspired by th marvellous era of English rock, the mid-sixties Kinks/'Love/John's Childr Who/Tomorrow/Manfreds/Pink Floyd/Troggs syndrome. Those delicious, melo

Pictured in transit at the Liverpool Street station (Central Line) of London's Underground are SPARKS. This world renowned musical aggregation (left to right: Ronald Mael, Russell Mael, James Mankey - crouching with umbrella, Earle Mankey and Harley Feinstein) is aurally represented on the current Bearsville pressing A WOOFER IN TWEETER'S CLOTHING. Ronald and Russell are brothers; James and Earle likewise are siblings. Harley is, as far as we know, unrelated to any other members of the group.

Publicity Department
Warner Bros. Records Inc.
44 East 50th Street
New York, New York 10022
(212) 832-0600

Distributed by
Warner Bros. Records Inc
3701 Warner Boulevard
Burbank, California 91505
(213) 843-6000

Publicity Department
Warner Bros. Records
44 East 50th Street
New York, New York 10022
(212) 832-0600

a little more like radio rock. I thought they needed a commercial hit to get people to listen. We agreed to do a test session at Wally Heider's on 'Girl From Germany', the song we decided would be best to get an idea of the sound for the album.'

41

It was a thrilling experience but, for Lowe, it was also a painful one. 'The night before the session, someone poured a cup of hot coffee in my lap and I was one notch below going to the emergency room. The next day I had to stand up the whole time at the 'Girl From Germany' session. But standing seemed to work, 'Germany' was a grinder and we agreed there was reason to proceed. We started on the album the next week.

'The songs are earthier on that album, and there was room to put some bass emphasis and bluesy vibration in there. I saw it as dark psych music, and that's how I tried to present it.'

There was room, too, for experimentation. Another of Ron's contributions, 'Batteries Not Included' was Sparks' idea of a radio or television commercial that could be used to promote the record itself, a short, but infuriatingly captivating jingle bemoaning the absence, of course, of batteries in a newly-purchased toy. 'They wanted to make a sort of commercial for the record during the sessions, and we needed a kid's voice. I think it was Earle Mankey that went out of the studio onto the street in Hollywood and, five minutes later, he reappeared with this eight-year-old kid and his mom. I remember the boy stepped up to the mike and said exactly what we wanted in one take.'

'Beaver O'Lindy' called out for an accordion, so Lowe called up his old Electric Prunes band-mate Mark Tulin and borrowed his 14-year-old brother Kip, an accomplished accordion player.

'Here Comes Bob', meanwhile, required a string quartet. Larry Dupont recalled that 'somebody said it could really benefit from a string quartet, so somebody else called out for one, like they were calling out for a pizza. And these four guys turn up driving Rolls-Royces, they got to listen to the basic track, they were given a little verbal direction as to what was wanted and where it was going to, and then they played the part and left. In and out, back into their Rolls-Royces, and away.' The arrangement was written by one of Lowe's associates, a Mr Vogel. 'It's a very youthful album,' Lowe contends. 'I think "Woofer..." has a wonderful band feel to it.'

Other songs told their own stories. 'The Louvre' allied Ron's original lyric to a French translation by another friend, Josée Becker, which was then delivered in impeccable French by Russell. After 'countless debates that threatened to delay the album's release by several decades over whether we should use the version where Russell sang in French, or the English one, we compromised and used half of each.'

A sleeve was conceived and a photo session arranged. Resplendent in their newly purchased uniform of Pierre Cardin suits, the band returned to Larry Dupont's lair in UCLA's Ethnic Arts Department, there to arrange themselves in a series of earnestly band-like poses for the camera. But the session dragged on and, looking for a moment of light relief, Feinstein, standing behind the seated Ron, suddenly pulled his band-mate's chair backwards. Ron flailed, the camera clicked, and when they looked at the negatives afterwards and saw the keyboard player disappearing into a shocked blur of movement, the band knew they had their sleeve. Dupont got to work with his hand-tinting inks, colouring in the band and recolouring Russell's suit as well. Bored with the red and black he normally wore, the singer asked for something different. Dupont gave him green and black. Like the record it enclosed, it was classy, distinctive and utterly unique.

But somehow, Sparks were not satisfied. At the end of July 1972, with the final mix of the album complete, Lowe was driving Ron and Russell back to their house when the conversation turned, quite naturally, towards the future. 'Ron asked me what I thought the next album should be about. I said, "How about love? Everyone can relate to that!" The thunderous silence told me I would not be doing the next album.'

Larry Dupont was not surprised. 'My greatest memory of Todd Rundgren in the studio was him sitting there with a drumstick up each nostril. As much as he liked the group, he wasn't really what the group needed. Jim was an improvement, in the sense that the band could do more what they wanted to do, but he couldn't realise what they needed, either. It was very frustrating, their whole early career to me is summed up by the thought that they were in the hands of people who didn't understand them, and that Ron and Russell were a lot smarter...and maybe *too* smart for their own good. Their music was way over the head of the people who listened to them, even management. The thing that Roy Silver brought to the picture was that he knew how to get things done. But the downside of it is that he didn't have a clue how to market the band, and where they fit.' Or maybe he did...

At the beginning of October 1972, with 'A Woofer In Tweeter's Clothing' scheduled for November release, Sparks made their East Coast debut, with a five-night residency at Max's Kansas City in New York. There, amid the Warhol freaks and wannabe circus that was the venue's nightly stock in trade, Sparks' bizarre appearance and even

more bizarre music at least dragged a few tables' attention away from whatever was being sucked, swallowed or injected that night, although Ron's later insistence that the waitresses loved the band should, perhaps, be taken with a pinch of salt. They liked every band that encouraged the punters to buy drinks, and songs like 'Green Thumb', 'Pardon My French' and 'We Will Make Great Pets' certainly did that.

Eschewing the chance to showcase either of their recorded albums in all their glory, Sparks instead insisted on peppering the set with new material, partly because it was fun to do so, but also because it relieved the monotony of playing 40-minutes-worth of the same songs twice a night, every night for the best part of a week. Old favourites like 'My White Bicycle' and the Equals' 'Baby Come Back' were set regulars, too.

Their performance was received with curiosity more than anything else. 'Sparks is a rock novelty act with a humorous approach... [and] a nostalgic feel despite the amplification,' cautioned the *Village Voice*. True, their 'Music Hall Rock' was distinguished by Russell revealing himself to be 'one of the most active of rock performers as he and [Earle] Mankey prance about throughout the set.' But still you got the impression that the reviewer really wasn't certain what to make of them.

One onlooker, however, a 19-year-old David Bowie fan named Joseph Fleury, was so he American....versus vice!" thus quoth Russ. So deep was their distaste for the All-American tan and brawn, that they totally ignored their local California vitamin D sunshine-rich beach, for fear of "getting a tan and being mistaken for the locals!" Satorially, they rejected out of hand, silks, satins, and sparkle, "That's for record company executives!", and they adopted that saviour of civilization: The Suit. "Frimpy, wimpy suits - now that's elegant!"

By now they were managed by Fanny manager Mark Hammerman, and had a close friend in Roy Silver (agent of renown) who suggested a change of name to S*P*A*R*K*S. So S*P*A*R*K*S they became.

And the stage act...
Russell energetically...
agressively harrasses...
RON!! Is that Ron? Ye...
up with his vegetables)...
image of Charlie Chapli...

He actually thought...
a T.V. appearance on ABC...
Charlie Chaplin's return...
believe that Ron wasn't...
Ron accordingly added Ch...
'dead-pan' allowing only...
behind the 'tache, but Ro...

In the States their...
having recorded S*P*A*R*K...

BIO

S*P*A*R*K*S

It had to happen! And it took two... Feinstein to do it. No, you do not mis... end of the last.....now start at the be...

For years it was English groups wh... influences as having been American. R... Now we ourselves in England over the ... added finesse to that catalyst and pr... affected the American scene. One spe... S*P*A*R*K*S.

S*P*A*R*K*S, two Maels, a coupl... to rumour, meet in a massage parlour... in the suburban splendour of Pacific... Angeles). There, two brothers Rona... marvellous era of English rock, the... Who/Tomorrow/Manfreds/Pink Floyd/T...

Distributed by
Warner Bros. Records
4000 Warner Boulevard
Burbank, California 91505

tuney tunes that in retrospect we all loved more than we knew. So Ron and Russ, in all innocence gathered a few songs in their hearts and answered an ad for a local studio.

The studio turned out to be Earle Mankey's living-room, where Earle possessed a $50 tape-recorder and a guitar. The two innocent brothers were much shocked by the deception in the ad (which had promised 16-track facilities for $2 an Hour!) but Earle was even more shocked with their undisciplined playing. "You need a guitarist", he said, picking up his guitar to join them. "that'll be $2.50 an Hour". And so he joined them. They called themselves HalfNelson, because it was a wrestling hold, and they refused to play live dates because they had no rhythm section. "We decided", said Russ, "to be a studio band".

So for two years (whilst they attended the University of South California, L.A.) they made tapes. Weird-sounding songs with titles like, "Johnny's Adventure" "Spider Run" "Do The Factory", were recorded often with the trio percussing on cardboard boxes and frying pans. Though the tape machine was cheap, it did have an...

Feinstein kindly, dropped his eye on an ad for a drummer in an L.A. student paper, sent to him by a 'liaison'. He packed his bags and flew straight home to reply in person. This was dangerous as the paper was months old. But then so were Ron, Russ and Earle by the time he arrived, and they were waiting for Harley. Harley had never played drums, so he was in.

And now they required a bass player. Many were seen who wanted to "boogie" (shudder!!) till Earle revealed that in earlier life he had a brother who was still a brother, in a "Blooze Band". Enter Jim, young of age and fiery of soul. He had just left a band called Three Day Blues, and was at first scornful of HalfNelson's strange approach. After he joined as guitarist/bass, he changed his mind.

The "NEW IMPROVED" sound reached mighty ears: the very Todd Rundgren and his lady of then, Miss Christine, of the infamous GTO's. Todd especially could see where our boys were at. After all he had spent time in the only other Anglophile American band, The Nazz. "I'm coming boys!" he wrote, "I'm coming!" And he did. And he signed them to Bearsville before you could say "Uncle Albert

An L.A. studio was hired, and though a little unnerved by the lack of homeliness compared to Earle's own 'studio', they recorded well and in quantity, whilst Todd produced. The produce was an album, singularly individual with songs like, "High C" and "Wonder Girl" (the former being about a fading opera singer's relationship with a rock star, and the latter not!) By the time Bearsville were ready to release the album, the live appearances they had so studiously avoided became a necessity.

"We wanted to look English. Just like English bands thought it was cool to

- 5 -

Clothing", decided to give S*P*A*R*K*S the chance of a lifetime, and send th... to the country that influenced them most to drink up the atmosphere. Which... Why S*P*A*R*K*S came here....merry on melodious music making.

If one were an academic, one would know that Russ had in fact paid a... visit to these shores in '66, as a guest of Ray Davies, and 1967 lent his... ability for high falsetto to such Kinks masterpieces as "Waterloo Sunset"... other tracks on their "Something Else By" album. One would also know th... and Russ's parents have settled here in Clapham Junction, but this is a... dental, for what concerns us is S*P*A*R*K*S....and they are flying....

# # #

December, 1972

44

impressed that he would wind up devoting the rest of his life to Sparks.

Fleury had great taste in music. Ziggy had broken through to the mainstream that same autumn of 1972, riding into America on the back of gigantic hype and proving, for once, that all the high hopes were justified. Fleury, however, had been following him long before that – more than two years had elapsed since Fleury paid his first membership subscription to Brian Kinchy's International David Bowie Society. Another early member, according to Kinchy, was John Mendelsohn.

Fleury was a Sparks fan as well, converted the day he picked up a copy of 'Halfnelson' on the strength of its cover design. He attended the first of the Max's shows, and then ran into the band themselves the following day in a nearby record store. He introduced himself, was invited back to the next show, and straightaway began work on a Sparks fan club. Within only a few months, membership stood at 200 plus – small fry compared with the organization's later success, but not bad for a band whose biggest ever hit had been scored in Montgomery County, Alabama.

Days later, Sparks left the United States for Europe. Although this was to be their first working look at their spiritual homeland, Ron, Russell, Dupont and Earle Mankey had all visited the UK in the past – on one occasion, in fact, Ron, Mankey and wife Elise travelled over together, leaving Russell and the rest of the band to their own devices back at the Doggy Factory. There, said Dupont, 'they started to do some sessions and play around in our absence, and they put together a really nice bit of music. It was a lot heavier than usual, very different.' Only when Ron and Earle returned from their trip did the song begin to take on more recognisably Sparks-like qualities.

With his press clippings file seemingly bubbling over with remarks about Sparks' distinctly English reference points – amongst others, *Sounds* made the point in 1970 and the *Village Voice* reiterated it two years later – Roy Silver convinced Warner Brothers that Sparks' greatest hope of making it might well lie in the UK. Or, more accurately, he did not so much convince them as force them into making that decision for themselves, relentlessly dropping by the offices every day until somebody gave him what he wanted.

'Roy's philosophy to get a record company to do something is to talk on a daily basis as though something is happening,' explained Larry Dupont, who found himself sitting in on several of the meetings. 'You don't ask for things, you talk about when they're going to happen, and sooner or later somebody screws up. And the screw-up here was extreme.'

Sparks were indeed given tickets to England, and placed in the care of Warner Brothers' London counterpart, WEA, under the watchful eye of former Beatles press man Derek Taylor. What Taylor was not told, and would not be for a surprisingly long time, was the size of the budget allocated to the band. In fact it was a comparatively paltry $10,000, enough to keep them in the country for a couple of weeks but not much more. Taylor, however, knew nothing of this; so far as he and his assistant Mandy Newell were concerned, Sparks had an open-ended meal ticket, and they were going to take full advantage of it.

Equipment was hired, hotel rooms were booked, living expenses were run up. There did come a time, Dupont recalled, when it looked as though Newell might just be about to figure out that the band had never been budgeted by either Warner Brothers or Bearsville, and he admitted that he was getting a little nervous about the possibility of being unmasked. But at the vital moment, responsibility for the group passed over to somebody else in the office, and he could breathe again.

'It was funny in a way, because the band was getting very upset that the record company wasn't doing enough for them, whereas my concern was that they might do too much and we'd be thrown out of England! Meanwhile, there was me, this guy in England pretending to manage the group...it was all very surreal.'

CHAPTER SIX

THE GOLDEN OPPORTUNITY
TO LOVE ME

Sparks, with Larry Dupont on board as both road manager and official photographer, flew into Heathrow Airport late in October 1972, to be met by their very own welcoming committee. The Maels' mother and step-father had relocated to London just a few months earlier, renting a home in Clapham Junction, and now they were waiting inside the terminal in full regalia; Miriam resplendent in a hat surmounted by either a silver skyscraper or an aeroplane (memories differ), Rogie as the archetypal Englishman with bowler hat and cane. A portable cassette recorder blasted Sparks' music through the arrivals lounge.

The band would not be staying with the Rogansons; their first halt was the up-market Constantine Hotel, near South Kensington tube station. They remained there for a month or so, then relocated to the Snows Hotel on Cromwell Road; 'cheaper and a little seedier,' as Feinstein puts it, and also prone to bolt its front door long before the average late-night reveller would be ready to go to bed.

Although they couldn't offer the band bed and board, the Maels' parents were gracious hosts, nonetheless. One evening Rogie took the entire band, including Dupont, out to the Playboy Club for what Feinstein described as 'the most lavish dinner I had ever had up to that point in my life.' Rogie was working in a shoe shop about halfway down the King's Road at the time; a fair chunk of his weekly wage was probably spent on that meal.

Sparks arrived in England to find the country still in the grip of its most enthralling musical upsurge since the Maels' beloved psychedelic era. It was the age of glam rock, the movement ushered in almost unintentionally by Marc Bolan and T. Rex at the end of 1970, and which he alone had propagated until the breakthrough of Slade a full 12 months later. Their 'Coz I Luv You', released at the end of 1971, proved to be the first of six UK chart-toppers over the next two years; T. Rex, by comparison, achieved only four. More importantly, however, it opened floodgates that neither critic nor prophet could ever have predicted.

Leading the field were the Sweet and David Bowie, of course, one a pantomime horror show which draped its bubblegum leanings in a series of ever more outrageous costumes, the other an emissary from some far-flung galaxy, fallen to Earth to let the children boogie. There was Gary Glitter, portly as he approached his rumoured middle-age but still capable of unleashing the most primal, stomping, tinsel-wrapped savagery. Even Elton John, the quiet, bespectacled, denim- and cap-clad bard whom UNI had so proudly signed around the same time as they didn't sign Sparks, had reinvented himself as some kind of rock'n'roll Liberace, his outlandish attire a riot of glitter and feathers.

Roy Wood, whom the Maels had so admired during his time with the Move, was back under an avalanche of hair and more war paint than the entire Cherokee nation. Roxy Music, Rod Stewart…you could barely turn around without bumping into another spangled peacock striding up in day-glo finery, and every one of them sounded just as good as they looked.

Simply walking down the street, the excitement was palpable. Back home, even the hippest kids dressed in T-shirt and jeans, James Taylor chic with just a hint of left-over hippydom. In

London, though, people barely left the house unless their trousers flared out over multi-storey platform boots, or their hair was teased to galactic proportions. A lot of it looked very silly, of course, but Sparks did not view it like that. All they saw was excitement, and they intended to soak it all in.

The band's schedule was leisurely – a couple of shows a week, with WEA footing the bill for everything, travel, meals, accommodation, the lot. It was, the musicians agreed, like Rock Star Camp, at least until their first review rolled in, a merciless assault spread over far more space than it ought to have been. But Roy Silver, paying the band one of his occasional visits, was delighted. 'They were absolutely ripped to shreds by the journalist,' recalled Dupont, 'and they were terribly upset. And Roy said to them, "You don't understand! This is wonderful! Any publicity is better than none."' He was right, too. The next time Sparks played, it was to an audience at least partially comprised of people lured along by the vitriol of that review.

Sparks would ultimately play around 30 shows during their European sojourn, although their date book was scarcely designed for convenience. Rather, they enacted virtual guerrilla raids on the cities they were scheduled to appear in, usually returning to London immediately afterwards. But Silver had done his job. In every new country, there was work to be done.

Sparks' London life kicked off with a residency at the Pheasantry, on the King's Road. A legendary artists' colony during the Sixties, when it played host to the likes of photographer Bob Whittaker, Australian film-maker Philippe Mora and feminist writer Germaine Greer, and where Eric Clapton and artist Martin Sharp wrote Cream's 'Tales Of Brave Ulysses', the old block of flats had since been converted into a nightclub and restaurant, and elected one of the hottest new venues in London.

A huge photograph of Sparks dominated the entrance, and the individual musicians were each provided with an expense account, all drinks and meals to be charged to WEA. It was heaven – especially when certain band members discovered that they only needed to point to their portrait on the wall to melt the heart of even the iciest local maiden. Even on the nights Sparks weren't playing, Feinstein at least was hanging out at the Pheasantry, often with Earle Mankey alongside him.

Jim, on the other hand, tended not to go out at all, preferring to remain at the hotel. 'It had to be so depressing for him,' sympathises Dupont. 'He didn't travel well. He used to disappear after a job and, at the beginning, we used to try and get him to come out with us. But after a while it was "where's Jimmy?" – "oh, he's in his hotel room".' The Maels, on the other hand, had their own itinerary to keep, either visiting their mother or touring the city and its museums and art galleries. Often the band members saw one another only at meal times.

Switzerland was the group's first continental destination, a trip to Zurich to film the *Hits A Go-Go* television show. They were given time to perform two songs, a punchy 'Wonder Girl' before playing the show out with a frenetic 'Do Re Mi', the five band members posing so perfectly for the cameras that there were moments when they seemed almost static onstage.

'That show was really fun,' recalled Feinstein. 'The kids all invited us over to one of their houses for a party afterwards. Most of them spoke only Swiss-German. But I found a girl that spoke French, which I spoke, so we were able to communicate. One young fellow asked me for an autograph. I was a jerk so I autographed his forehead with a marker. He proudly posed and Larry snapped a photo. I still have it.'

The band found further entertainment at the expense of Gary Glitter, a fellow guest on the show but, seriously, one of the flabbiest excuses for a rock star they had ever seen. 'He and his manager [Mike Leander] were so creepy,' Feinstein shuddered. 'They talked like east-coast gangsters. Glitter was out of shape, yet he wore those skin-tight silver lamé suits and platforms. It was all we could do to repress our laughter at him. He was a joke.'

From Switzerland, the band moved onto France; it was there that they finally got their hands on the newly-pressed copies of 'A Woofer In Tweeter's Clothing', specially delivered from Bearsville to London, and then forwarded on by the ever-obliging WEA.

The party arrived in the Netherlands on 10th November, stepping off their plane at Schipol airport to be met by journalist Constance Meijers of *Aloha* magazine. He would conduct them first to a photo session for his publication, and then onto the studios of Radio North Sea International, a thriving neo-pirate station whose evening-long English language broadcasts were essential listening for a generation of British teens, static and interference notwithstanding.

Christmas was still six weeks away, but disc jockey Alfred Lagarde led the band through both the scheduled interview and an improvised Christmas jingle, before waving them off for their next stop, another outing for 'Wonder Girl' on the nationally broadcast *Top Pop* television show in Hilversum. It was there that they encountered their first ever hysterical audience. Meijers reported that their visit was highlighted by 'dozens of girls…fighting over an autograph. One of them requested an autograph on her forehead. This sort of audience was totally new to them and it utterly surprised them.' Nobody had ever asked Sparks for an autograph on their head before; now they'd done two in a week.

But a gig in Scheveningen that same evening brought the group back down to earth. A tiny club with an atrocious sound system, the Tiffany's management then compounded Sparks' discomfort when they

revealed that the scheduled support act would not be appearing, and that Sparks would need to fill in for them, as well as playing their own show. Looking out at the tiny audience that was surely present more through curiosity (or the absence of any alternative entertainment in town that evening), Ron agreed, but insisted that they'd play the exact same set both times.

Journalist Meijers recounted the rest of the evening. 'The gig is poorly attended, the quality of the band unworthy. But...we are all in a very optimistic mood. For me personally, this is even increased by hearing, after many years, their version of Tomorrow's "[My] White Bicycle". Noticeable is Russell's phenomenal singing, who seems to have a control over his voice which has seldom been heard. This particularly applies for his modulations, of which he makes ample use, especially during the magnificent "Girl From Germany", which ends yodelling. Ron Mael's act consists of taking various poses for several seconds each, thereby carefully avoiding any contact with the audience. This however, results in a lot of laughter. Most of the songs are (still) new to me, but the band plays with full spirit.'

Back in London, Sparks made their UK television debut on 21st November 1972, guesting alongside the recently re-emergent singer-songwriter Neil Sedaka (and some film footage of Bill Withers) on the *Old Grey Whistle Test*. 'Wonder Girl' and '(No More) Mr Nice Guys' were the evening's fare, but it was not a happy introduction to the country. Just months after the show's genial host, Bob Harris, told the world that he thought Roxy Music were an unimpressive hype, and almost exactly a year before he described the New York Dolls as 'mock rock' and so lit the slow-burning fuse of punk, the bearded whisperer condemned Sparks as a cross between Frank Zappa and the Monkees, and the worst thing he'd ever seen. It seemed that even England, the land which had inspired so many of their hopes and aspirations, wasn't ready for the Maels.

Sparks watched the broadcast back at the Snows Hotel, seated in the television room with all the other guests, one of whom, an older gentleman, appeared to be present simply so he could shout rude and insulting things at whoever might be appearing on the screen. No matter what programme he was watching, something would set him off, and often at such a volume that he completely drowned out the sound of the television itself. Sparks' *Old Grey Whistle Test* performance inevitably prompted one of his outbursts.

Feinstein recalled, 'The band assembled in the TV room of the hotel and, sure enough, the man who yelled was there. We came on and he was yelling insults at us on the TV.' He didn't even seem to be aware that the objects of his derision were sitting all around him. He simply shouted. 'We couldn't shut him up. So we never really got to hear the show.'

Neither did they hear much of what Neil Sedaka had to say, as his interview followed Sparks' performance and the moment he appeared the old man bellowed out his hatred for the podgy American veteran. But what they did hear prompted Sparks to take up arms as loudly as their fellow viewer. 'We couldn't hear much over the old guy's yelling, but I remember hearing Sedaka say that we represented a certain kind of band that was becoming more prevalent in music...a kind of band that he didn't like. The host didn't disagree. I wondered what kind of band he was talking about. I didn't know what kind of band we were.'

Harris and Sedaka's harsh words notwithstanding, the *Old Grey Whistle Test* turned Sparks' entire visit around. Their earlier sporadic gigging suddenly became a flood of dates, both in London and further out into the provinces. The crowning glory, however, came when WEA called up to inform them they would be playing a block of four shows at London's famous Marquee Club, every Thursday night throughout December, treading the same hallowed boards as so many of their own past heroes.

The opening night of the residency was 7th December 1972. The evening before, Sparks were at the wonderfully-named Growling Budgie in Ilford, playing to a small, but genuinely enthusiastic audience that appeared to be comprised almost wholly of *Whistle Test* viewers. The Marquee audience, too, contained just a couple of hundred people, but the venue's window was festooned with photographs and the distinctive red brick facade of the first album sleeve, and when the show was over, the band simply stared at one another in amazement. 'It was the best gig the band ever did while I was with them,' Harley Feinstein insisted. 'The place was packed. The crowd was very receptive.'

Everybody was looking forward to the following week's gig. Then Russell fell ill. It was nothing serious, just one of the cold or flu bugs that always circulate during the winter. But it robbed him of his voice and, while Dupont is adamant that 'If Russ could have made a squeak, he'd have been out there', the band had no alternative. They cancelled their second Marquee show.

'It was a disaster,' Dupont laments. 'Afterwards, we heard there'd been queues around the block to get in. Everybody was so excited to see them, and they couldn't play.' Seventeen-year-old Derek Paice was among the luckless hundreds who queued that night to see Sparks, but ended up watching a hastily-arranged replacement.

Paice had watched the *Whistle Test* with disbelief and amazement. This was what he had been waiting for; this was the band that actually made listening to rock music a worthwhile pursuit. Like the later acolytes who declared the New York Dolls' appearance on the show completely rewired their musical futures, Paice happily admitted 'Sparks' appearance proved to be a life-changing experience.' He could scarcely believe his good fortune when he opened the *Melody Maker* and discovered Sparks were playing at the Marquee. Or his *mis*fortune when he then realised that they weren't.

'A totally forgettable first band came on, followed by a marginally better second one, but I have forgotten any details. The second band was announced as the main band of the evening. I found a member of the house staff and asked them about Sparks, but they didn't seem to have a clue as to who Sparks were, or that anyone might be expecting them to play that night. I couldn't find anyone who could confirm whether Sparks were actually playing, although I did find someone on the door who said they weren't. The atmosphere was choking with smoke and I was feeling very claustrophobic in the crush, so I left. The music wasn't good enough to stay for. It was a huge disappointment. I just hoped they would return, so I could see them another time.' But they didn't.

With Russell recovered, gigging continued to devour the band's time. Back from a short tour of the American east coast, the Kinks embarked on a handful of dates around the UK; Sparks were added to the bill for one show, at Bournemouth's Winter Gardens, a serious thrill for the Anglophile contingent even if Kinks main man Ray Davies did keep himself to himself for the evening. The remainder of the headliners were friendly, though, and Harley Feinstein still remembered sitting down with drummer Mick Avory to discuss drum pedals.

Another trip outside London took Sparks to the University of East Anglia, to open the show for the Electric Light Orchestra, the band formed by another of the Mael's heroes, Roy Wood, following the demise of the Move. Wood had moved on from ELO as well by now, putting together a new group called Wizzard and leaving ELO to the mercy of Jeff Lynne. At this stage it was still uncertain whether ELO would ever truly get off the ground.

Laughing with the benefit of hindsight, Feinstein recalled, 'Many people, including Ron and Russell, thought that the essence of the Move was Roy Wood. They had placed their bets on Wizzard being the band that made it, not ELO.'

A barely heated furniture storeroom acted as a dressing room for both bands. The gig itself was in a small room in front of just a few hundred people, but Sparks went down as well as they could have hoped, and ELO were simply blinding.

Sparks were having the time of their lives. 'We were on [that] one TV show [*Whistle Test*], then they booked some club dates and, as a result of that one TV show we were selling out these clubs,' Russell marvelled. 'We thought "God, this is so easy here. People actually respond to what you're doing..."'

A new face appeared on the scene. John Hewlett was heading up the UK end of Roy Silver's Tetragrammaton agency, but that wasn't the only reason why Silver wanted him on board with Sparks. Hewlett also had a track record that itself might once have caught Silver's managerial eye. As a self-confessed tone-deaf teenager, Hewlett had been the bass player in John's Children, an anarchic Mod combo that gnawed around the edges of the UK psychedelic scene during 1966-1967, and might have shattered leaving behind nothing more than a string of broken instruments and outraged club owners had their guitar player, Marc Bolan, not gone on to become the biggest British star since the Beatles.

Hewlett had not followed in his old band-mate's footsteps; never comfortable as a musician (primarily, he laughed, because he wasn't one), he instead allowed John's Children manager Simon Napier-Bell to lead him into the business side of the music business, with a job in the publishing department of the Beatles' Apple empire.

There he discovered and signed a pair of Glaswegian songwriters, Benny Gallagher and Graham Lyle and, when Hewlett left Apple to take the Tetragrammaton job, Gallagher and Lyle accompanied him. An attempt to place the duo into a new band, the Cups, failed – the band released one single, 'Good As Gold', and then folded. Hewlett, unperturbed, decided to move into management a little more seriously ('well, it seemed serious at the time'), and set about forming a new band, McGuinness Flint, around his dynamic duo. The group scored a couple of UK hit singles, 'When I'm Dead And Gone' and 'Malt And Barley Blues', before Gallagher and Lyle were finally ready to take their first steps as a self-sufficient duo. Hewlett, too, was moving on to new things.

Reuniting with John's Children drummer Chris Townson and Trevor White, a guitarist who himself would have joined John's Children had the band not broken up first, Hewlett recruited bassist Ian Hampton and singer Ian Kimmett to form a new band – which Derek Taylor, Hewlett's old friend from Apple (and Sparks would-be nemesis at WEA!), promptly christened Jook.

Boasting a deal with RCA, making them label-mates to the likes of the Sweet and David Bowie, and with their debut single 'Alright With Me' on the shelves, Jook were fascinated to learn of Hewlett's latest clients, never realising just what a profound impact this peculiar American band was about to have on their lives.

Hewlett: 'I first saw them live at the Pheasantry, and really liked the band. However, I felt that though Harley, Earle and Jim were competent musicians, and nice people, they did not "rock" as I saw necessary for a unit required to balance the quirkiness of Ron and Russell.' At the time, he filed those reservations away and simply resolved to do all he could for the group.

'Ron and Russell I found very easy to get on with, we shared similar views and tastes. I think we felt respect for one another and realised that we were a good combination. I found them both smart, funny, interesting and focused plus I particularly admired their song writing abilities and, at that time, we shared a common vision for their music.'

Ian Hampton: 'Because of the John Hewlett connection, we went to see each other several times. Initially, I didn't know what to think. Chaplinesque Ron with his long curly locks, they didn't seem like siblings. The pretty one and the accountant one. But we hit it off socially, we went to all their gigs, and they came to ours.'

Unfortunately, Sparks' date sheet was about to come to a very abrupt halt. One night in London, Russell met a girl, a Swiss tourist, whose father owned a club, the Post, in Zermatt. Somehow, she persuaded him to book her new friend's band into the venue, and to throw in bed and board as well.

Dupont was furious. 'I was so opposed to that show. It was a huge mistake, because all I could think of was – they've already blown one gig off at the Marquee, they're about to break in England, they're going to be big, it's finally happened. Three months in this country and, at long last, they're somebody. "A Woofer In Tweeter's Clothing" was about to be released...and, instead, they hopped on the plane and went to Zermatt.'

He was right to be furious. British crowds were still small, but there was an enthusiasm at large which the band members had simply never witnessed at home. Part of it, the group knew, was the sheer novelty of their sound and appearance. But it was wider than that. All around them, the British pop scene was exploding, likewise with a vigour that America could never have matched. It was a genuinely exciting time and Sparks were poised to be part of it.

Yes, there were frustrations. Larry Dupont: 'Considering how much WEA had now spent on Sparks, you'd think they'd have expected a whole lot of performance out of them. And that's what was so damn sad. All they had to do was release one cockamamie single during the three months the band was there. They had the single, it had already been released in the States, and it had been a hit there. WEA would have had a hit on their hands. But they didn't. Sparks had finally found their niche, and WEA blew it.'

Not only that, but WEA actively contributed to the situation by gleefully agreeing that the band were right to ditch the Marquee show in favour of a trip to Switzerland – because it meant that the label executives could go there as well. 'That was the only reason the record company wanted to send them there, so all the executives could write off a trip to Switzerland.'

And so the third Marquee concert, on 21st December 1972, went the same way as the previous week's, and it was all for nothing anyway. 'We got to Zermatt to find there were all these technical issues,' said Dupont. 'Day after day, Harley and the others would go off to ski while they waited for something to happen, and then we got slung out of the hotel because somebody accused them of burning the rug in their hotel room.'

They ended up in a hotel in a neighbouring town, and that brought its own set of problems as Sparks suddenly found they were reliant on the promoter's son to get them to the show. 'And the guy drove them off the road into a ditch,' gasps an incredulous Dupont. 'I wasn't with them at the time, so I got a phone call from the promoter asking where the hell they were, and I think by this point in time I was really worn out. Day after day of things going wrong, and me being angry that we were there instead of London, and he started getting on my case about the band not showing up. I didn't scream, but I said "If your goddamned son hadn't driven them into a ditch, they'd have been there." And that was the end of the gig in Zermatt.'

Sparks returned to London, arriving just in time to attend the Christmas party at the WEA offices, where everything seemed concealed behind a thick wall of marijuana smoke. Christmas day itself was celebrated with Rogey and Miriam. Meanwhile, more gigs were being scheduled to keep them busy. The festive season drifted by...Boxing Day, the day after that...now it was 28th December, the last night of their Marquee residency and the band were all looking forward to it. A chance to redeem themselves after two cancellations, an opportunity to show the world what they were made of...

'And that,' said Dupont, 'is when the magic moment came. The record ['A Woofer In Tweeter's Clothing'] was released and they had the Marquee show that evening, but that same day the band was taken to the airport and put on a plane home. Because the day before that, WEA finally got the budget through from the States – $10,000. The band was on the plane like greased lightning, it was just unbelievable.'

'Oh, WEA were pissed. There was no discussion at all. Once they found out there was only $10,000 in the budget, there was no discussion. It was as if you were dead. I cannot imagine the grief that flew around that place.'

Even a conservative estimate of the total cost of Sparks' visit, including three months of travel, accommodation and food, a band's worth of equipment and an expense account wherever they wanted one, would dwarf that figure many times over. Sparks were back to square one.

They celebrated their return to the US with two nights at the Whisky-A-Go-Go, 29th and 30th January 1973. They had been gone for three months, and the Whisky ads welcomed them with a banner announcement: 'From London, Sparks', cried the advertisements, and nobody was sure whether the club was simply referring to where they'd been, or if somebody thought that's where they were from. Had Los Angeles really forgotten them so quickly?

Maybe it had. The rest of the country certainly seemed to have. 'A Woofer In Tweeter's Clothing' had been released just ahead of the Christmas rush, and it was doomed, once again, to die in the record stores. Russell was speaking with the wisdom of hindsight when he suggested that the most obvious choice for a follow-up single, 'Girl From Germany', was passed over in favour of releasing nothing at all, 'in order to avoid the risk of failure, and thereby relieving us of a lot of anxious moments.' But he was correct, regardless.

'We were doing things we thought were special,' Ron reflected on Sparks' Stateside profile, 'and six waitresses were all that would come to see us. That kind of brought us a certain reality that we were working in a kind of fantasy land, and then the reality of the situation that there's a record company, but nobody hearing what you're doing. That kind of clashed with our dream of how the whole scheme of things was gonna be.'

Warner Brothers did pull one song, 'Moon Over Kentucky', for inclusion on the 'Days of Wine And Vinyl' album, a promotional set mailed out to every worthwhile radio station in the land to showcase the best of the label's recent releases... Roxy Music, Jethro Tull, Captain Beefheart and a vintage David Bowie cut were also featured. But there was little advertising for Sparks in their own right, few reviews, no television and, because Sparks weren't even in the country at the time, no chance of rectifying any of that.

Producer James Lowe was devastated by the album's failure. 'I thought it was a hit and would get Sparks some recognition. I was completely wrong.' He simply couldn't understand how his instinct about the group had let him down so badly. Even his friends were nonplussed.

'To be honest not many of them "got it". Russell looked so much like Marc Bolan that they just thought it was a T. Rex copy band. The material was exactly what rock'n'roll should have been to me...fresh and different. Sometimes the supposedly hip music biz has no guts.' And he had no more time for it. He had already promised wife Pamela that, if 'A Woofer In Tweeter's Clothing' didn't take off, he would find something else to do with his life. He just never expected to have to live up to that pledge, but he did it anyway.

'It was my disillusion over this that actually made me shift my focus from music to television. I decided if my gut feeling about this was wrong, it might be time to change fields. So I did.'

He never lost his affection for Sparks, however. 'The Maels are brave, clean and reverent. They dance to a drum we can't even hear, and then bring it back around to give us a treat. Did I think they would survive? Not on your life. Recording acts were like disposable tissues at that time in Los Angeles. Their foundation is brotherhood, a unique talent and hard, hard work. I am proud to have been involved with them. I love their album covers and their music. For me, that is saying something. Just one thing – how do you get those lyrics out of your head? I still hear them after forty years!'

Sparks limped on. Alice Cooper got in touch to ask if he could borrow the 'I'm the girl in your head, the boy in your bed' lyric from 'Beaver O'Lindy'. He was refused permission, so he borrowed the title from '(No More) Mr Nice Guys' instead. 'Well, at least somebody discovered this song and made a buck or two out of it,' was Russell's weary rejoinder, but how it stung, sitting around in Los Angeles with nothing to do, while one of their song titles, at least, flirted with the top of the charts.

A spring 1973 tour of America supporting Todd Rundgren was proposed, but fell through, while a trip up to Bearsville to begin work on a new album, or at least a new single, fizzled out with just one song, 'I Like Girls', in the bag. Russell shrugged, 'Nick James produced the song, but it didn't come out as well as expected. [It] was due to be a single but was never released.'

'We got some measure of a buzz going [in Europe],' Ron said. 'We came back to the States and had zero; we couldn't get a gig anywhere.' They played a handful more shows at the Whisky, and each time seemed more desultory than the one before. 'When we did play, it was supporting people like Heads, Hands and Feet and five people would show up. We were really up against a wall.'

Not that the band were themselves impressed by the opportunities that the Whisky offered. 'Apart from the four waitresses and three twelve-year-old groupies, we were playing to nobody,' Russell sighed. But at least they were playing. By early spring, however, even the Whisky was refusing to book them again. Ron recalled, 'They just said "We can't have you anymore because nobody's coming to see you." Also, we were too loud. It was a funny kind of sound we had. It was a combination of being not ballsy, but really loud at the same time. It probably irritated a lot of people.'

The Whisky's decision was a devastating blow, but worse was to come. 'Our manager said "There's nothing else I can do for you." It was like the end of the line. Usually, a manager gives you pep talks. Our manager was saying, "There's no place you can play, no record company is interested in you, and I don't think that much of you myself." It was devastating.'

Earle Mankey agreed. 'The break-up of the band was caused by lack of response, really. We got signed after playing for a million people who didn't like us. We went to England and had some success, then came back to Los Angeles and a record label that kept giving us these blank stares. We played the Whisky for the umpteenth time. Finally, I got a part-time job as a recording-console designer.'

Yet there was one glimmer of hope. England liked Sparks. Maybe, Ron and Russell mused, it was because the UK is a much smaller country; it was easy for a band to go 'national' when they had no more territory to contend with than a single small American state. How many times would the UK fit into Texas? The idea of abandoning America altogether, relocating permanently to Britain, was growing more attractive with every passing day, until finally a casual conversation they'd had with John Hewlett regarding where the band saw itself to be heading turned into a concrete decision.

The Maels phoned John Hewlett to find out if he would be interested in taking over the running of their affairs. But only theirs... The remainder of the band, Harley Feinstein and the Mankey brothers, Earle and Jim, would not be making the journey with them.

CHAPTER SEVEN

IT'S WINTER, IT'S RAINING, YOU'RE TIRED

If Ron and Russell Mael required any further evidence of just how low their stock had sunk in the United States, even among the people who professed to love them, they found it now. John Hewlett was certainly up for taking over the band's affairs, but he needed the necessary legal documentation to prove that they were now free agents. Neither manager Roy Silver nor Bearsville head Albert Grossman even batted an eyelid as they released Sparks from their contracts.

While the Maels gathered the required paperwork, Hewlett got to work, drawing up a shortlist of labels that might be interested in the Maels and then, starting from the top, introducing the group to the right people. He struck lucky with his first call.

'I spoke to David Betteridge, who was the MD of Island Records, and explained my ideas for the development of Sparks.' Betteridge then brought in Muff Winwood, the label's head of A&R, and it was Winwood who would have his work cut out for him, playing the tape Hewlett had give him to label head Chris Blackwell, and then sitting back while Blackwell outlined all the reasons why he didn't like Sparks.

Winwood was not unduly worried. From the dawn of his career at the label, Winwood had grown accustomed to such differences of opinion. Sometimes he won through, other times he was forced to take a pet project elsewhere, as when Blackwell turned down the chance to sign the group Patto but allowed Winwood to produce them for another label, Vertigo. Now it was happening again.

'Blackwell didn't hear them. They were so weird that Los Angeles hadn't been able to handle them, and they had come to London.' Finally, at least acknowledging that Winwood's instincts were usually spot-on, Blackwell agreed to cut a deal. He would release £500 for pay for airline tickets, accommodation and any other expenses. Bring them to England, cut a few tracks, and we'll see what happens.

That was enough for the Maels. They boarded the next flight they could out of Los Angeles and didn't look back. 'The old group never actually broke up,' Russell insisted. 'We were at a stalemate. Sparks weren't getting any bigger and we wanted to change the outside elements surrounding us to see what would happen. So we changed members and changed countries, record labels and managers. The one element we didn't want to change to gain acceptance was the music.'

He was convinced the UK would have no problem with that. 'There's no real scene in Los Angeles. The so-called "West Coast Scene" has so much mystique in England and Europe, but for us there was no real scene here. It was the folky people in Laurel Canyon and then Topanga Canyon steel-guitar stuff, and there was no scene like the days of Jan and Dean and the Seeds and all that. That was one reason why we wanted to go to England, because at least there's some drive going on among bands. You're constantly bombarded by magazines with colour band photos, and everybody's in a band and rock'n'roll's just really important for kids. It's not important for everyone in LA.'

British heroes, the brothers had discovered on their last visit, were not 'the legendary figures like Dylan and Clapton and Crosby, Stills and Nash and all that,' Ron marvelled. 'It's all new people who probably only get heard for a couple of months and then fade away. That makes it really silly in a certain way, but exciting too.'

Sparks had been out of the country for just six months, and already the charts and, consequently, the teenybop press was overflowing with a heap of new faces. Who had even heard of Nazareth at the end of 1972? Or Mud? Or Suzi Quatro, another American who moved to the UK to make it after America shrugged its collective shoulders? Now all three were threatening to take over from the very bands that had seemed all but inviolate at Christmas. And, if they could do it, so could Sparks.

Not that the Maels were under any illusions of competing with all of them. Their music was not easy to understand, they knew that, and their own interpretation of their art scarcely even considered the possibility of racking up hit after hit on the notoriously fickle British hit parade. Mud, Sweet and Quatro could sleep soundly at nights on that account. If the Maels identified with any of their soon-to-be competitors, it was the likes of Bowie, Roxy Music and even Elton John – artists whose greatest statements were their long-playing releases, but whose singles sold healthily regardless. The fact that Roxy Music were also Island recording artists only added to their excitement.

The Maels' reasons for leaving everything behind, then, could not be faulted. But still it was a betrayal that left both the Mankeys and Feinstein reeling, even if they understood every nuance of it. The Maels had already proved that, when it came to their career, their loyalties extended only as far as their personal interests demanded. If Sparks were to continue, and the brothers were adamant that they would, it would be in a new land with a new crew. A fresh start in every sense of the word.

Moving into John Hewlett's home in Croydon, the Maels quickly settled into London life. There was just one cloud on their horizon. They had no songs. Ron had written little since the completion of 'A Woofer In Tweeter's Clothing' – one reason for the failure of those final sessions for Bearsville was the fact there was no new material to work on, or none that Ron had any interest in pursuing further.

Even the songs with which Sparks befuddled the audience at Max's Kansas City had been abandoned. Again, it was to be a fresh start; the version of Sparks that Ron and Russell envisaged creating was to be very different from the somewhat haphazard and deliberately quirky outfit that Bearsville had accepted, a view that Muff Winwood readily confirmed the first time he met them.

They were in the big league now, he explained. Island Records had endured a few soft years in the half-decade since the label's initial emergence at the forefront of the post-psychedelic folk and prog movements, when the likes of Traffic, King Crimson, Fairport Convention and Emerson Lake and Palmer epitomised the company's musical policy. Most of the bands that Island's success had been built on had either broken up, moved away, or simply faded out of the limelight, while one of their most stubborn failures, the four-album-old Mott the Hoople, had repaid the label's doomed perseverance by switching to a different label and scoring one of the biggest hits of 1972 with the David Bowie-penned 'All The Young Dudes'.

Only Roxy Music now flew the Island flag on the charts with any regularity, while other recent signings – former Velvet Underground mainstays John Cale and Nico, ex-Roxy man Brian Eno, folkies Sutherland Brothers and Quiver and Canterbury prog hero Kevin Ayers – might have looked good in the music press, but they were scarcely likely to become household names. Indeed, in the 12 months ending in September 1973, only four out of 66 singles released on Island and its affiliated labels had been Top 20 hits and, while Roxy Music seemed guaranteed to maintain that presence, Bryan Ferry insisted that it would take place only once a year, when a single might be culled from the latest album to help it on its way.

Similar strictures now seemed likely to bind Ferry's own solo career, and it appeared that any further hits that Island were to have would continue to come almost by accident – the recent

JOOK

reactivation of Free's 'All Right Now' and 'Wishing Well', for example. Island needed a hit-making machine, and Winwood wanted Sparks to provide it.

The first songs Ron wrote in England found him accompanying himself on guitar. It worked, but it was not comfortable; he pined for a keyboard, and luckily, he knew where to find one – at his mother and step-father's house in Clapham Junction. Every Sunday, then, he would travel across town, ensconce himself in their living room and work.

An album's worth of new material flourished during those first weeks, songs like 'Marry Me', 'When I Take The Field Friday', 'I'm About To Burst', 'Alabamy Right' and 'My Brains And Her Looks'. 'They were recorded with just the two of us playing,' he recalled. 'It sounded just like a Simon and Garfunkel album throughout.'

Not everything he wrote was solid gold, and one song in particular, 'Too Hot To Handle', struck him as especially uninspiring. For a start, it reminded him too much of 'Simple Ballet', from the 'Halfnelson' album, and he didn't have any words for it either. Even the title only came about because it fitted the syllabic requirements of what would be the opening line.

But there was something about it that intrigued him. Maybe it was the fact that he wrote it in the key of A, and it amused him to think of Russell trying to strangle his vocal chords up to such a pitch. The song was written in A, 'and by God it'll be sung in A,' he insisted. 'I just feel that if you're coming up with most of the music, then you have an idea where it's going to go. And no singer is going to get in my way.' Besides, as a lyric finally began to fall into place, he knew Russell would have to agree.

He was watching, or at least thinking, about the Hollywood Westerns that he once loved so much, when his mind tripped over the line 'this town ain't big enough for both of us'. It was the traditional prelude, of course, to a gunfight and maybe that was something the song could feature, the crash of gunfire. But rather than head off down the obvious route and have the song's protagonists duelling, how much more entertaining if the lyric had nothing whatsoever to do with violence and was, in fact, an unabashed love song in which the size of the town was more or less immaterial? Tinkering away at it for days before he finally presented it to his brother, Ron now knew he had written something special. Even if it was still stuck in the key of A.

'Ron could only play it in that key,' Russell agreed. 'It was so much work to transpose the song, and one of us had to budge, so I made the adjustment to fit in. My voice ain't a "rock" voice. It's not soulful, in the traditional rock way; it's not about "guts". It's untrained, unschooled, and I never questioned why I was singing high. It just happened, dictated by the songs. Ron has always written Sparks' lyrics and never transposed the songs into a rock key for me to sing. He always packed each line with words, and I had to sing them as they were.'

Of course, writing new songs was not the only task that faced the brothers. They also needed to put together a new band to play the things. And the obvious solution, they decided, was to keep everything in the family and hijack Hewlett's other managerial clients Jook.

A year into their RCA career, Jook were still searching for that elusive first hit, and growing increasingly desperate as they did so. They had no shortage of admirers – producer, publisher and self-made record company supremo Mickie Most was a fervent fan, and so was label-mate David Bowie. Ian Hampton recalled, 'Bowie was a chum to Jook. We were both signed to RCA and met often. Although he was a mess at that time, [so] perhaps we were more chums to him...'

Jook, however, were not interested in jacking it in, dismissing their own singer, and becoming Sparks. Their records may have stubbornly refused to sell, but they were a dynamic live act and that made it all worthwhile. They'd been through a lot together already, but they felt as though it was only just beginning. Chris Townson agreed to help the Americans out rehearsing and auditioning new musicians, but onstage with Jook, it was obvious where his, and his band-mates', affections really lay.

Ian Kimmett: 'Ron and Russell came to a couple of our recording sessions and gigs and hand-clapped on a couple of tracks, and I remember seeing The Harder They Come with them.' But that was as far as it went. Jook had too much else going for them.

'We would thrash the show out for between one-and-a-half and two hours,' Ian Hampton recalled. 'It was a very sweaty experience!' A monthly residence at the Edmonton Sundown, in

Major Recording Label Artists

SPARKS

require

DRUMMER

Must be an exciting, inventive drummer with a really good face that isn't covered with a beard.

(Previous applicants need not apply)

Auditions:
SATURDAY, OCTOBER 13
12 noon

SPARKS

require

LEAD GUITARIST

Must be incredible looking and an exciting, accomplished guitarist
(Previous applicants need not apply)
Auditions:
Sat, October 6th

STUDIO
S.E.1

at the Tu
74 Gt.
Bring

ORGANIST

required by major label recording band.
Image extremely important
(no beards or bulges)
Auditions:

Date: Saturday, February 16th

Place: Furniture Cave
(basement)

533 King's Road - 01-352-3796

Time: 1 p.m.-6 p.m.
Hammond C3 and Leslie will be supplied

North London, was their main stomping ground. There, the predominantly skinhead audience that the band had attracted turned out in the sort of numbers that even Slade, at the height of *their* early flirtation with the crop-top masses could only dream of. 'Oh, if only they'd known what sort of people we really were,' Townson smiled. 'They'd have slaughtered us.'

Still, it could be construed an intimidating look. One of the band's fans was an aspiring young bassist named Martin Gordon, who recalled; 'Jook always seemed to be nice, middle-class boys. But I remember seeing their picture, boots and braces *et al*, and being rather nervous when I met them for the first time. I soon caught on that their image was just that, an image. But I [still] had them pegged as "bovver boys"...'

One can only imagine his surprise, then, when he answered an advertisement in *Melody Maker* one Wednesday in July 1973, calling for young, good-looking and out of work (or otherwise) musicians to make themselves known to a certain telephone number, and found himself face to face with the ringleader of the "bovver boys", manager John Hewlett. And that was before he clocked the other people in the room, one tall and thin with ethereal curls that cascaded over his angelic face, and the other one skeletal beneath a vast Afro hair-do, with a manic moustache to match.

The Maels had given up on the idea of co-opting Jook and were casting their eyes elsewhere. They may have been joking when they claimed to have offered Todd Rundgren first refusal of the guitarist gig – according to Ron, 'We phoned him once we'd got to England. It was still going to be firmly our band, but with him as the guitarist...I mean, we could have made him a star, y'know , but Todd said that he was going in another musical direction.' But they were certainly looking far and wide.

One luckless contender was a 21-year-old Canadian drummer named Warren Cann. A few years later, he would make a name for himself in Ultravox, a band whose musical debt to Sparks simply ripples through their debut album. He didn't pass muster, however, and that despite at least being able to talk intelligently to the brothers about their music – he was that rare thing in England at the time, an already-confirmed Sparks fan. Perhaps that's what counted against him... The Maels wanted a fresh start.

Out of luck, too, was a New Yorker named Salvatore 'Sal' Maida, who had moved to London around the same time as the Maels, and had spent the months since then looking for a band. He had been a Sparks fan since the Bearsville days, catching one of their shows at Max's Kansas City and, before that, befriending Joseph Fleury via their mutual love of record collecting. Indeed, Maida recalled, their first ever meeting let him know just how devoted to the hobby Fleury was.

'I'm talking '71-72, somewhere in there. Joe wrote a rave review of a record I loved, and which still is one of my favourites to this day, "We Are Ever So Clean", by Blossom Toes. So I decided to contact Joe, and we discussed our love of said LP and other British bands. So I invited him over to see my Brit 45 collection and he brought [journalist] Alan Betrock with him. We're in my room, looking through my 45s and listening, having sandwiches and soda from my mom.

'Now, I had a crazy habit of putting my 45s in these old boxes without the sleeves. As they're looking at my stuff, I notice a look of horror on both their faces. I'm thinking "Wow, I thought I had some great records, but I guess not." Finally, I had to ask "Is something wrong?" They both kind of stuttered and said "Oh, no, nothing." Then finally, after seeing some more rarities, or whatever, both blurted out "Why don't you have sleeves?"'

Now Maida was calling the Maels after seeing their advert in *Melody Maker*... 'Obviously I knew who they were. I saw the ad and I believe it said "English musicians only", but I thought I'd

61

call anyway, and they were like "Hmm, we're here looking for English guys, because we don't want to go through the work-permit thing, the visa thing," so I said okay, and that was it.'

There was more to their determination that that, however. As John Hewlett explained, 'The stroke of genius lay in the pairing of Ron and Russell with English rock musicians creating an Anglo-American blend that has worldwide appeal.'

One such Englishman, Martin Gordon, was certainly promising. He was working as a technical author at the time, 'writing manuals about how to stop oil tankers sinking'. Just 19, and with musical experience to match, Gordon's biggest moment to date had come when he and his drummer friend Tony Sprinks joined visiting American bluesman Eddie 'Guitar' Burns onstage for a lunchtime gig at their local college in Hitchin, during January 1973. The last time Burns had played the UK, his pickup band in Cambridge included Syd Barrett, Jack Monck and Twink. This time, however, there were fewer legends to be cast, and while the long-haired Gordon was captured in full beaming smile by the local paper, it was clear that he wouldn't be giving up his day-job just yet.

'I called an ad in *Melody Maker*, and left the number of a pal, drummer Bob Sturt, who was also after a gig. One day, he called me and told me that someone called Russell had called him, and that I should call back. Bob and I were invited to visit.' On 20th August 1973, the pair drove down to Croydon.

The Maels were unimpressed. To be fair, the advertisement hadn't really said much about applicants' appearance – later, the brothers would become very specific about their requirements, with both beards and bulges, those banes of Halfnelson's early existence, warned off before they could even pick up the telephone. They'd never really considered that long hair might be a problem. But Gordon, by his own admission, was suffering from a certain amount of 'post-hippydom', and the hirsute vision that was now standing in John Hewlett's kitchen did not bode well for the Americans.

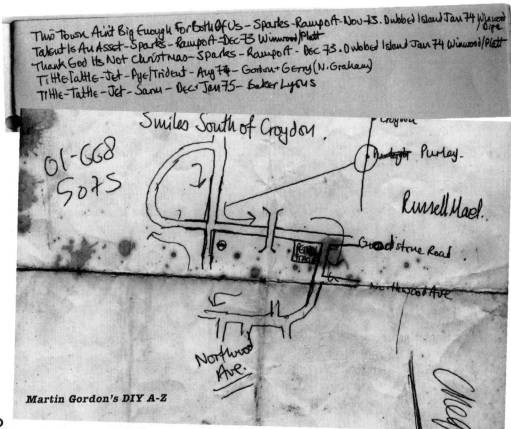

Martin Gordon's DIY A-Z

Neither did the fact that Gordon and Sturt were several hours late in arriving. Russell, when he arranged for the pair to visit, was very specific about the time they should arrive. It was not Gordon's fault that the American's accent translated *Godstone* Road, which was the correct address, into the non-existent *Guardstone*.

Nevertheless, something about the buoyant, and clearly enthusiastic, Gordon did appeal to the Maels and, while Bob Sturt was never in the running for a place in the band, the bassist was invited back to jam with the Maels at Barnet Cricket Club eight days later. He arrived to discover two of Jook now awaiting him, guitarist Trevor White and drummer Chris Townson (who conveniently lived just around the corner), and, with introductions out of the way, the team learned its way around three songs, 'Girl From Germany', 'Wonder Girl' and 'I Like Girls'.

Adrian Fisher

ADRIAN FISHER is a young Spark (22 in August) from Dulwich who plays guitar, takes the occasional solo and revels in a (deliberate and possibly defensive, I think) exaggerated uncouth character.

"I'm not embarrassing you am I?" he'd bellow across a hotel lounge buzzing with hushed conversation. He plays the young James Dean and like that actor his rebellious nature has a likeable naivety which make his few real excesses immediately forgiveable.

Ade started playing guitar after he "got me Bluesbreakers LP. Started at Clapton and I worked me way back from that." A real blues freak, he says.

He started in the music business when "I got slung out of school on a Thursday and started at (Robert) Stigwood's on the Monday. I was the office boy. It was good fun. All yer heroes worked at Stigwood's. It wore off after a while. Gettin' sandwiches for Ginger Baker."

Whenever he had any time spare at Stigwood's Ade would "scive off down to the kitchen and play bottleneck. Robin Turner heard me playing down there once and when he left Stigwood's to join Island he phoned me up one day about three months later and said 'There's a geezer here wants a guitar player'."

The geezer was Andy Fraser in post-Free vacuum. Fraser heard Fisher and after a brief audition Ade joined Fraser's band, Toby.

After Toby split, Fisher sat at home for around seven months. Then he thought about getting another job. He then joined Brush, led by the Irish musician who gave the band its name.

In all, Ade was with Brush for 18 months with a break of two to three months. Finally their management said the band owed them "this incredible amount of money." And that was the end of it.

Fisher did some jamming around. "There was no money or anything. They were just a couple of bands that weren't gonna do anything. I just couldn't stand it. And so I showed up for the auditions with Sparks."

Did he find it difficult to restrict himself to the fixed structure of Sparks' songs after a career, albeit short, in loose-blowing bands.

"We all chip in with arrangement ideas. But he (Ron) doesn't write songs where they've got a verse, chorus, verse, chorus, middle, end and stuff like that. Each song you just have to remember as it comes.

"I couldn't sit down and play them now. I just have to remember it as it comes. I'm a complete blank before they knew me and my guitar playing and everything.

"They asked me to do it when they first came over. John suggested it. He knew I wouldn't do it then."

Trevor's second offer to join Sparks and Ian's first came simultaneously. They went along to a "two-way audition" and if both parties dug what they played then they'd join.

"It fitted in straight away. In an hour we did 'Hasta Manana' and 'This Town' and they were perfect and it sounded great and we thought 'Well what have we been doing for the last few years.'"

'They were good songs,' Townson reflected. 'I didn't really have to learn them, it was more a matter of just keeping a beat and throwing in a fill every so often so I looked busy, but I enjoyed playing with them.' Vague conversation about him filling the drum stool on a permanent basis, however, passed him by. 'I wasn't interested. I had Jook. Plus, I don't think my real playing style would have fitted in with what the Maels were looking for. I wanted to be Keith Moon. They were thinking more in terms of Ringo.'

Gordon was impressed. 'I liked "I Like Girls" a lot, with its pointlessly chromatic riff and unpredictable modulation.' But did the Maels like him? As the days went by, and the phone steadfastly refused to ring, Gordon assumed not. For the next few weeks, he recalled, 'I was back with my manuals and *Melody Makers*, until one day the Maels just called me up out of the blue and asked me to go along again, by which time I'd had my hair cut and was able to make a far better impression.'

This time, the meeting was being held at the Island Studios on Basing Street, where the

Maels had booked two days (22nd/23rd September) in which to record a clutch of demos. Pink Fairies guitarist Paul Rudolph and Roxy Music bassist John Porter were there as well, with Porter also handling production, but Gordon was more impressed by his surroundings. 'I was very chuffed to find that the session was in the basement studio, which I recognised from the cover of a [former Spooky Tooth singer] Mike Harrison album, so that was my pay-off for the event. I photographed the area where he was sitting for the cover shot.'

Across the four songs recorded that day, 'I Like Girls', 'Barbecutie', 'In My Family' and 'Marry Me', the band sounded good. But Gordon knew that it was not a permanent line-up. 'I had the feeling that these guys were never in consideration as band members, although I was indeed introduced as the bass player. Rudolph was about thirty, it seemed to me at the time, and that was Very Old Indeed.' No matter that Ron, at 28, was himself nearing the same age; Sparks required a clean-cut, fresh-faced, youthful image. One that matched Russell's, in fact. Porter and Rudolph were indeed too old.

Further auditions were lined up; and, in the meantime, Gordon was kept busy working out arrangements for the vast number of songs which Ron was now turning out. It was not, he pondered idly, exactly what he'd been expecting when he was told the brothers needed 'an equal partner to help Ron do a Lennon/McCartney'...he may even have wondered why that offer was made in the first place, being as Ron was already prolific enough in his own right. But it was certainly a more involved position than that which would be afforded the rest of the band, once they finally materialised.

'Auditions began. We would play two chords, D and G, and encourage people to play along with them. I tried to get my pal Tony Sprinks in on drums, at a rehearsal in King's Cross. He was a big fan of Billy Cobham, but his enthusiasm hadn't extended to learning to play like him.'

A new Melody Maker ad was placed. 'Sparks require lead guitarist. Must be incredible looking and an exciting, accomplished guitarist. Bring guitar and look sharp.' The audition was set for noon on Saturday 6th October, at the Tunnel Rehearsal Studio on Great Suffolk Street, in one of the old railway arches close to Southwark Bridge Road.

It was a damp, inhospitable venue, and its owners were not especially punctual, either. Ron, Russell and Martin Gordon arrived a few minutes early so they could set things up before the applicants started arriving, and they were still standing outside at 12.30, waiting for someone to come and unlock the door.

Derek Paice, the luckless teen who turned up at the Marquee on the night Sparks didn't, was waiting for the band with them, although he wasn't looking for a job. He was a fan.

'I was working in the West End of London on the Saturday morning when they were auditioning for guitarists across the river in Southwark in the afternoon. I thought I would go and see if I could meet Sparks, assuming they were "my" Sparks, and not some other band stealing the name. I "borrowed" the company truck, with all the builders' paraphernalia I had been delivering and collecting that morning along with several bags of rubble on board that I'd spent hours sweeping and shovelling, and that I should have taken to a waste disposal site.' Instead, he took it to the Tunnel Rehearsal Studio.

Ron and Russell were already there when he arrived. 'I said hello and they were charming. They introduced me to Martin [Gordon], who had no eyebrows and a beautiful jacket. Apart from that, I ignored him, which was horribly rude of me. Then, when the door of Tunnel was unlocked, Ron invited me in. I wasn't expecting that, but I was too excited to turn back by this time!'

The first applicants had already arrived, and Paice made his way over to sit with the most approachable-looking of them all, a wiry young man named Adrian Fisher. 'I didn't know him or his work before that day,' Paice admitted. 'I cringe to think how irritating it must have been for someone trying to prepare for an audition to have to put up with a twittering eighteen-year-old, especially one who'd just walked off a building site.'

But Fisher seemed happy to talk. After all, he didn't know anybody else in the room either and besides, for all he knew, the twittering teen might well have been a part of the Sparks team. He certainly wouldn't have put it past them. 'The first time I saw the brothers, yeah, I thought they were weird. The whole band was,' Fisher recalled around a decade later. Not that he was at all daunted by that prospect.

Straight out of school, he had landed a job as tea-boy at impresario Robert Stigwood's RSO organisation, hanging in the shadows of some of the grand old men of British blues – Eric Clapton was a regular visitor to the offices, and his influence rubbed off. Fisher had replaced Gary Moore in Skid Row, played alongside former Free bassist Andy Fraser in Toby and had been playing the blues for as long as he could remember.

'I wanted to do something that was different...I mean, stay within my framework, but expand out of it. I remember listening to the other people at the rehearsal, and the things they were being asked to try, and I thought to myself, this could be it.'

'The audition was a bit disorganised from what I could see,' Derek Paice continued, 'but that was par for the course at the time. Inside there were two rooms. Candidates waited in the first room, while Ron, Russell, Martin and a couple of others went through to the second room. After a while the first candidate went in. We could hear everything, unfortunately. The bass and drums struck up with a 'Whippings And Apologies' groove and this poor guitarist had to play along with them. Unfortunately, he was not a very experienced player and his soloing was falteringly slow and didn't match the two-chord sequence of the groove. Adrian made no comment about this player's lack of skill. I thought that was really decent of him. Others found it hard to stifle their contempt.'

The first contender came out, packed his guitar and left. A few minutes later, Russell emerged. 'Has he gone?' Then he asked whether the others had heard anything '...because if you can't play any better than that, will you go now?'

Derek Paice: 'I waited for the next person to go in. It may have been the Steve Peregrin Took lookalike, all dressed in purple velvet, or it could have been one of the bearded ones, but I realised I needed to leave these guys alone to get on with their job so I wished Adrian the best of luck, bade him goodbye and left.' Fisher got the job.

A drummer arrived the following week, on 14th October, following a fresh round of auditions at the Tunnel. This time the ad pulled no punches. Chris Blackwell had finally given his approval to Sparks joining the Island roster, and the Maels were swift to broadcast the news. 'Major-label recording artists Sparks require drummer. Must be an exciting, inventive drummer with a really good face that isn't covered with a beard. Bring sticks only. Previous applicants need not apply.'

Norman 'Dinky' Diamond had been playing the German cabaret circuit and, by his own admission, 'I was not really expecting this audition to be any different to any of the others I'd been to. Just another band trying to be either Led Zeppelin or David Bowie, so I was amazed when they started to play and it didn't sound like anything I'd ever heard in my life.' A handful of other players went through their paces on either side of Diamond, but the Maels knew the moment they heard him that they had found their man. Sparks was complete.

A technical author, a cabaret drummer and a tea boy. They were hardly the 'unknown band' that the Maels would soon be maintaining they had discovered at a party thrown by their biggest fans, the Kennedy family. In fact, they were barely even worthy of the other tale that Russell told, that John Hewlett had discovered the trio already playing as a band only to then learn that they were dedicated Sparks-o-philes, 'fanatical about what we had done. They were doing Sparks songs in a pub. It was amazing. And we found we could get along on a personal level, so they became our band. They were English, and they could even play!'

Once again, Ron and Russell, with an astute grasp of the power of the media, were more than aware that a good story could sell as many records as anything else. And this one – provided nobody gave it away – was certainly a good one. It was also a lot more glamorous than the truth and in England in 1973 glamour still held a lot of appeal.

Sparks' first full rehearsals kicked off the following week, in a wooden-floored dance studio in Clapham. The room was lined with mirrors, and the acoustics were deafening. Martin Gordon was especially impressed. 'Hearing the songs for the first time was often a stimulating moment. Some were immediately better than others, and some were a real grind to get through, 'Lost And Found', for example, and 'Equator', which seemed to go on for ever.'

But the good songs certainly outweighed the so-so ones, and the optimism that built up around them even overcame the negativity that permeated the band's personal reality. Gordon continued, 'Rehearsal would begin with elaborate greeting rituals. Arms would be thrown around each

SPARKS   Dinky Diamond

SPARKS   Martin Gordon

other's shoulders, backs would be slapped, enquiries about the health of one's nearest and dearest would be made and then, and only then, would the merest hint of "Let's hit it!" emerge. Oh, hang on, that's another group, sorry.'

Sparks was a different proposition altogether... 'The various musicians would wander in, on time of course, and eye contact would briefly be made. Mutual acknowledgement would take place. Descriptions of last night's meal in an Indian restaurant would be delivered, along with pictorial evidence. Interest would be feigned, or not, as appropriate. Bafflement would shortly set in, perhaps driven by cultural misunderstanding. Conversation would slow and then stop.'

Finally, Ron would gesture towards his unoccupied piano and propose that 'We...er...could maybe...shall we...?'

'Heads would be tilted first towards one side and then the other. "Ah, yes," we would say, and disappear in the direction of the toilet, the cake shop or the reception area. Eventually, and inevitably, we would reassemble and the real work would begin. Better get to work, people, otherwise the singer will start to talk in his fake English accent, which is most amusing unless you happen to have a sense of humour and then, frankly, you are buggered.'

Still they hung together and when the Island Records contracts arrived – an individual contract for each member of the band – four of the five signed without a second glance. Only Fisher refused, instead proceeding to take what Gordon remembered as 'ages to (very sensibly) get legal advice from his lawyer.' At the time, 'there were choruses of disapproval from all and sundry. But later, when he left the band, he reaped the benefit of his wisdom by getting exactly what he was due, on an ongoing basis.' Gordon and Diamond would not be so fortunate.

Slowly, an album's worth of songs was being teased to perfection. It wasn't always easy, though. Ron, who had now assumed full control of Sparks' songwriting output, even to the exclusion of his brother, wrote great songs, but scarcely conventional ones. Signatures would shift, weird breaks would manifest, and peculiar chord changes loomed unexpectedly. Later in the process, Gordon would explain 'we all chip in with arrangement ideas. But [Ron] doesn't write songs where they've got a verse, chorus, verse, chorus, middle, end and stuff like that. Each song you just have to remember as it comes.'

And then there was 'This Town Ain't Big Enough For Both Of Us,' which rapidly proved to be an absolute law unto itself.

'We'd drive [Adrian] crazy,' Ron confessed. 'A lot of the chords in that song are keyboard chords which don't come easily on a guitar. And it turned out that some of the time signatures are a bit weird, too. I only found that out when the sheet music was published. There were all these weird three-beat bars thrown in among the four-beats.'

Martin Gordon: 'When Ron brought in 'This Town Ain't Big Enough For Both Of Us', the chords were scribbled down, and we all began to construct parts to play. I heard something revolving around the D/A chord movement, and began to play the riff with which the song opened. Adrian expanded it with a change every second repetition and it worked very well. I threw some offbeat bass and drum punctuations, straight out of the Yes canon, or so I imagined, and when the rehearsal finished, Ron said to me "It's funny, I hadn't heard that riff as a part at all..."'

Other songs fell into place, although not always to everybody's satisfaction. 'Complaints', for example, saw Gordon devise 'a coda for the ending, which we rehearsed and recorded onto a cassette player.' The following day, however, the brothers announced that they weren't going to use it. According to the bassist, they felt it overshadowed the song itself, 'to which I responded "so let's make the song itself better, then!"

'Alas, they weren't falling for that old ploy. My ending was removed, becoming a fade. I did not hide my disappointment at having my contribution rejected.'

Other battles flared, even as the songs improved. Gordon: 'Arrangements became more exaggerated and focused, as parts were endlessly discussed and argued over, and fought for. On one occasion, I spread the *Daily Telegraph* [then a broadsheet] across my amp and read it thoroughly from beginning to end while playing, to show my disapproval, again, of something or other. Of course I didn't *really* read it, as I was totally focused upon playing as well as I possibly could, while giving the impression that I was actually reading the newspaper. But I would turn the pages during the legato notes, and I noticed out of the corner of my eye that Ron was watching me with keen interest.'

Gordon found a willing co-conspirator in Adrian Fisher. The Maels, he recalled, 'always expressed disdain for the kind of musician who would actually have to establish eye contact with the drummer at the end of a tune, in order to synchronise the final beat. So Adrian and I would make a point of exaggeratedly looking at Dinky at the end of tunes, and we would both do the Big Waggle of the guitar neck on the last beat, just to irritate them.'

With the distorted hindsight created by knowledge of how both Gordon and Fisher's tenure with Sparks would end, many Sparks historians have seized upon moments such as this as evidence of just how fragile the first London line-up of the band was. In fact, the opposite is true. The musicians were getting to know and understand one another. The petty high jinks and blazing rows were all a part of that process, as the individual chemistries came together and fused, and Sparks literally began sparking. They were truly becoming a band.

'There really was camaraderie within that first line-up,' Dinky Diamond reflected a decade later. 'Yes, Ron and Russell wanted everything their own way, but that was only because they were so devoted to the music, and the reason for the arguments was because we all felt the same way. We were all pulling together, creating something from scratch that we knew was completely unique, and we all wanted everything to be as good as it could be.

'Ron and Russell won most of the arguments because, at the end of the day, Ron wrote the songs, and it was their concept to begin with. But even if that hadn't been the case, somebody had to make the final decision, or else we'd still be arguing now. And that's what being in a band is all about. Everybody throwing their best ideas in, and then stirring them around to make the best music they can. Which is exactly what we did.'

CHAPTER EIGHT

IT'S THE SOUND OF TODAY
PLAYED SO LOUD

From Clapham, the rehearsals moved to the basement beneath the Furniture Cave, at the World's End limit of the King's Road in Chelsea, a cold and clammy subterranea on which the single-bar electric fire could barely make any impression. A rapidly diminishing pile of coins beside the electricity meter let the band know how much longer each rehearsal would last but, said Gordon, 'things were getting pretty good, musically. When manager Hewlett, and later producer Winwood would show up, we would run through the latest songs for them and they, and usually at least some of us, would laugh aloud with glee at the sheer effectiveness of the result. And it was fucking loud as well, which of course helped.

'For rehearsals, we had only the RMI electric piano, rather than the battery of keyboard delights which were available in the studio later on. This being the early days of technology, the RMI had one sound, or perhaps only half a sound, and it wasn't remotely touch-sensitive. But this made it all sound quite tough really, and not at all "a tinny cabaret act", as it was later to be described by *Melody Maker*.'

Tiring of the Furniture Cave, the band's next haunt was a studio in Battersea. 'Musically, the thing just kept getting better and better,' Gordon continued. Muff Winwood was now around a lot of the time, listening enthusiastically as the repertoire came to life and attentively as the Maels laid out their own hopes for the record.

Still enamoured by what Roy Wood was accomplishing with Wizzard, the brothers were insistent that he should produce their next record. Wood's garishly painted but exquisitely stylised rock'n'roll revival band sounded sensational, a spirited blend of primal rock'n'roll and Phil Spector's Wall of Sound that was exactly what Sparks thought they ought to sound like.

The call was made, but Wood was unavailable, and with the Maels unable to come up with any other ideas, Winwood suggested that he handle production duties instead. Sensibly, Sparks agreed – turn him down, and any failure that might follow would be squarely on their shoulders. But if the blame could be shared with the man who was, effectively, their boss, then there would always be room for a second chance.

For all their faith in the new songs, there were still no guarantees whatsoever that Britain would be any more receptive to the new incarnation of Sparks than America (Montgomery County, of course, notwithstanding) had been to the old. The music had moved on, and there was definitely a more commercially-astute air to the likes of 'Amateur Hour', 'Barbecutie', 'Thank God It's Not Christmas' and 'Talent Is An Asset', than there had been to, say, 'Saccharin And The War' and 'Moon Over Kentucky'.

But, if Ian Hampton's young son was any indication, audiences today were going to be just as hard to please as they ever had been. Jook bassist Hampton laughed, 'I got a call to ask for something to be delivered to the rehearsal room in Battersea. I don't recall what, it may have been my Fender bass. Whatever, I drove Jook's orange van up there to deliver it, with my four-year-old son on board. We went down to the dungeon, and I said to my kid "did you ever hear a rock band before?" He ran out screaming!'

True to his word, and certainly true to the plan, Ron's writing had soared onto a new plane.

CHARTS

SINGLES

(Week ending Tuesday 25th June 1974)

This	Last		Weeks in Chart	Highest position
1	(2)	ALWAYS YOURS .. Gary Glitter (Bell)	3	1
2	(1)	THE STREAK Ray Stevens (Westbound)	5	1
3	(3)	HEY ROCK AND ROLL Showaddywaddy (Bell)	5	2
4	(23)	SHE .... Charles Aznavour (Barcley)	2	4
5	(4)	JARROW SONG .. Alan Price (Warner)	5	4
6	(19)	I'D LOVE YOU TO WANT ME Lobo (UK)	3	6
7	(5)	THERE'S A GHOST IN MY HOUSE R. Dean Taylor (Tamla Motown)	7	4
8	(6)	A TOUCH TOO MUCH .. Arrows (Rak)	4	6
9	(11)	LIVERPOOL LOU ... Scaffold (Warner)	4	9
10	(7)	JUDY TEEN ..... Cockney Rebel (EMI)	7	6
11	(9)	ONE MAN BAND Leo Sayer (Chrysalis)	3	9
12	(24)	KISSIN' IN THE BACK ROW Drifters (Bell)	2	12
13	(16)	GUILTY .... Pearls (Bell)	3	13
14	(26)	GOING DOWN THE ROAD Roy Wood (Harvest)	2	14
15	(8)	THIS TOWN AINT'T BIG ENOUGH FOR BOTH OF US ...... Sparks (Island)	8	2
16	(13)	SUMMER BREEZE Isley Brothers (Epic)	4	13
17	(30)	THE WALL STREET SHUFFLE 10 c.c. (UK)	4	17
18	(15)	DON'T LET THE SUN GO DOWN ON ME .... Elton John (DJM)	4	15
19	(21)	THE MAN IN BLACK Cozy Powell (Rak)	5	19
20	(25)	OOH I DO .... Lynsey de Paul (Warner)	3	20
21	(—)	BEACH BABY .... The First Class (UK)	1	21
22	(—)	DIAMOND DOGS David Bowie (RCA)	2	22
23	(12)	I SEE A STAR Mouth & McNeal (Decca)	6	9
24	(10)	SUGAR BABY LOVE Rubettes (Polydor)	9	1
25	(14)	CAN'T GET ENOUGH Bad Company (Island)	6	14
26	(17)	THE 'IN' CROWD Bryan Ferry (Island)	6	7
27	(—)	BANANA ROCK ..... Wombles (CBS)	1	27
28	(—)	FOXY FOXY ... Mott the Hoople (CBS)	1	28
29	(—)	EASY EASY Scotland World Cup Squad (Polydor)	1	29
30	(28)	YOUNG GIRL Gary Puckett & the Union Gap (CBS)	2	28

ALBUMS

(Week ending Tuesday 25th June 1974)

This	Last		Weeks in Chart	Highest Position
1	(1)	DIAMOND DOGS David Bowie (RCA)	5	1
2	(2)	THE SINGLES 1969-73 Carpenters (A & M)	24	1
3	(6)	BAD COMPANY Bad Company (Island)	4	3
4	(5)	KIMONO MY HOUSE Sparks (Island)	5	4
5	(3)	JOURNEY TO THE CENTRE OF THE EARTH Rick Wakeman (A & M)	8	2
6	(8)	TUBULAR BELLS Mike Oldfield (Virgin)	44	4
7	(7)	BAND ON THE RUN Paul McCartney & Wings (Parlophone)	28	2
8	(9)	GOODBYE YELLOW BRICK ROAD Elton John (DJM)	36	1
9	(4)	QUO .... Status Quo (Vertigo)	8	3
10	(14)	SHEET MUSIC .... 10cc (UK)	2	10
11	(10)	BEHIND CLOSED DOORS Charlie Rich (Epic)	14	5
12	(19)	REMEMBER ME THIS WAY Gary Glitter (Bell)	2	12
13	(16)	THE STING .... Soundtrack (MCA)	13	8
14	(12)	SUPER BAD .... Various Artists (K-Tel)	8	9
15	(21)	DARK SIDE OF THE MOON Pink Floyd (Harvest)	65	1
16	(13)	AND I LOVE YOU SO Perry Como (RCA)	52	5
17	(17)	GLEN CAMPBELL'S GREATEST HITS .... (Capitol)	12	10
18	(20)	THE WAY WE WERE Andy Williams (CBS)	2	18
19	(15)	DIANA AND MARVIN ... Diana Ross & Marvin Gaye (Tamla Motown)	22	5
20	(18)	EASY EASY Scotland World Cup Squad (Polydor)	5	18
21	(11)	BY YOUR SIDE Peters & Lee (Philips)	9	11
22	(—)	ATLANTIC BLACK GOLD Various (Atlantic)	1	22
23	(—)	PHAEDRA .. Tangerine Dream (Virgin)	11	13
24	(23)	NOW AND THEN Carpenters (A & M)	51	1
25	(—)	THE PSYCHOMODO Cockney Rebel (EMI)	1	25
26	(26)	INNERVISIONS Stevie Wonder (Tamla Motown)	24	8
27	(—)	HAMBURGER CONCERTO Focus (Polydor)	3	19
28	(—)	WOMBLING SONGS Wombles (CBS)	6	22
29	(—)	BETWEEN TODAY AND YESTERDAY Alan Price (Warner Brothers)	2	23
30	(—)	BEST OF BREAD .... (Elektra)	2	30

Where once he revelled in obscure idiosyncrasy, now he pursued the most everyday (well, maybe every week) occurrences, and then gave them a little twist... things like arranging to meet your girlfriend on the equator, but forgetting to specify exactly where. 'All of the gifts are now melted or dead... you see I've been halfway round this place.'

Or, as Madeline Bocaro, long-time editor of *Sparks International Official Fan Club Newsletter* put it, 'You simply can't follow "Equator", so it closes the album. This is the closest Russell has come to singing the blues, and the saxophone he is seemingly battling with is clearly losing the fight. I'm sure that his date was there waiting for him on the equator, he just didn't walk around far enough to meet her! This is the song you put on when a friend has overstayed his welcome. It clears a room within two minutes, guaranteed.'

Another song dealt with a lovers' leap, where he jumps and she stays behind. In 'Hasta Mañana, Monsieur' we hear about the pitfalls of dating a foreign girl, with whom language is only one of the things you don't have in common: 'You mentioned Kant and I was shocked... where I come from, none of the girls had such foul tongues.'

But still they shuddered when Winwood suggested that 'This Town Ain't Big Enough For Both Of Us' become their debut Island single, and mourned the loss of 'Barbecutie' to its B-side. Everyone who heard it agreed that 'Barbecutie' was a guaranteed smash hit, from the rampant bass that kicked it into gear to the chorus that leaped out of nowhere to skin you. 'This Town Ain't Big Enough For Both Of Us', on the other hand, was just plain weird.

'You are as relieved to find [the] lyrics,' Bocaro continued, 'as a drowning man is to find a raft and, ten years later when you've turned twenty-five, you realise what it all means. Walter Mitty, eat your heart out! The uneven tempos and sudden changes might even classify this as the very first three-minute opera.'

With Winwood at the helm, recording kicked off on 22nd November 1973 at Ramport Studios in Battersea, an old church that the Who had recently converted into their own studio. It was (although the term was mercifully not in use at the time) a state-of-the-art affair, but it still relied upon electricity to make the machinery work, and that was something that was in short supply at the time.

The United Kingdom was in the grip of so many political crises that it was amazing that anybody got any work done, and the fact was a lot of people didn't. With new strikes seemingly being announced every week, Britain was in the throes of both an energy crisis and the three-day week. A six-hour booking in the studio could be halved as the National Grid rationed power, shutting down the network to great swathes of the country between this hour and that. You couldn't even sit and read for a while, waiting until the power returned, because candles, batteries and torches were in short supply as well.

For two Americans raised in sunny California, where everything ran at full tilt 24 hours a day, life in England with the winter closing in, and the country's natural grey now plunging into blackness, was like stepping back in time a hundred years.

There were also fears that, even if the album was completed, there might not be enough vinyl to press it on. Britain was not the only nation struggling to keep the lights on, after all. A dispute with the oil-producing moguls of OPEC had seen the entire Western world hit with an oil embargo, leading to lengthy queues at the petrol pumps and a sharp reduction in the use of oil in every industry in the land, including the music industry.

Tours were being curtailed or even cancelled, top-name American visitors were being forced to remain at home, and vinyl – whose primary ingredient was, of course, oil – was rapidly becoming an endangered species. It was certainly getting thinner and thinner every time a new disc left the pressing plant in an attempt to make dwindling stockpiles stretch as far as possible.

Labels were even looking to drop new and recent signings from their rosters rather than risk precious resources trying to break them, all of which gave the Maels good reason to be

71

grateful they'd decided to work with Muff Winwood. Outside producers might come and go, but the boss was there to stay.

Besides, it wasn't as if Winwood was a beginner. He might not, like his younger brother Steve, have been a household name, but the pair had played together in the Spencer Davis Group as they racked up two successive Number 1 singles in 1965; then, when he moved to the other side of the mixing desk, he'd cut his producing teeth on three marvellous albums by Patto, and as many again by the Sutherland Brothers and Quiver. He knew what he believed great music should sound like, and it was a testament to his genius that it usually wound up exactly the way the musicians intended in the first place.

The first set of sessions for the new album ran until the end of 1973. Eight songs were completed at Ramport: 'Barbecutie', 'Falling In Love With Myself Again', 'I Like Girls' and 'Talent Is An Asset', all recorded with engineer Tony Platt, and 'Complaints', 'In My Family', 'This Town Ain't Big Enough For Both Of Us' and 'Thank God It's Not Christmas', with Richard Digby-Smith.

There was a break for Christmas, before the whole team, with Digby-Smith again in attendance, shifted over to Island's Basing Street studio to put the finishing touches to the record. The Basing Street sessions started well, and saw the completion of 'Equator', with Ron duping his Mellotron into believing itself to be a saxophone while Russell's vocals ran riot through a varispeed machine, the oddly inconsequential 'Profile' and 'Hasta Mañana, Monsieur', with Winwood firmly and correctly insisting that he wanted to hear castanets clacking throughout the song, a little aural pun that most people might not even notice but which keen listeners would certainly celebrate.

But it was one of the last of the Basing Street recordings that sealed the line-up's fate. 'Amateur Hour', Ron's breakneck ode to the joys (or otherwise) of puberty, was the flashpoint. In particular, the bass line which Martin Gordon gifted the recording.

The song was already complete when Winwood, emerging from the control room, declared himself unhappy with it and asked the bassist to overdub a replacement. Gordon thought the demand was unnecessary, but worse was to come as he was told to abandon the Rickenbacker 4001 he'd been playing with such distinction throughout the rest of the album and run through on a Fender bass that just happened to have been delivered to the studio by Jook's Ian Hampton.

'The stupid thing,' Gordon explained, 'was that it wasn't the bass line itself, but the *sound* of the bass line. Very pre-post-modern, you might say.' Disgruntled, but obediently, he replayed the existing bass line note for note on the Fender, while demonstrating his contempt for the entire proceedings by staring fixedly out of the studio door's glass window, watching the comings and goings in the outer offices. And it suddenly dawned on him, he hated being in Sparks. 'Out there was real, out there was art. Not what was going on inside the studio – lifeless reproductions of things that were much better, in order to satisfy the paranoid fears of colonials and a Northerner.'

But Gordon's travails were not over. Next, he was subjected to a Ron Mael tirade over the nature of the bass line on 'In My Family'. It was, Ron insisted, 'wimpy'. Gordon, who probably couldn't have coaxed a wimpy sound out of that Ricky if he'd wanted to, was understandably furious and gave back as good as he got. Maybe even better.

Adrian Fisher, too, was finding the Maels to be considerably harsher taskmasters than he felt they ought to be – 'beyond perfectionist' was his succinct summary of their approach. He smoked and he drank, and they found fault with both habits; he retaliated, he laughed, by insisting on adding a guitar solo to every song, and particularly to the fade-outs, whether one was required or not. Winwood, who became as exasperated by this as the Maels, responded by either deleting or drastically reducing the volume of every unauthorised note Fisher played, including some fiery contributions to the dramatic bombast of 'Falling In Love With Myself Again'. And that became another flashpoint for Gordon, who demanded that the guitar be brought back up in the mix. It was another battle that he lost.

At the same time, however, Fisher acknowledged that his love for the rock'n'roll lifestyle, in all the manifestations that the early- to mid-Seventies made possible, was also completely at odds with his band-mates in general, and the Maels in particular. He enjoyed London's nightlife and he liked hanging out with other musicians. Ron and Russell, on the other hand, had no interest in hobnobbing with the stars.

One day, during the Ramport sessions, Roger Daltrey dropped by the studio to listen, but apparently fled when Russell's sole means of engaging him in conversation appeared to be a litany of every Indian restaurant he'd visited. On another occasion, Free guitarist Paul Kossoff came by to see Winwood. Gordon recalled, 'He was greeted warmly by Muff, was eyed with awe by me and was roundly ignored by Ron and Russell. After he left, he was scorned by them for not having neat hair.'

Finally the album was complete. A title, 'Kimono My House', was decided upon, a phrase lifted from 'Hasta Mañana, Monsieur' that itself parodied the old Rosemary Clooney standard 'Come On A-My House' (co-written, incidentally, by Ross Bagdasarian, better known as the creator of the Chipmunks). All that remained now was to mix the thing, a process that the band naturally assumed they'd be invited to witness, and even contribute to.

They were wrong. Winwood refused to allow them into the studio, and the Maels backed him up. The band would not hear their handiwork until the final mix had been completed, when they were invited to what Gordon described as 'a *fait accompli* listening session in Air Studios at Oxford Circus, when the whole thing was finished.'

It was there that Gordon delivered his fateful opinion of the guitars in 'Falling In Love With Myself Again'. 'A silence fell upon the assembled throng. The guitars stayed as they were, and there were no more listening sessions.'

Disgruntled, but not willing to rock the boat too hard, Diamond, Fisher and even the increasingly unhappy Gordon went along with their masters' dictates, relying upon manager Hewlett to smooth out any difficulties that simple conversation was unable to salve. The Maels appeared to have settled down as well, now the album was complete and sounding spectacular. Island wanted them out on the road as quickly as possible after the single's release.

'This Town Ain't Big Enough For Both Of Us' was scheduled for a mid-March 1974 appearance, and everybody who heard it was thrilled. Ian Kimmett recalled, 'John Hewlett and Trevor White were very excited about "This Town Ain't Big Enough...". John was so high on it that he actually played the song in the middle of one of our sessions at RG Jones Studio!'

Attention turned now to just how accurately the band might be able to reproduce their sound on stage. So far as the British contingent was concerned, there was no problem. Ron, however, was stymied. Extra keyboard parts were the rule, not the exception, across the completed album, far more than he could ever play alone, but all of them integral to the songs they graced. It was time to return to the back pages of *Melody Maker*: 'Organist required by major label recording band. Image extremely important – Saturday February 16th, Furniture Cave. No beards or bulges.'

Enter Peter Oxendale – or *Sir* Peter, as Adrian Fisher quickly dubbed the musically over-qualified player after discovering that his visiting card suffixed his name with a string of initials. Unfortunately, while Oxendale was unquestionably a great player, his band-mates also delighted in describing him as their ugliest member by far...so ugly, in fact, that they were uncertain whether he should even be seen on stage with them, or if he should be hidden away behind curtains, to provide his accompaniment in total seclusion.

In reality, Oxendale's stay with Sparks was so short – just a matter of weeks – that he didn't even get beyond the live rehearsals at the disused Fulham church that Emerson, Lake and Palmer had converted into their own Manticore rehearsal space. But, sure enough, his Hammond was kept right at the back even there, invisible behind the PA column. He was forced to keep walking up front after every number simply so his watching girlfriend could see that he really was a member of a band.

The rehearsals were not designed solely to nail down the sound of the group. Visually, too, everything needed to match the Maels' expectations, and Adrian Fisher was once again in their sights. An inveterate smoker, he had long ago taken to sticking his cigarette onto one of the loose ends of guitar string that wound out of his machine heads, and it annoyed the hell out of them. It looked cheap and corny, they complained. It looked like he was trying to be cool. But Fisher didn't care what it looked like. 'Eric Clapton does it,' he shrugged, 'and that's good enough for me.' There really wasn't much you could say in reply.

There were other changes. At rehearsal one day, Ron announced that he was heading off to Gotama, a trendy hairdresser's on the King's Road, and that he was going to get his hair cut short. He left the room with a thick, long, mass of curly black hair. He returned a suave approximation of Adolf Hitler. Strangely, band-mates Gordon, Diamond and Fisher all turned down the opportunity to follow him to Gotama.

Clothing was next. One day a tailor, Andrew, arrived at the Furniture Cave to measure the band members for new outfits, most of which matched one another when the initial order was placed but later, as wardrobes expanded, any chance of co-ordination fell away. Which is why, Gordon laughed, 'The band often appeared in photographs as a rather odd collection of individuals, including a polo player, a second-hand car salesman, a public school drop-out, someone who had just got out of bed and who wanted to return to it as soon as possible, and a strip-club drummer. It was odd that nobody ever suggested a bit more integration....'

The Maels, with the full support of Island's marketing department, had already determined that a major component in the beckoning media onslaught would be pictorial. One early photo shoot deposited Sparks at *Vogue* photographer Barry Lategan's studio in Flood Street, Chelsea. It was Lategan who'd shot the first, and most famous, images of Twiggy, although Gordon rather caustically remembered the experience more for Russell's 'dreadful cream cardigan' and the 'variety of silly wallpapers' in front of which the band were forced to pose.

Another photo shoot set about preserving the group's new look for the album jacket. Gordon: 'The photographer came down to rehearsals, and shot Adrian, Dinky and me individually. We were actually playing during the pix, so it was quite easy to look "real". The original plan, as explained to us, was that on the back of the album cover there would be a large colour picture of the band, by which was meant *all* of the band. And indeed some pics along this line were taken', the five of them, with the Maels of course in the foreground, pinned to a backdrop by a vast white spotlight beam.

According to Gordon, however, it quickly became apparent that those pictures were not going to be used. 'So a panacea was suggested. Hewlett said that the British, reduced from their previously full-colour band-pic status to a token presence in minute black and white snaps on the back of the sleeve, could at least select their own pictures. Okay. I chose mine, so imagine my surprise...well, it was not great...when I was eventually presented with an album featuring an entirely different picture!'

In truth, the band photographs, and that includes the larger, and very distinctive shot of Ron and Russell that dominated the back cover, were simply there for the sake of convention. It was the front cover image that would give 'Kimono My House' its lasting reputation as one of the most striking LP sleeves of all time.

Ron had devised the image the previous year, seizing upon a Second World War vintage photograph of a pair of Japanese geisha girls pointedly holding their noses while apparently clutching a copy of 'A Woofer In Tweeter's Clothing'. It was a captivating notion; what he could not have envisaged, however, was that Island would recruit Karl Stoecker to bring it to life – the same Stoecker who had already done so much to revolutionise British album art with his work with Roxy Music.

All three of their albums to date, 'Roxy Music', 'For Your Pleasure' and 'Stranded', had been dominated not by any conventional album art or band photograph but by pin-ups, apparently torn freshly from the pages of some high-class glamour magazine. The geishas would match their glamour, but dismiss it too – their make-up was smeared, their faces distraught and their clothing as bulky and form-obscuring as the Roxy girls' was skimpy and alluring.

Michi Hirota and Kuniko Okamura, the two women selected for the shoot, were members of the Japanese Red Buddha Theatre, a 35-strong entourage of musicians, dancers and singers that had been working with percussionist Stomu Yamash'ta (the company's producer, director and composer) in London and Paris since the previous summer. At the time of the photo session, they were back in London for a month at the Chalk Farm Roundhouse.

Hirota, who would later (1979) provide the Japanese vocals on David Bowie's 'It's No Game', told Madeline Bocaro, 'We were both actresses. [The] record company approached our director looking for Japanese women, and we were asked to do the modelling.' It was a lengthy session, four or five hours, made all the more difficult because neither of the women knew the precise way to arrange their hair or even fix their kimono. 'There was nobody to dress us!'

Neither was Hirota especially happy with the finished photograph; 'I thought that I looked a bit ugly.' There were far more satisfactory shots taken, she thought;

especially since the selected photograph was in fact one that Stoecker initially regarded as an outtake, shot towards the very end of the session.

The girls were the only image on the front sleeve; even the band's name was omitted, at the Maels' request. 'We were very happy that Island Records allowed us not to have the name of the band nor the album title on the front cover,' Russell celebrated. 'We thought the image alone would speak loudly enough. Try to get a company to go along with that concept today.'

The music was ready, the album sleeve was ready and the band was ready. It was time to unveil the package to the world.

'Without drawing overworked comparison,' announced Island's first press release, 'we believe that Sparks, with their music and unique visual identity, will capture the imagination and affection of roughly the same audience sector which has made Roxy Music such an overwhelming success.'

With John Hewlett meanwhile declaring that Sparks were 'trying to recapture the excitement of the Small Faces and the Who', two rather different sets of expectations had thus been nurtured. But few listeners could have been adequately prepared for the reality, as Sparks' first British single, 'This Town Ain't Big Enough For Both Of Us', was unleashed in March 1974.

'Our music is a weird combination of gutsy backing and Russell's falsetto,' Ron told *the Sun*, while Russell elaborated on the latter, and most distinctive, quality for *Record Mirror*. 'The singing is dictated by the way the songs are written. When Ron writes, he happens to use the right hand a lot on keyboards, and he comes up with songs without any regard as to whether they can be sung like that. He'll go from high notes to low notes without singing it himself, so he doesn't even know if a person can possibly sing like that. But it's quite interesting occasionally, to force yourself to sing like that, and not transpose it to a key that's easier. The result is that I sing whatever's there.

'Actually, my voice hasn't changed since I was twelve. It hasn't broken yet, and I'm keeping my fingers crossed that it doesn't, otherwise we're going to be in for a lot of trouble.'

The press was fascinated, then, and the very first stirrings of public interest, too, could be felt. Sensing that his job was going to get a lot busier over the next few weeks, John Hewlett arranged for Joseph Fleury to be flown over to work as his assistant, and to begin putting together the band's fan club.

He also contacted Larry Dupont, to ask whether he would be interested in taking the helm of Sparks' American career. Dupont turned him down. Life was good at that time; not only was his career as a photographer and illustrator taking off, he had sufficient free time to head up into the mountains with Harley Feinstein and ski to his heart's content. Hewlett was astonished by his reaction. 'So what do you want from life?' he asked Dupont. 'Happiness or excitement?' Dupont replied 'Happiness', and that was the end of the conversation...

Joseph Fleury, on the other hand, had no qualms whatsoever about uprooting himself and flying to a foreign land. Derek Paice, who quickly became one of Fleury's closest friends in London, recalled the New Yorker being installed 'in a gloomy bed-sit', and then presented with 'a desk and cupboard space at Island Records in Basing Street. The first time he took me to Basing Street, he pulled out lots of the old photographs, various issues of the Sparks fanzine he produced in New York, drawings and scribblings he'd done. He was the perfect interface between the band and the fans.'

Those fans were very thin on the ground right now. 'This Town Ain't Big Enough For Both Of Us' was painfully slow to take off. Nicky Horne became the first British disc jockey to play it during his local (London) Capital Radio show on 18th March; Radio One's John Peel took it national with another airing later that evening. But Elton John was so shocked when he heard it that he bet Muff Winwood that it would not be a hit and, for a while, it seemed his money was safe. For six weeks, the record simply hung in a void, receiving just enough airplay to keep it alive but not sufficient to make any difference to the sales.

'There was this real big push to try to make 'This Town Ain't Big Enough For Both Of Us' work,' Russell recalled. Island were pulling out all the promotional stops, but 'there was resistance... because it's a pretty unique song.'

Slowly, however, it became apparent that they were making headway and suddenly, a month and a half after the single was released, Capital Radio selected it as part of their weekly People's Choice poll. Every day for five days towards the end of April a different single would be played, with listeners then asked to call in and vote for their favourite. 'This Town Ain't Big Enough For Both Of Us' swept to victory. Days later, it poked its head into the Top 50, hitting Number 48 in the first week of May.

Top Of The Pops were on the line, inviting the band onto that week's show. 'And all of a sudden,' Russell continued, 'Island Records were rejoicing that they'd done it finally, and this was going to be the massive break for Sparks in the UK.'

Unfortunately, it was not to prove quite as easy as that, as Russell recalls; 'We went to re-record the song [a Musicians' Union requirement at that time] and the producer of the show, a guy named Robin Nash, came down to meet us. A very British gentleman, and he says with a perfect BBC accent, "Hullo, Robin Nash, *Top Of The Pops*" and I went, "Hi, I'm Russell from Sparks" with my best American twang. And he said, "Oh. Oh... Excuse me, I must make a telephone call." And they

pulled us off of the show, because they'd assumed we were British and we weren't part of the Musicians' Union here.'

Sparks were removed from the show's line-up and replaced by the Rubettes – whose own single, the similarly falsetto-led 'Sugar Baby Love', had just entered the chart at Number 27. 'Robin Nash, bless him, said "quick, get another band",' recalled Rubette Alan Williams. 'There were two or three bands bubbling under and [we] got the call.' The following week, Sparks were themselves at Number 27, and the Rubettes were Number 2. But the necessary paperwork had at least been filed, and Sparks finally made their debut on the show on 9th May.

Martin Gordon recalled the aftermath; 'Having recorded the show, we left and I began the long haul back home to Hitchin, carrying my bass – Rickenbackers are notoriously heavy. It was raining as I left the hallowed BBC portals and trudged across the road to White City underground. A long black limousine glided past me. A languid wave came from the back.' It was Ron and Russell, luxuriating in their first taste of stardom.

One can't blame them, of course. Having already played at least a handful of television shows that could, according to sundry industry analysts, make or break them in their respective territories, the Maels did not expect too much from *Top Of The Pops*. They understood of course, the importance of image, and the ability to project a look – as Ron reflected, 'On TV you could make an impact with a small, subtle action that would have had no effect in concert, in a big hall. You could strike people in a big way, a raised eyebrow, a changed expression, a moustache. I'd done them live before, but nobody had noticed,' and he'd done them on television, too. If *American Bandstand*, the *Old Grey Whistle Test*, *Top Pop* and *Hits A Go Go* couldn't break Sparks out of obscurity, why should this show be any different?

Because it was, of course. The single most watched music television show in Britain at that time, regularly commanding an audience in the region of 14 million viewers, *Top Of The Pops* was the pulse of British pop, not just musically, but stylistically, too. When Marc Bolan went out on that stage with the first flash of glitter on his face, he single-handedly created glam rock. When David Bowie went on, and draped an arm around guitarist Mick Ronson's shoulders, he let everybody in on his bisexual secret. And when Sparks went on and the camera focussed for the first time on Ron's unsmiling face, his tiny toothbrush moustache bristling defiantly back at the lens, he created a sensation. Pop stars had looked like a lot of things over the years. But had one ever looked so much like Adolf Hitler? Or, at least, Charlie Chaplin?

When asked to elaborate upon their past by the handful of British journalists who had already passed through their orbit, the brothers delightedly claimed that their mother was Doris Day. Now Ron was having to deny that Chaplin was his father, and taking it all in surprisingly good spirit. Because, although people *asked* about Chaplin, they were *thinking* about Hitler, still a shockingly potent bogeyman in a society which, 29 years after his death, still bore the scars of the war he had ignited.

London remained scarred by the bombsites of the Blitz; television constantly picked over the ashes of that recent history; children's comics routinely echoed to the clash of Nazi jackboots marching up to drag another English Pig-dog off to Gestapo HQ. The war was over, but both the conflict, and the rogue's gallery of German politicians who masterminded it remained very real. But it would be another 20 years before Ron discovered, while talking to the fans who flocked around Sparks during their mid-Nineties renaissance, just how terrifying that image appeared.

'People told me they used to hide behind the sofa when I came on television,' he said, with just a hint of contrition. And, when outlining all the achievements for which he was justly proud, his resemblance to the Fuehrer did give him pause. 'Perhaps I'm not quite as proud of that.'

What he could, and does, take pride in was the knowledge that he had reasserted a role in rock'n'roll that had grown all too rare in recent years, that of the genuine outsider, looking in with rage, not envy; with malice, not greed. Gene Vincent had it, his gnarled, crippled leg dragging uselessly behind him, a heart attack for everybody who assumed rock'n'rollers should be glamorous and chic. The early Rolling Stones almost had it, at least appearing dishevelled enough to send a chill of despair through every self-respecting parent in the land. And Jethro Tull's Ian Anderson had it, a one-legged hobgoblin, his flute disappearing into a bearded mouth as he half-balanced, half-crouched, in readiness to attack. All three, appearing on television for the first time, seemed to suggest some fundamental breakdown in the rules by which pop music was played.

The Seventies, however, offered none of that. Everybody was beautiful now, tarted up in the top glam fashions, even when their music should have pointed them in another stylistic direction altogether. The magic Marc Bolan had promised was delivered not only through his music, but throughout every level on which he operated. Even a simple photograph captured it; Bolan was absurdly photogenic, a trait which, above all others, was to be aspired to by the bands that sprang up in his wake. Not for the first time in rock history was the music a poor second to the packaging, but in the past only a privileged few could have got away with it. Bolan, however, liberated the halt, the lame, the ugly and the hopeless; suddenly a sprinkling of glitter and a pair of platform boots were all one needed to bring a hint of glamour to the most disparate of careers.

When Van Der Graaf Generator vocalist Peter Hammill in the guise of nihilistic pop genius Rikki Nadir condemned 'all those jerks in their tinsel glitter suits, pansying around...' he bemoaned not Bolan and the handful of names who actually enlarged upon his original vision, but those who emerged from stage left simply to borrow a handful of glamour.

When the hyper-hairy Strawbs went on *Top Of The Pops* with false cheekbones, they created Glitterfolk, prompting a disbelieving Martin Gordon to quip, ' I remember seeing a pic in some teeny mag with the singer's gleaming red-lipsticked lips peering moistly out from his bushy beard. A truly horrible sight.' When Edgar and Johnny Winter took to smothering themselves in rhinestones, they were no longer Bluesmen, they were Glitterbluesmen. And so on...Labelle hatched Glittersoul; Parliament birthed Glitterfunk; Silverhead created Glittermetal (and what a mediocre beast that turned out to be).

In every instance, the Glitter was nothing more than a visual aid, a convenient peg upon which to hang a career or two, but it worked. And, had Sparks comprised just one Mael brother, the cute one with the curly hair, it would probably have worked for them as well. But it would not have been half as effective, nor half as successful.

'Sparks were one of the few pre-punk bands who gave an inkling of what was to come,' declared the Adverts' singer TV Smith. 'Smart lyrics, devious tunes and an image that was so unlike the usual pop fodder around at the time. Hardly ever before had there been, like Ron, a pop star whose image was actually scary and threatening. Maybe Alice Cooper was the only other one...and that was it until Johnny Rotten.'

Ron was certainly enjoying himself at the time. As the umpteenth journalist of the day

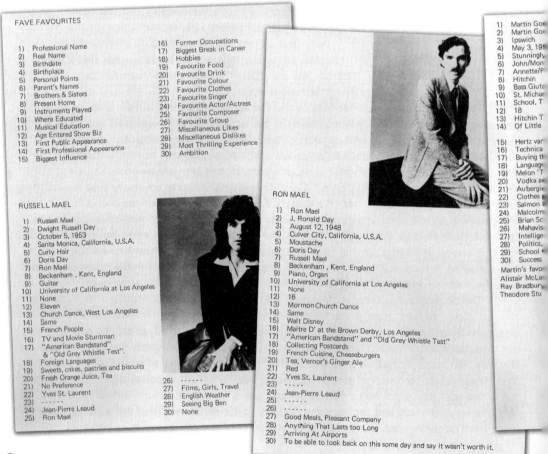

FAVE FAVOURITES

1)	Professional Name	16)	Former Occupations
2)	Real Name	17)	Biggest Break in Career
3)	Birthdate	18)	Hobbies
4)	Birthplace	19)	Favourite Food
5)	Personal Points	20)	Favourite Drink
6)	Parent's Names	21)	Favourite Colour
7)	Brothers & Sisters	22)	Favourite Clothes
8)	Present Home	23)	Favourite Singer
9)	Instruments Played	24)	Favourite Actor/Actress
10)	Where Educated	25)	Favourite Composer
11)	Musical Education	26)	Favourite Group
12)	Age Entered Show Biz	27)	Miscellaneous Likes
13)	First Public Appearance	28)	Miscellaneous Dislikes
14)	First Professional Appearance	29)	Most Thrilling Experience
15)	Biggest Influence	30)	Ambition

RUSSELL MAEL

1) Russell Mael
2) Dwight Russell Day
3) October 5, 1953
4) Santa Monica, California, U.S.A.
5) Curly Hair
6) Doris Day
7) Ron Mael
8) Beckenham , Kent, England
9) Guitar
10) University of California at Los Angeles
11) None
12) Eleven
13) Church Dance, West Los Angeles
14) Same
15) French People
16) TV and Movie Stuntman
17) "American Bandstand" & "Old Grey Whistle Test".
18) Foreign Languages
19) Sweets, cakes, pastries and biscuits
20) Fresh Orange Juice, Tea
21) No Preference
22) Yves St. Laurent
23) - - - - - -
24) Jean-Pierre Leaud
25) Ron Mael
26) - - - - - -
27) Films, Girls, Travel
28) English Weather
29) Seeing Big Ben
30) None

RON MAEL

1) Ron Mael
2) J. Ronald Day
3) August 12, 1948
4) Culver City, California, U.S.A.
5) Moustache
6) Doris Day
7) Russell Mael
8) Beckenham , Kent, England
9) Piano, Organ
10) University of California at Los Angeles
11) None
12) 16
13) Mormon Church Dance
14) Same
15) Walt Disney
16) Maitre D' at the Brown Derby, Los Angeles
17) "American Bandstand" and "Old Grey Whistle Test"
18) Collecting Postcards
19) French Cuisine, Cheeseburgers
20) Tea, Vernor's Ginger Ale
21) Red
22) Yves St. Laurent
23) - - - - -
24) Jean-Pierre Leaud
25) - - - - - -
26) - - - - - -
27) Good Meals, Pleasant Company
28) Anything That Lasts too Long
29) Arriving At Airports
30) To be able to look back on this some day and say it wasn't worth it.

1) Martin Go▪
2) Martin Go▪
3) Ipswich
4) May 3, 19▪
5) Stunningly
6) John/Mon▪
7) Annette/P▪
8) Hitchin
9) Bass Giuta
10) St. Michae
11) School, T
12) 18
13) Hitchin T
14) Of Little

15) Hertz var▪
16) Technica
17) Buying th
18) Language
19) Melon 'T
20) Vodka a▪
21) Aubergie
22) Clothes ▪
23) Salmon ▪
24) Malcolm
25) Brian Sc
26) Mahavis
27) Intellige
28) Politics,
29) School ◀
30) Success

Martin's favo▪
Alistair McLe▪
Ray Bradbury
Theodore Stu

passed through, observing that the gentleman with the black, slicked-back hair, toothbrush moustache and thoroughly English cricket pullover in no manner resembled a rock'n'roll star, Ron would simply glance at the schedule in front of him to double-check who he was talking to... Chris Welch of *Melody Maker*, on this occasion... and then replied.

'Thank you, Mr Welch, that's the nicest thing anybody has said to me all day. It's another case of a failure acting as a strength, because I always really had a desire to look like Alvin Lee. But something happened. I'd look in the mirror and put spikes in my hair, and look gaunt, and I'd have a fag hanging out of my mouth and say, "Ta. Fanks very much." And I had my teeth rotted away a little bit, but I still couldn't look like [Ten Years After guitarist] Alvin Lee.'

And teeth became the topic *du jour*, at least for the benefit of the now sadly departed *Melody Maker*. 'I have a tooth missing and that goes over really well,' said Russell proudly. 'You see in the States, most of the English groups that come over appeal because there seems to be something about English teeth. We haven't yet found the exact solution to the problem, but English teeth appear to be different from American. Something happened to one of mine, and when I went on stage and smiled, they said, "God, the guy must be English..."'

'The secret of English bands is having rotten teeth,' added Ron, baring his own draft-eluding gnashers. 'Everybody thinks it's their boots or some mystical heritage. But it's definitely not the boots. If you ever have a better dental service, then the English balance of payments will be in a lot worse shape, because none of the English bands will be making it.'

Not every member of the group revelled in their new-found celebrity, however. Adrian Fisher had baulked at the need to dress up for the cameras even before 'This Town Ain't Big

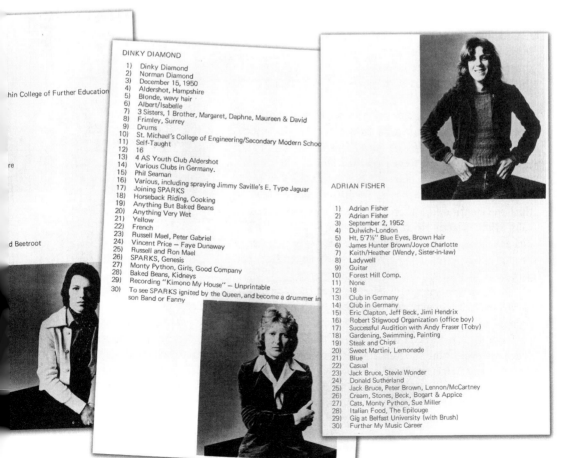

hin College of Further Education

re

d Beetroot

DINKY DIAMOND

1) Dinky Diamond
2) Norman Diamond
3) December 15, 1950
4) Aldershot, Hampshire
5) Blonde, wavy hair
6) Albert/Isabelle
7) 3 Sisters, 1 Brother, Margaret, Daphne, Maureen & David
8) Frimley, Surrey
9) Drums
10) St. Michael's College of Engineering/Secondary Modern Schoo
11) Self-Taught
12) 16
13) 4 AS Youth Club Aldershot
14) Various Clubs in Germany.
15) Phil Seaman
16) Various, including spraying Jimmy Saville's E. Type Jaguar
17) Joining SPARKS
18) Horseback Riding, Cooking
19) Anything But Baked Beans
20) Anything Very Wet
21) Yellow
22) French
23) Russell Mael, Peter Gabriel
24) Vincent Price — Faye Dunaway
25) Russell and Ron Mael
26) SPARKS, Genesis
27) Monty Python, Girls, Good Company
28) Baked Beans, Kidneys
29) Recording "Kimono My House" — Unprintable
30) To see SPARKS ignited by the Queen, and become a drummer in son Band or Fanny

ADRIAN FISHER

1) Adrian Fisher
2) Adrian Fisher
3) September 2, 1952
4) Dulwich-London
5) Ht. 5'7½" Blue Eyes, Brown Hair
6) James Hunter Brown/Joyce Charlotte
7) Keith/Heather (Wendy, Sister-in-law)
8) Ladywell
9) Guitar
10) Forest Hill Comp.
11) None
12) 18
13) Club in Germany
14) Club in Germany
15) Eric Clapton, Jeff Beck, Jimi Hendrix
16) Robert Stigwood Organization (office boy)
17) Successful Audition with Andy Fraser (Toby)
18) Gardening, Swimming, Painting
19) Steak and Chips
20) Sweet Martini, Lemonade
21) Blue
22) Casual
23) Jack Bruce, Stevie Wonder
24) Donald Sutherland
25) Jack Bruce, Peter Brown, Lennon/McCartney
26) Cream, Stones, Beck, Bogart & Appice
27) Cats, Monty Python, Sue Miller
28) Italian Food, The Epilouge
29) Gig at Belfast University (with Brush)
30) Further My Music Career

Enough For Both Of Us' began its rise. Now he grew positively rebellious, even to the extent of calling in ill on the days when a magazine shoot was scheduled to take place.

On one occasion, the quintet were handed half a dozen large plywood letters which, when suitably re-arranged and turned towards the camera, spelled out the band's name. Fisher, however, was unimpressed. He picked up his piece of lettering, the final 'S', and then turned his back on the cameraman, and nothing could tempt him to turn around again. It was still a striking photograph, rolled out for the advertisements and a promo poster that preceded the album's release, and then reused for the inner-sleeve artwork atop the LP's lyric sheet. But Fisher's disdain for the burgeoning circus was growing ever more pronounced. And it was only going to get worse – both the circus, and his disdain. Seven days after Sparks made their debut on *Top Of The Pops*, 'This Town Ain't Big Enough For Both Of Us' entered the Top 10.

Martin Gordon, however, did not enter with it. The band was still rehearsing for the tour, now less than one month away, when Ron and Russell announced that they were tired of listening to Gordon's Rickenbacker, and wanted him to revert to the same Fender he'd played on 'Amateur Hour', no matter how purposefully amateurishly he may have played it.

Gordon refused, still smarting over the Maels' refusal to allow him full rein with his own ideas. Angry, too, that the early promise of him being allowed to contribute his own songs to the band had been quashed after one perfunctory run-through of his exquisite 'Cover Girl', Gordon had been growing more and more fractious every time the Maels made another decision that was then handed down to their band-mates like an Imperial diktat.

Now he snapped. According to Joseph Fleury, who watched nervously as the row grew fiercer, the argument really was about nothing more than a preference for the Fender's sound. But to Gordon, it was far more sinister than that. Dogmatic to the last, he told Ron that, if he couldn't use his own bass, he'd rather not be in the band at all. And from three 'o clock the

following morning, when Fleury phoned him up ('John brought me over to be his personal assistant. It meant I could do all the dirty work while he carried on being a nice guy'), he wasn't.

The Maels themselves admitted that Martin's tenure within Sparks had not, perhaps, lived up to the bassist's expectations. But they denied that he was ever promised anything more than a bassist's role. As Russell said, 'Why would we want another songwriter when we already had Ron?'

Perhaps because Martin was also a great writer and even the band's biggest fans would admit that there were times when Ron's own compositional abilities clearly valued quantity over quality. 'Martin did bring some good ideas into the band,' Joseph Fleury acknowledged. But that was not what they were

looking for. 'Ron and Russell always knew what they wanted.' And a democracy was not part of it.

'It was a stupid mistake,' John Hewlett admits. 'The rehearsals prior to the recordings had sounded fantastic and led to them signing a contract, but, either to due to my inexperience or lack of self confidence, I accepted the opinions of Ron and Russell. That was the beginning of the end of a potentially truly great rock band.'

Gordon's final act as a member of the band, however, was certainly a memorable one. He shot Russell Mael.

Keen to exploit the foreign markets that the band would hopefully be too busy to tour, Island hired directed Rosie Samwell-Smith (wife of ex-Yardbird Paul) to make a promotional film to accompany 'This Town Ain't Big Enough For Both Of Us', at a time when such extravagances were scarcely at the top of many artists' minds.

David Bowie had shot a few promos at that point, and so had the Sweet and T.Rex. But it was almost unheard of for an all-but-unknown band, just enjoying their very first hit, to go to so much trouble or expense, and even rarer for the resultant video to step far from those other acts' simplistic notions of miming their instruments in front of the cameras.

Samwell-Smith's vision, however, placed Sparks in a series of considerably more expansive settings. The video was shot at Beaulieu, the stately dwelling of Lord Montague, and home to one of the greatest car museums in the world – an instant thrill for the car-mad Ron. There, the band members drank wine and walked the beautifully appointed rooms, scampered across the grounds

island records ltd ·

Mr Adrian Fisher
Mr Martin Gordon
Mr Norman Diamond
Mr Ronald Mael
Mr Russell Mael

(Professionally known as "Sparks")

22 November 197

c/o John Hewlett
73 Northwood Avenue
PURLEY
Surrey

Dear Sirs,

We hereby confirm the Agreement between us for your exclusive recording services the terms of which are contained in this letter and our Artist Recording Contract Standard Conditions ("the Conditions") a copy of which is attached hereto : -

1. The territory referred to in Condition 1 shall be the World.

2. The period referred to in Condition 1 shall be two years from the date hereof or until ninety days after you shall have satisfactorily recorded for the company sufficient acceptable recordings to comprise four 33 1/3 rpm double sided long play records (hereinafter called "albums") in accordance with Condition 4(D), whichever shall be the later date (hereinafter called "the initial period") pro- vided that we shall have an option (such option to be exercised by notice in writing prior to the end of the then current term) to extend the initial period for a further term of three years from the expiry of the pre- ceding term or until 90 days after you shall have satis- factorily recorded for the company sufficient further acceptable recordings to comprise six (6) albums in accor- dance with Condition 4(D) whichever shall be the later date (such further term being called "the renewal term").

3. a. The royalty referred to in Condition 2(B) shall be : -

   i. In respect of records manufactured and sold in the United Kingdom of Great Britain and Eire excluding records so manufactured but sold for export to other territories) (hereinafter called "the U.K. area") ten per cent (10%) calculated in accordance with Condition 2(B) but where the sales of any one album in the U.K. area exceed 50,000 units then the royalty shall be increased to eleven per cent (11%) calculated in accordance with Condition 2(B) in respect of all sales of albums thereafter in the U.K. area.

22 St. Peters Square, London W6 9NW. Telephone 01-741 1511. Cables: ACKEE Telex : 934541
Directors: David Betteridge John Leftly Charles Levison Tim Clark Tom Hayes Muff Winwood
Regd. No. 723336 England Regd. Office: 25 Gilbert Street, London W1Y 2NU

Please confirm your acceptance of these terms and conditions by signing and returning both copies of this letter.

Yours faithfully,

for and on behalf of
ISLAND RECORDS LIMITED

ACCEPTED AND AGREED

Adrian Fisher

Martin Gordon

Norman Diamond

Ronald Mael

Russell Mael

ió costs incurred by the Artists in fulfilling the commitment to in paragraph 2 hereof shall be paid for by the Company ed against the Artists royalties to accrue hereunder.

and then ran down to nearby Studland Bay for some shots against the water.

Adrian Fisher, perhaps predictably, spent the day in a bad mood. But still the video was a jewel, mere snatches of performance blithely tying the vision in with the sound, while a closer eye zoomed in on literal interpretations of the scenarios that unfolded through the lyric.

And that included the memorable moment where Russell stood in a garden gazebo staring fixedly ahead, while Gordon raised his double-barrelled shotgun and fired. The singer collapsed slowly to the ground, his white suit bloodless, but clearly mortally wounded. Except it wasn't the town that wasn't big enough for both of them, it was the band.

Gordon sighed with comic drama. 'It subsequently transpired that I hadn't really shot the lead singer. It was only acting.'

CHAPTER NINE

THE CRITICS ALL SAID 'RIVETING'

The Island label's attempts to breathe some fresh life into things notwithstanding, 1974 was fast shaping up to be a year of almost startling mediocrity, at least when compared to its immediate predecessors. The sudden rush of new faces that had begun in the summer of 1972, and which was at its peak the last time the Maels visited England, had quickly dissipated. Now only Bowie, Elton John and Gary Glitter survived with anything even remotely approaching their previous invincibility. Marc Bolan's reign was over, Slade and the Sweet were bottoming out, in terms of sales if not musical quality, and it was left to the power of television, through the soap opera *Crossroads*, the talent show *Opportunity Knocks* and a sudden obsession with the martial arts, to challenge the seemingly eternal chart residence of aged French balladeers, country and western singers and 'Y Viva Espana'.

Into this dismal musical climate, Island plunged two totally dissimilar Californian brothers whose avowed ambition was to be 'as big as General Motors'. And, by God, we needed them. When the hottest new act of the year so far is the Wombles, you know there's a problem, but even they were to have their thunder stolen by the return of the Bay City Rollers, a band that most people thought had shot their bolt with a solitary hit in 1971, but who had just been reborn in dramatic fashion with a look that the Jook boys thought was remarkably familiar.

Playing a show early in 1974, Jook were introduced to what Chris Townson recalled as 'a very hairy, very scruffy' Edinburgh band who dropped by the dressing room to rave about Jook's image. A few weeks later, Jook stared in horror as those same scruffy hairies, scruffy and hairy no more, cavorted around *Top Of The Pops*, clad in almost precisely the same clothes as Jook had been wearing for years.

'Ian Kimmett and I both knew Tam Paton, the Rollers' manager, from the early Sixties, when he was the leader, singer and keyboard player of an Edinburgh band called the Crusaders,' Ian Hampton reflected, 'plus I knew most of them from the Scottish circuit. I recall Tam and the band being blown away by Jook's image.' Addind a dash of tartan to Jook's boots, braces and turned up trousers, the Bay City Rollers had arrived, and that, concluded Chris Townson, 'was the end of Jook.'

In fact, there was still one final tragedy left to play out, as a country-wide, and solidly sold-out British tour supporting the Sweet was cancelled at the very last minute after the headliners' singer, Brian Connolly, had his throat slashed in a street fight.

Despite this body blow, Jook's supporters remained upbeat – they could still do it, they assured them, they could still break through... But there's a big difference between 'could break through' and having already done so. When John Hewlett phoned Ian Hampton and Trevor White to appraise them of the disarray in the ranks of the country's currently most popular band – to let them know that Gordon had already gone, and Fisher was likely to follow him – it took them no time at all to put Jook, and all its possible potential, behind them and launch into a life where fame and fortune were already on the plate. They might even get to fulfil a promise that White had made to one of the teenybop magazines two years before – 'If we ever make any big money, we're going to buy the most ridiculous cars.'

Melody Maker

GUST 31, 1974 — 10p weekly — USA 60 cents

SPA

SPARKS hit the road
The band embark or
of concert dates in
second British tour this
And the new Sparks' alt
be released to coincide wi
Concerts start at York
2, continuing at Newcastle
fort Hall, Leicester (4). Li

SPARKS' EXILE IS OVER: BIG TOUR

SPARKS RETURN to Britain for a major tour
autumn, ending their year-long exile from this cou
The band's last British tour was in November,
after which Sparks announced plans to concentrate
efforts in the United States and Europe. They comp
their American tour in June and, in September, S
will be playing in Europe as a prelude to the B
series of concerts.

The band's tour will start at the Newcastle City
on October 15, continuing at the Edinburgh Odeor
17), Glasgow Apollo (18), Manchester Palace (19),
mouth Guildhall (21), Taunton Odeon (23), Oxford
Theatre (24), Hammersmith Odeon, London (26), Ip
Gaumont (28), Leicester De Montfort Hall (29), Sh
City Hall (30), Liverpool Empire (31), Leeds Univ
(November 1), Coventry New Theatre (2), Bristol C
Hall (4), Birmingham Odeon (6)

Sparks fail to ignite

RKS: atrocious balance

parks: just tinny abaret act

Michael Watts

OOM can a band have had such encouragement
from critics and audiences alike and been so
on the big night as were Sparks at the Rainbow
nday. The tedium fell like fine drizzle on the
around me in the circle, and well before the end
were sloping off in whatever direction offered
hing that approached entertainment. In short,
y was running at a new high.

be, as their defenders will assert, they have been
too fast and too soon, but all the same, they
d next to nothing. What seems on the records to
mlnor masterpiece of wit and invention, emerged on
as a tinny cabaret act, a gimmick pushed to extremes.
r Russell Mael has an interesting and penetrating
that works well on the album, where the songs
ly sound strong enough to complement him, but
performance that piercing shriek going on ad infinit
gets up your ass.

erformance, furthermore, isn't helped by some of
st banal patter between songs since the formation
kefield Theatre Club.

thing on the lines of, "now here's one called . . ."
ah. He should really try to learn something about
e-handling. It's one thing to play Stockport Town
nd another to get yourself across at London's most
venue.

Sparks/ Rainbow

WHEN AN audience
consists of Bowie rejects,
juvenile fashion followers,
weenyboppers, some
couples in the over forty
age bracket and jean-ies,
you know something spe-
cial is expected.

Sunday night was Sparks
night, but somehow the world
was not set alight.

Instrumentally nothing was
amiss, the band were tight —
very. Adrian Fisher reproduced
the fresh guitar licks that ab-
ounded from the album with
gusto; Dinky Diamond's enthusiasm was visible.

It was the vocals that provided the downer. The mix was
bad, and at times, Russell
Mael's authentic voice was
completely submerged by the
band.

The opener was "Hasta Ma-
nana Monsieur" from the "Kimono" album, which provided
the majority of songs, exceptions being: "Wondergirl,"
"Something For The Girl With
Everything", "Bar-B-Cutie",
and "Girl From Germany".

The highlight was "Here In
Heaven" where Mael's voice
could be heard almost clearly

antics were a show in th
selves. As one person remar
"Sparks should've been the s
port".

Shyama Per

Refugee, String Driver Thing/ Manchester

IT WOULD have been hard fo
any band to fail with an au
dience as high-spirited as th
one that turned out for R
fugee's first visit to Manches
ter's Free Trade Hall. Heart
cheers were awarded for jus
about anything that happened
on stage.

The lights went down as the
cheers went up, and the M.C
announced, "We've got a
couple of hours of really good
music lined up for you," and
although the hall was less than
half full, there was a lot of noise
made to welcome String Driven
Thing.

Displaying their new line-up,
they played a good opening set
which featured some haunting
licks on electric violin, blending
with fine lead guitar work. The
vocalist, who was in excellent
form, sounded more than a little
like Paul Rodgers and t

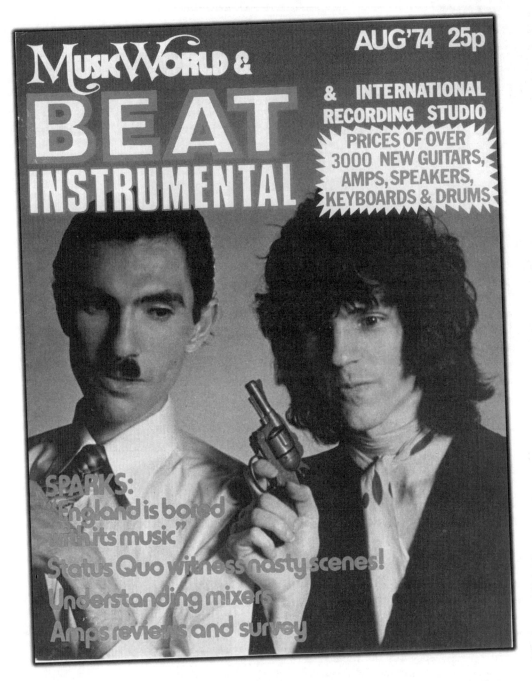

AUG'74 25p

MUSIC WORLD &

BEAT
INSTRUMENTAL

& INTERNATIONAL
RECORDING STUDIO
PRICES OF OVER
3000 NEW GUITARS,
AMPS, SPEAKERS,
KEYBOARDS & DRUMS

SPARKS:
"England is bored
with its music"
Status Quo witness nasty scenes!
Understanding mixers
Amps reviews and survey

'We went along to a two-way audition,' explained White. 'If they liked us and we liked them, we'd join. But it fitted in straight away. In an hour we did "Hasta Mañana, Monsieur" and "This Town Ain't Big Enough For Both Of Us", and they were perfect. It sounded great and we thought "'Well, what have we been doing for the last few years?"'

Its reception buoyed sky high by the single, which everybody now seemed to love unreservedly, 'Kimono My House' was released to an almost unprecedented reception in mid-May 1974. The *New Musical Express*'s Ian MacDonald declared it 'an instant classic'; *Sounds*, in a May 1974 issue, with Ron's face beaming from the cover, announced, 'it's got the musical extravagance

BRIGHT SPARKS!

With an almighty flash, Sparks burst on to the pop scene and knocked everybody out! But how did these lads take the pop scene by storm? Read on . . . and see . . .

UNIQUE, astounding . . . a band unlike any other group to hit the British pop scene, that's Sparks! And these lads have a style all of their very own!

But it's only recently that their talent has been recognised.

In the beginning there was Ron and Russell Mael, two brothers from California, both overflowing with talent, not merely musical, but literary and artistic talent too. But they didn't quite know what to do with all their good ideas.

Ron was makin' a living as a bit-part actor, whilst Russell was singing his way thru' the modelling scene.

In between his acting career Ron had learnt to play the piano and of course Russell had been keepin' his voice in good trim practising his arpeggios (singing scales to you!) in between posing for the photographer. Then the lads decided to form a group which they called Halfnelson, with some other musical mates of theirs.

Three years later they reckoned they'd set at least one record — by collecting the largest collection of record company rejection slips possible for any struggling pop musicians! In fact Ron papered his bedroom wall with them!

Then luck — and recognition — finally staggered their way! A record company accepted them, recorded them and changed their name to Sparks. They made two albums with this record label and toured Europe and much of the States. But, disillusioned with the American pop scene, the band split up.

Not for long, tho'! An English promoter got hold of the lads, boosted their morale, and Sparks Mark II with their current line up of the Mael brothers, Dinky Diamond the dancing drummer, bass guitarist Martin Gordon and lead guitarist Adrian Fisher were formed! (They have another organist for live gigs, who plays under the name of Sir Peter Oxendale!)

And that's the Sparks we know! Their first tongue-twisting smash hit was "This Town Ain't Big Enough For The Both of Us", taken from their album "Kimono My House." And their new single "Amateur" is heading the same way.

It's hardly surprising — these boys have definitely got something new and different to offer the pop scene — and the fans appreciate it. Could you call it a 'spark' of originality?!

of Wizzard, the sophisticated feel of Roxy and the menacing power of the Third Reich.' And they were not alone. The other music papers bent over backwards to accommodate Sparks' vision, while the letters pages, too, found room to praise the Maels' achievement.

'Today,' wrote Steven Morrissey of Stretford, Manchester, in a letter published in the NME's 14th June issue, 'I bought the album of the year. I feel I can say this without expecting several letters saying I'm talking rubbish. The album is "Kimono My House" by Sparks. I bought it on the strength of the single. Every track is brilliant, although I must name "Equator", "Complaints", "Amateur Hour" and "Here In Heaven" as the best tracks and in that order.' Thirty years later, that same Steven Morrissey would arrange for Sparks to headline a Meltdown Festival concert at the Royal Festival Hall, London, performing 'Kimono My House' live in its entirety for the first time ever.

Indeed, such was the fervour surrounding the music that, when Gordon's departure was announced, just days after that first Top Of The Pops appearance, nobody even seemed to notice. They were too engrossed in inventing new epithets to bestow upon 'Kimono My House'.

With a second Top Of The Pops appearance on 23rd May behind it, 'This Town Ain't Big Enough For Both Of Us' finally peaked at Number 2, kept off the top by those usurping Rubettes. And, while its disappearance from the Top 20 was precipitous, to say the least, from Number 9 to nowhere in the space of a week, Island lost no time in following it up. Only a fortnight after its predecessor left the chart, 'Amateur Hour', that beginner's guide to adolescent sex, entered the Top 50 at Number 42. The following week it was at 17, the week after that, Number 7. And this time it did it without Top Of The Pops, pulled from the screens

by a BBC technicians' strike that left the music industry to fend for itself for seven weeks.

Still, it was all very confusing for the new boys. White and Hampton both still speak of the absolute disorientation of the world into which they were so suddenly flung, and the sense of frustration that went with it. To be appearing on countless television shows, performing the hits they had no part in creating, admitted White, was even worse than hearing one or other of the album tracks on the radio and thinking, 'That's the biggest band in the country, I'm a member of it, and nobody even knows.' But that was all to change as Sparks went out to meet their new adoring public for the first time, a 16-date tour that ran from 20th June to 7th July 1974.

20th June – Winter Gardens, Cleethorpes
21st June – Hull University
22nd June – Leeds University
23rd June – Town Hall, Cheltenham
24th June – Top Rank Suite, Birmingham
25th June – University of Lancaster
26th June – Top Rank Suite, Swansea
28th June – Flamingo Ballroom, Redruth
29th June – County Ballroom, Taunton
30th June – Pavilion, Torquay
2nd July – Mobile Theatre, Home Park, Plymouth
3rd July – Victoria Rooms, Bristol
4th July – California Ballroom,Dunstable
5th July – Corn Exchange, Cambridge
6th July – Kursaal Ballroom, Southend On Sea
7th July – Rainbow Theatre, London

Arranged by Alec Leslie Enterprises, promoters who also operated out of Island's Basing Street headquarters, the tour was a lot shorter than demand for tickets insisted it should be. 'Why no Manchester or Liverpool or Glasgow or Newcastle?' asked the fan mail that every day's post brought. The simple answer was because nobody knew those places would care. The tour was booked before 'This Town Ain't Big Enough For Both Of Us' even started to take off – in fact, the first show to be confirmed, back in March, was at the University of Hull, where the original bill had Sparks headlining over Cockney Rebel and the Rubettes.

Now all three bands were in the charts (Cockney Rebel's 'Judy Teen' had just broken through at the beginning of June), and the bill splintered. It would be completed instead by veteran jazz humorist George Melly and a local female folk singer.

'It was...a bit of a Sparks Free Trial Offer Tour, in that everybody was still feeling their way and nobody knew what the reaction was going to be,' admitted Russell. 'Nobody knew if anybody would show up to some of the gigs. It was a learning process for everybody, for The Real Tour.'

Tickets for the Hull gig cost £1, and it sold out within 90 minutes. At the other end of the itinerary, tickets for the London Rainbow gig were gone within a week.

The band's own budget, too, was tiny. Mother Miriam attended most of the shows, glorying under the pseudonym of Doris (for Doris Day, of course) as she wandered out to chat with fans. But even Joseph Fleury had to be left behind in London for some of the gigs, or asked to make his own way there. Derek Paice, who chauffeured Fleury to a handful of the shows, recalled, 'It struck me as strange that someone who seemed so important to the continuing life of the band, albeit behind the scenes, often had to make his own way to and from shows.'

The stage set was Spartan. Russell explained, 'we...discussed it with the lighting crew and said that we wanted it to feature us in a way that wasn't overtly theatrical, but would present us really well as just our personalities.' Simple bright white spots picked out Ron and Russell, said *Melody Maker*, 'a little like the convicts captured in the copper's torch beam.' 'We wanted to create the atmosphere,' Russell continued. 'We wanted to be the atmosphere and we did it, I think, by using just those two spots, because we're really concerned that we didn't get into elaborate presentations and outdoing everybody with elaborate Busby Berkeley-choreographed settings and all that stuff.

'People have said that our music is really theatrical at times, but...we wanted it to come from the songs having a theatrical tinge to them. Rather than combining rock and the theatre. It's better to go see the Royal Shakespeare Company than to see a rock band trying to be theatrical.'

But it worked. TV Smith caught the band in Torquay and marvels, 'I was impressed with how they managed to play those fiendishly clever songs note perfect on stage.' Joe Elliott of Def Leppard attended the Leeds show and the experience inspired him to want to put his first band together.

For White, Fisher, Hampton and Diamond, meanwhile, the tour was the first chance they had ever been given to play at being rock stars, and they threw themselves into the lifestyle with abandon. Hampton: 'It was a culture shock. We'd never had to play anything other than the three chords before that. But it was an amazing experience. We didn't have long to rehearse the set, not much more than a month before the first gig, and it's not the easiest music to learn. But the audience was mad, it was the biggest audience I'd ever played to, and the maddest.'

SPARKS

Travelling on a 41-seater coach, dodging the water pistol fights that kept Fisher and Hampton amused during their down time, the biggest shock for the newcomers was to discover that the Maels did not want to join them in exploring the wild pastures that were suddenly opening up for them.

'It was very rare that they would let themselves go,' Trevor White recalled. 'We used to have this thing that if anyone fell asleep on the coach, they would wake up to find that the rest of us had "decorated" them. All apart from Ron and Russell, who would sit quietly up at the front.' Nobody ever decorated them.

Adrian Fisher agreed. 'My memory of Ron and Russ on the road is the two of them sitting at the front of the bus with their noses buried in

93

APPLY FINANCIAL SUPPORT & PUBLICITY TO TOUCH PAPER & STAND BACK

SPARKS

★ WARNING ★
THIS COULD BE A DAMP SQUID — IF IT DOES NOT GO OFF PLEASE APPROACH QUICKLY WITH MORE PUBLICITY + CASH ETC ......

Tony Bonyon

SPARK PLUGS

TODAY I bought the album of the year. I feel I can say this without expecting several letters saying I'm talking rubbish. The album is "Kimono My House", by Sparks. I bought it on the strength of the single. Every track is brilliant — although I must name "Equator", "Complaints", "Amateur Hour" and "Here In Heaven" as the best tracks, and in that order.
STEVE MORRISSEY, 384 Kings Road, Stretford, Manchester.
■ Migawd. Conviction

oozes from every sentence like the very ichor of life itself from the metal life-support systems of the **Bronze Giant of Fangorak**. The eyes of Mr. Morrisey gleam with a missionary zeal that shames into submission the cringing doubts of those yet unconvinced. Me? I dunno. I ain't 'heard the thing yet. S'pose it's all right, though. — C.S.M.

I WOULD like to apologise for the startling void in "Gasbag" last week. That was my brother's letter. He is noted for his lack of musical taste (he likes Bad Comapny and ELP), and his musical appreciation is

equalled only by his brains: Sparks are the biggest sound since flexi-discs, and, with lyrics that slice layers off Sinfield's quill, how can they fail?
"Kimono" is a great record. Heavy vibes, babe. A mantlepiece — SALLY NUTH, Esher.

■ Who's **Sinfield**, anyway? —CSM.
■ **Arthur Sinfield**, born Stoke Newington, 1871, to a family of horse-knackers, became famous in later life for his fantastic predictions. "Peace in our time", he said in June 1914. — WHO'S WHO.

magazines, or talking quietly to each other. We'd be laughing and joking, pulling faces and shouting things out of the windows at passers-by and they just ignored us. It was like being on a school trip sometimes, because if things did get too loud they'd send Hewlett down to tell us to be quiet.'

Relaxing offstage, too, the brothers rarely indulged themselves. Ian Hampton remembered, 'We used to go to the Speakeasy quite regularly, and Ron and Russell would sit there and have their steaks and things with the rest of us, but we'd drink and they wouldn't.' Thirty-plus years later, nothing has changed. 'They live like monks,' laughs latter-day Sparks drummer Tammy Glover. 'They eat fresh fruit, they eat vegetables, they work out, they wear sunscreen. They do all the things you're supposed to do.' Touring America with the string of Los Angeles based club groups that sustained her throughout the Nineties, crammed into the back of a van with her band-mates, Glover reached the point where simply the sight of an open bag of Fritos could make her feel ill. Touring with Sparks thereafter, she came to appreciate the finer points of life once again. 'They're very disciplined people.'

Journalists asked the Maels how they saw their future careers panning out. Acting, they replied, was definitely a possibility. But so was authoring a cook book. Russell explained, 'Originally we had a project to do an entire cook book, our favourite meals that we cook at home, and we found there so many favourite meals and so many favourite after-meal things, that we decided to limit the book to being an after-meals thing.'

He was not, he admitted, a good cook, 'but I continue to make things because I enjoy it.' In an age when most rockers, his band-mates included, saw food simply as another projectile to

94

hurl across the room, the idea that one could possibly dream of preparing it was another indication that here was a group that had little to do with rock'n'roll.

At the same time, Ron in particular could be lethally amusing when the fancy took him. White recalled, 'If we were in the coach, and people started looking in to see who we were, Ron would start doing these horrific gorilla impersonations, hanging by one arm and pulling faces through the glass.'

Ian Hampton added a memory of his own from the band's first visit to Germany later in the year, the occasion when 'Ron got his pretend phrase book out and asked the guy at the gas station "My grandmother needs new combat boots." What you don't get from Ron is his sense of humour, it's absolutely wicked, the greatest sense of humour. Brought tears to my eyes many times, just by ad-libbing.'

Place him in charge of a video camera and his comedic gifts went even further. Sequestered away within Ron's personal home movie collection is footage of him sitting at Walt Disney's desk, lip-synching 'When You Wish Upon A Star' with such becoming sincerity you could believe it's him singing; and a madcap vamp through Sinatra's 'Chicago, My Kind Of Town', filmed with the Eiffel Tower in full view of the camera.

'But Ron and Russell did get this reputation for being weird, and the only reason for that was because they weren't weird at all,' White continued. 'They were just so straight that everyone thought that they *had* to be weird. And it wasn't an act, they were really like that. As far as they were concerned, we were just a bunch of guys who toured and recorded with them, and who had these riotous after-gig parties without them. They would never join in anything like that.'

For the most part, the tour was as successful onstage as it was at the box office. But when things came crashing down, they did so in a big way. The London Rainbow gig was the big one, the largest venue on the tour, and the one that the music press was waiting for. And the critics' verdict was merciless. 'A tinny cabaret act,' opined *Melody Maker*'s Michael Watts. 'Seldom can a band have had so much encouragement from critics and audiences alike, and been so dismal on the big night. The tedium,' he explained, 'fell like fine drizzle' and, long before the show was over, he was watching the audience as it drifted away.

The *New Musical Express* was no more enthusiastic. 'When an audience consists of Bowie rejects, juvenile fashion followers, weenyboppers, some couples in the over-forties age bracket and jean-ies, you know something special is expected. But somehow the world was not set alight.'

What went wrong? The show got off to a bad start when Adrian Fisher tripped as the band were being guided onstage by torchlight, crashing his prized Gibson Flying V guitar into the stage. The instrument was undamaged, but the upsets continued all night long.

Michael Watts blamed Russell's 'banal patter' between songs, while the 'piercing shriek going on ad infinitum really gets up your ass.' The *NME*'s Shyama Perera thought the band looked bored, if not downright 'mutinous...towards their masters.'

But the true real villain of the piece was a sound system that rendered Russell all but inaudible. It wasn't the first time the PA had let the band down – it was pretty atrocious in Cambridge as well. But, with all due respect to that city, Cambridge isn't London, and the Corn Exchange isn't the Rainbow. 'Without lyrics, Sparks are charmless,' *Melody Maker* declared. 'Sparks should have been the support', sighed the *NME* (GT Moore and the Reggae Guitars had opened the show).

Of course, one disappointing gig does not a career break. The 2,000-plus fans who attended, determined to enjoy themselves, did so with abandon and, besides, so many of them were there intending to scream that they didn't particularly care what the music sounded like. Just so long as the objects of their adoration were on stage.

Trevor White: 'The first gig we did was in Cleethorpes and it was just incredible, total pandemonium. I spent the entire gig in a daze, trying to relate to the fact that I was onstage with all these screaming kids out front, and thinking "two months ago, I was playing to total apathy at some Top Rank place. Now look at it.'"

It was mayhem, and it had only just begun. 'There were girls screaming and hopping up on stage,' Russell remembered, 'clawing you and pulling your hair. It was exactly like the fantasy you've had about those types of bands, and it was happening to us! We had the screaming girls and the other fans who thought there was a deeper side to what we were doing... They didn't like the screaming girls.'

Neither did the band's detractors, as Ron later noted. 'We got into trouble, because we never thought of ourselves as a pop band with a teenybop following. Audiences became ninety-five percent screaming girls, and we were doing these songs with about ninety-five chords in them. People that could stick with us musically, didn't because they saw all these girls and assumed we were a teenybop band. The same thing happened with the press, so we were no longer able to retain that following. We loved being grabbed onstage, but it scared away a lot of people who ordinarily would have come to our shows.'

'What we were doing,' Russell continued, 'despite being a bit musically challenging – though totally accessible too – was being received as though it was the Bay City Rollers, as far as crowd reaction goes. It was a bizarre phenomenon for us to be performing songs in concert with lyrics such as those in 'Talent Is An Asset', about a young Albert Einstein growing up, and in turn having fans throwing themselves at us on stage. They'd run on stage and try to grab you, although if they got hold of you they weren't quite sure what to do next.'

In fact, Russell's invocation of the Rollers, in June 1974, was just a shade premature. The Tartan Terrors were just a couple of hit singles into their reign and, while they had certainly reawakened what sundry media observers termed 'the age of the screamagers' after a few years in the doldrums (only the Osmonds and David Cassidy could top them in terms of hysterical outpourings, but *their* visits were few and far between), Sparks' new-found following matched them decibel for decibel.

And why not? In Russell Mael, the band not only had a good-looking front man, they had an Adonis who could match any matinee idol of old and, if the still-Bolanic curls continued to remind older viewers of an earlier age, for the kids who pinned his picture on their wall even the corkscrew hair was a whole new phenomenon. Of course that was a facile reason for falling in love with any artist, and a year later, Ron would write a song about his little brother's predicament: 'It's not very hard to make history...as long as you're long on looks.'

CHAPTER TEN

A QUICK RETURN TO MY FRIENDS

Britain was only the first step. A European tour was already being lined up, while Joseph Fleury was now on the phone trying to set up an American excursion. Although his nominal role remained that of Hewlett's assistant, the band swiftly discovered he was a lot more than that. 'Joseph was omnipresent,' Ian Hampton reflected. 'His role was never clearly defined. He was kind of like a tour manager, always present and willing to do all the local management crap like dealing with the Union monsters. And always on hand to kick ass, cajole and generally be there for us.'

Right now, he was hounding David Bowie's MainMan management offices, demanding that Sparks be added to the bill for the West Coast outing that Jook's old buddy would be launching in September 1974. 'Sparks are very interested,' a 6th June 1974 telex to MainMan supremo Tony DeFries declared. 'Their manager [sic] Joseph Fleury keeps ringing me. What's your reaction, before I give him an answer?'

DeFries shook his head. Bowie didn't need a support act.

No matter. By the time they got to America, Sparks would probably be headlining in their own right anyway.

The UK tour was followed by a handful of continental performances, including a triumphant show in Paris. And afterwards, as they retired to the most luxurious hotel in the city, the Hotel George V, they knew that all of their dreams so far had been leading up to this night. And it wasn't over yet. While Ron and Russell went to bed, Hampton and Fisher took one look at the bar prices ('absurd,' laughed Hampton) and set out into the darkened streets in search of cheaper sustenance.

'We ended up somewhere on L'Île de la Cité, arms around each other, singing, among other popular ditties, "The Sun Has Got His Hat On, Hip Hip Hip Hooray". It was at this point that we were joined by two young Floridian ladies who had been at the concert and recognised us. Of course, they joined in the singing. Somewhere close to Notre Dame Cathedral, the French police appeared. Officers were not impressed and arrested us. The girls were sent on their way. After the police finally believed where we were staying, they released us both, to a riposte of "Ton soleil ne porte pas du tout de chapeau!" or whatever the French is for "your sun doesn't have a hat at all!"'

Back in London, Sparks returned to the studio to begin the awesome task of following up 'Kimono My House'. Recording had already begun – just days before the tour kicked off, with White and Hampton still finding their feet in the midst of what Hampton described as 'a week of intense rehearsals for the live shows', the band and Muff Winwood taped one song for the new album, 'Something for the Girl With Everything'. An acetate of the performance was in their hands on the day of the Hull concert, and was promptly handed to the DJ at the local discothèque that the band descended upon after the show. Cue pandemonium. If anybody, even a watching *Melody Maker* journalist, had wondered whether the ten songs on 'Kimono My House' were a fluke, this latest offering – a wordy inventory of, indeed, some things for the girl with everything – dismissed any such doubts out of hand.

Still, the temptation for the Maels simply to adhere to the same formula as the last album must have been immense. The reception 'Kimono My House' had received was still prompting people to discuss the record with the kind of reverence usually reserved only for long-established super-heroes.

But even the super-heroes were struggling to come up with the goods. Summer 1974 had brought eagerly-awaited follow-ups from a host of tried-and-trusted icons, from Mike Oldfield (with 'Hergest Ridge', the successor to the mega-selling 'Tubular Bells') to Elton John ('Caribou'), and almost all of them had been disappointing. 'Diamond Dogs' was not a patch on 'Aladdin Sane', 'It's Only Rock'n'Roll' was the most boring Stones album ever, John Lennon seemed determined

Every Thursday

Kid Jensen

Exclusive Look-in 45 Competition!
Meet Kid Jensen with his guests in the 45 studio ☆ plus 25 signed Sparks albums to be won!

22   Russell and Ron Mael

GRANADA'S exciting new pop programme "45" is proving a huge success. Already Alvin Stardust, The Glitter Band, 10cc, Showaddywaddy, and Kiki Dee have appeared on the show, and in this week's exclusive Look-in competition you have the opportunity of an all-expenses paid trip to the Granada TV studios in Manchester to see the programme being made and to meet "45" host Kid Jensen and his guests for that week. The 25 runners-up in our fabulous competition will each receive a copy of Sparks' new album 'Propaganda' as soon as it is released ...and each copy will be autographed by Ron and Russell Mael. Sparks are appearing on this week's show (Thursday at 4.50, except for London area when the programme will be shown on Saturday 12th during 'Saturday Scene') together with Labi Siffre and Dave Dee, Dozy, Beaky, Mick and Tich. Granada viewers will also have a second chance to see the programme on Saturday morning.

ALL YOU HAVE TO DO to enter our exciting competition is read over the five questions on the right-hand page, and enter your answers in the spaces provided on the coupon - not forgetting to include your name, address and age, then send it to: Look-in, "45" Competition, PO Box 141, London SE6 3HR. The sender of the first correct entry drawn from the postbag after Tuesday 22nd October 1974 will be invited to meet Kid Jensen in the "45" studio. The senders of the next 25 correct entries drawn will each receive a copy of 'Propaganda' autographed by Ron and Russell Mael.

to completely self-destruct, and so it went on.

Instead, it was the bands at the other end of the spectrum who were trying the hardest. Acts like Cockney Rebel, who followed the psychotic sheen of 'The Human Menagerie' with the decadent beauty of 'The Psychomodo' and Queen, whose grandiose self-titled debut was now completely out-bombasted by its successor, 'Queen II'... 'Something For The Girl With Everything' suggested that Sparks were determined to complete that triumvirate, and noises from the studio confirmed that they might go even further. 'Kimono My House' looked like it might be just the beginning.

Trevor White knew that duplication was the last thing on the Maels' minds. Sensibly realising and accepting that 'Kimono My House' was going to be the yardstick by which all subsequent releases would be judged, they opted instead for a completely fresh start. 'The way they looked at it was, the last album had been a success, but everyone had heard it, so now we had to do something different, something that they won't have heard. They felt that they always had to be one step ahead of what people expected from them, so they would just veer off in a new direction whenever they felt like it.'

Russell agreed. 'Artistic freedom is one of our strengths. We are doing exactly what we would be doing in the ideal situation. On the first couple of albums, there was some thought of studio time as the only limitation.' Now that wasn't a concern – with Muff Winwood back behind the controls, and Basing Street at their disposal through the summer, they could labour as long and hard as they liked. 'You get a chance to see what you can get away with in the given album structure. We spend a lot of time on things. We're song oriented as opposed to working from an image. When an album is done, the slate is clean, and it's time to start again.'

Yet these sessions were also difficult, as Ron admitted afterwards. 'There was a lot of pressure. "Kimono My House" was incredibly popular in England, and we were under the microscope. Anything we did was going to be judged. We went into the studio with a lot of songs, but a bit scared. We kept thinking about the Beatles and their constant rise. We tried to make "Propaganda" a little more complex than "Kimono My House".'

Joseph Fleury was convinced they succeeded as well. Heading up the band's fan club meant more to him than simply sticking a few photographs and a quarterly glossy newsletter into a stamped addressed envelope, and banking the £1 postal orders (which was, in truth, a lot more than most bands charged – 10cc's fan club was only 50p) that came flooding in.

On the road, going out of his way to meet the band's audience, Fleury thought nothing of devoting great chunks of an evening to his fellow fans, exchanging stories and anecdotes in return for their thoughts about Sparks. And, while there were certainly some people who would have been content simply to listen to 'Complaints' and 'In My Family' rewrites for the rest of time (or, at least, until the next thrill came along), the true fans expected, and deserved, far more than that. 'People would have felt cheated if they'd just recorded "Kimono My House" again. They wanted new sounds and fresh ideas, and that's what they got.'

Yet the process was complicated, not by the need for fresh invention – Ron saw that merely as one more challenge to rise to and defeat – but by the absence of intention. Recording 'Kimono My House', Sparks had seen themselves as a *band*, no matter how undemocratic that unit might ultimately have revealed itself to be. Arranging the songs and rehearsing hard, the five musicians pulled together for the team. But one of those five, Martin Gordon, was now gone, and a second, Adrian Fisher, was on his way out – even if he wasn't yet fully aware of the fact. No matter how hard White and Hampton worked to fill the resultant voids, both were well aware that the intangible chemistry that bound the old group together in the studio was gone.

Looking back from the dawn of the next decade, manager John Hewlett recalled, 'in Martin, Adrian, and Dinky, they had three excellent musicians all gelling perfectly with one another. Everybody was throwing ideas around, and when you've got as much talent as that all in one pool, it's really going to seethe.' Stripping out that talent, looking back upon the departed (or depart*ing*) individuals as little more than guns for hire, the Maels lost that chemistry at precisely the time they needed it most.

Sparks was their vehicle, their concept, everybody was aware of that now. Where they overstepped was in ensuring that everybody *remained* aware of it. A decade after his time with Sparks, Dinky Diamond still mourned the fact that Ron and Russell 'furiously discouraged' anything more than the most elementary working rapport which might have looked like developing between the new line up. 'It was their band. They had taken control.' But for all their confidence, they didn't seem to know quite what to do with it.

Trevor White: 'I think they took the heart out of the band. They really softened things down. Ian had a far more standard bass sound to Martin, and Adrian was just pushed right out of things. I remember when I joined, I'd thought it a bit strange that they should want two guitarists, especially when they already had one as good as Adrian. But I think it had been on their minds for a long time to get rid of him, they were just waiting for the right moment. Maybe they thought it would cost them money if he went too soon, it was that sort of situation.'

Instead, Fisher was marginalised. 'They wiped nearly all of his guitar parts off the new album, so that all that was left were my rhythm parts. A typical example was 'Achoo', which ended with this really great, really characteristic long solo from Adrian. And they wiped it off, and put on all these horrid multi-tracked sneezes. I don't know if they were deliberately trying to be irritating, but those sneezes were the ultimate in... I don't know what! They figured that everyone had heard a guitar solo, but they hadn't heard us all sneezing.'

Fisher was well aware of what was happening. He told Finnish journalist Petteri Aro, 'I just wanted to butch it all up and get a blues lick in everything.' During the 'Kimono My House' sessions, his plan worked. 'It went well. Martin Gordon, I think, was the only one who had a clue what I was up to.' This time around, he was less successful.

The sessions were by no means bogged down in seriousness and recrimination, however. One of Ian Hampton's favourite recollections is of 'Russell, Trevor and I wasting huge amounts of expensive studio time by "corpsing" while doing vocal harmonies. Sometimes it simply went from bad to worse – mere eye contact would render us completely incapable of speech, far less song!'

Besides, most of the criticisms that can be laid at 'Propaganda's door are obvious only with hindsight. All three British musicians admit that the sessions raced by in a blur of enthusiasm and excitement and, when the reviews of the record came in, even the absence of the man whom some writers were already describing as 'the inventor of the Sparks sound,' Martin Gordon, wasn't that noticeable, as the Maels proved to be quite capable arrangers after all.

Once again the sleeve art was striking, but clearly less strikingly anonymous; although the band's name did not appear, the Maels' faces did, trussed up in a speedboat as it raced off the coast of Bournemouth.

WITH valentine

TERS FROM DAVID OSMONDS BOWIE RUSS MARTY QUEEN

21st DEC., 1974

mirabelle

REVEALED!
The
SECRET LIFE OF RUSS AND RON

DONNY'S 4-PAGE PHOTO PULL-OUT

ROLLER DEREK TELLS ALL!

GET READY FOR CHRISTMAS!
* HAVE YOU GOT MISTLETOE MAGIC?
* PLAY OUR PARTY GAME OF LOVE

Letters at it

d. "I ever mpy oke

at our village hall I saw this gorgeous fella who looked the spitting image of Leslie McKeown. My friends and I are all enthusiastic Bay City Roller fans so we thought we'd ask for his autograph. We still weren't

sure though him, so me volunteered You can ima barrassed I took my piec wrote down Gilles. I wen

RUSS' DEL TA

to walk e with he car er the 't be ask my She but as to

trot back fo We had sle ments in the what a disa old Trevor above me, a know how m Not only tha a restless spent most looking abov

Russell detailed the experience in his weekly column in the magazine *Mirabelle*, a publication aimed squarely at the heart of the female teenybopper. 'The front pic features Ron and I in a speedboat, travelling at ninety miles an hour. We are also bound and gagged. Very pleasant? No! We rode down to the coast in a minivan and the weather was totally chaotic. The wind was so powerful that we had to walk backwards. When I saw this little boat, I decided that a nice studio shot of me would be just as effective an album cover.' No such luck. 'The photographer wanted his realism' and so the brothers were bound,

...ealed !!!

THE SECRET LIFE OF RUSS AND RON

OUR SECRET REPORTER FOUND THE MAEL BROTHERS IN THEIR SECRET HIDEOUT PREPARING FOR THEIR OWN, VERY SPECIAL XMAS. AMID GREAT EXCITEMENT THEY TALKED OF THEIR PLANS . . . .

At this point Ron entered the room, looking exactly like he does in his photos—right down to white shirt and tie.

Russ said: "I was just explaining my diet plan, care to add anything?"

"Yes," Ron answered. "Brush your teeth after every meal." I could see things were getting a bit off the beaten track, so I finally settled them down to a serious interview, or as serious as you can get when the Maels are in 'one of those moods'.

Mirabelle: Christmas is right on hand, are you doing anything special for the holiday season ?

Ron: We finish our tour on the sixteenth, so we may spend Christmas in Vienna, Austria. You know, great pastry, snow, sleighs and stuff. We had an offer to tour the Holy Land, but they wanted the band to stay in a stable in Bethlehem, without central heating.

Russ: I'd love to go to Los Angeles. It's strange to be

FILL YOUR
XMAS STOCKIN
WITH AL

---

and Russell Mael
xcitement and joy
day season, and
non-stop cover-
1 runs from buy-
s to Christmas
s sort of like one
en-course meals !
interviewed the
rs right before
to Sweden to
irst ever Euro-
to get their
the festivities
n.

ed their flat,
diately chirped
d if I'd like
came out with
tray of elabor-
this interview
tre around the
Christmas, I
et in the mood
me seasonal
e tray were
gingerbread
nd pine trees
mond paste,
scuits in the
akes and an
which Russell
traditional
n Germany."
ood played a
s Christmas
of course !
at, and some
n others."
on why are
demanded.
bit. I eat
ealthy. My
cake and
g fattening
meat."

---

gagged and placed in their positions; the signs warning that the seas were too rough for any kind of boating were ignored; and, for the next 'hour or two', the pair were battered by the waves, drenched in sea salt and generally abused by the elements until the photographer had finished his work. And then it was time to shoot for the back cover. The Maels had just one thing to be grateful for. Ron told the Sparks fan club magazine, 'the photographer had originally suggested that we be bound and gagged and dropped from an airplane with parachutes on, and he would photograph us from the air as he too descended. We declined his kind offer.'

The songs that Ron brought to the 'Propaganda' sessions were certainly as strong as almost anything on its predecessor. True, the greatest extremes of that record, 'This Town Ain't Big Enough For Both Of Us' and 'Equator', were absent. In their place, however, the multi-layered vocals of 'Propaganda', the soaring ballad 'Bon Voyage', the staccato breathlessness of 'Something For The Girl With Everything' and the compulsive two-step 'Reinforcements' all sparked with vigorous energy and invention, but even these highlights fell deferentially behind what is not only Ron Mael's most beautiful composition, but one of the loveliest songs anybody has ever written, 'Never Turn Your Back On Mother Earth'.

It was a song, Ron revealed, that simply appeared to him 'fully formed. I never even had to go to the piano for that one.' He also knew that there was nothing to compare it to, not in Sparks' universe, nor anybody else's. Perhaps David Bowie's 'Life On Mars?' might venture close, in terms of a lovely melody, a mystifying lyric and a peerless performance that stepped out of the artist's expected milieu to illustrate abilities that went beyond simple pop writing. Bob Dylan had also shaken up the constituency once or twice in the past, tearing up the form book simply because he could.

But Bowie did it at a time when he had nothing to lose, on the 'Hunky Dory' album that simply announced his intentions long before he got to deliver on them; and Dylan did it later, in an age when his success was already inviolate. Sparks weren't merely going out on an artistic limb, they were venturing out on a commercial one as well.

Nonetheless, 'Never Turn Your Back On Mother Earth' swept imperiously to Number 13 in October 1974 – lower than its predecessors, but respectable all the same – and the following month, 'Propaganda' peaked at Number 9, again, not as impressive as its predecessor's Number 4, but with only six months dividing the two albums' release dates, a lot of people were still catching up on the earlier disc when its follow-up hit the shops. Not only that, but a two-for-one repackaging of the Bearsville albums was inevitably rushed out to capitalise on the band's success and, when British record sales were tallied up at the end of the year, Sparks had no difficulty whatsoever waltzing into the Top 10 best selling artists of 1974. Bowie, Dylan, Queen and Cockney Rebel weren't even in contention.

SPARKS   Ian Hampton

'Propaganda' was Fisher's last hurrah. No sooner was the band out of the studio than Joseph Fleury was sent to make the necessary phone call. Fisher was fired, his photograph was removed from the projected new album sleeve and his guitar was mixed down even further. The group's next bout of gigging, including their first American tour as superstars, was due to start in less than a month.

'Things were getting really difficult with Adrian,' explained Fleury. 'Adrian hated the band and he hated the music – he was simply in it for the money.' The final straw had come at the Cambridge Corn Exchange on 5th July. Throughout Sparks' first British tour, Fisher had been growing more exuberant on stage, but on this particular night he crossed the line.

'That was the night Adrian's 'lack of inhibition' led to his dismissal,' remembered Derek Paice. 'I was standing at the back with Joseph and he was aghast that Adrian was dashing all over the stage and playing in Russell's face. "What does he think he's doing?"'

SPARKS   Trevor White

The night before, Fleury witnessed what he described as one of the best Sparks shows he'd ever seen. Now he was watching one of the worst. Paice recalled, 'I believe they had to stop the show and try to sober Adrian up a bit. Personally I didn't see the problem. I thought it was an even more exciting performance than usual.' The Maels disagreed, and Fisher, a decade later, just shrugged.

104

'I knew I wasn't going to be in the band for much longer, and it didn't really bother me. Ron and Russ wanted good little boys who would do what they were told, stand in their place so they didn't get in the spotlight; even on TV, they used to shunt us off to the back somewhere and tell the cameras to concentrate on them. But what's the point of being in a rock'n'roll band if you can't rock'n'roll? It was the other guys I felt sorry for, the ones who were still stuck in there.'

More vehemently, he told Petteri Aro how shocked he was when Martin Gordon was sacked, and how outraged he was that John Hewlett delegated Joseph Fleury to actually break the news. He warned Hewlett at the time, 'You do it to me that way, I will kill one of them. When the time comes, you fire me in person.' Hewlett did so. 'John came to my house and said, "Well, you're expecting this... Want your lawyers to look over these [papers]?" We had a laugh and a drink.'

So why didn't he just quit in the first place? That went back to his foresight in having his lawyer inspect the original Island contract. 'If I walked, I would have broken my contract. I had to make them break their side of it.'

Again, Hewlett could only watch with impotent fury. 'The band still was very good and still rocked because with Adrian there, it could not fail to rock. He was a truly great rock'n'roll guitarist and his presence gave a credibility to Sparks' music that elevated it up among the greats – his playing won over many fans who otherwise would have dismissed Sparks as a pop band.' With his departure, the band's detractors could have a field day.

Looking around for replacements, Fleury was convinced that there was only one guitarist Sparks needed to look at. Ian North was the young and good looking figurehead of Milk'n'Cookies, a New York band that was clearly influenced by Sparks and associated glam-rockers, and whom he and Hewlett had recently taken under their joint managerial wing. Quite what the loss of their guitarist would have done to the rest of Milk'n'Cookies doesn't seem to have crossed management's mind, but the Maels turned the idea down very quickly. North was a decent enough guitarist, but he was also a songwriter. Reflecting upon Martin Gordon's brief sojourn in their ranks, the brothers decided bringing in another songwriter was the last thing they wanted to do.

Besides, they had their own ideas. At that moment in time, there were just three guitarists in the country who mattered: Mick Ronson, former lieutenant to Bowie's cosmic cowboy, Ariel Bender, the man who put the 'heh' in Mott The Hoople (before he left to be replaced by Ronson... small world!), and Brian May, he of the corkscrew-perm style and glowering good looks, with a guitar sound that could make your heart race. Ronson and Bender were both busy at the time, so they gave May a call instead.

In the year or so since their emergence, Queen had made quite a name for themselves. Their debut album won widespread acclaim, while the follow-up spawned a hit single – 'Seven Seas Of Rhye' – that was coincidentally slipping down the chart at exactly the same time as 'This Town Ain't Big Enough For Both Of Us' was on the way up.

Since that time, though, Queen seemed to have fallen on hard times. Yes, they'd recorded a new album, ominously titled 'Sheer Heart Attack', and yes, they had a new single, the seemingly self-referencing 'Killer Queen', ambling up the chart. But clearly Queen had already peaked. It could only be downhill from here.

The press despised them. George Tremlett, author of the band's first biography, 1976's Queen, reflected on the band's early years by remarking upon their 'total rejection by the critics'. Queen publicist Tony Brainsby remembered being told by one heavyweight rock journalist that 'he wasn't going to write about a load of poofters'. Another paper even came up with a new category to lump Queen into. It was called 'Supermarket Rock.' Nobody, the Maels determined, could be happy trying to operate in that kind of environment. So they popped round to visit May.

It must have been a tempting offer. 'I did like the band,' Brian May reflected. 'I loved "This Town Ain't Big Enough For Both Of Us". Anyway, they came round, the two brothers, and said "Look, it's pretty obvious that Queen are washed up, we'd like to offer you a position in our band, if you want it." I said, "Well, I don't think we're quite dead yet..."' And today – does he have any regrets? 'No, not a lot...'

Fleury did. 'Brian [was] very tempted,' he revealed. 'He's an incredible guitarist, and a very intelligent, kind person. Too bad I dislike Queen.'

The clock was still ticking. The Maels were considering recruiting a new keyboard player as well, but they were horrified by the prospect of having to sit through a series of interminable auditions, knowing that any decision they made would as likely be based on desperation as any other consideration. Finally, the brothers made the move that, perhaps, they should have thought of at the start. In the same week that the 4th October release of 'Never Turn Your Back On Mother Earth' was announced in the music press, it was also revealed that Fisher had gone. A spokesman told the *Melody Maker*, 'They felt the band was stronger without him. There's no ill feeling, however. He will not be replaced.'

In fact, an approach was made to Ian Kimmet, the now bandless former frontman with Jook. With Trevor White promoted to lead guitar, Kimmett recalled, 'I had the offer to join Sparks after Jook broke-up. John told me the offer to play rhythm guitar was from them and I respectfully declined the offer on the grounds that I was not at one with their style of music...hee hee!' Instead, Kimmett moved to the other side of the musical fence, taking up a position at Bearsville Records in Woodstock. One of the first things he did upon arrival was add the first two Sparks albums to parent company Warner Brothers' ongoing series of 2-for-1 reissues, 'Two Originals Of...'

Remaining a quintet, Sparks headed across to Europe for a handful more television appearances. It was not going to be easy. Songs that had been recorded and rehearsed with the two guitar line-up needed to be pared down accordingly. Witnesses to Sparks' appearance on Germany's *Musikladen* show, one of the first live television appearances they made without Fisher (a 28th September appearance on *Disco*, performing 'This Town Ain't Big Enough For Both Of Us', had them miming to the regular single), would be horrified by the weedy sound emanating from the band, the way 'Amateur Hour' in particular simply plodded, while Russell appeared to struggle to even maintain his falsetto.

Practice would see the band adjust, of course, and improve beyond words. But was America really the best rehearsal platform they could have selected?

CHAPTER ELEVEN

NOISY BOYS ARE HAPPY BOYS!
LET IT OUT!

Back in London, 5th October 1974 saw Ron and Russell spend their morning guesting on television's *Saturday Scene* (not broadcast until 11th November), before boarding a flight to New York with the band. It was time to revisit the homeland which, the Maels maintained, had rejected them once before, but would now have no alternative other than to sit up and pay attention to the conquering heroes.

It was a short visit, and a tightly budgeted one. Even Joseph Fleury wasn't certain that he'd be travelling until the last minute, despite Ron and Russell actively campaigning for him to join them if only for the sake of his health. His first English autumn was not treating him well, a stubborn dose of flu combining with sheer overwork to the point that, at one point, he even suggested he leave the UK altogether and hand his duties on to somebody else. He was eventually talked down from that particular precipice, but he clearly needed a break. Finally, Hewlett relented and agreed he could travel.

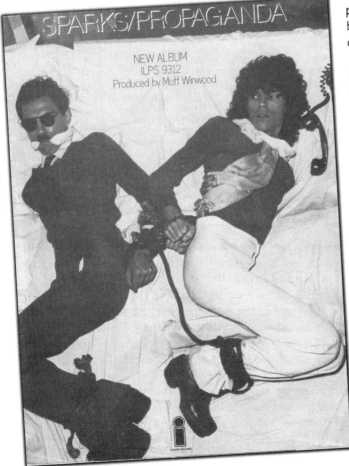

Still it was a slimmed down entourage that flew into Toronto, Canada, on 2nd October, made it to Los Angeles five days later and then jetted straight out again to appear on Greek songstress Nana Mouskouri's TV show back in London.

America eyed Sparks warily. *Rolling Stone*, at that time America's most influential music magazine, welcomed them with a review of 'Kimono My House' that basically comprised little more than an account of Gordon Fletcher's difficulty in understanding the lyrics, a reasonable observation in its own right but sadly the theme that subsequent *Rolling Stone* reviewers would reprise with almost Pavlovian loyalty.

Island Records had certainly done their job on the promotional front, however.

Also WORKING

Sparks

Title: *Hello Young Lovers*

Due: February 2006

Producer: Ron and Russell Mael

Songs: Dick Around, As I Sit Down To Play The Organ At The Notre Dame Cathedral, Here Kitty

The Buzz: "It's the bigger, uglier, more commercial brot[...] to *Lil' Beethoven*," gasps a spokespers[...]

Morrissey

Title: *Ringleader Of The Tormentors*

Due: February 2006

Production: Tony Visconti

Songs: TBC

The Buzz: Rejoined by guitarists/ c[...] writers Boz Boorer and Alain Whyte [...] declares his new one "the most bea[...] ful – perhaps the most gentle, so fa[...]

Isobel Campbell and Mark Lanegan

Title: *Ballad Of The Broken Seas*

Due: February 2006

Producer: Isobel Campbell

Songs: The Circus Is Leaving Tov[...] Hard To Kill A Bad Thing, Rambli[...]

The Buzz: "It's sun-bleached an[...] chedelic, with a little bit of folk and country," says Campbell, who admits she's a big fan of the albums of Nancy Sinatra and Lee Hazlewood.

SPARKS
Ron and Russell Mael are two of the most eccentric lookin' American musicians ever to cross the Atlantic. Also the most talented!

Sparks first came to England because their career was not going too well [...] home . . . And here we were knocked out b[...]

It looked lik[...] Sparks were s[...] for good.

But no such . . . they went to the States but with a pr[...] to visit us oft[...]

Amateur Hour

[...]corded by **SPARKS** on Island Records

[...]e lawns grow plush in the winter lands
[...]e perfect little settings for the one night stands
[...]e drapes are drawn and the lights are out
[...] the time to put in practice what you've dreamed about
[...]I she can show you what you must do
[...] be more like people better than you

[...]rus
[...]teur hour goes on and on and when you turn pro
[...] know she'll let you know
[...]teur hour goes on and on and when you turn pro
[...] know she tells you so

[...] grow tops to go topless in
[...] we sit and count the hairs that blossom on our chins
[...]oices change at a rapid pace
[...]d start a song a tenor and then end as bass
[...]ose your partners everyone
[...] hesitate the good ones are gone

[...] Repeat

[...]r hour goes on and on and when you trun pro
[...]ow she'll let you know

[...] laugh, wine, dine, talk and sing
[...]e cannot replace what is the real thing
[...] like playing the violin
[...] not start of and be Yehudi Menuhin

[...]epeat to Fade

[...] Limited

9. Achoo by **SPARKS**

Alex Kapranos (Franz Ferdinand): One of the best chord progressions ever. Enigmatic vocals which jump from the repetitive rhythmic onomatopoeia of the word "achoo" to a narrative that creates vivid characters through impressionistic suggestion. It comes close to being the perfect song – it's immediate, like the best pop, yet you can listen to it repeatedly, because as you try to look beyond its shiny black surface you realise you'll never know the true depth.
Propaganda (Island)

The tour was limited to a string of television performances – in quick succession, Sparks recorded a six-song set on *Don Kirshner's Rock Concert*, a four-song blast on *Midnight Special* (broadcast on 15th November), and a similar burst on ABC's *In Concert*.

All, of course, expanded the band's local fan base, and all played their part in opening the group's delights up to the more esoteric corners of the American music press. The magazines *Hit Parader* and *Creem* both became staunch Sparks supporters and, even if the US as a whole was to remain stubbornly impervious to the appeal which had so swiftly brought England to her knees, the tour witnessed the first stirring of the cult following that would sustain the band through the remainder of the Seventies.

Long-time fan Sharon Hottell spoke for everybody who discovered Sparks that autumn. Like so many other 14- and 15-year-olds, she was bored with the state of American music and fed up with the endless conveyor belt of funk, easy listening and lacklustre rockers who traipsed out every time the television cameras focused on what they considered a rock show.

108

And then... 'One blessed night it happened. Thank you *Don Kirshner's Rock Concert*! A sassy man came out with the look of a rock star, but an attitude unlike any of the singers I had seen. Enter Russell Mael. Instead of making love to his mike stand, he stomped about with a pout and quick glances across the audience. The keyboard player, Ron Mael, looked more like a businessman turned marionette, but the music was heavenly, the lyrics were witty, and the singing superb and unique. Sparks had entered my life.'

Drummer Hilly Michaels, he who was so enamoured of 'Wonder Girl' back in 1970, had left Omaha. Now he was living in his home state of Connecticut, and he too was watching *Don Kirshner's Rock Concert*, sitting in the front room with his older sister.

'Suddenly Sparks took the stage. "Something For The Girl With Everything", "This Town Ain't Big Enough For Both Of Us"...The band was tight as hell and Russell was jumping around, taunting Ron who was sitting there rolling his eyes around playing the Wurlitzer. My sister and I were in tears, laughing. I had a big smile on my face for that entire broadcast. We laughed and laughed and I remember thinking, "Wow, this is so, so, great, this is fresh, this is super entertaining."

'Russell was in top form with his vocals and I was simply astonished. A mind-blowing musical experience. My sister and I brought up that moment many times for weeks after, and always had a good burst of laughing together. I had to go out and buy their entire catalogue. I brought the records home, and just sat there for hours, listening and studying the artwork. My sister walked through the door, came over to me and said "Whaddya buy?" I said, "Sparks, remember we saw these guys?" She said "Oh yeah!" I played her my favourite tracks and again we giggled and laughed and just felt happy and good, listening for hours. I remember thinking I'd be in heaven to drum for this band! I had always been "marching to the beat of another drummer" my entire life.

'The creativity in their music and artwork kept me staring at the artwork while I listened, shaking my head up and down thinking "Cool! Amazing! Brilliant!" Up to that time, I thought I was the only quirky, loony guy I knew amongst my friends. Sparks had a positive effect on my life and music from those days on. I knew I was not alone in the world liking offbeat, zany music and creative ideas.'

Sharon Hottell shared Michaels' evangelistic fervour. 'When my other friends would come over, I put Sparks on for them to hear. The normal reaction was a side look, a wrinkled nose with an occasional "I can't understand a word that guy is saying." However, they usually liked looking at the band members with the typical "He's cu-u-u-te!" for Russell, and "What is *up* with this guy?" for Ron.'

Don Kirshner's Rock Concert reached out and grabbed a lot of people. The band's own memories of the show, however, linger more on the offstage activities. Ian Hampton explained, 'Ringo [Starr] and Mooney [Keith Moon] were hosting. Bastards cut off our ties! Although that wasn't broadcast... Mooney was also playing on that show. I don't remember who with, but he had a clear acrylic kit, the toms filled with water and goldfish. Pretty gruesome. And, after the show, Mooney asked us to his dressing room for a "little drink". He had at least twelve bottles of Cognac, twelve of Jack Daniels, twelve of Southern Comfort and twelve of just about anything else you could mention. I'm surprised he lived as long as he did.'

After the mayhem of the United Kingdom, it felt strange to suddenly be in a land where Sparks were completely unknown, and could head out to the shops without fear of molestation. 'Kimono My House' did make it onto the American chart, but rose no higher than Number 101, and Trevor White remembers that a lot of the early enthusiasm was directed not at Ron and Russell, but at Ian Hampton and himself. For they had been members of Jook and, to those areas of America most afflicted by Anglophilia, Jook had been anything but the struggling no-hope tax loss that they had become at home.

Walking down the streets of Los Angeles with the rest of the band, White recalled how

674. Sparks

SPARKS   Serie P - Prii

680. Sparks

757. Sparks

the pair would suddenly find themselves besieged by 'all these kids with Jook stuff: posters, photos, records, which they wanted us to sign. It was amazing; we'd hardly been heard of at home, and to find we had this great big following in America – apparently they'd been writing over to RCA for all of the stuff – was just unbelievable!'

Returning to the UK, Sparks launched their second British tour in November 1974, with a feature in *Melody Maker*'s 16th November 1974 issue highlighting the logistics of the outing:

Concerts – 25

Cities – 25

Touring party – 16, comprising five musicians, one manager, one agent, one coach driver, two equipment men, three lighting men, two PA crew, one truck driver.

Transport – Group travel in luxury coach and road crew in 12-seat Mercedes bus. Equipment by 40-foot articulated lorry.

Equipment – 13 tons worth £35,000

Potential audience – About 50,000

Money – Ticket prices 60p – £2. Gross potential takings around £50,000

Incidentally – Island Artists estimate that each day on the road costs the group £1,300 in hire of halls, hotel bills and crew wages.

2nd November – York University
3rd November – Newcastle City Hall
4th November – Leicester de Montfort Hall
5th November – Liverpool Empire
6th November – Bristol Hippodrome
8th November – Reading University
9th November – Exeter University
10th November – Coventry Theatre
11th November – Hammersmith Odeon
13th November – Swansea Brangwyn Hall
14th November – Oxford New Theatre
15th November – Blackburn St George's Hall
16th November – Lancaster University
17th November – Stoke on Trent Victoria Hall
18th November – Southport Theatre
19th November – Edinburgh Odeon
20th November – Dundee Caird Hall
21st November – Glasgow Apollo Theatre
22nd November – Manchester Free Trade Hall
23rd November – Hastings Pier Pavilion
24th November – Croydon Fairfield Hall
25th November – Torquay Princess Theatre
26th November – Bournemouth Winter Gardens
27th November – Birmingham Town Hall
28th November – Dunstable California Ballroom

Throughout the outing, they received a reception which, to an outsider, seemed just as ardently fanatical as the last one. Only to the band themselves was a small, but appreciable, reduction in the level of hysteria noticeable – a reflection, maybe, of the sheer number of heavyweight tours that were criss-crossing the country that autumn. Alongside a double bill of Lynyrd Skynyrd and Golden Earring, fans could catch Supertramp, 10cc, Thin Lizzy, Humble Pie, Jethro Tull, Queen, the Strawbs and the ubiquitous Bay City Rollers all strutting their stuff in the closing weeks of 1974.

Perhaps it also symptomatic of the lower chart placings that their records were now achieving – Trevor White certainly felt salt being rubbed into any attendant wounds when the support band Pilot, who had started the trek completely unknown and considerably out of pocket, were suddenly catapulted into the limelight. Their new single, 'Magic', effortlessly eclipsed 'Never Turn Your Back On Mother Earth' in the Top 20. 'No wonder,' White mused grimly, 'they could afford to send us Christmas cards that year.'

If there was disappointment in England, however, a single show at the Paris Olympia on 30th November 1974 quickly restored the Maels' equilibrium.

Even more than England, France was a spiritual home for the brothers, a land of endless sophistication and elegance, whose language, food and lifestyle epitomised everything that they most valued in life. Sometimes, when he talked, and often when he sang, Russell even seemed to pack a slight French accent and, although lots of cities in lots of countries have roads that they call 'boulevards', when he sang that word in 'Thank God It's Not Christmas', it wasn't the wide open highways that scar American cities that came to mind, it was the leafy café-lined streets of Paris.

The impression was universal, too. While preparing for the concert, Russell recalled, 'We were discussing, with a guy from Island Records in Europe, fun things to do that weren't involved

with being in a rock band and how to just kind of expand the whole thing. [Movie director] Jacques Tati's name was brought up and we just kind of laughed it off. Anyway, he approached Jacques Tati and somehow got him to come meet us. Jacques Tati didn't know anything about Sparks because he was sixty-seven years old and doesn't listen to rock music.'

But he was intrigued by the Maels, who in turn were suddenly presented with an opportunity to fulfil one of their greatest ambitions. They would be thespians, and they were thrilled when Tati found roles for the pair of them in his proposed next movie.

Confusion, outlined Ron, would tell the story of 'two American TV studio employees brought to a rural French TV company to help them out with some American technical expertise, and give them some input into how TV really is done.'

France held other treats in store, too. The opening act at the Olympia gig was Philippe DeBarge, a wealthy young Frenchman who, back in 1968, had recorded an entire LP with the 'SF

Sorrow'- era Pretty Things. The album was never released, but DeBarge and the Pretties remained in contact and, in 1974, reconvened for a handful of French concerts. This was the biggest of all of them and, though a seriously-fanatical French Sparks audience probably didn't appreciate the historic importance of the event, the music thrilled the crowd and the headliners alike.

Taking the Olympia stage, Sparks faced a totally hysterical crowd that made even the first English crowds look restrained. Afterwards, not even the pain of the ribs he'd cracked while being hugged by one particularly zealous female fan could wipe the smile from Russell's face. Record sales were booming and the media was as curious as it had been in London. An entire new market was opening up for the band.

Sparks rounded off 1974 with a special Christmas show at Leeds Town Hall on 20th December, announced alongside the warning that it was likely to be their last UK date for 'almost a year'. *Melody Maker* reported that US tours had already been scheduled for February-March and September-October 1975, European and Far Eastern dates would be slotted in when possible, and the band was also planning to record its next album in the United States.

In the event, the proposed schedule quickly unravelled. The first part of 1975 was indeed devoted to the United States, but they played only a handful of shows before the band returned to Europe, then headed back to America for further dates in May and June. They came home to London in late June, then announced new tours of Europe and the UK for September and October – in between times, they would be going into the studio in London to begin work on a new album...slated, declared *Melody Maker*, to include 'Confusion', 'the song written by Ron and Russell Mael as the title track for a forthcoming Jacques Tati movie.'

In fact, the movie never happened, and the song was mothballed too, although it would reappear on the following year's 'Big Beat'. Tati's declining health pulled him away from the camera shortly after the release of *Parade* in 1974, and he never made another movie. Years later, Russell admitted 'The biggest disappointment of our career? Not making the film with Jacques Tati...'

Touring the United States, Russell once laughed, was a matter of 'playing the two coasts and ignoring everything in the middle'. Los Angeles and New York were, of course, the major

centres, music industry hubs that also possessed what most bands acknowledged to be the most open-minded, and aware, audiences.

Again, it was on the streets that Sparks made the greatest initial impact. In Seattle, walking into the long-vanished Campus Records store on University Avenue, teenaged Queen fan Mike Sharman recalled spotting 'a big display of 8-tracks of 'Kimono My House' and the newly released 'Propaganda'. I didn't know what Sparks were, I'd never heard of the band, but the guy in there told me a bit about them, so I picked up one of the albums and that same night I was back there for the other one.'

In Los Angeles, a young drummer named Danny Benair actually camped out overnight to be sure of the best tickets for the Sparks show. He had been listening to Sparks since the day in early 1973 when he picked up a used copy of 'A Woofer In Tweeter's Clothing', 'most likely at a record store like Aaron's in Los Angeles. It was probably one of those Saturday afternoons when I trudged in and bought it for probably a couple of bucks, saw the cover, heard about them, really liked it... instantly I was very smitten with it... then worked back and bought both versions of the first LP.'

It would be another 18 months before he saw the band live, by which time Sparks had two more LPs in the stores and Benair had hooked up with songwriter Steve Hufsteter in the Quick, a group whose most obvious influence was indeed Sparks, with some Queen, Sweet and Bowie stirred into the mix.

'Sparks were playing Santa Monica Civic Centre, and I remember sleeping outside the venue to be first in line for the tickets, and looking at the people who were out there with me and thinking, "I know that all these people would like my band. But they don't know my band because we don't play live," because at that time we were still just rehearsing and learning. And the funny thing is, all the people I met at that show ended up becoming huge Quick fans.'

Los Angeles also brought the Maels out of the protective shell in which they spent their London lives. Ian Hampton recalled how the group took up residence at the Hyatt House Hotel on Sunset Boulevard, the Riot House of popular rock mythology. 'One day Russell and I were playing pinball and feeding the jukebox when two ladies came up and befriended us. Before it went any further, "Uncle" Ron found us and took us to one side. He said "Have you noticed the five o'clock shadow yet?" I bless Ron to this day!'

On the other side of the country in New York City, Anglophile Jeffrey Ross Hyman was likewise among the first in the queue for Sparks' 9th May 1975 performance at the Academy of Music – years later, as Joey Ramone, Hyman invited Ron and Russell to appear in his band's video for 'Something To Believe In'.

Talking about his formative musical influences in the early Nineties, Ramone explained, 'Sparks were amazing because they didn't sound like anything else, but they really had that glam rock thing going – you'd listen and you'd know they were English, and then you found out they weren't and that was the greatest thing. It meant there was hope for the American music scene after all.' At one point, the Ramones came close to recording their own personal tribute to Sparks, a cover of 'Nothing To Do' from the 'Big Beat' album, but sadly the idea was never followed through.

Sparks celebrated their New York appearance with an after-show party at a nearby Burger King...'black tie optional', the Island Records invites suggested. Other parties on that tour were held at the nearest local branch of the International House of Pancakes – it was all a far cry from the wild bar-room scenarios that awaited other touring bands, although Russell caused a stir regardless, turning up at the New York bash in a white tennis outfit, complete with the shortest shorts he could lay his hands on.

NEW YORK ROCKER

No 4 $1.00

Cherry Vanilla
and
Russell Mael   the
                                           Runaways

                                           MILK 'N' COOKIES

                                           Orchestra
                                           Luna

Sailor

the
Heartbreakers

Cyrinda Foxe and
David JoHansen

Fans travelling home from the gig could buy a special souvenir of the evening's entertainment, as the latest issue of the *Soho Weekly News* had splashed a picture of Russell, reclining in the arms of singer Cherry Vanilla, across its cover.

'It was supposed to be a jungle shot,' Vanilla recalled. 'It was so cheesy and funny ... it was supposed to be. Photographer Leee Black Childers took it at a plant store on 8th Avenue in Manhattan, so those are the leaves around us ... the plants were all out on the sidewalk, and I had a leopard print something or other on ... maybe just some fabric cut and tied (not even sewn) to look like a Jane of the jungle outfit, and we had a fake stuffed snake. It's very funny. Russell was shirtless and I think I am trying to make the snake attack him. He was very sweet, and that was it, a half-hour or so together on the streets of New York, the jungle.'

Again there were a few television appearances, including their long overdue return to *American Bandstand*. With 'Propaganda' heading towards a chart peak of Number 63, they performed 'This Town Ain't Big Enough For Both Of Us' and 'BC', while Russell paraded around in the horse riding outfit that later became his stage attire for the 'Indiscreet' tour. At that time, the band themselves were probably only dimly aware that, by the time the show was actually broadcast, on 12th July 1975, they would be back in the UK, not only promoting a brand new single but a brand new sound as well.

Following the final show of the tour, in Philadelphia, the band headed to Los Angeles to shoot the promotional film for their upcoming single, 'Get In The Swing'. Hampton, White and Diamond then flew home, leaving the Maels behind in Los Angeles for another few weeks.

CHAPTER TWELVE

THEY'RE ABOUT TO LEAVE
AND WE WILL STAY

'**G**et In The Swing' was a joyous celebration of a cocktail set whose hectic social lives had led them to reject all but the most materialistic values and, like the rest of the band's forthcoming album, it was recorded with Tony Visconti wearing the producer's hat. The song featured one of Ron's finest lyrics to date married to one of Sparks' most intriguing backing tracks, a cross-pollination of styles and movements that simply screamed out to be spread over a few extra minutes and, maybe, heralded with a little more fuss and fanfare.

Ruthlessly ambitious, soaringly dramatic, almost operatic – 'Get In The Swing' was all of these things, but somehow fell on deaf ears. It would be another four months before Queen put together almost precisely the same ingredients, added a few lines of cod-Italian and created 'Bohemian Rhapsody.' But while Queen topped charts all over the world, Sparks watched their latest effort stall at Number 27 on the UK listings, their poorest showing so far.

Sparks put a brave face on the summer single's failure. 'The chorus was very commercial,' Russell acknowledged. However, 'the song was a little bit different in structure, and the words were kind of different too.' And those were difficulties, apparently, that even an appearance as 'star guests' of the Bay City Rollers on their tea-time *Shang-a-Lang* TV show, alongside the now requisite *Top Of The Pops* performance, could not overcome. 'I guess Ron just wasn't obvious enough,' Dinky Diamond sniffed when reminded of its fate a decade later. 'If he'd called it "California Rhapsody" or something, and had Island make a fuss about it, who knows where it could have gone.'

The decision to use Tony Visconti, while the catalyst for a friendship that has endured to this day, also marked one of the Maels' most courageous moves. Although the Brooklyn-born producer is now regarded among the giants of his trade, in 1975 he was simply one of several studio men fighting to re-establish their names and reputations after their most-lauded glam-era clients, in Visconti's case Marc Bolan, had gone seriously off the musical boil.

Three years had passed since Bolan and T. Rex had enjoyed their unprecedented success, during which time another of Visconti's former clients, David Bowie, had led the usurping pack. But Visconti had had nothing to do with that – he and Bowie had stopped working together in 1971, around the same time as Bolan's rise to fame truly went into overdrive, and they had only just reconnected, working together on Bowie's latest album, 'Young Americans'. In between times, Visconti's production work for artists such as Carmen, an Anglo-American flamenco rock band, and folkies Ralph McTell and Tom Paxton, had raised few listeners' temperatures, prompting at least one former associate to describe Visconti as 'an ordinary producer with some extraordinary friends'.

Ron and Russell Mael, however, had no qualms about working with him, and Visconti repaid them with an album that still stands among the most inventive of their entire career. It's also the most controversial. Ian Hampton readily confessed that 'I hated that album for years. I think it was Tony Visconti, it was almost like being in a chamber orchestra at times, "Under The Table With Her" and things, where is it coming from?'

Yet 'Indiscreet' is now his favourite of them all, a reinstatement of all the values that had

On the road with Sparks — this time sur le continong. Read how . . .

SPARKS KNOCK PARIS DEAD

by Jan Iles

SPARKS on stage, they go down like sensational, as they say in France.

RUSS MAEL est un chic type. The fans are outside the stage door of the Olympia in Paris, but he doesn't try to escape them by masquerading as a gendarme.

Instead he mingles with the crowd, smiling like a true star and pleasing them by speaking the lingo.

Russ's French is indeed fluent as he learnt the language at school.

Tucked

Sniffed

Fagged

Explained

Appreciated

Illuminated

Headed

Linked

RUSS MAEL . . note the next plastic footwear!

---

set 'Kimono My House' so far above its peers, yet at the same time offering absolutely nothing that a fan of that album would immediately recognise. If people thought that 'Propaganda' had thrown a curve ball, 'Indiscreet' was bowling googlies.

John Hewlett shared Hampton's reservations, utilising the album's sheer versatility as a stick with which to beat it into submission. His own relationship with the Maels was becoming increasingly difficult, as they turned more and more to Joseph Fleury for guidance and ideas. Fleury himself once described Hewlett as simply 'the guy who signed the cheques, and he wasn't happy about doing that too often, either'. Hewlett clung on now because it was his job, but his

OADSHOWS
gh energy
arks . . .

Fairfield Halls,

BABY-faced onky tonking tage centre in ol-boy jacket, rbockers and n boots.

im the astute g every inch 'ood Forties your Mother on over plays nky, Ian and nstrate mu- he on their struments.

The Swing speed at the followed by hout Using ords of the complete o, but it r too much trics are so manding

to be seen the energy ake some look like rocks re-

and their improved

100 per cent. Even the light show is pretty - if the music doesn't appeal the colours grab you in all the right places.

Russell, throbs, reels, rolls and yodels his way through the numbers. One minute he's a paramour with svelte hand on equally svelte hips. The next he's a twelve year old - maybe little Albert - marching on the spot like a kid playing at soldiers.

Suffice to say the musicianship in the band is A1. Trevor White on lead guitar plays some fluid licks, especially on In The Future and Tits.

Old favourites like This Town and Amateur Hour cause tumultuous applause, but in my opinion it's the slower-paced Hospitality On Parade which causes weird sensations in the belly that wins out.

For the encore, Russell comes on stage clad in boiler suit and Ron strips down to his Marks and Sparks vest.

RON: Forties pin-up?

During Looks, Looks, Looks, a fearless jezabel from the audience dodges the bouncers, races on stage and hugs Russell to death.

Aptly, How Are You Getting Home brings the show to a halt. But for the most part the crowd could stay and listen to the band all night long.

One marvels at the Sparks professionalism. Although their music is intricate and complex they still manage to sound almost as good live as on disc. And that's some mean feat! **JAN ILES**

words suggest that it wasn't one he enjoyed too much. 'They were so desperate to keep one step ahead of what everyone expected them to do that they simply weren't giving anyone a chance to make up their mind about them. And in the end it got so predictable, you knew that they were going to do what you didn't expect them to do. It got so boring that finally people just gave up on them.'

Wrong. People did not give up on them, and the Maels' sheer longevity proves that point. But the marketplace did. In the light of subsequent releases, it is now possible to see that the Maels, far from being in the process of artistic decline, were always capable of coming up with a new 'Kimono My House'. But it would happen only on their own terms, and by the standards that they believed made that album so special, which, for every Sparks album that has been, or could be, described as 'the new "Kimono My House"', has entailed ripping up everything they'd done in the past and starting all over again.

'No. 1 In Heaven' would do that. So would 'Lil' Beethoven'. But 'Indiscreet' was the record that started that sequence, an album that might at the time have been regarded as the death throes of a truly unique talent, but was, in retrospect, an exercise in artistry at its most undiluted and pure.

Russell detailed the reasons behind Visconti's recruitment. 'We loved Tony intensely as a real musician, and as an engineer and producer. [But] the decision was more about the fact that he could do those big-band arrangements and could arrange outside instruments.' Even in their earliest demo form, Ron intended that the new songs should be performed as far outside of the 'Sparks sound' as was physically possible.

Strings, brass, fiddles, even an entire orchestra would be called upon to ease the new songs to completion, and Visconti, whose orchestral talents, as utilised by the likes of the Move, Procol Harum and Paul McCartney's Wings, had never been in doubt, was one of the few available, London-based producers who could offer all of that and more. He was also one of the few, the Maels deduced, who would truly appreciate what they were trying to accomplish.

'Russell and Ron Mael are truly avant-garde,' Tony Visconti explained. 'They're both ex-art students, like so many rock stars, but they really are artists, and they wanted to make a completely different, left-field, bizarre album. With all due respect to Muff Winwood, he's very straight ahead and down the line – "let's double track this, put harmonies here, mix it, and get it out". He's a very singles-oriented person, and he helped Sparks immeasurably in the beginning. But they still had these weird ideas in mind, and they were looking for someone like me to help them put them across.

'There were a lot of bizarre things on that album, and a lot of tangents from the main line way of recording. There was nothing on it that was remotely like "This Town Ain't Big Enough For Both Of Us".'

More than 20 years later, interviewed for Sparks fan club newsletter, Visconti continued, 'Sparks have to be placed in the unlikely category of "Thinking Man's Rock". Lyrically, you need a thesaurus to even attempt to glean what Ron is writing about. When the penny drops, the imbedded humour in the lyrics hits you a like a whack in back of the head. There aren't many groups that can hold a candle to the intellectual rock outpourings of the Mael

Official Programme

SPARKS

brothers. There is no singer out there with Russell's vocal agility and aplomb, which are necessary to deliver such potent lyrical and melodic content. He can sing and appear like an angel, making the mangled, tortured wordscapes sound like a Sunday psalm on acid.'

Recalling the 'Indiscreet' sessions for the BBC's 1982 radio series *The Record Producers*, Visconti clearly had many happy memories of the project; 'One of the tracks which was a complete surprise, because it became a Top 30 single, was "Looks Looks Looks". We did it with a Thirties band arrangement, and it was an absolute delight to record. We did it at the Who's studio, Ramport, and we got all the old faces in from the Ted Heath Band. I did some research by listening to all my old records from the Thirties, listening closely to the harmonies and the way you have to write for saxophones, and for the things that I wasn't sure about I rang up a friend of mine, Bruce Lynch, who's a brilliant arranger and, with a little help from him, I wrote this arrangement.

'And it was so great to walk into the studio, and see all these grey-haired guys, who hadn't seen each other for years, with their Harman cup mutes, and a big double bass, and this guy with an old F-hole electric guitar – it was great! The first take that we did was excellent, but we did a second one, and then sent them all home.

'None of the band played on it, not even Ron, because we hired an old piano player to play all that Count Basie type stuff. All you hear on that track is Russell and the backing vocalists, who were Russell, Mary Hopkin [Visconti's wife] and myself, doing those Frank Sinatra, skylark type of harmonies.'

Two of the brass players even accompanied the band onto television's *Supersonic*, where the song's lightweight jazzy vibe certainly stood out from the remainder of the show's customary fare.

With tricks like that up his sleeve, Visconti was not at all surprised when Dinky Diamond went 'behind my back' to complain to Muff Winwood, still the band's A&R man despite being replaced in the studio, 'that

the rest of the band wasn't featured enough'. Nor when Trevor White reacted furiously to the release of 'Looks Looks Looks' as a single – he hadn't even wanted it included on the album. White failed to stop either happening, but with the single eventually peaking at Number 22, both sides of his argument were partially vindicated. It had done better as a single than 'Get In The Swing', but a far more impressive showing might have resulted had they opted to release one of the less unconventional numbers they had available.

It was ironic, then, that possibly the strongest contender, outside of 'Hospitality On Parade' and the closing ballad 'Miss The Start, Miss The End' – which itself only made it onto the record at Tony Visconti's insistence, the Maels having been quite prepared to leave it in the can – was one of the songs ultimately dropped from the album...

'Gone With The Wind' looked at the film of the same name from three different angles; the lovers who fall asleep and end up spending the night in the cinema – 'it's history, it drags on and on, it wasn't my fault it lasted till dawn'; the stuntman selected as Vivienne Leigh's stand-in – 'Cut! Now we want you to fall down the stairs without breaking your fall, using no hands at all'; and finally, in a verse that Joseph Fleury described as 'inexplicably cut' from the song when it eventually appeared on vinyl, from the point of view of Margaret Mitchell, the book's writer.

Neither was it the only casualty of such productive sessions. Just as they had during the recording of 'Kimono My House', Sparks taped far more material than they could fit on a single LP. But whereas most of the earlier album's out-takes were then utilised as B-sides, those from 'Indiscreet' were less fortunate.

The brief and largely pointless 'The Marriage Of Russell Mael To Jacqueline Kennedy' would appear on the flipside of the American 'Looks Looks Looks' single – Mary Hopkin supplied Jackie Kennedy's vocal contribution. But Ms. Hopkin's own, serenely beautiful rendition of 'Never Turn Your Back On Mother Earth' remained archived until she finally released it on a rarities collection, 30 years later.

The laconic nightclub sleaziness of 'Tearing The Place Apart' joined the abridged 'Gone With The Wind' on the 1979 'Best of Sparks' package. But a wild calypso ride through 'Intrusion', which in turn became the putative movie theme 'Confusion', would be abandoned long before the song was re-recorded for the next Sparks album, while Joseph Fleury admitted he could never understand why the Maels did nothing at all with a song called 'Looks Aren't Everything'. A decade after 'Indiscreet' was completed, he still regarded it as one of their most sensational songs. Both 'Intrusion/Confusion' and 'Looks Aren't Everything' were later appended as bonus tracks to the

2006 '21st Century Island Masters' reissue of the 'Big Beat' album.

Yet it is unlikely that any of these songs, replacing any of those that were selected for 'Indiscreet', would have silenced the album's critics. At the same time as the Maels must be applauded for the sheer nerve of 'Indiscreet', the puzzled frowns that greeted its release are easy to understand. Lively and spirited it may have been, but this was an album that catapulted the listener haphazardly, and without any concession to the concept of continuity, from straight rock ('In The Future'), to the big-band swing era. It seemed that nothing could knock the Maels off course in their quest to produce something strikingly different...

The Maels' greatest musical failing, after all, is also one of their greatest strengths – the apparent inability to realise that not everybody thinks along the same lines as them, and their refusal to adapt their own course in the slightest to make up for that. Songs which, for Ron and Russell, might merely have been a little joke or, at worst a display of compositional virtuosity, were to an outsider a complete musical aberration – with the inevitable consequences in the marketplace.

There are a few artists whose following is willing to sit through even their most bizarre idiosyncrasies – Bowie, Frank Zappa and Neil Young spring to mind, and, at that time, even Young's audience might have raised an eyebrow at the thought. Sparks would one day make their way into that same lofty company, but in 1975 their fans simply wanted a new 'Kimono My House', or at least a revised 'Propaganda'. Instead they got a reborn Ted Heath Band. There was no comparison.

But of course, there wasn't meant to be. 'Indiscreet' evoked a world as far removed from those of its predecessors as was possible, one which opened with a tribute to the brothers' American homeland as it stood poised, 200 years before, to break away from its colonial overlords, and which then painted its subsequent progress with bold splashes of every imaginable colour.

No two songs sounded the same; few of them even sounded like Sparks – 'How Are You Getting Home' at a pinch; 'The Lady Is Lingering' if you really tried hard. But what to make of 'Under The Table With Her', all string quartets and that neo-French accent again, 'It Ain't 1918', with its

Depression-era America vibe, 'Pineapple', apparently a love song to a tropical fruit...or 'Tits'?

'Tits' was worth infinitely more than its title (referred to as 'T*ts' on the sleeve to avoid complaints from any passing moral guardians) suggested, as Russell acknowledged. 'Some people do snigger [when they hear the title], as I did when I first heard it. But if they listen carefully to the lyrics, there's more to the song than they think.'

'Tits' took its cue from 'Propaganda's 'BC', thematically if not lyrically – and certainly not musically, as bass and brushes conjured up a smoky *film noir* nightclub, where every drink tastes of betrayal. However, while 'BC' approached the subject in the characteristically frivolous Sparks fashion, all breakneck word play and charming punning, 'Tits' dispensed with even a semblance of humour as, for perhaps the first time in his songwriting career, Ron threw aside all the pretences, the irony and the jokes, and got straight down to the matter in hand.

The song revelled in its own desolation, with the protagonist telling his friend Harry about his wife's infidelity. It started small, with her announcement that her tits – which, 'for months, for years, were once a source of fun and games at home' – were now there only to feed their son. But things quickly deteriorated until finally he caught her on the phone as well, talking with her lover, plotting to leave her husband. And who was the home-wrecker who had sailed into his life? None other than Harry himself.

But no hard feelings; 'Let's drink, Harry, drink till we can't drink no more.' It was a truly remarkable song, and one which, even if straightforwardness were its sole virtue (which it wasn't), still stood head and shoulders above the rest of 'Indiscreet'. 'Tits' even became an instant live favourite and it deserved every cheer. 'I explained it in my very rusty French,' Russell smiled following the band's triumphant return to the Paris Olympia, 'and the crowd responded in "*ooh-la-las*"...'

So 'Indiscreet' was an adventurous concept, but it was more than that. In its renouncement of Sparks' musical and social heritage, at a time when both of those things were still a frontline attraction in the marketplace, it was possible the bravest move the Maels have ever made. Visconti certainly adores it still. 'We had a ball doing that album, and we all loved it,' he concluded. 'It's one of my favourite albums, totally uncommercial, but so creative.'

Now the search was on to find people who agreed with him. 'Indiscreet' drifted no higher than Number 18 on the UK chart, and was in and out of the charts within a month. Reviews were openly hostile, with *Rolling Stone*'s Ed Ward claiming that even his dog 'sighed audibly... as the last bars faded into the night. It was over'.

Russell's vocals, Ward complained, were 'a lot of high-frequency twittering', Ron's lyrics were 'clumsy polysyllabic obscurantism... a sneer is not an insight', and the music was 'busy-busy. Sparks' melodies are getting better, it is true, but better melodies are of hardly any use in a band where there are no outstanding instrumentalists'.

If the UK and United States no longer had any time for Sparks, however, Europe was another matter entirely. Early autumn 1975 saw Sparks set out on what would become their final tour. It was a difficult one to prepare for, and Ian Hampton recalls rehearsals spent 'trying to fill in for the brass and strings and everything, without using them – it was very difficult.' In fact, great swathes of 'Indiscreet' were not even be attempted live, so complex were the studio arrangements. Nevertheless, the tour was destined, like the album, to become a far grander undertaking than anything that had preceded it, a 21-strong road crew including an on-the-road laundry, official photographer Richard Creamer and no less than four lighting crews to handle some of the most spellbinding effects the band had yet envisaged.

They had their work cut out for them as well, as one memorable moment, the conclusion of 'Without Using Hands', proved. As the song came to an end, the band and backing vocals faded away, leaving Russell alone, simply whispering the title over and over. Two spotlights concentrated everybody's attention upon him and Ron, then began to focus in on Russell's mouth and Ron's hands alone. Then, as Russell finally hushed, his spot would blink out and all that could be seen in the darkness were Ron's hands on his keys.

The tour started with sold-out shows in France and Scandinavia before winding up in Brussels. Everywhere was pandemonium and in Sweden, particularly, there were again scenes reminiscent of the UK tour that followed the release of 'Kimono My House'. *TOPP* magazine rewarded the group for topping their 'Best New Band' poll by presenting them all with a wooden horse trophy. 'Indiscreet' went gold, 'Get In The Swing' topped the chart, and even the year-old 'Propaganda' made a fleeting entry into the lower reaches of the album listings.

'They're an amazing audience to play to,' Russell said of Sparks' Swedish following. 'All I can ever see is a sea of blonde hair. And they all wear the same clothes. Those anoraks, usually blue or red, rubber boots and jeans.'

Fans followed the band back to the hotel which they were invariably sharing with a party of businessmen who were completely ignorant of the devotion that these pop stars were capable of inspiring in the nation's youth. Trevor White remembered one hotel where, every time one of the band stuck his head round the curtains at the bar window, the crowd assembled outside would immediately start screaming. The businessmen would then break off from whatever else they were doing and rush to see what calamity had befallen this inexplicable gathering of teenagers.

At other times, a cigarette butt thrown casually into the melee could provoke outbreaks of fighting, everyone scrambling for the hallowed object. And backstage in Stockholm, away from the multitude of ecstatic fans in the auditorium, the promoter happily informed the band that the next time around, they would need only play one-off stadium gigs, flying into the country for just a single show and then flying out again straight afterwards. For Trevor White, Ian Hampton and Dinky Diamond, however, there was to be no next time.

Sparks' final British tour was a 19-date outing that again proved that predictions of Sparks' commercial demise should be taken with a pinch of salt. Their record sales may have declined, but the gigs sold out as fast as ever and, if the crowds were less prone to screaming, they remained more enthusiastic than most bands of the age could routinely expect.

15th October – Newcastle City Hall
16th October – Edinburgh Odeon
17th October – Edinburgh Odeon
18th October – Glasgow Apollo
19th October – Manchester Palace
21st October – Portsmouth Guildhall
23rd October – Taunton Odeon
24th October – Oxford New Theatre
26th October – Hammersmith Odeon
28th October – Ipswich Gaumont
29th October – Leicester de Montfort Hall
30th October – Sheffield City Hall
31st October – Liverpool Empire
1st November – Leeds University
2nd November – Coventry New Theatre
4th November – Bristol Colston Hall
6th November – Birmingham Odeon
7th November – Lewisham Odeon
8th November – Brighton Dome
9th November – Croydon Fairfield Halls

'People were saying that we were on the way out,' Dinky Diamond shrugged, 'but they weren't the people on the road with us, who were queuing up for tickets or storming the hotel, hanging around backstage.'

Several times, roadies were sent out of the venue, disguised as Ron and Russell, to dive into a waiting limo and be whisked away in the hope that the kids crowded outside might follow them into the night and allow the real Maels to leave unmolested. 'It worked the first couple of times,' he laughed, 'and then the fans got wind of it. So half of them would chase the car and the rest would hang around and wait.'

The final night of the tour was also the most hysterical. The brothers had reiterated the fact that this would be their last tour for at least a year, and Record Mirror's reviewer awaited them with as much excitement as the crowd. Sparks' stock may have fallen in the more self-consciously serious music papers, after all, but Record Mirror still adored them. Ron and Russell would even be the cover stars of the magazine's Christmas annual, and that would never have happened unless the editors believed the band was still worthwhile. The review confirmed that view.

'Russell throbs, reels, rolls and yodels his way through the numbers. One minute he's a paramour with svelte hand on regally svelte hips. The next he's a twelve-year-old...marching on the spot like a kid playing at soldiers.... The crowd could stay and listen to the band all night long. Although their music is intricate and complex, they still manage to sound almost as good live as on disc, and that's some mean feat!'

Filmed footage from the concert bears out the review. With the sound mixed by Tony Visconti, four songs were broadcast on British television, and they show Mael mania at its undiluted height, with the audience rushing the stage, wrestling Russell to the ground and hugging Ron throughout the performance.

There was little time to rest following the end of the tour. Just four days later, Sparks were due on stage for the opening night of their next North American sojourn, the first of a string of shows that carried them deep into December.

14th November – Philadelphia, PA, Tower Theatre
17th November – Pittsburgh, PA, Stanley Theatre
19th November – New York, NY, Philharmonic (Avery Fisher) Hall
20th November – Detroit, MI, Masonic Temple
21st November – Chicago, IL, Rivera Theatre
22nd November – Cleveland, OH, Music Hall
23rd November – Buffalo, NY, New Century Theatre
24th November – Toronto, Canada, Maple Leaf Gardens
25th November – Ottawa, Canada, Civic Arena
26th November – Montreal, Canada, Plateau Theatre
28th November – Kansas City, MO, Soldiers & Sailors
29th November – St. Louis, MO, Ambassador Theatre
30th November – Indianapolis, IN, Rivoli Theatre
1st December – Denver, CO (cancelled)
3rd December – Los Angeles, CA, Santa Monica Civic
4th December – Los Angeles, CA, Santa Monica Civic
6th December – San Francisco, CA, Berkeley Community Theatre
9th December – Portland, OR, Paramount Theatre
10th December – Seattle, WA, Paramount Theatre
11th December – Vancouver, Canada Vancouver Gardens
14th December – San Diego, CA, Civic Arena

Again, Island's marketing department had been busy. 'Indiscreet' was promoted with life-sized cut-outs of Ron and Russell which could be seen everywhere. Seattle fan Mike Sharman spotted them for the first time outside a record store in Hawaii. Things were slowly beginning to pick up in America, it seemed. Audiences were more responsive than before – there were less people coming to simply stare curiously, and more who seemed to know the songs. 'The American audiences surprised me,' Russell said as he looked forward to the outing. 'They really freaked out the last time we played there.'

Los Angeles gothic rock supertsar Rozz Williams never made any secret of his love of British Glam Rock, and how it sustained him through his teenage years in the remote desert town of Victorville. Most commentaries on his career concentrate on the influence David Bowie had on him, but Sparks had a profound effect, too, the dichotomous faces of Ron and Russell Mael opening his eyes to the concepts of 'ugliness and beauty living side by side in one body, one soul. Sparks helped me through a lot of ugliness. Sparks were amazing.'

Talking in the early Nineties, Williams still regretted having sold his copy of 'Sparks' in 1982, and, shortly before his death in 1998, he was considering the possibility of recording a version of 'Moon Over Kentucky'.

The first genuine fanatics began to emerge, people who were now treating Sparks like others once regarded Jook, writing to England and elsewhere to buy the latest singles, stockpiling back issues of the UK music press, delving deep into the band's history and mystery in search of hidden meanings. The fan club, now run by the Maels' mother Miriam under the quickly-unmasked semi-anagrammatic pseudonym of Mary Martin, was overflowing with American members.

Sharon Hottell recalled, 'I had a pen pal who lived in the UK. She would send me posters and clippings of Sparks from UK magazines. And aware of how important music was to me, and knowing that Sparks could use some American support, my mother let me join their fan club. I received their newsletters, which had articles typed, cut and pasted along with photos, which were then photocopied on coloured paper. That is how it appeared anyway. They were wonderful! Thanks Mary Martin!'

Hottell still recalled the day she opened her mail box 'and found a handwritten post card from Russell. It was amazing that he took the time to write to a fan! Later – about thirty years later – I met a lady from New York who had the same experience.'

Pockets of support were springing up on both east and west coasts, but somehow it wasn't enough. It wasn't the big time. Audiences responded well, but the band was losing money hand over fist. Worryingly, Island's American office appeared not to have a clue who Sparks were; one night, Richard, the group's road manager, found himself deep in conversation with Island's head of radio promotion who was convinced he was actually talking to Ron Mael.

'Any excitement we generate is lost on a label which doesn't like [our] stuff, doesn't know Ron from our roadie, and can't support [us],' Joseph Fleury reported bitterly, and, if he was distraught, the Maels were positively seething.

Watching his band-mates as they continued to endure their homeland's apathy, Trevor

White was astonished at just how deeply hurt the brothers were. In his mind, the Maels' hearts lay anywhere but in America.

'The places they seemed most at home in were places like Paris, trolling up and down the Champs d'Élysées, that was really where they were at. Or even in England; they were really into the English way of life. They used to get up in the morning, have a cup of tea, and then look up an Egon Ronay restaurant to have lunch in. That whole upper-class, sophisticated decadence thing that they put over, that was what they were really like, and that was what Sparks were all about.'

But he understood how they felt. Three years earlier, the Maels fled the Californian sunshine with their tails figuratively, if not literally, between their legs. Now they were returning as conquering heroes, but where were the ticker-tape parades? Where were the presidential-style motorcades? Where the keys to the city? And what did they have to do to secure them?

Talking with Hewlett and Fleury every day, it sometimes felt as if one last, major push really could achieve that coveted breakthrough. Discussions had already been opened with Rupert Holmes, the Maels' choice to produce their next album.

Holmes had an impressive track record, writing, recording and producing a string of solo FM radio hits in the early Seventies. His 1974 album 'Widescreen' had brought him to the attention of Barbra Streisand, who covered some of the songs from it, and soon afterwards used more of Holmes' compositions in the movie *A Star Is Born*. Ron and Russell had recently been listening to Streisand and were favourably impressed by the lush wall of orchestration which backed the lady up; they were intrigued, too, by Holmes' recent work with Sailor, a band generally seen as nothing more than CBS's answer to both Sparks and Roxy Music.

Joseph Fleury explained, 'The initial idea was for Holmes to oversee a duet between Russell and Marianne Faithfull on "I Got You Babe". That came up around the time of "Indiscreet", and everybody was really keen on it, apart from Island, whose only response was "who's Marianne Faithfull?" Then Marianne turned round and said she didn't want to do that song because it was so close to her own era, so Ron wrote a new song, "Room For Two".

'Now Marianne loved that one, but Island still weren't interested – they still thought Marianne was a has-been.' Ironically, less than three years later Faithfull signed to Island in her own right. Meanwhile, the idea of doing the duet faded, but the Maels kept Holmes in mind. If anybody could translate the sound of Sparks into something that mainstream America might fall in love with, it was Holmes.

Unfortunately, the British contingent of the band disagreed. 'The mention of Rupert Holmes put me right off,' Ian Hampton admitted. 'I didn't want to work with bloody Streisand's producer.'

They disagreed, too, with the possibility of the entire band relocating to Los Angeles, much as the Maels had expected they would. A concerted assault on the hearts and minds of America would require uprooting the three Englishmen from their homes and families for months on end. Would they really want to make that sacrifice for a band they knew was not really theirs? Even before they posed the question, the Maels knew the answer. America was a great place to visit, but that was the end of it. If Sparks wanted to break America, they'd need to break up the band as well.

Five months earlier, appearing on *Shang-a-Lang*, Sparks had been introduced on stage with the words 'the great American twosome', a description that must have shocked the rest of the group. But maybe Roller Alan Longmuir knew more than he, or the twosome themselves, were letting on.

Nothing was ever said as the American tour rolled along, but in hindsight it was clear that something was going to happen. The tour climaxed in Los Angeles across two nights at the Santa Monica Civic Centre, on 3rd and 4th December. From there it was up the coast to San Francisco, Portland, Seattle and Vancouver BC, before hurtling back to San Diego for one final show, on 14th December. And that was where the axe fell, at least for Dinky Diamond and Trevor White.

John Hewlett recalled; 'I found out about Ron and Russell's decision to dismiss the band during the US tour and I believe I told the band prior to their return to the UK. Ron and Russell may have given them some glimmer of hope for a possible future, but my recall is that the decision was made and there was going to be no turning back. I recall their reaction as deeply saddened, especially Dinky's. He was devastated because he regarded himself as a founder member of Sparks. He was devoted to the band and proud to be their drummer.'

The pair flew home immediately afterwards, still reeling from a blow from which one of them, at least, would never recover, as John Hewlett reminds us.

'Sadly, the scars of rejection do not always heal. Dinky committed suicide on 10th September 2004, and Adrian Fisher died of a heart attack on 31st March 2000.' Both men, of course, had got on with their lives after they were summarily sacked from what could have been the biggest British band of the age. But for both, the pain of that dismissal had lingered on.

Ian Hampton did remain in the Maels' plans, at least for a little longer. He'd been invited to stay at bluesman John Mayall's house in Laurel Canyon while its owner was elsewhere, and while he waited to see what was going to happen next. He was not in suspense for long. One evening, the Maels came round for dinner and it was clear, Hampton recalled, that there was something on their mind. 'We sat down and they said "where do you think we're going?"

'I said "I really don't know," and they said "we don't either..."'

And that was it. Hampton flew up to Woodstock to spend a few days with his old Jook friend Ian Kimmett, who now worked for Albert Grossman's Bearsville operation, and then headed home. 'I recall flying back to the UK on Christmas Eve that year, dressed for the Californian heatwave. Boy! Did I regret it when I arrived at Heathrow!'

CHAPTER THIRTEEN

OUT OF THE DOORWAY, INTO THE MORNING

'**W**e'd got sick of England,' said Ron. 'The weather was disgusting, the food was terrible, and we got tired of the provincial atmosphere. What at first had seemed quaint later got really annoying.' Partly, he admitted, the decision was informed by the knowledge that their success 'did begin to tail off'; that the fickle pop hearts that drew them to London in the first place had already begun moving on to other fancies. The week Ian Hampton flew back into London, 'Bohemian Rhapsody' was into its fifth week at the top of the chart, ensuring nobody could ever employ another falsetto voice over a constantly shifting backdrop again without being immediately compared to Queen.

Other new bands, Jigsaw, Stretch, Smokie and the oddly-enduring Sailor, were riding waves almost as large as the one that Sparks had swept in on, and if their musical content was scarcely comparable to anything the Maels had aspired to, the fate of 'Indiscreet' suggested that quality might not have been the essential ingredient the Maels believed it was. 'Looks Looks Looks' was sounding more ironic every time Ron thought about it.

But disappointing record sales were only a part of it. Given time and a little bit of luck, Sparks could turn the tide at any moment, maybe even with their next album. Ron started writing songs for Sparks' sixth LP during that break in Los Angeles in July; home again for Christmas, he was working even harder, and the new songs that were piling up around him were as good, he believed, as anything he'd written. Maybe even better. No, the real reason why Sparks abandoned London was because they were homesick.

'There were certain creature comforts we'd become used to back home and really missed,' sighed Ron. 'We were used to sun. We were [in England] for three years and I was getting chilblains.' And not even the red-hot summer of 1975, a dress rehearsal for the unprecedented heatwave that all but overpowered the UK the following year, could dissuade them.

Ron was right to be confident about the new songs. Tracing his development over the five preceding albums, it was fascinating to watch as he slowly (and perhaps, at first, a little unwillingly) abandoned the madcap abstraction of his earliest compositions in favour of a more personal, even confessional, style. 'Moon Over Kentucky', way back on 'A Woofer In Tweeter's Clothing', had begun the trend: the cry of the the lunatic, in the classical sense of the word, looking up at his tormentor and pleading for her to 'leave this mooring and seek some new rendezvous', but to make sure she takes him along as well. Both, after all, had had enough of being trampled on.

'Equator' had followed, with its idiosyncratic imagery of loss and being lost set against a musical backdrop as disconcerting as the actual landscapes in which the traveller found himself. More recently, the chilling trilogy of 'In My Family', 'BC' and 'Tits', had examined accepted familial traditions in all their unspoken, dysfunctional glory.

Even at the time, few critics could claim Ron Mael chose 'typical' themes for his songs, but in allowing the humour and irony that was a vital component in his songwriting to obscure the glimpses of personal revelation that lay underneath, the critics consistently missed the point. Film, stage and television had long ago learned to accept humour as a valid form of self-expression, cloaking serious issues with a veneer of irony and laughter in order to press the point home further. After all, what was the so-called satire boom that swept through British entertainment in the early Sixties – making superstars of David Frost, Peter Cook and Dudley Moore and, ultimately, the Monty Python troupe in the process – if not an attempt to dismantle the hypocrisy of one world and replace it with the idealism of another, *and smiling as it did so?*

Yet rock music still took itself far too seriously to allow for that. Frank Zappa had dented that self-importance a little, but Zappa was little more than a well-respected cult figure in the mid-Seventies. 10cc, whose own domination of the UK chart both bookended and coincided with Sparks', also made a virtue of cynicism and irony, but only after they first warned their listeners what they were doing, painstakingly spelling out their mission in interview after interview, until everybody was in on the joke – at which point, the joke really stopped being funny.

Sparks, however, didn't puncture the imagery. Ask a direct question about a song, and Ron might deliver a direct answer. But, with so many other burning issues to be discussed, from Doris Day to Adolf Hitler and even Russell's shorts, few people ever got around to asking the questions that counted, and so Ron wrote on, building the world of words in which Sparks would reside, and only cursing in private when his meanings were misconstrued.

'Indiscreet' was the album where those mutterings finally broke free, song after song reflecting the alienation of an individual struggling against the tide of conventional society in a desperate attempt to live life in the style of his own choosing...and failing every time. In 'It Ain't 1918', for example, Johnny and his wife fight desperately to preserve the standards they believe in, while the world around them races ahead. Their neighbours do their best to try and pull the misguided couple into the modern world, bombarding them with fancy gifts, replacing their old jalopy with a shiny new car, and telling them all the while that they'll be much happier with all these wonderful new appliances. Johnny turns them down, and the neighbours turn nasty. 'It ain't 1918, for us or for you,' they tell him in the song's denouement. 'And if we can't enjoy it, then neither will you.'

The same storyline resurfaces at the end of the album, with the stark insularity of 'Miss The Start, Miss The End'. Again it is a song of rejection, of putting aside the distractions and obsessions of the outside world and living instead wholly in the companionship of one other person. But whereas 'It Ain't 1918' is seen entirely from the viewpoint of a dispassionate outsider, 'Miss The Start, Miss The End' is relayed from that of a close friend – or, at least, someone who is close enough to understand *what* the song's subjects need from life, but not so close that they understand *why*. It is autobiography seen from the outside, a reader's eye view of a personal narrative and, as such, it is still a personal pronoun or two away from stark confession, as though Ron was still not quite ready to take that leap.

Now he was. The songs that make up what became 1976's 'Big Beat' are Ron Mael at his most raw. He is still disguising his innermost feelings with irony and humour, of course – a song like 'I Want To Be Like Everybody Else', for example, could only be taken seriously if its meanings were totally flipped, while 'I Bought The Mississippi River' is such a joyous slab of silliness that only by stripping away its surface meaning and pondering the type of person who *would* buy 2,340 miles of inland waterway does its true intent reveal itself. It's the same sort of person who would be buying the BBC 18 years later. In neither case does he have the foggiest notion what he's going to do with it; he buys it because the world demands that he owns something, so it might as well be the most grandiose thing he can find.

'Big Beat' was the first Sparks record that offered the contemporary listener a clear portrait of the character that Ron was creating. Hindsight reveals its development across the earlier albums, and subsequent Sparks releases would allow him to build and further round out the image that he wanted to present to the world. What was, and remains remarkable, is the sheer consistency of that image.

Once they hit their musical stride most songwriters discover the core characteristics that lie at the heart of their public persona, and work to develop them over the course of their career. But most are also unable to sustain the effort. External distractions, internal revisions, and the pressures of their career itself can all affect a writer's grasp of his personal strengths, and one only needs to look at the creative ups and downs of David Bowie to understand how the drive for continued success can utterly skew a genuinely gifted performer's ability to harness his abilities.

Arguably, Bowie spent 25 years, from 1973 to 1998, denying his true musical nature. The young man who recorded the career-best albums 'Hunky Dory' and 'The Rise and Fall Of Ziggy Stardust and the Spiders From Mars' then went off on a series of musical tangents, and it was not until 'hours...', in 1999, that he returned to base – which is not to demean the work that appeared in between, simply to observe that it was not Bowie at his most honestly bare.

Bob Dylan, on the other hand, found his true voice as early as 1964, when he released his fourth album, 'Another Side of Bob Dylan', and had stepped fully into his chosen role by the time of his fifth, 'Bringing It All Back Home'. He has never truly abandoned it since then – there have been missteps, and a well-publicised dalliance with born-again Christianity, during which he denied the validity of almost everything he'd ever said in the past. But overall, the Bob Dylan we listen to on record is indistinguishable from the Bob Dylan we imagine cleans his teeth every morning, watches TV every evening and talks baseball in the bar with his buddies. And that is something few other songwriters have ever achieved.

Nobody, for example, believes that Neil Young is truly as bad-tempered as his best records suggest, any more than they used to believe that Slade went to the supermarket wearing the same clothes they donned for *Top Of The Pops*. Bono may be a sanctimonious twerp when the cameras are rolling and the microphone is on, but away from the glare of publicity he's probably a bundle of fun.

But Ron Mael, like Dylan, *is* the character he creates in song, or at least we truly believe he is, because we simply cannot imagine him being anything else. And it is that simple quality which, more than any other, defines a great songwriter. Others, in the short term, may write catchier melodies; others, equally sporadically, may craft more captivating hooks. But to sustain a consistent standard, both in a musical sense and in terms of unswerving public perception, over the course of a lifelong career (2009 marks the fortieth anniversary of Sparks' formation), is truly the hallmark of rare brilliance. And all of that started with what is widely still regarded as one of Sparks' lesser releases.

John Hewlett: 'The idea in Ron and Russell's mind at the end of the 1975 tour was that Sparks was now a hot enough name to create interest on its own, and they could put any group of musicians together to perform on new material and the result would be a new Sparks album... in my opinion, this was a flawed temptation which has led to an lot of inferior product being released over the years since "Kimono My House" and "Propaganda". The "Big Beat" album and its cover both reveal the path of selfish vanity chosen by Ron and Russell.'

'"Big Beat" is 180 degrees different from our last album, and a lot of that has to do with the time we've had back in the States,' Russell said at the time. 'The songs still retain the ideas that have characterised Sparks, with titles like "I Like Girls", "White Women" and "Everybody's Stupid", but the music's changed. The album is very guitar-oriented, very hard rock. It's obvious, like rock should be, and more accessible than anything we've ever done before.'

'Big Beat' had a lengthy gestation period. The decision to depart Island's American wing presented the Maels with their first stumbling block. A handful of suitors stepped forward and, by early March 1976, it seemed certain that Sparks' next album would be released in the United States by Columbia Records – 'the greatest American label,' Russell enthused. 'We are obviously optimistic and very happy....'

That all came tumbling down on 8th March when Island turned their back on three months of negotiations and announced that they were not going to release Sparks from their contract after all. The matter was eventually resolved, but not before all of Ron and Russell's optimism and hopes for their immediate future were dashed, and they never quite managed to regain the sense of excitement they'd enjoyed at the beginning of the year.

The relocation to the United States, too, was going slowly. The Basing Street office had been abandoned, but its contents – past promotional materials, fan-club paraphernalia, all the accumulated detritus of three years of operations – were still *in situ*. Somebody, Joseph Fleury mused, needed to get over there as soon as possible to clear out all the drawers. Undoubtedly it would be him.

Ron and Russell, too, were unsettled. They initially intended returning to Los Angeles, and building the new Sparks from there. They even reunited with Earle Mankey, settling into his home studio to record a new song, a caustic glance at their recently-concluded exile, titled 'England'.

It was a stirring little number, one that described the Maels' erstwhile home in much the same way as Neil Armstrong might have treated the moon had he landed there only to discover that McDonalds had beaten him to it – 'England's just like everywhere I know.' Add a typically quirky Mankey production and, had the two parties agreed to stick together for a full LP, the results might have been remarkable.

Unfortunately, there was a growing sense that Sparks needed something more than Los Angeles could offer, and that going home would be taking the easy way out at a time when the band's continued existence required far more radical thinking.

The notion of working with Rupert Holmes remained at the forefront of their minds. During the ongoing negotiations with Island, the idea of recording a Russell Mael solo single came up, along with the concept of a vastly over-orchestrated cover of the Beatles' 'I Want To Hold Your Hand'.

'So they took it to Rupert Holmes,' explained Fleury, 'who also loved the idea. He wrote a complete orchestral score for it, brought Melissa Manchester in on backing vocals, and the next thing we knew was when he called Russell into the studio to do the vocals.' Even Ron sat it out.

'We still wanted to put it out as a solo single,' Russell continued, 'but Rupert loved the song so much that he persuaded us to put it out as Sparks, figuring perhaps that it would stand more of a chance that way. As it was, Island weren't keen on it, and the record was only released in Scandinavia.' In fact, it *was* issued by Island in the UK, backed by the recently completed 'England', but it was doomed to obscurity. Released on 19th March 1976, then mysteriously withdrawn from sale just days later, 'I Want To Hold Your Hand' clocked up the Mael's first truly unsuccessful single since they'd arrived in England three years earlier. But it wasn't going to be alone in this respect for long.

It was Joseph Fleury who suggested the Maels try relocating to New York City. It wasn't a completely unselfish notion. He and John Hewlett were now working towards setting up their own record company, to be christened JJ from their shared first initials, and the two bands already earmarked for the label, the Marbles and Milk'n'Cookies, were themselves both based in the city.

But Fleury was also aware that New York was itself in the grip of a major musical renaissance, with a growing tide of new sounds flowing out of the city's vibrant club scene. Before the year was out, critics on both sides of the Atlantic would have labelled these new sounds punk rock and new wave; right now, however, the simultaneous existence of the Ramones, Television, the Patti Smith Group, the Heartbreakers and so many others was simply one more of those odd coincidences of mood and momentum that shake (and sometimes shape) a local scene from time to time. These bands were just the tip of the iceberg – the city was seething with new talent, and if the Maels couldn't find what they were looking for in New York they might not find it anywhere.

Sal Maida, the bassist they turned away in London three years before because they didn't want to work with American musicians, was their guide to this new world.

Maida's own career had seen some exhilarating ups and downs since that phone call. Weeks after the Maels turned him away, he landed the job of bassist in Roxy Music, as that band headed out on the road to promote their 'Stranded' album. One world tour later, in late 1974, he was back in New York, where John Hewlett and Joseph Fleury sought him out and offered him a gig with Milk'n'Cookies.

'The Roxy Music tour was over, so John and Joe said "Hey, what you gonna do now?" I hadn't really thought about it, so they asked if I wanted to join this new band they were working with – "They sent us their demo and they're fantastic, and the first thing we want to do is put you in the band..." They played me the stuff, and I said okay, and they said "They're like seventeen years old, and really good, really raw. They need some work, but with you in there that would be a great addition, give them some musical credibility." Whatever! So I listened to the tape and said "Yeah, these guys are great." I still didn't know if it was right for me, but they talked me round, they gave me this whole sales pitch, so I went down to play with them and the chemistry was through the roof. It sounded great, so they were like "You gotta do it..."'

Things moved quickly. Just as he had with Sparks, Hewlett piqued the interest of Muff Winwood at Island. Only this time, it was Winwood who flew to America to see the band, travelling to their Long Island base to witness the quartet going through its paces. Maida continued, 'He immediately said "Let's do it, I'll sign it, I'll produce it…." We went over to London, Island put us up in a big house, Muff produced, Rhett Davies was the assistant, it was pretty amazing.'

And then everything that could go wrong did go wrong. 'We made the record, but Chris Blackwell hated it. He didn't want us on the label. The single ['Little Lost And Innocent'] came out before the LP and it got absolutely destroyed in the *NME*. Apparently Blackwell read that, and it was the first time he'd ever even heard of us! He was like "They're on my label? Who is this?" He didn't even know he had us!'

The Milk'n'Cookies album would eventually be released the following year, but it was too late for the group. 'We were dropped and sent back to New York, and started playing the whole CBGBs scene. We were doing these gigs in New York, and John [Hewlett] was trying to get us a deal with Bell; Sire was kind of interested; we did demos for Warner Bros. There was interest in us, but nothing panned out. And then one day John mentioned that Ron and Russell were coming to New York and wanted to use New York musicians, all this stuff, and would I be interested?'

Maida had met the Maels by this time, backstage at a Roxy Music gig at the Rainbow Theatre in London late in 1973. He was still a huge Sparks fan as well, so of course he said yes.

The Maels fell in love with New York. Some of the bands Maida introduced them to they liked, some they didn't, but there was no denying the sheer energy and drive that was exploding everywhere. Their next album, they decided, should reflect some of that – and as for Rupert Holmes?

'After a couple of weeks in New York, they'd completely forgotten about Rupert Holmes,' said Joseph Fleury. 'Now they wanted Mick Ronson' – who, as it happened, was a good friend of Maida's cousin. Phone calls were made and addresses were exchanged. Ronson and his family were living in an old brownstone on the Lower West Side at the time…and one day early in the summer, Maida remembers, 'Ron and Russell, Joe and I went to his loft to run the songs, and Hilly Michaels was there.'

Michaels, the veteran Sparks fan who fantasised about one day playing with his dream band, picks up the story. Since his teens, Michaels had been in and out of bands and projects with a then-struggling singer named Michael Bolotin (later Bolton). One day in 1973, Bolton's piano player, Patrick Henderson 'talked Ronson into coming to New Haven to hear Bolton perform. I walked into our rehearsal house and there he was, my idol…Mick Ronson sitting together with his exquisitely beautiful wife Suzi. I remember turning into a statue when I walked into the room, and saw Mick and Suzi. They came to our live show on a floating party barge, and disappeared after the gig. I guess Mick was interested in listening to Michael sing as a possible front man for his own band.'

Ronson would return, and he and Michaels quickly became friends; at one point, Michaels was living with the guitarist and his family, sharing their brownstone, writing songs and playing with Ronson nearly every day. They worked together on John Cougar Mellencamp's debut album, rehearsed constantly and dreamed of the band they'd form together.

Then one day the buzzer sounded and Danny Shea, the Ronsons' other room-mate, stuck his head out of the window to look down to see who was at the door. 'He said something like "Hey Ronson, those guys Sparks are here for you" and I remember a gush of excitement came over me. Sparks were here? Oh my God! I loved them, and I had every record they'd released up till then.'

Ronson knew that as well. 'He turned to me and said "Hey Hilly, do you want to play drums with us? Sparks want me to produce and play guitar on their new record." Mick always kept things he was doing to himself… I guess he knew they were coming over but he didn't mention it to me.'

The initial contact, Ronson later said, was made through management, the Maels just one more in the long list of artists who'd contacted him since he split from David Bowie in the hope

RECORD MIRROR

1976 ANNUAL

Britain's brightest pop annual

Photos, Stories and the best pop information

SPARKS
NOT ABOUT TO FIZZLE OUT

SPARKS ARE more than just a flash in the proverbial pan—cisterns are being broken right left and centre whenever their name springs forth, and not only that, these oddities of popular music are beginning to steal the limelight (not to mention fans) from other great celebrities. It's true to say that they're the freshest thing since Casanova and his merry band of men, and it's undeniable that their music is so unique it cannot be compared with anyone elses. Thus they're in a class all their own. Right? Wrong, they're more than that—nobody, but nobody, can say that Sparks are just a hype and that it's just luck and a little dash of rouge and a handful of hair pins that has made them what they are today.

Just listen to their sparkling, fresh melodies and the high, hyaline vocals (courtesy of ritzy Russ Mael) and you'll see what we mean. Their overall sound is pure magic. Ron Mael's writing is amusing as well as interesting and the rest of the band are all capable of playing fine crisp and concise music on their respective instruments.

Ron says about his songwriting. "I'm inspired by lots of things. It can be the simplest theme in the world, so long as it gets to me. I like my songs to be short and sweet, why say something in twenty minutes, when it can be summed up in three?"

Their albums have all been successful, their stage acts more so.

"It can be frightening playing to pent-up teenagers whose sole aim is to grab you", exclaims Russ, the one who has to face the danger out in front. "During our last British tour I got whacked about a bit by fans, it was mind-blowing. But they don't mean to hurt you of course, it's just that they're so intent on getting you off stage they don't think they're doing you any damage."

If you haven't been to a Sparks concert, then you haven't lived (or been near to death!). The fans go balmy. They don't believe in being kitch an' all that hip stuff—If they wanna cry they cry and if they wanna wet their knicks, they wet their knicks! "I've always liked audience reaction, it helps us entertainers", opines Russ. "Like we know whether or not the audience are really digging us. If they are sombre

4

and solemn throughout a concert then it's nigh on impossible to tell what they're thinking!"

Well at least Sparks have no problems there. The kids would tear the clothes off their idols if they could, and if they did catch a glimpse of Russ's lily white flesh Gawd knows what might happen?

"We have come very near to being raped", Russ laughs casually, "but they never seem to be able to pull it off successfully."

Sparks supporters average about 15 to 16 years of age, but there has been older folk in their audiences, enjoying the band's antics (especially cherub looking Russ) just as much as their younger counterparts. Often young and old alike can be seen miming to Sparks more popular toons such as "Amateur Hour", "Girl From Germany" and "Never Turn Your Back". It's almost like a disease—the teen mania we mean. It has now spread further afield to their native America, and today they have as big a following there as they do in the British Isles.

When these two paragons of pop aren't sitting in 5 star hotel rooms waiting for their next gig, or busy over some dazzling ditty, they can be found at home, aprons on, utensils out. Ron and Russ are mad about cookin', folks (no, not actually cooking people, sweet delights more like).

Says Russ, "My speciality is sweet-after-meal-treats. When we have parties, Ron and myself usually make all these weird and delightful dishes for our guests. I'm sure most of them only come to sample the food!"

Ron also loves to collect colourful bawdy posters—and we're told he has quite a selection!

"Usually it saves writing long letters to people saying how much you miss them, when you don't. You just send them an interesting, colourful postcard and that says it all for you."

Characteristically, the two Maels are worlds apart. Russ summed it up adequately when he once said: "He's the drip", to which brother Ron replied, "Yeah, and he's the bouncy, vibrant dancey type."

If anyone cares to look into their crystal balls they'll clearly see that Sparks in general and the Mael brothers in particular are heading for super stardom—whether they planned it that way or not!

5

that he might want to work with them. Some he agreed to meet, others he passed on. Sparks, though, intrigued him.

'They were a good band,' Ronson said. 'I'd liked the singles, thought they had a good look and I knew they'd broken up so I wouldn't be stepping on any other guitar-player's toes, so I told them to come on over.' Today would be the first time he met the brothers face to face.

'The Maels, Joseph Fleury and Sal Maida marched upstairs,' Michaels continued, 'we sat and chatted, and Russell said to me something like "So you play drums?" I nodded and Mick interjected with "Hilly's a great drummer and he's in my band we're starting." Russell said "Can we go downstairs and play, and we'll show you some of the new material we're working on?" I thought, sure, let's go play!

'We plugged in and the music and the energy was just incredible! We played for about two hours working on songs like "Big Boy", "Everybody's Stupid", "Throw Her Away" and, I think, "I Want To Be Like Everybody Else"', all for the benefit of a small mono cassette recorder in the corner. 'I kept thinking to myself, this is it, Mick and I need not look for a band any more. Sal was thumping away and locking in with me as if we'd been playing for years together, Mick was coming up with some great arrangements... everything was flowing so nicely, and I thought for sure that we would all just join forces and become Sparks featuring Mick Ronson!'

Ron Mael: 'We still have the cassettes of the really rough demos of Mick Ronson playing a lot of the songs. And they sound really great because he plays with a lot of abandon.'

'Mick's manner was more easy-going than we expected,' Russell told Ronson's biographers, Weird and Gilly. 'Mick the musician didn't let us down with the image we had of him from his work with Bowie. His guitar work was every bit as musicianly, flashy and cool as we had expected. Certain pop musicians stand out above the crowd. Mick was one.'

The Maels departed, but Michaels and Ronson continued talking. Ronson was clearly enthusiastic about the project, loved the songs and liked the brothers. Michaels asked when it would all be kicking off... 'Pretty soon, I think,' replied Ronson.

And then it all went sour. Michaels again; 'The following day, Mick was acting kind of strange. I asked him "What's up?" He said that Sparks' management had contacted him earlier, and told him that if he were to produce the record and play guitar on it, they required him to become a permanent member in Sparks. Mick Ronson is a tough act to follow, and Ron and Russell knew that, if he didn't join the band, who on earth was going to fill his shoes and play guitar like him live?'

Michaels didn't see a problem. 'I said to him, "Well, why not? We sounded fantastic yesterday. Why not do it for a while?"'

Ronson, however, was adamant. He would do the gig on his own terms or not at all.

'I would have liked to have done it,' Ronson said a decade later, 'but I was still involved with Ian Hunter and the Dylan thing.' In fact, his recollection of the sequence of events was inaccurate – Dylan's Rolling Thunder Revue, of which Ronson was a member, had played its last show a few weeks earlier in May, while he would not tour or record with Hunter again until 1979. But he *was* talking with both David Cassidy and John Cale at the time, and he *was* playing occasionally with ex-Winkies guitarist Phil Rambow's band. Ronson rarely had to look for work – work came to him – and he was certainly right when he claimed 'There just wasn't time to devote to a full-time project like Sparks were asking me to do.'

While Ronson moved on, Michaels was left hanging – so near, but so far. Then one day about a week later, the phone rang; it was Russell inviting him to join the Maels for lunch. 'We were sitting at some outdoor café talking, when Ron and Russell looked at me and first said, "You know, we've got to do something about your image as the drummer of Sparks, Hilly. Do you have any ideas?"' He was still thinking of an answer when they dropped in a few thoughts of their own. 'Like maybe cutting off all your hair, maybe dying it with a purple kind of henna, and perhaps have you wearing white painters' pants and some kind of contrasting shirt for a "Hilly Boy" kind of thing, you know?'

Michaels knew. Among his more recent gigs was a stint playing alongside Cherry Vanilla as she slipped onto the New York club circuit with her band, the Backstreet Boys, every one of them festooned in so much face paint that Ronson once came backstage and swore Hilly was wearing more make-up than even the Spiders From Mars had. 'So when Ron and Russell suggested me doing something to create a distinct image, I was all too eager.' But Russell, still wondering whether the allure of Sparks was sufficient to drag Michaels away from Ronson's embryonic new group, had one final ace to play.

'Well you can either stay here in New York, and keep doing these intensive and endless auditions for Mick's band...' he said, 'or, you can join us and play for thousands of screaming Sparks fans, with hundreds of young girls trying to rip your clothes off.'

Michaels never did get the screaming fans, he laughed. But the Maels were right about one thing. When he and Sparks parted company at the end of the year, Ronson still hadn't got a band together.

The priority now was to seek out a new lead guitarist. Who else was there? For a time, the Maels were seriously considering Cheap Trick guitarist Rick Nielsen. He turned up for the audition with bassist Tom Petersson in tow, and Hilly Michaels recalled, 'I know they were trying to talk Rick into joining the band, and he almost did it. He would have joined, except for the fact that he insisted on being included as a songwriter. But I remember Ron and Russell discussing how it would alter their style if they let him in and write songs.' Nielsen was passed over.

Other auditions came and went without turning up anybody suitable, and the Maels were growing frustrated. Sal Maida recalled; 'I got word that Ron and Russell were considering pulling the plug on the whole New York scenario, and maybe going back to Los Angeles, or back to London, so at that point I suggested Jeff Salen from Tuff Darts, and they were like "Oh he's great", and that's how we wound up doing the record. He was a pretty great guitar player.'

'But it must have been awful for Jeffrey,' shuddered Fleury. 'Ron and Russell would play him the Ronson tape and say "play like that".'

In fact, Salen was quite comfortable with the comparison, as Hilly Michaels explained; 'I had met and played with Jeff several months before at Ian Hunter's home in Connecticut one day. Mick brought me up to spend the day and jam with him and Ian, and Jeff was already there. We all went down to Ian's basement and played together.'

Still, he admitted that Salen did experience 'a bit of a tough time remembering all the changes and parts to the songs at rehearsals, and he sounded a bit unsure of how and where to play the guitar parts. But Ron and Russell were very patient, and had faith in him to fill Mick's shoes.'

Ronson's influence, brief though it was, did linger, however. 'We all took what we could remember from what Mick played, and where he was going with the music when we all played with him that one day, and we tried to remain faithful to his overall vision of it. The Ramones and tons of other punk music was happening around this time, and we were somewhat influenced by those sounds as well.' Michaels, for his own part, 'always kept Dinky Diamond's drumming style in mind, and always tried to keep faithful to his type of drumming, thinking to myself "How would Dinky Diamond approach this one?" I thought he played some nice creative drum parts when he was with the group.'

With Ronson out of the picture, the need to seek out a producer raised its head again, and suddenly Rupert Holmes was back in the frame.

Michaels: 'Rupert finally arrived at our rehearsal one afternoon. He was a "no show" the day he promised to come by, so when he arrived a day late, he handed Ron and Russell a bouquet of red roses, and a box of chocolates, and apologised profusely to them for being absent the day before. Ron and Russell, I think, were biting their lips from cracking up laughing about "the tardy gift" from Rupert and when he left after listening to our worked-up material, we all let out the laughs we were holding back in his presence. Roses and chocolate?

'But he listened to us perform, and he loved our sound. He realised he was now going to produce a completely different-sounding Sparks from when he last worked with them ['I Want To Hold Your Hand']. This is high adrenalin rock'n'roll now. He was slightly taken off guard, thinking he was going to be writing all these big, lush orchestration charts for the band. We really threw him for a loop, to put it mildly. As I recall, he had a slightly concerned expression on his face!'

It was time for producer and band to have a 'getting to know you' session, ducking into Mediasound Studios to record a version of a song that seemed fated to a kind of half-life existence, the long-mothballed 'I Like Girls.' 'It was just a try-out,' explained Fleury, 'to see if Rupert would be suitable for the next album. But it worked out okay, and that was it.'

CHAPTER FOURTEEN

ALL OF THE GIFTS ARE NOW MELTED OR DEAD

With recording scheduled across a few weeks in August 1976, Rupert Holmes was duly engaged to produce 'Big Beat', and the Maels have lived with the consequences ever since. The sessions themselves were good-natured, while Ron and Russell's own spirits soared as word got around that they were recording at Mediasound, and the first fans began appearing outside the studio hoping for autographs and a chat. Hilly Michaels recalled, 'Despite the lack of attention Sparks was receiving in the States, every time we walked along the streets in New York City Ron and Russell were instantly recognised and approached several times a day.'

They did not change their habits, however. Meals were generally taken at Serendipity, an uptown restaurant that thoroughly merited its name, while a typical order at lunch was an iced tea with Sweet-n-low, and a low-fat pastry. And, if a fan or two should join them at their table, they would natter away like old friends.

Only as 'Big Beat' neared completion did its faults seem to become apparent. 'So much of a record has to do with the circumstances surrounding it,' Ron said a decade or so later. 'There was no atmosphere around "Big Beat". That was really a miserable time for us. I don't know if it's for musical reasons or what, but I don't especially like that album. The demos we did with Mick Ronson were so much better than the finished thing. While Rupert Holmes might be really good for someone like Barbra Streisand, I don't think he's a rock'n'roll producer.'

Sal Maida nods in assent. 'I always thought Rupert Holmes was a weird choice for a big American hard-rock record. I think, for the most part, it was a pretty good experience; it seems in recent times to have got its due, that record. I don't think it's Ron and Russell's favourite record, but I talked to Russell [in 2008] and he said that when they worked it up for the London shows they really fell in love with the songs again, and they were like "Yeah, it was great".

'But the production was weird. It was almost as if they squashed the guitars. They should have been really big, but things hadn't worked out too well in the studio with Jeff, and in the final mix the guitars were kind of squashed down and lost.'

Hilly Michaels, too, agreed that the production let the record down badly. 'Rupert Holmes may have overdone it a bit with the super-compressed drum sounds, and he could and should have used a trifle more room sound on my drums. I'd love to go in and re-mix that record, and show off just how awesome it really is. It was way ahead of its time, I think.

'But I still like the record a lot. "Big Beat" is an intense, hard-edged, beefy record, and the entire LP is devoid of any lukewarm tracks. Every single song is very catchy, and sung and played with such unique passion and energy. I know it's not a typical Sparks-sounding record but the thing just rocks and rocks.

'I'm very proud of my drumming on that LP and I think Ronnie wrote his heart out for it. I'm well aware that Ron and Russell like to throw musical curve balls all the time, and that "Big Beat" was only one of the many throws, but I'm so partial, and so happy how it turned out. I think it's a very underrated record.'

'Rupert was, in retrospect, the wrong choice,' Joseph Fleury concluded. 'He tried to make a rock'n'roll record and it just didn't work. But it wasn't only because of Rupert that things came out as they did. We were having trouble on a personal level as well. John Hewlett refused to come out to the States with us – the only contact we ever had with him was by telephone, and that was rare. We'd call him up and leave a message; he never returned a call. He even appointed a new assistant, Bill Siddons, to stand in for him in the States, he seemed that disinterested.'

He did indeed. Asked for his own opinion of 'Big Beat' and the circumstances that surrounded it, Hewlett sniffed, 'They went for a harder, rock sound. It was a contrived attempt by producer Rupert Holmes to... well, it was "Rupert's a big name", it was swanning around New York. I think the best comparison is Bob Ezrin and Alice Cooper, but with Sparks it was just a bunch of session musicians in New York....'

With the record complete, the Maels decided to rebuild the band more or less from scratch. Jeff Salen was let go, and Sal Maida had already declared that he intended to remain in New York and see out the last days of Milk'n'Cookies. But Hilly Michaels was retained, 'and we went on a guitarist hunt across New York City. We ended up jamming with Jimmy McCallister at some loft he was in that had a makeshift rehearsal room. He was no Mick Ronson or Jeff Salen, but Ron and Russell liked him a lot as a rhythm guitarist. He just sounded steady, precise, a quick learner, a hell of a nice, laid-back, good sense of humour kind of guy. I think Jim was inducted into the band the very next day. Ron and Russell really thought he'd fit in well.'

From New York, the band's base switched back to Los Angeles, where, with Michaels and McCallister installed in the Sunset Marquis Hotel, the hunt was launched for a lead guitarist.

A lot of time was spent auditioning; a lot of time was spent watching new bands. Los Angeles, just like New York, was experiencing what the music critics would soon be calling a grassroots renaissance, a new generation of bands coming out of the clubs and gutters of the city to rephrase the lessons they'd learned during their own musical upbringing. A bunch of kids who'd spent their time dancing to the latest British glam imports at Rodney Bingenheimer's English Disco, or hanging around outside the Riot House, they too would ultimately be saddled with the punk-or-thereabouts epithet. Where things might get interesting, the Maels decided, was if you tried to blend the Los Angeles version of that term with its New York counterpart. Even under the same brand name, the ensuing clash could be startling.

Right now, the biggest local band in Los Angeles was the Runaways, a teenage all-girl band launched by the ever-entrepreneurial veteran Kim Fowley, newly signed to Mercury Records and about to head off on their first nationwide tour. Fowley already knew who would replace them at the top of the local tree, an all-teenage boy band called the Quick whose drummer, Danny Benair, had been first in line for tickets when Sparks played Santa Monica the previous year and whose influence had rubbed off on his band-mates too.

'It was so stupid of me,' songwriter and guitarist Steve Hufsteter lamented. 'Of all the bands to copy! If I'd decided to copy Led Zeppelin, we would have been huge. But I was such a huge fan of Sparks.'

But it was the older, 'Kimono My House'/'Propaganda' era Sparks that intrigued him. 'Indiscreet' had not made nearly as great an impression on him and, though he had yet to hear a note of the new music, he doubted whether 'Big Beat' would either. 'I just didn't like where their music was going anymore, and I badly wanted to do something that brought the sound of their first few records back.' It was, he told journalist Mark Spitz, 'just a misunderstood, carried-away fan thing.'

Ron and Russell Mael would not fall into that category. Benair had already tried to put his band onto their radar when he marched up to John Hewlett at the Hyatt House the previous year, and handed him a copy of the band's first demo tape. They never heard back from him. A year later, however, the Quick could not be ignored.

Produced by Earle Mankey ('that Sparks connection again,' laughed Benair. 'We also tried

SPARKS

Luke Zamperini, Hilly Boy Michaels, Ron Mael, Russell Mael, David Swanson, Jim McAllister.

to get James Lowe'), the Quick's album 'Mondo Deco' was released at much the same time as 'Big Beat' and the Sparks comparisons were the first thing from every critic's pen.

'One can hardly imagine a more straightforward copy of Russell Mael's distinctive vocal style,' wrote *Rolling Stone*'s Teri Morris, but the most damning word was left to Robert Hilburn, the king of local Los Angeles journalists. He wrapped the two albums into one review, and, shuddered Benair, 'basically said that we're everything that's good, and that Sparks have let themselves down and are everything that's not good. So the article is saying, we've picked up where they left off and I'm thinking "Oh boy", because I think Sparks are brilliant. That's the last thing I want!' A few nights later, Ron and Russell were spotted in the audience at a Quick live show at the Starwood. They left without saying a word. 'I think they hated us.' But perhaps they did have the last laugh.

'With my last band, the Three O'Clock, I ended up playing on some bills with Sparks in 1982 and 1983, where they were sort of mean. So I often wondered, maybe they know someone from the Quick is in this band. We never got soundchecks from them. It was ridiculous; we played a San Francisco gig with them, then we played the Country Club in the San Fernando Valley, and literally, it was five minutes to eight, the doors would be opening at eight and they're just coming off the stage after soundchecking for two hours. Their manager Joseph Fleury was a wonderful guy, I loved him, but it's the worst thing that can happen to a support act.'

The Quick were not the only local band with an eye for the Sparks sound. The Cigarettes, the duo of John Clancy and future Fear mainstay Philo Cramer masquerading as an art-drenched quartet, had the 'Kimono My House' sound down to a tee as well. In fact, their debut single 'Gimme Cigarettes' now regularly appears on underground Sparks rarities collections (usually under the title 'Cigarettes And Politics'), labelled as an authentic period out-take.

Hilly Michaels' happiest memories of this time, however, revolved not around the continuing search for musicians, but the manner in which the Maels lived their lives. Every day, they would descend upon their old haunt at the Farmers Market on Third and Fairfax, where the iced tea could be accompanied by a bagel with ricotta cheese on the side. 'We'd sit and chat,' Michaels laughed, 'and see who could peel the skin off a bagel the best, and who had the nicest-shaped bagel left over. We would never eat the doughy part because of the calories and, to this day, I still peel my bagels the way Ron and Russell showed me.'

The auditions continued. They unearthed lead guitarist Luke Zamperini, but the ongoing lack of a bassist finally forced them to contact a player they had actually turned down while in New York, David Swanson. He was flown to Los Angeles and launched, said Hilly Michaels, into 'an intensive rehearsing schedule, until we all felt great about the band. The music rocked, and I had the most fun time in my life. We played and tackled the old favourites with an intense, frenetic energy and we sounded awesome. The "Big Beat" era was a lot about breaking the band in the US,' he reminds us, and nobody had any doubt that it would...until they got out on the road.

Before the tour began, Russell counselled, 'Our new stage act will revolve mainly around the songs. We're staying away from props and such because we feel now that we have enough theatricality just in the way we are naturally.' The result would be a stripped-down act, with its emphasis on reclaiming the strength and energy that the album perhaps lacked.

Sparks' new configuration made their live debut opening for Boston in Santa Barbara on 6th November 1976, with the headliners already riding the crest of the wave unleashed by their recently released self-titled debut album. And when Sparks' performance lacked the vitality and dynamism it had had in rehearsal, they initially put it down to first night nerves. A couple of days, and concerts, later, however, it became clear that the problems were deeper-rooted than that.

Hilly Michaels: 'David was a good bass player, but it was just not a good match, me and David as a rhythm section trying to reproduce the feel and energy of the "Big Beat" record live.' After one more desultory show, Michaels took his concerns to the Maels. 'I said to Ron and

Biography

Ron Mael
Isolationism.

Russell
Yeah. That's exactly it. England's really a small town, in many ways quaint, and open to the strangest forms of music. After our initial success with "This Town" and *Kimono*, which was fabulous…

Ron
The songs started getting weirder and weirder. We felt, well, if *that*

Ron   Russell

worked, and it's weird, wait'll they hear *this*.

Russell
You get locked up, really, in your own little world—recording and touring without a break to think. You're

always
and tl
idea c
our ta
clear
Colu

Ron
We r
that
sinc

Rus
The
rele
mo
thi
all
di
lo
we

R
B

R
T
r
t

♪PARKS

Biography

Ron
With less frenzy.

Russell
Yes. It's obvious, like rock should be, and more accessible than anything we've ever done before. Our stage act will revolve mainly around the new songs. We're staying away from props and such because we feel now that we have enough theatricality just in the way we are naturally.

Some not-so-hard facts about the Mael Bros.

AGE: Ron-28; Russell-23
BORN & RAISED: In Los Angeles
LIKES: Russell — Good restaurants; Girls; Shopping around the world for clothes; Movies; The New York Yankees.
Ron — Orson Welles; American International pictures; Any film made on a budget of less than $30,000; The New York Yankees.

Russell, we have to do something about the bass or the lack of it and get Sal back. David burst into my motel room back in Hollywood on the verge of tears, asking me why I was all about Sal and not him. He was so distraught. I felt so sorry for him, but I felt like I was having to play extra hard and furious, just to make up for him.'

'Hilly was just losing his mind,' Maida laughed. 'Ron and Russell weren't happy, so I got the call from Bill Siddons, "Do you want to come out and do this tour with us, this guy's not

147

working out," so I was... okay.' He flew out to Los Angeles, was installed in the Tropicana and, when he turned up at the rehearsal studio that first day, Michaels recalls, 'We all lit up. I felt like a huge weight had been lifted off me. You can't lose as a drummer when Sal Maida is playing with you. Other than Dan Hartman [with whom Michaels has also worked], Sal was my all-time favourite bass player. We had a certain simpatico

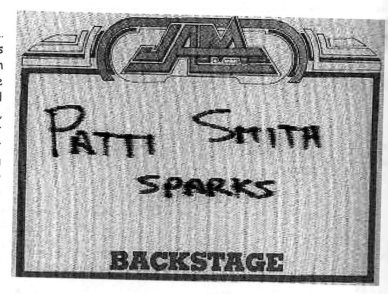

together. He just knows how to hammer the foundation of the rhythm section to the floor.'

What Maida didn't know was that he was about to be plunged into what remains one of the most ill-judged (although, at the time, most welcomed) developments yet in the Maels' career, their movie debut.

'I asked Bill Siddons what the first gig was, and he said it was for a movie. So we went out to Magic Mountain and I think it took two days to film two minutes.'

Neither was it a low-rent indie project, or some high-class art-house effort, the celluloid fate of so many bands who dare to step into cinema land. The film Siddons had wangled the group into was Hollywood's latest monster-budget disaster movie, *Rollercoaster*.

Sparks were not director James Goldstone and his backers' first choice; according to reports in the teenybopper press, the Bay City Rollers were originally scheduled to appear before manager Tam Paton decided that his tartan-clad Jook clones could probably find a more suitable vehicle for their big-screen debut. Sparks stepped into the breach, lip-synching furiously before an invited audience in what was destined to be a short interlude, totally irrelevant to the movie's plot, in which a blackmailer sets out to blow up a rollercoaster, and George Segal tries to stop him.

'Yes,' Russell confessed a few years later, 'you did see Sparks performing "Big Boy" and "Fill 'er Up" in the film *Rollercoaster* during your last airplane trip. And no, we didn't know that the film was going to turn out like that. *Rollercoaster* proves that you have to be continually careful about what you do. You never know what's going to last and what's going to fall by the wayside – and man, does that last!'

Pre-release, the Hollywood buzz was that *Rollercoaster* would become the new *Jaws* that the industry had been waiting for, $12 million-worth of action and special effects that audiences would die for. Instead it nosedived, and Sparks' dreams of cinematic success nosedived with it.

'It was about being in a film during a period when our band was just directionless,' Russell confessed later. 'Unfortunately, the film seems to get played on every airplane and in every country round the world, year after year. So we get "Oh, you're the guys from *Rollercoaster*." It's a shame that, as a document of Sparks, that has to be the one that keeps resurfacing, and we can't get away from it.'

But worse was to follow. Back on the road, the band found themselves having to contend with what Michaels promptly dubbed 'the road manager from hell'.

Jim Seiter was old-chool California music industry. Back in the Sixties, he was an integral

Columbia Records
Press and Public Information
51 W. 52nd St. New York 100
1801 Century Park West, Los Angeles
Telephone: (212) 975 - 4321
(213) 856 - 4770

part of the Byrds camp, as they made the transformation away from their Beefeaters days via a fateful meeting with Terry Melcher. Seiter was a key player in some of the most exciting and influential moments in Californian rock history, and where was he now? Driving bands he'd barely heard of back and forth across the country.

'He was just a bitter guy that had been around and now he was stuck with us,' reasoned

Maida. 'And it wasn't so much that he was stuck with us personally – it would have been the same with anyone – it was that he had to be in a car being a tour manger driving people around after being a player in the Sixties. He got that job through Bill Siddons, so there was this kind of Los Angeles Sixties situation going on and it was completely the wrong combination for Sparks. It was a different world.'

'We didn't get along with him,' Michaels continued, 'and he didn't like us. In fact, he detested us. It was unreal, because it made getting what we required almost impossible. We'd get to a hotel on the road, and he would toss our room keys at us saying 'here', 'here', 'you' and 'your's', throwing them at us. We were beside ourselves with him working with us, and our sound man wasn't much nicer, either. But… we prevailed, kept a cool head and would vent to each other about our treatment by the people who were supposed to look after our well-being.

'It was so bizarre a circumstance to deal with. Ron and Russell handled the situation so diplomatically and coolly. I was very impressed with their restraint from clobbering this guy. It was a totally surreal situation, because they were so frustrated. I recall feeling bad for the way things were being handled. Hewlett was hell-bent on breaking Sparks in the US, but we felt like we were being thrown to the wolves, and Ron and Russell just didn't know how to overcome being treated so disrespectfully.'

Matters were worsened by the tour itself. Sparks had encountered their fair share of unsuitble tour billings in the past – gigs with Dr Hook and the Medicine Show stuck in Ian Hampton's mind, for example – while this outing would include a night spent opening for the prog band Nektar at the Capitol Theatre in Passaic, New Jersey, on 27th November. But which genius was it that thought Sparks could ever share an audience, or anything else for that matter, with the Patti Smith Group as they toured America on the back of their recently released 'Radio Ethiopia' album?

Michaels remains astonished by the pairing, even today. 'Sparks and Patti Smith on the same bill for a good dozen shows? Fellini couldn't have thought up anything that weird. It was like a grandiose travelling musical oddities tour for a while.'

Smith's guitarist Ivan Kral admitted, 'I'm embarrassed to say that I don't remember much about Sparks, except I thought they were original and nice guys.' But Michaels insists, 'there was a lot of friction between the Patti Smith Group and us.' Some nights, Sparks weren't even granted a soundcheck before the doors opened, but they retaliated, he recalls proudly, by blowing Smith off stage as often as they could.

'Sometimes they were so intimidated by the response and applause from the audience for us… two or three encores… that they would intentionally wait and wait until the excitement from our show had subsided before they'd dare take the stage. Thirty-five or forty minutes some nights. Ha! We sounded up, peppy and supercharged, they sounded dark and broody. I respect her artistry but haven't listened to her music since touring with her.'

The one concession made to the distinctly different audiences that the two bands could expect to attract was the agreement to alternate the headline slot. Michaels continued, 'Depending on the city, either she or we would open first. We had our pockets of places where we were stronger, where the crowd went absolutely wild when we took the stage, and Patti had hers.'

In Montreal, Canada, a solidly Sparks-loving crowd was making so much noise before the show started that Smith, having agreed to open that evening, wouldn't even come out of her dressing room, she was so wary about going out on stage. At the Masonic Auditorium in Detroit on 12th December, on the other hand, a fanatically devoted Smith audience greeted Sparks' arrival on stage with a hail of abuse that swiftly graduated to flying bottles.

It was inevitable that somebody was going to get hurt, and sure enough, they did.

'A beer bottle was tossed from the audience,' Michaels recalled. 'It was meant for Russell, but it split my head open above the left eye, during our last crescendo note being played at the

end of the set. I couldn't see the blood pouring down my face onto my snare drum until that last chord was hit, but then the bright lights went on. I remember Russell looking over at me with a kind of astonished look on his face after the song stopped. My snare drum was a pool of blood. I looked at it and almost fainted. I was rushed to hospital, but luckily I only suffered minor concussion and had to wear a couple of butterfly-stitch bandages for a week or so.'

Another night, Michaels confessed, brought one of the scariest experiences of his entire onstage life. Again they faced a loyal Patti Smith crowd, and as they ran out on to the stage, the entire venue erupted into a chorus of catcalls. 'There was this thunderous "Boooooooo" resonating from over three thousand people just as we were getting ready to start. We were all a bit paralysed by that! But we ignored it and, by the end of the set, had won over about half the theatre. But it was an uphill struggle from the outset, and we had to perform our asses off for every single show.' It was with some relief that the two bands finally parted company following a show on 19th December at Seneca College in Toronto – Sparks territory once again.

Still, tempers were beginning to fray. Early in the tour, Ron had taken to smashing his piano stool to pieces during the closing 'Big Boy'. Maida laughed, 'Here's Ronnie doing that whole act, tilting his head and really being immobile and then, all of a sudden, right at the end of "Big Boy", he's standing up, grabbing his piano bench and smashing it all over the place, just going nuts.'

It was an ironic gesture at first, but as the tour went on, it became a crucial one as well. He was venting. And it wasn't always the piano stool that came off the worst.

'One night in Chicago, we were playing on a really high stage. It was the end of "Big Boy" and Ronnie went to smash the bench and one of the legs came off in his hand. The entire rest of the bench went flying off the stage and, with his adrenalin, he jumped off the stage to continue smashing it. He landed and fucked up his leg, and then the police moved in. They thought he was just some fan, so they were grabbing at him and we were yelling "No, no, he's part of the show!"'

'Poor Ron,' Michaels sympathised. 'He damaged his leg so bad that we took all the canned sodas and beers out of a new plastic garbage container and he stuck his entire bruised and bloody leg into the ice-filled can. We were very worried about him hurting himself whilst going nutzoid on piano benches.'

Having recovered, Ron quickly returned to his auto-destructive ways. Playing the Bottom Line in New York City, twice a night for two nights across 21st and 22nd December 1976, Ron was so engrossed in demolishing his stool that he lost his balance and landed on the one table in front of the stage where the Columbia VIPs were seated. Everything on the table – drinks, food, ashtrays, the lot – went flying.

Sparks' 1976 American tour finally wound down with a New Year's Eve bash at the Santa Monica Civic Centre. Flo and Eddie and a new metal act called Van Halen, who stepped in at the last minute for the scheduled Ramones, opened the show; Ron closed it by smashing his piano stool once again – and only a handful of sharp-eyed observers seem to have noticed that he was breaking much the same piece of furniture every night, then having his roadies tape it back together for the following evening.

Remaining in Los Angeles, the Maels began looking towards the future. Across the world, 'Big Beat' had flopped resoundingly, and both record and live reviews were harsh. Hilly Michaels recalled, 'The un-Godly abuse we were taking was diabolical and deflating. I was kind of in a mild state of shock, myself. I thought and viewed Sparks as the eighth wonder of the world, and just couldn't figure out why everyone was so mean to us.

'I just couldn't make sense out of it. I thought at the time that everyone loved Sparks and everything. That they were a band saying "C'mon everyone lighten up, laugh and have a good time here." But Ron and Russell weathered the whole thing rather well' – and so did Columbia. The label was already talking about the band's next album, all the more excitedly now that the Maels' commitment to Island in Europe was over and they could sign with the label worldwide.

There was some thought given to releasing a live album, using a recording made at the Cleveland Agora Ballroom on 13th December 1976 that captured the band in especially fiery form. Ron and Russell, however, were swift to scupper that notion. The show might have been great, but the band wasn't perfect and they had no intention of preserving that imperfection on vinyl.

'As I remember it,' said Maida, 'Ron and Russell were disillusioned with Luke, so they wanted to change the band around.' Zamperini departed, quickly followed by Michaels and Jimmy McCallister as funds ran out and it became impractical to keep them on the payroll any longer. Both returned to New York. Maida, however, stayed on, living at the Tropicana Hotel and, almost every day, joining the Maels as they began planning the next record.

There was talk of teaming up with Bob Ezrin, the Canadian producer whose widescreen vision had been responsible for some of the most distinctive-sounding records of the past few years, amongst them Lou Reed's 'Berlin', Kiss's 'Destroyer', Peter Gabriel's debut outing and a string of Alice Cooper albums. That plan, unfortunately, fell by the wayside following a meeting at which the Maels played him their latest batch of songs. The ever-loyal Joseph Fleury described the new material as 'very varied and bizarre'. Ezrin, however, listened impatiently, then turned around and said 'Okay, now play me your A-sides.'

That was the end of that, and the end of Maida's time with the band as well. 'The whole thing was dissolved, they couldn't afford the expense any more, and I went back to New York too.'

Sparks were at an impasse. '"Big Beat" had been a stiff, sales-wise, which shook our confidence a bit,' confessed Ron. Bob Ezrin dented it even further. For the first time in their career together, the Maels did not know what to do, and hindsight suggests they should have waited until they did. Instead, they allowed Columbia to take up the reins and, when it was suggested that they permit the label bigwigs to do what they did best – that is, build a record from the ground up and create a product that they knew would sell – the Maels simply agreed.

The Maels would write and sing the songs, as usual. But the album that Columbia decreed should be called 'Introducing Sparks' would be introducing a very different act to any that the band's old fans might recognise. Only the title seemed at all characteristically off-kilter, as Russell later acknowledged. 'We just felt it *apropos* to title our seventh album "Introducing Sparks". Most bands don't name their seventh album "Introducing...". That's probably what appealed to us. In fact, most bands don't even have a seventh album!'

It wouldn't have a conventional cover, either, just two matching portraits of the brothers, shot and coloured in the manner of an old-style matinée idol's latest waxing. Russell: 'We liked the idea of there actually being no front or back cover, that they were in fact the same image but with a different one of us on each side. We liked the idea that in some shops, Ron would be on the front cover, while in others I would be on the front.'

But such a sleeve was never going to float at a time when the western world was turning punk rock, and, if any indication of the record's dismal sales performance is needed, it's the fact that the limited-edition red vinyl pressing was, for many years, more common than the 'regular' black, meaning that the album barely even sold out of its first short pressing.

They were completely stranded. Joseph Fleury and Bill Siddons continued to do what they could, but everything had ground to a halt.

Russell: 'Bill was kind of a temporary situation, I believe he was going to be sharing the duties with Hewlett for America, but we were only with him for a short period of time, and then Joseph took over.' John Hewlett was still officially the band's manager but, for all other intents and purposes, the kid Sparks first met in a record store in New York City, back before they were anything, was now in total control of their destiny. He was also, Russell admitted, probably the only person left who actually cared enough to do the job properly.

'Joseph was always there, always around,' said Hilly Michaels. 'He was such a positive, passionate fellow, not to mention one of the nicest guys in the music business I'd ever worked with.' Whether he was cut out for the vicious thrust of music-industry management was an issue they would deal with later. For now, it was enough simply to have one person whose faith in what the Maels had to do never wavered.

'The Columbia period was interesting,' Fleury explained, 'because there were a few people there who really cared about Sparks, but a lot more who didn't even know they were on the label. We used to sit around and ask each other what we had to do to be noticed, but the problem was that the people at the label who would really have been able to get things done were either busy elsewhere or were chasing projects of their own.'

He also acknowledged that Sparks in 1977 were completely out of their depth. It was the era of new wave, in full effect in the UK, but beginning to make inroads in America as well. Fleury himself was working with two other bands, the still-fighting Milk'n'Cookies – reconvened after Ian North fled to England to work with Martin Gordon in a new band called Ian's Radio – and a New York group, the Mumps. He and Hewlett were also courting a Los Angeles band, the Dickies, whose front man Leonard Philips once contributed keyboards to an early Quick demo (small world!), while Fleury's dream of establishing his own label was finally coming to fruition with a solo EP by Earle Mankey. 'Mau Mau' was released on the Bomp Exhibit J label, set up through fellow former Halfnelson supporter Greg Shaw's Bomp label.

'There was a lot going on during that period, and it was hard sometimes to see where Sparks fit in with it all,' Fleury admitted. 'If "Big Beat" had taken off, it would have been very different, they would have become accepted as part of the new scene, but it didn't and I think everybody just panicked.'

Columbia took over completely. Rather than even attempt to follow up 'Big Beat', stylistically or sonically, the label announced that the next album would be recorded with a strict line-up of seasoned session men, while the Maels' attempt to lessen that shock by at least picking a producer they admired came to an end with Ezrin's rejection.

SPARKS

Instead, Columbia gave the job to the band's A&R man, Terry Powell. He would co-produce the record with the Maels and, no matter how subdued Ron and Russell might have been feeling as they sat and listened to their new record taking shape, the only consolation (in the most ironic sense, of course) was that the session players weren't any happier.

A stellar line-up gathered to record 'Introducing Sparks'. Canadian keyboard player David Foster, jazz guitarist Lee Ritenour, harmonica player Ben Benay, pianist Alan Broadbent, bassist Mike Porcaro – there might not have been a household name in sight, but nobody could doubt the sheer wealth of talent gathered together in Larrabee Sound Studios in Universal City. So why was there so much complaining going on?

'Those guys were getting a quarter of a million dollars a year,' said Ron, 'and they bitched constantly. Most of our songs aren't three chords… [but] they reckoned they couldn't play in the keys we wanted them to, or said things like "wouldn't it be better to use a sax instead of a guitar", things like that. It was a joke.' *Rolling Stone*'s review of the finished record bore out his remarks. It was 'as if each musician were waiting for someone else to take the lead,' yawned writer Charley Walters. But no-one ever did.

'I'd never do it again,' Ron pledged. 'They are a totally different breed than I was used to working with, and it's a totally different idea of what music is to me. These people are incredibly crafted, but there's absolutely no feeling or personality in anything they're doing. After fifty minutes of recording everybody said, "I gotta take a break because of the Union." By the end of the sessions, the Maels were so downhearted that, if they'd been given the opportunity to scrap the whole thing and start again, they'd have grasped it with all four arms. Unfortunately, Columbia had spent huge sums of money hiring the *crème de la crème* to make the record. They weren't going to spend more to make it better.

155

The label did stump up for a couple of videos, stylish shoots to accompany the album's first two projected singles in America, 'Forever Young' and 'Occupation' (oddly, 'A Big Surprise' was the choice of 45 for the UK), but even they seemed somehow bland as Russell stood in jeans, clip-on earrings and check shirt and Ron barely snarled at the camera once. The first single bombed, the second was abandoned and the videos have scarcely been seen since.

There were no live concerts to help promote the record, precious few interviews and no television appearances. Factor in that kitsch sleeve, and 'Introducing Sparks' appeared just about as relevant as the Fifties. As the year rolled on, so it became increasingly obvious that any band whose fame pre-dated the punk explosion needed to pull something really special out of the hat if they wanted to make any kind of impact. Precious few of them succeeded – of Sparks' own early Seventies contemporaries, only David Bowie seemed to have an inkling of what was happening, and he responded with a brace of albums, 'Low' and "Heroes", that ensured that he would live to fight another day.

But almost everybody else was just washed away, particularly those who had nothing more with which to counter the new insurgency than a clutch of ballads, some overwrought Beach Boys harmonies and just one song that even glanced towards the eccentric fields of old, the Cossack fiddle-led 'Goofing Off'.

Later in Sparks' career, 'Introducing Sparks' would become one of those albums that simply demanded rediscovery, and which would, ultimately, receive it. But even the compact-disc revolution ignored 'Introducing Sparks' until its thirtieth anniversary in 2007, when the Maels re-released it on their own Lil' Beethoven label.

When future Sparks drummer Tammy Glover singles out its closing track, 'Those Mysteries', as one of the songs that she regards as 'quintessential Sparks, quintessential Ron', she does so with the benefit of over 30 years of hindsight. It is quintessential Sparks, quintessential Ron, an unending series of unanswerable questions that, ultimately, can only be shrugged off with no answer at all. In 1977, however, you needed to wade through a great deal of less alluring music in order to reach that final track and, at that time, people simply didn't have the patience.

When more than one reviewer intimated that Sparks truly were washed up, very few dissenting voices were heard. How wrong could they be?

CHAPTER FIFTEEN

SOFT PASSAGES CAN GET YOU INTO TROUBLE

Giorgio Moroder and Pete Bellotte had been quietly operating out of their Musicland Studios, in Munich, since the early Seventies, but made very little impact outside Germany until the end of 1975. True, they had written the smash-hit 'Son Of My Father' for Chicory Tip, and Moroder had taken his own version of the song into the American charts in 1972, but apart from two further British chart entries for the outlandishly-clad Maidstone-based band, 'What's Your Name?' and 'Good Grief, Christina', further success eluded them until they teamed up with American soul singer Donna Summer. Having scored a Dutch monster with 'The Hostage', the trio went on to enjoy a world-wide hit with 'Love To Love You Baby', a lush production featuring wall-to-wall orgasms set to a gentle disco beat and spread out across one entire side of Summer's latest album.

A year of indifferent form followed, but summer 1977 saw the Musicland sound really come into its own with the release of 'I Feel Love', a groundbreaking recording that featured Summer's breathy vocals over a repetitive and hypnotic synthesiser pattern. The European disco scene never looked back.

This new sound might have revolutionised the world of dance music, but, aside from David Bowie and Iggy Pop, no established rock artists seemed to have considered applying the possibilities it offered in the rock'n'roll arena. So, when the Maels first conceived of working with Moroder, purely on the strength of hearing 'I Feel Love', they found themselves in a situation where they were free from any preconceptions of what would happen, simply because 'no-one had any idea of what a disco producer working with an eccentric rock band would end up sounding like.'

Russell Mael: 'After "Introducing Sparks", we were doing as we do every so often, just journeying to find some new kind of context in which to place what we're doing. We were really excited about "I Feel Love" – we'd become bored with working with bands, thinking we'd tapped out all we could at that particular point from the traditional band context and format. We wanted "o try some other approach and, coincidentally, we'd heard 'I Feel Love" and thought that this was something amazing, and that it might be interesting for us to see if there would be a way to put Ron's songwriting and lyrics, and my singing, into a completely different framework than we'd been working in the past. So, at some point during that period we contacted Giorgio.'

Actually, he corrected himself, that wasn't quite true. Being interviewed for a German magazine in Los Angeles one day, the brothers mentioned that their next project would see them working with Giorgio Moroder. "We told the journalist this, and we were caught in a lie because, of course, of all the people living in Los Angeles, she happened to be close friends with Giorgio and she was… "Oh really?" But she was instrumental in helping us to reach him, and he was really keen to work with us too, because he'd not worked with a proper band and a band sensibility. So he was up for the challenge. He thought it would be interesting for him to branch out in another area. It was a really interesting collaboration.

'Working with Giorgio opened up new ideas for us. For one thing, it showed we weren't tied to the guitar, bass and drum format, and it showed you could work in other ways, in a non-band context. Making that record also showed that you could use electronics and then, after that, you

157

IT COULD have been appropriately titled "Rock 'n' Roll People In A Disco World", after one of its tracks, but "Terminal Jive" does have a sophisticated ring that is entirely complementary to Sparks' current mood.

The album marks the second phase in the collaboration between Moroder and Sparks. They joined forces initially with the first new-age Sparks album, "Number One Song In Heaven", last year. Yet the news that the partnership was to be sustained was worrying. They had, after all, achieved what they set out to do with that album, which was to merge Moroder's unique Euro-discoism with the voices and songs of Sparks. What would be the point in sustaining the formula?

More than we could have hoped for, as it turns out. "Number One Song In Heaven" saw Ron and Russell Mael as rock 'n' roll people in a disco world, bowing to Moroder's superior experience and technique. "Terminal Jive" reverses the terms of the partnership and has Moroder playing in Sparks' court, applying his skill to the production of a rock album. It's an even more compelling venture than last year's.

It was essential that Moroder should display his versatility outside disco, and here he shows that his militaristic discipline can be applied to hard rock too, with his synths programmed to apply to traditional rock dynamics. The hard rock bands who've attempted to merge electronics into their music (e.g. the Skids) might take notice.

The guitar, well and truly condemned by Ron and Russell Mael last year ("Guitarists are jokes"), makes a comeback, and nowhere more effectively than on "Stereo", where it tumbles in behind a neat synthesizer line and gradually imposes its rude character on the track. The guitar playing on the album generally has a spareness and sympathy too often heard on rock albums.

Disco isn't dead, however, and certain disco identification marks are retained. The sharp rhythm of the drum is the heartbeat that Moroder feeds off, and his synthetic wall of sound is still there, though less prominent this time. The single, "When I'm With You", doesn't indicate the pattern of change on the new album, but it's the first track and the change only becomes evident as the album progresses, especially on the second side where rock becomes the dominant partner in the relationship.

The inclusion of the instrumental version of the single seems superfluous until placed in the overall context of the album. The album's intention is defined for the first time, with the hard rock guitar chopping ferociously alongside the mannered synthesizers.

"Terminal Jive" is given further depth via the quality of the Maels' songwriting, with additional credits occasionally to various members of the Moroder entourage. Still obsessed with adolescence, Ron and Russell emerge with a series of memorable pop tunes, any of which would make fine singles. "Young Girls", "Noisy Boys" and "Stereo", the three tracks that open side two, are persuasive arguments in favour of this being their best-ever album. — **HARRY DOHERTY.**

could go on to use electronics with guitars. So I think in terms of finding a new way to present our songs, he really opened up things for us.'

'Few people had worked with computers in pop music, and he taught us everything,' Ron continued. 'Also, we had been locked into three-minute songs and some of the things [we did with Moroder] were more extended. Even though we liked what he had done on that one song, "I Feel Love", we went in without really knowing what the end result would be. And those are the most fun albums to make.'

It was also, as Russell pointed out, 'one of the first times that what was considered a band was now just a duo.' In years to come, the likes of Soft Cell, Blancmange, Orchestral Manoeuvres In The Dark and the Pet Shop Boys turned that notion into a tradition, but when Sparks entered the studio with only session drummer Keith Forsey for company, there was very little in the mainstream with which they could be compared. 'Some people were confused. They'd say "Are you a band?" Because bands have more than

Ron and Russell: guitarists were last year's joke.

two people. It kind of opened the door, and said it was okay to not have to worry about being a five-piece band with drummers and bass players.'

Work on the next Sparks album had already commenced by the time Moroder was finally introduced to them. Two songs left over from the 'Introducing Sparks' sessions – 'Kidnap' and 'Keep Me' – had been earmarked as possibilities, while Ron and Russell had also recorded demos of a handful of new songs. They were going nowhere, however.

Among the multitude of unauthorised Sparks recordings floating around, or at least being referenced on the Internet, a set of six songs labelled the 'Arista Demos' is often regarded as representing Sparks' activities at this time. 'After Dark', 'Biggest Party In The World', 'B.R.E.A.T.H.E.', 'Get Laid', 'I Wish I Could Dance Like Black People Do' and 'Trying Day' were all possibilities for the next Sparks album and Russell acknowledged that Arista was one of the labels to which they were sent. Those same songs, however, went to more than one label before the Maels scrapped them.

Russell complained, 'That thing that's floating around the Internet, the "Arista Demos", from our point of view there was *never* an Arista demo. There were demos that we recorded at that period, but you could easily say they're the RCA demos, the Warner Brothers demos, the Capitol demos. For some reason, they've been given this mythological title of the "Arista Demos", but if someone's going to have illegal copies of some of our songs, they should at least credit the other 22 record labels that turned them down, and not just feature Arista.

'They're just a bunch of songs that... we do lots of songs, lots of times, and those particular ones just got out there. To be honest, we prefer people not having copies of things that weren't made to be heard at that time, so to elevate those songs to some higher plateau is weird for us. It's bizarre that there's six songs given such a place of honour. Come to my bedroom sometime, and I've got four hundred of the same sort of songs and some even better!'

Moroder certainly had no use for any of the songs which the Maels presented to him. Just two numbers, 'Academy Award Performance' and 'Beat The Clock' accompanied the duo when they set off for Germany, and they were radically altered before they made it on to vinyl. '"Beat The Clock" was basically like a Velvet Underground song when I wrote it at the piano,' Ron explained, 'and if you listen to it with that in mind, you can kind of tell. But what Giorgio did with it was amazing.

'Actually, "No. 1 In Heaven" was pretty exciting to make, because... This was the only album we've ever gone into with almost no material. Giorgio wrote the music for at least half the other songs. We tried to get as much of us as we could on [to the album], but at the same time, we wanted an outside influence. Obviously, we got it.'

The Maels struck up an immediate friendship with Moroder, signing to his production company and allowing him to take on the arduous task of securing Sparks a new recording deal.

It was not a swift process, as Russell recalled; 'I don't know how much time elapsed, but the album was recorded with Giorgio in 1978, and even at that point it wasn't on the public radar because it took a year before someone even in Giorgio's position could place the album.'

Three years had passed since Sparks were last considered a power in the land and their most recent deal, with Columbia, had ended ignominiously. On the face of it, there was no reason why any self-respecting record company man should even glance at them again, while the handful who did pop the cassette into the player were probably quick to take it out.

Russell: 'A&R people and record companies are often times way out of sync with what they think they can work with on a commercial level, and I know there was some head-scratching at that time because people understood Sparks to be a band, a rock band with a slightly different sensibility. So, when you throw into the mix that it's now not got guitars and it's icy electronic music....'

ite a lot

PIC: PAUL COX/LFI

Moroder to be — but Giorgio is crazy. He spent about a week in the studio with us asking every five minutes what we thought of his hair transplant!"

So is this the big romance for Sparks now they've backed the winner?

"Uh-uh," Russell shakes his head. "I doubt whether we'll be making another album after this next one with him."

What's the new one called? "Terminal Jive," he answers with a broad grin.

A couple of years back Russell Mael wouldn't have been able to put his tongue that firmly in his cheek.

It's still a risky move to team up any artist with Moroder, however. Even though the up-coming album was in the main written by the Maels, anything which Moroder and Bellotte handle inevitably, and indelibly, comes out the other end of the computer bearing the duo's own distinctive stamp.

MY TIME with Russell meandered on but apart from being encouraging in his new readjusted state of mind, his conversation never escaped from his politeness and determination to push product.

On leaving I got a tape of their excellent new single from "Terminal Jive" called "When I'm With You" — a deceptively twee sounding semi-ballad that grows into what is without doubt the finest moment of the reborn Sparks. Out have gone the over-the-top sound effects and self indulgence in their new electronic toys that occasionally took the edge from the last platter, and their sounds have become more paced and melodic.

It must remind the Mael Brothers of a song they once wrote . . .

ALBUMS TO BE WON

The music industry was still only just beginning to come to terms with punk rock, more than two years after it first began to make waves. Very few in the business would have been comfortable with the idea that the music scene might be about to undergo another radical change in direction, abandoning the napalm savagery of punk for the frozen vistas of electronica. True, there had always been room for the occasional novelty. 'I Feel Love' had proved that, and at almost exactly the same time as Moroder started sending the Sparks tape around, another continental disco producer, Cerrone, was tasting success with the similar-sounding 'Supernature'.

But at a time when the biggest records in the universe were the singles that had spun off the soundtrack to *Grease*, and Rod Stewart was wondering how sexy he was, the idea that

161

computers were about to take over wasn't simply preposterous, it was unimaginable.

Russell: 'And the irony is, there were more hit singles on that album than on any of the ones before it. It's kind of ironic that things like that happen, where people who supposedly know what they're doing, don't know maybe as much as they think, and they certainly don't give the public as much credit as they could, because the public obviously liked it.'

A stroke of good fortune finally came to Sparks' rescue. 'It really was one of those classic cases where the cassette of the album was sitting on some guy's desk in Germany, an A&R man at Virgin Records. He saw it had Sparks written on it, so he picked it up and played it, and thought it was amazing. Then Virgin in the UK picked us up, and that was it. So the long gap between "Introducing Sparks" and "No. 1 In Heaven"

wasn't a case of us twiddling our thumbs. It was this period of waiting to see where it was going to surface, and on what label...'

Once the deal was done, however, Richard Branson's rapidly-growing label really pulled out all the stops. Ron recalled; 'Virgin were really good to us, they really had faith in what we were doing. Our first single for them, "The No. 1 Song In Heaven", took eight weeks to get into the chart, but they never lost faith in it. They just kept pushing it all the way.'

They were aided in their quest by those recent, and quite remarkable, sea changes in the British market, most notably the breakthrough of Lene Lovich, a Detroit-born, Balkan-themed vocalist whose utterly idiosyncratic vocal style and eye for pop with a quirky rhythm would soon prompt even *Rolling Stone* to point out 'stylistic twists that even the chronically manipulative Sparks would admire...[while] a neo-yodel reminiscent of...Russell Mael further heightens [her] idiosyncrasies.'

Lovich's debut single, 'Lucky Number', was released in January 1979 and quickly pushed into the Top 30, at precisely the same time as another rock band, New York new-wavers Blondie, took their own bite at the dance floor cherry with 'Heart Of Glass'. Suddenly a musical movement that had not even been conceived six months earlier was making an impact on the charts. 'The No. 1 Song In Heaven' finally entered the UK Top 40 on 21st April 1979. It would be another month before the artist that many musical histories credit with having ignited this new wave, Gary Numan, made an appearance in the lower reaches of that same chart.

'The No. 1 Song In Heaven' ultimately climbed to Number 14, Sparks' biggest British hit since 'Never Turn Your Back On Mother Earth' five years earlier, and immediately, people who had written Sparks off just a year or so before started singing their praises once more. The record was indeed a true return to form – not only that, but it also finally afforded some genuine credibility to a white disco market whose main exponents to date had been the disciples of *Saturday Night Fever*.

In the wake of Sparks' success came a host of what looked suspiciously like imitators, some new to the scene, others who had seen in Sparks' astonishing renaissance ingredients which might help to revive their own careers. The week that Sparks appeared on *Top Of The*

Pops with their second Virgin single, 'Beat The Clock', the band was joined in the studio by two such purveyors of this hip new sound, M, with the hyper-excitable 'Pop Musik', and the reborn Mike Oldfield, with 'Guilty'. Gary Numan's 'Are "Friends" Electric?' was top of the charts, while the Flying Lizards' harshly computerised revision of the old R&B chest-beater 'Money' was lurking in the background. Behind them, the floodgates were strained to their limits.

Russell confessed to being impressed. 'I don't get much chance to check out the current British scene, but when I'm here I like to go out to gigs occasionally.' He was especially intrigued, he said, by the Human League, a starkly electronic band from the Midlands city of Sheffield who had themselves just signed with Virgin Records. 'They're a pretty special band,' he enthused, adding that electronica 'is more or less the future of rock.'

The Human League repaid the compliment two or three years later. 'There are some terrific records that get out, and that people just will not buy because of the image,' said singer Phil Oakey. 'For instance, Sparks. They were always one of my favourite groups, they had a man with a silly haircut and that was great for one record – see the man who looks like Hitler. But three records on, they're making really, really great singles and things, and lyrics that said a lot about what was going on, but no-one wanted to go into a record shop and buy something by a man who looked like Hitler. It was stupid.'

'They cited ['The No. 1 Song In Heaven'] as the thing that got them excited and focused on what they were doing, showed the possibilities,' Russell said proudly.

'Beat The Clock' made it to Number 10 on the UK chart, while the Maels also made their mark on one of the summer's most distinctive dance

records – composer Adrian Munsey came calling, recruiting Sparks to join him in creating a very tongue-in-cheek take on the disco movement in general, and New York dance supremos Chic in particular. Their 'Le Freak' had been one of the biggest hits of 1978 – now Ron and Russell were co-producing 'C'est Sheep', in which the characteristic vocal sounds of the New York dance band were replaced with those of... a flock of sheep.

Another day, another project, as Virgin introduced Sparks to Noel, a female singer for whom they had very high hopes. 'But that flopped as well,' Joseph Fleury mourned, possibly because nobody believed that Noel actually existed. They thought she was a pseudonymous Sparks. 'It's really a coincidence that Russell's tonal range was similar to hers,' Ron shrugged. 'A lot of people think there isn't a Noel.'

There was greater local success as the Maels went into the studio with the French band Bijou to produce their third album, 'Pas Dormir', but it was ironic that the one pairing the Maels were offered that might have paid serious dividends was one that was turned down.

'Stiff Records were really keen for Ron and Russell to record with Lene Lovich,' Joseph Fleury recalled. 'Lucky Number' was followed onto the chart by the equally captivating 'Say When', and Lovich made no secret of her love of Sparks. 'But either Virgin or Giorgio, or maybe both of them together, wouldn't go for it. Lene was on another record label, and they didn't want Ron and Russell moonlighting. Or maybe the money wasn't right. But it was a real disappointment when they passed on it.'

A third single, 'Tryouts For The Human Race' (a song about sperm, Ron acknowledged later, although the video depicted the brothers transforming into werewolves) made it to Number 45. Inexplicably, however, the album from which all three came (and of which 50 per cent was now available in 45rpm form), 'No. 1 In Heaven', did not do so well. One week at Number 73 was all Virgin had to show for their efforts, and that despite an advertising campaign that encompassed not only the conventional media but the run-off groove of 'Beat The Clock' and 'Tryouts' as well.

'Virgin told us they were going to try and push the album with the singles, so they asked us if there was any television personality who we particularly liked, who they could ask to put a little 'now buy the LP' message at the end of the single. We said Peter Cook, because we think he's really funny, but we never thought anything would come of it. But they got him! You can hear him at the end of the twelve-inch single.'

Virgin also released the latter two singles in coloured vinyl – and not just in the one single colour that most bands received. 'There must have been about ten different colours,' Russell marvelled. 'I don't know if we even got them all. I went into the office one day and they had them all up on the wall. It looked really good.'

Yet, while Sparks seemed to be cleaning up on the dance floors, the music critics were less certain about their rejuvenation. Indeed, while the media lavished praise on a newly emergent Scots band called Simple Minds, who openly acknowledge that their debut album 'Life In A Day' owed much to vintage Sparks, Sparks themselves were treated like pariahs.

'We went to England,' Ron shuddered, 'and had so much criticism thrown at us that it was terrible.' Just one question seemed to await them – 'why did you make a disco album?' And Sparks really didn't have an answer – 'We thought it had a disco element,' Ron admitted – but they'd hoped people would see past that, and applaud them for their true achievement. 'Nobody had made an album combining disco with other elements.'

The band's original British fan base, too, seemed perplexed. Disco music was the enemy in those days, a facile American import that seemed capable of reducing even talented performers into polyester-clad poseurs. No matter that the accompanying insurgence of new bands would swiftly transform disco into the effervescence of early Eighties' synthipop; neither the Rolling Stones nor Rod Stewart had yet been forgiven by their critics for 'going Disco', and Sparks weren't going to be allowed to get away with it, either.

Sparks off the old block

SPARKS
'No. 1 In Heaven'
(Virgin V2115)***½

NEVER MIND the artist, check the producer. Sparks started out in the early 70s as Halfnelson, with a flop album on Bearsville under the aegis of whizzo Todd Rundgren. Fractured pop, with lyrics that delighted in rubbing the listener's nose in the smartass verbals shrieked out by cutesy pie Russell Mael and mainly penned by hit Hitler-lookalike brother Ron.

The record did a little better when it was quickly withdrawn and reissued in a vastly inferior sleeve under the name of Sparks. At this time the band included future Beach Boys engineer and all-around maestro Earle Mankey, and things looked rosy till the rock mags got bored and a second elpee bombed . . . Sparks resurfaced in England while later, as Ron & Russell and a clutch of Anglo boys, including Martin Gordon (now ex-Radio Stars). The brothers came up with their single greatest statement in 'Kimono My House', an album of speedy yelps and crazi-spiralling guitars/pianos that predated punk in its energy, wry lyrical content and visual flash. Russ on TV pop shows wearing a shirt with no collar and knitted gloves donated by some lovelorn girl. A hit single, critical acclaim (press coverage, especially in NME, was over the top; they were treated as being Right Up There With The Greats). Lots of people hated 'em too, just to prove how much they mattered. After progressively less suc-sful singles and albums followed (you can't have minor hits after major hits: not allow-ed), Sparks did a couple of crashing failures for CBS. And now here they are again, as mimic as a chocolate eclair. A cunning ploy. No guitars.

Merely synthesizer, drums and voices. Cool graphics, coloured plastique, only six tracks on the album, the whole meringue schlepped into shape by Giorgio Moroder, emperor of respectable disco electronics and the diode behind Donna Summer. Think about it.

In one foul sweep, the brothers Mael dust off their faded image, revibe their stance and reassert their (supposed) importance in the scheme of things. Hey kidz, didn't we bridge the gap between glam and new wave? Sparks: the group you can eat between meals!

Now, with Moroder composing too, the Maels have the credibility to stick their noses in the air right along with Alternative TV, Pop Group, Pere Ubu and all those other dingbat bands who uneasily straddle the fence between avant-bored muzik and the big beat. Incompetence and lack of talent are easy to get away with when you don't have to play in tune, come up with real songs, or even be entertaining.

Dumb rock audiences don't know about the Nonesuch label, so baffle 'em with science! Ulp, so why does this album get 3½ stars?

Because Sparks can sing, can play, have found in Moroder the best filter for their ideas since Rundgren, and have exhibited a laudable talent for survival and staying on top of the heap (something I thought was quite beyond them these days). Ethereal vocals and shimmering tubes and wires come across like a mating of Popul Vuh and music for dancing fools. Yep, this lot do got riddum.

Naw, I don't think 'No. 1 In Heaven' will go down in history as one of the all-time hot 100 albums, but it's icy sharp and fresh. And don't weep for Sparks' rock phase, please. The Quick did it better, and look what happened to them . . . Ambiguity on the road to ruin.

'Beat The Clock' Sparks sing. They've done it, too. Whoosh! Don't mean a thing . . .

SANDY ROBERTSON

SPARKS

'"No. 1 In Heaven" was blasted by fans,' Russell recalled. 'They called us disco traitors, when in fact we saw it as a chance to work with Moroder who was into electronics with a neat beat like nobody else. It wasn't the pejorative "disco music" – call it "dance music" today and it's cool again!' And besides, although they may not have been traditional Sparks fans, the people who did understand 'No. 1 In Heaven' really understood it. 'England really picked up on that album.'

Sounds journalist Sandy Robertson was one of those who were quick to applaud the brothers' guile. Moroder, he declared, was 'the best filter for their ideas since [Todd] Rundgren', while Sparks themselves were credited with having 'exhibited a laudable talent for survival and staying on top of the heap (something I thought was quite beyond them these days). Ethereal vocals and shimmering tunes and wires come across like a mating of Popol Vuh and music for dancing fools.' He doubted, he said, whether 'No. 1 In Heaven' 'will go down in history as one of the all-time Hot 100 albums, but it's icy sharp and fresh. "Beat The Clock", Sparks sing. They've done it, too.'

'Moroder's finest achievement,' agreed another UK magazine, *Smash Hits*, 'must be in picking up the shambolic, played-out remains of the once-fine Sparks, plugging the dubious twosome into the mains and making them what the music business would term a "viable proposition" once more.'

Viable indeed. The brothers had long since decided that they would not tour the record, simply because there was no way of recreating it on stage at that time without hiring an army of supplementary keyboard players. Television appearances were also limited, not only by the similar lack of instrumentation but also by the paucity at that time of shows they could even appear on. But it didn't seem to matter and, with so grand a renaissance taking place around them, the band's old friends at Island Records lost no time in leaping aboard to remind people where Sparks had started.

Dinky Diamond recalled, 'Somebody at Island called me up and said they were thinking about putting together a "Best of Sparks" collection, and did I have any ideas? Obviously the singles had to go on there, but was there anything else I could think of that would interest people who maybe had all the other records? So immediately I thought of some of the tracks we hadn't released, like "Gone With The Wind" and "Tearing The Place Apart", and I think we came up with a pretty good package.'

In fact, it was when 'The Best Of Sparks' failed to chart that the Maels first understood the downside of their dalliance with dance music – the fact that disco audiences at that time had very little loyalty. They bought the beat, not the artist, and so long as what they wanted was available on a single – preferably a 12-inch, with the attendant extended mix – they had no time at all for albums. All but the very biggest names on the late-Seventies disco scene relied upon 45s to further their careers – their albums were essentially afterthoughts, and they were usually treated as such in the marketplace. Sparks, then were being treated with no more or less respect than anyone else who brought a neat beat to the dance floor that year – Hi-Tension, the Michael Zager Band, A Taste of Honey and Sylvester... Where Sparks and Virgin went wrong was in thinking that they might be treated any differently.

Nevertheless, the comparative failure of the 'No. 1 In Heaven' album, and the similar lack of success which greeted 'Tryouts For The Human Race', disheartened neither Virgin nor the Maels. A new Sparks album was already recorded and scheduled for release less than two months after the final single from 'No. 1 In Heaven' had run its course and, when the tapes for 'Terminal Jive' first arrived at the label, that confidence seemed very well founded.

A rave review in *Melody Maker* upped the ante even further, with writer Harry Doherty declaring that 'the three tracks that open side two ['Young Girls.' 'Noisy Boys' and 'Stereo'] are persuasive arguments in favour of this being their best-ever album. "No. 1 In Heaven" saw Ron and Russell Mael as rock'n'roll people in a disco world, bowing to Moroder's superior experience and technique. "Terminal Jive" reverses the terms of the partnership and has Moroder playing in Sparks' court. It's an even more compelling venture than last year's.'

Nobody doubted that the year's most unexpected comeback would continue unabated, and fears that the Maels would, as so often in the past, turn their backs on a winning formula and go shooting off on some absurd tangent instead, proved totally unjustified.

Yet closer examination of 'Terminal Jive' revealed it to be possibly the least Sparks-like album they had ever made, perhaps because there were only a couple of songs in sight that were written by Ron alone. The remainder of the set paired him with Moroder and members of his crew. He was not even permitted to play keyboards on the record, 'and as I've always seen myself as the keyboard player of Sparks, it was a little rough'.

Joseph Fleury: 'Ron was never happy about that arrangement, but you have to remember that Giorgio was very powerful at that time, and had done a lot for Sparks, so there was a feeling that he knew the market and what it wanted a lot better than we did. So when he said Ron's writing was sometimes a little on the crazy side, and that people needed something else, we thought "Well yeah, and you're the guy who can provide that, because you've had all these hits"... Forgetting that whenever Sparks have been the most successful, it's because Ron is completely off on his own tangent and not paying any attention to the market. We forgot that, but we were reminded of it very quickly, once the record came out.'

Although Moroder was nominally overseeing the sessions, the actual work was this time passed onto one of his protégés, German composer and keyboard player Harold Faltermeyer. Ron was not impressed. 'Harold could play better than me or Giorgio, but the songs were more heavily screened. We submitted twenty songs, and only one ['When I'm With You'] passed muster. And even then the middle eight was changed. I was hurt.'

Despite this, 'Terminal Jive' was to be a considerably more organic recording than its predecessor. Recording 'No. 1 In Heaven', Russell confessed, 'we got so into it that we suggested guitars were obsolete'. This time, however, 'There's a whole load of guitars and any other suitable instruments that came to hand. We considered what to use carefully, and decided that it would be ridiculous to close off everything but synthesiser possibilities. The big danger was making 'No. 1 In Heaven' Volume Two, and I think we've avoided that.'

In France, the single 'When I'm With You', one of Ron's most unashamedly romantic numbers, struck such a chord in the hearts of the populace that it sold 750,000 copies and topped the national charts for six weeks.

The video, director Millaney Grant's stylish slow dance through a roomful of glamorous mannequins (interspersed with the peculiar notion of Ron the ventriloquist putting words in Russell's mouth), was a genuinely classy affair that seemed barely to be off the television screens for a moment. Within one six-month period, the brothers appeared on some two dozen different French TV shows, while offers came flooding in for them to spread their magic further afield.

Lio was an 18-year-old singer, and one of the biggest selling female stars in France. According to Russell, her first album spawned three separate million-selling singles, but with Sparks threatening to eclipse even that achievement, her producers, the Belgian band Telex, had no qualms about asking the Maels to help break her internationally. The brothers wound up writing an entire album's worth of English lyrics for Lio's second album, and then going into the studio with Telex themselves to Anglicise their next LP.

Sales throughout the rest of Europe ensured that 'When I'm With You' became Sparks' best-selling single ever. Yet in the UK it bombed. It was followed into the bargain bins by both 'Terminal Jive' itself and the exquisite 'Young Girls,' an upmarket homage to underage sex, and it now seemed hard to believe that only six months earlier Sparks had been riding on a wave almost as big as the one they'd arrived on in 1974.

'A lot of people really hated what we were doing,' Ron reasoned. 'People suddenly started aligning us with the whole disco thing. We were no longer a real band, we were a synth duo and, at the time, there was no room for synth duos.'

Russell went even further. 'I think that reaction really damaged our reputation in [Britain]. People thought we'd sold out; they questioned our motives for making records. They seemed genuinely bothered by our existence.'

Ever philosophical, the Maels took it all in their stride. It was the unpredictability of the UK market, where reputations counted for nothing, that had attracted them in the first place, and it was only the present time that mattered. Where they would feel the pinch as the early Eighties passed by was in the knowledge that a lot of the bands that had risen in recent years, from failed Sparks auditioner Warren Cann's Ultravox through to the distinctly glam-influenced new romantic crowd that was just beginning to break through, had grown up listening to and absorbing Sparks.

A word or two from them might have made all the difference to the Maels' UK profile, and Russell mourned, 'We've found that most English bands we meet say to us "We like what you're doing, you've been a great influence on us", but no one will ever go out on a limb and say anything publicly about Sparks, because it might not be cool for their image. When they're doing an interview, it's always David Bowie that's their influence. It's a funny thing, that.'

By the end of 1980, Sparks were back in Los Angeles, their disco experiment over, and looking now for their next sonic adventure. They would find it in Bates Motel.

CHAPTER SIXTEEN

AN EMOTIONAL CORE, AIN'T THAT WHAT SONGS ARE FOR?

David Kendrick, a Chicago boy who'd played drums in a succession of local bands, first encountered Sparks in 1974, and immediately fell in love with what he heard. 'I was kind of an Anglophile – David Bowie, Roxy Music and so on – and for me Sparks were nothing like any other band from California. I was playing in bands, and in those days it was harder to get a gig if you played original music. There was a big club scene where you had to play a lot of covers, but in Chicago you could get a little more eccentric, so I convinced one of the bands I was in to do "Talent Is An Asset".' The performance, he said, 'went over so-so', but the song remained in the set.

He relocated to Los Angeles in 1977, lured to the city by the chance of hooking up with Kim Fowley's latest project, Venus and the Razorblades. He lasted about a week before realising that it wasn't what he wanted to be, a puppet drummer in the master puppeteer's theatre, so he picked up various other bands to work with – he was with the Continental Miniatures for a time – and, by 1980, wound up as a member of Bates Motel.

Featuring guitarists Dave Draves and Leslie Bohem, bassist Bob Haag and Kendrick on drums, Bates Motel were named after Norman Bates' lair in Hitchcock's infamous movie *Psycho*, and, as Kendrick explained, 'were all movie buffs, a lively young band...we were very movie orientated. In fact Les Bohem is now a screenwriter! We were all into Hitchcock and French film and *film noir*; we were all very big on that and still are, so we called ourselves Bates Motel. One of our little promo things was a Bates Motel keychain!'

It was a great name for a band, but movies were not their only obsession. They were also what Kendrick calls 'café buffs', hanging out together at the Farmers' Market, and falling into conversation with the other regulars. 'There was an espresso stand there and, in 1980, that was rare. There were hardly any around. And we started to see Ron and Russell there. They have always had a spot they go to mid-morning, their break time, and they would go there and me and the others would end up meeting them, and we'd sit and talk about movies.'

Bates Motel were a strictly Los Angeles concern. 'We were just playing locally.' They did contribute a song, 'Love Among the Dancers,' to the regional 'Sharp Cuts' compilation, 'but we didn't have a record deal. We could play pretty well, though, so besides hanging out together at the market, Ron and Russell started to come to see us.'

One thing led to another. The Maels had already mentioned in passing that they were thinking about working with a band again – the impersonal 'Terminal Jive' experience had soured them on a lot of their more recent interests. Maybe Bates Motel would fit the bill? Kendrick was thrilled. 'I was pushing for it to happen more than anybody else, because I liked Sparks so much.'

In part, his fascination was personal. He was intrigued by the Maels. 'One thing I thought was so amazing about them, to me it was very unusual to have a set of brothers that weren't only in an ongoing working relationship, but who also literally spent all their time together. They were almost like a symbiotic set, where they kind of made one complete person. Russell was far more the social half, the outgoing one, whereas Ron was very reserved... Amazing to talk to, and so

Russell Mael   Ron Mael

SPARKS

ATLANTIC

funny, but he was always a little more reticent. There were very few times when they were apart. Russ went to China for a time, and Ron was completely at loose ends.'

But professionally, too, the opportunity was tempting. Bates Motel was approaching a career crossroads as guitarist Draves announced he wanted to move away from the city and out to the desert. They could replace him and soldier on together, or they could break up and find some other bands to play with. Or they could become Sparks. Finally, the remaining trio reached their decision – they'd do it.

It was the first time that the Maels had worked in a band format since the dissolution of the 'Big Beat' line up, but they threw themselves into things with gusto, booking a month's rehearsal time in Los Angeles. There, said Kendrick, 'we ran through the songs from scratch. Ron brought in a blackboard and had the chords up. They hadn't worked with a band for a few years in a writing sense, so learning that way was very organic.

'We learned a lot of songs, a few more than we recorded. One of them was called "One Nut" – "one nut is all it takes". That was a great one. Some of the songs were eliminated because they were maybe similar to other songs, others just didn't work. The thing that amazed me, though, was the way some of them would be worked up as songs, with verses and choruses, but there wouldn't be words. Russ would psychobabble through what would become the verses, and that's what we would learn.' It was only once they arrived in Munich, to begin recording at Musicland Studios, that the final lyrics would arrive.

'Ron wrote words sometimes literally a day or two before in his hotel room, the final version of the lyrics. I thought that was so unusual, because they were so fully formed. His lyrics sound like he should slave over them for months, and I don't think that was really the case.'

Overseeing the sessions was another of Giorgio Moroder's more in-demand protégés, engineer Reinhold Mack (his 1981 diary also included stints with Queen and the Electric Light Orchestra). 'Musicland was a really cool set-up,' recalled Kendrick. 'It was in the basement of a hotel and, adjacent to it, they were working on a subway route, and there were all these huge concrete rooms.'

Of course the band had to utilise them. Recording 'Upstairs', for example, Kendrick was essentially set loose in those vast, echoing hallways to bang on anything he fancied. A few years down the road, such activities would fall under the auspices of 'industrial music', and praised to the skies by journalists tired of conventional rock instrumentation. 'Upstairs' deserves recognition as one of the technique's pioneering recordings.

'Mack was a real rock guy,' Kendrick continued, 'but there was a cool, trashy sound to what we were recording which I really liked. We were very much a rock band and when we interfaced with Sparks... As a fan of theirs all these years, I think the first two records we did together, are one of their very best periods...if I may say so!'

The new material that Ron and Russell brought to the sessions was far removed from that which had characterised their last two albums – once again, Sparks had changed course dramatically. Of course they retained their fascination with electronic dance music – you didn't go to Germany to record in the early Eighties if you didn't want those beats. But they had been paying attention to everything else that was being played on the radio at the time – during their time in England, they noted the sudden rise of the new wave and the likes of Lene Lovich and the Flying Lizards. They took in recent offerings by Blondie and David Bowie, and club hits by the new romantics and Toyah... Even Hilly Michaels, their drummer for 'Big Beat', was getting in on the act, scoring a solo hit with the insanely contagious 'Calling All Girls'. When the video channel MTV launched in mid-1981, Michaels was all over it – Sparks, Ron and Russell declared, would soon be joining him.

At Moroder's insistence, they had parted company with Virgin Records by now. 'Whomp That Sucker' would be released on RCA in the US, although its British appearance would be somewhat lower-key, as RCA had linked the band not with its main label but with Why-Fi, a small and newly-formed subsidiary.

According to Joseph Fleury; 'Virgin had been really keen to keep Sparks, and I think that if "Terminal Jive" had been a hit, they would have. But Giorgio was asking for too much money, and Virgin didn't even have American sales to fall back on to justify paying what he wanted because the album hadn't been released there... Which was a shame really, because Giorgio had made that record purely with America in mind.' The French success had been nice, he said, but it hadn't really brought in much money. Virgin really did support Sparks, though. They were as surprised as anybody when "Terminal Jive" flopped. They'd been so sure Sparks were going to be enormous.'

The new album, according to Ron, was 'a return to traditional values, a really conscious effort to get back to the Sparks of old. [It] was an explosion for us. We had been working in tight little ways with session people and real bourgeois types. We wanted to rebel against that and make an album that had real character to it, a lot of songs, really rocky.' In fact he was so determined on that score that, he recalled, 'When we got to Munich, it was just a case of getting a good sound, then my taking the basic track and figuring out extra parts for the songs.'

There was certainly something in what he said. 'Whomp That Sucker' was a return to the Sparks of old, but with sufficient sonic updating to ensure there could never be a sense of *déjà vu*. The lyrical sparseness of the past two albums was more than compensated for as the humour returned with a vengeance, together with an almost anarchic sense of musical indiscipline that kept the songs bubbling energetically from beginning to end.

'Tips For Teens' and 'Wacky Women' both continued Ron's preoccupations with the problems of youth, and problems with women. 'All they like is sex and sitcoms,' sang Russell in 'Wacky Women'. 'Try to be suave, they'll kick you in the bonbons.'

Elsewhere, the deliciously melodic 'That's Not Nastassia' commented upon the western world's then-ongoing obsession with actress Nastassja Kinski. A fearless examination of the media's obsession with passing fads and 'a modern Hula Hoop', it might also have been a commentary on Sparks' own long-ago moment on the tip of every commentator's tongue. 'She is on the news again tonight, someone looking like her stole a bike, if I wasn't masculine, I would join the craze, dye my hair and take on those Nastassianic ways.'

SPARRRKKK

photo: Michael Ratney

Sparks. Russell and Ron Mael.

by Brian Dall

"It's been five fucking years," somebody yelled at Sparks's recent rare Paradise appearance. "where have you been?"

Russell Mael, Sparks's curly haired vocalist (and brother to the moustached keyboardist, Ron) looked surprised, but took the compliment well. "Did you really miss us that much?" he laughed. The rousing response from the crowd answered his question.

Originally from California, the Mael brothers' first taste of show business came with a child modelling job for Sears and Roebuck. After a few musical ventures Ron and Russell, along with Jim and Earl Mankey (another brother team) and Harley Feinstein formed the group Halfnelson. Demo tapes sent to various companies resulted in rejection until Todd Rundgren's then-girlfriend fell in love with one of the tapes, and convinced Todd to sign them to his Bearsville label.

After the release of the first album, entitled *Halfnelson*, Bearsville decided that the group's name was not commercial enough, and asked them to change it. They changed it to Sparks and the first record was repackaged and retitled *Sparks*. The second album, *A Woofer in Tweeters Clothing* was released in 1972. Both albums were phenomenal—but neither sold well and subsequently they were out of print shortly after their release.

After a two year absence from the recording studio, the Brothers Mael left Bearsville and decided to move to London for a fresh new look and sound. After recruiting a new band, Sparks signed with Britain's Island Records.

"All of a sudden there were all these thirteen year old girls at our concerts," Ron recalls. "This frightened off the crowd of people who were easily frightened off by thirteen year old girls. We had no idea why they came. Our single 'This Town Ain't Big Enough for the Both of Us' became a number one British hit, which we though was rather bizarre. We didn't consider ourselves pop artists."

Three albums were released on Island. All were big hits in Britain and parts of Europe, but never sold well in the U.S. From there, they switched to Columbia, released two more long-players and then hopscotched over to Elektra records.

Sparks's first and only Elektra release, *Number One Song in Heaven* was produced by disco maestro Georgio [...] the time we didn't think we c[...] those songs live," says Ron, '[...] touring."

"But we now do 'Beat th[...] 'Number One Song'," Russe[...] really missed touring during [...] always been one of our strong[...]

Considering the current suc[...] like the Human League, Tho[...] and other dance-oriented grou[...] help but think that *Heaven* wo[...] a dance smash if it were releas[...] stead of 1979. The single "Bea[...] one of their finest efforts, was[...] ada, but elsewhere it went v[...] cognized. "People in Europe [...] realizing what a special album [...] reports.

The Mael brothers enliste[...] services for their followup alb[...] *Jive*. What's that you say? It'[...] Schwann catalogue? That's rig[...] *Jive* was never released in the U[...]

In the middle of their own p[...] sell and Ron had time to take [...] prodigy allegedly named Noel[...] more dance music with vocals [...] surprisingly like Russell Mael. [...]

'Funny Face' was almost as good, the tale of an extraordinarily good-looking boy who tires of 'looking a lot like a *Vogue* magazine, perfect and smooth'. Disfigurement follows and his greatest dream is realised: 'Doctor Lamaar says your face is a mess, I've got my one request, I've got a funny face.' And, if the song was bizarre, the accompanying video was even better.

MTV was still only available in a handful of American locations, and it would be several years more before the channel could claim to have reached every corner of the nation. But its influence in those areas was already profound, with once-hostile record labels ('what do you mean, we *give* you free videos to show on your station? What do we get out of it?') now falling over themselves to feed the monster. Sparks, for whom the possibilities of video had always been an inevitability waiting for technology to catch up, leapt into the new arena feet first.

They had to tease their paymasters first, though. Ron recalled being handed 'a certain amount of money' and sent away to do what they wanted with it. A few weeks later, the Maels submitted their finished video. Ron laughed, 'We dubbed the song over four minutes of a porno film, so when RCA played it at their high-level meeting, they'd think that was the actual video.

Then, after it, we put the real video on. They didn't think it was remotely funny.'

The 'real video' itself was unconventional enough, though. A panoply of rubber masks and lecherous leering, it showcases Ron spying on a trio of innocent little girls as they dance around the head of a recently decapitated pantomime cow before he is chased away by their disapproving mother after offering the children a cream bun. Another shoot, to accompany 'Tips For Teens', then placed the brothers in the boxing ring together, hunky Russ versus skinny Ron. Was it just a lucky punch? Or a genuinely calculating move? Ron gets the knock-out and every watching underdog cheered aloud.

Sparks' tenth album, 'Whomp That Sucker' was released in October 1981, and was immediately treated to that rarest of phenomena, an approving review from *Rolling Stone*.

'California's version of the Katzenjammer Kids', wrote Parke Puterbaugh, had created an album that combined 'the droll wit of a James Thurber to music that can only be described as John Philip Sousa meets the Beach Boys. One can almost picture the Maels at home: Russell in his bedroom preens for a hot date, while Ron, downstairs, crabbily reclines in a Naughahyde easy chair and thinks up awkward situations to put to music.'

American sales were slow, but France, once again, leapt on the album. Released on the Underdog label, a subsidiary of Carrere, it was the follow-up, after all, to one of the biggest hits of the past few years, and news that the group would be touring to promote the new album only raised the temperature even further. The Maels had not, of course, hit the road at all for their past three LPs.

'It's weird,' muses David Kendrick. 'There was a total backlash against Sparks in Britain at that time, we had no traction in that period. We played on the continent, and we had a deal for England but that record didn't do anything there. They were huge in France, and there was nothing anywhere else in the world.'

The tour was booked and Sparks went into rehearsal. At Ron's request, Joseph Fleury introduced a new keyboard player for concert work – Jim Goodwin was a friend of his from New York City, most recently sighted in John Cale's band. Later, as the Bates Motel trio relaxed between Sparks projects, Goodwin would join them in a new group, Gleaming Spires. Right now, though, all eyes were on France.

'The tour was pretty involved,' declared Kendrick, 'a lot of shows all over the country. Someone had booked them an incredible amount of shows. What I liked at that point was that we were doing some older songs as well as the new. We did "Here In Heaven" and "Hospitality On Parade". I got them to do "At Home, At Work, At Play", which they'd never done live. I was pushing for other earlier songs because, frankly, I just wanted to play them.'

The band was still in rehearsal when, suddenly, all hell broke loose. Joseph Fleury; 'They were all set to take off for France, when suddenly K-ROQ radio in Los Angeles began playing "Tips For Teens" and "Funny Face"...'

Like MTV, K-ROQ represented a whole new way of listening to music. The station itself had

been around since the early Seventies, when the old KBBQ country music station had decided to adopt a new Top 40 formula. It carried on through the Seventies, just another radio station from Los Angeles, until the arrival of a new program director, Rick Carroll, saw another change in format in 1979. Tired of merely playing the Top 40, K-ROQ would now create it, switching over to an almost exclusive diet of new-wave music, and welcoming the end of the Seventies by declaring itself 'the Rock of the Eighties'.

Missing Persons, the Go-Gos, Adam and the Ants, Josie Cotton, Oingo Bongo, Romeo Void... if it was new and new wave, K-ROQ would be riding it, and there was no doubt that the latest Sparks album fit the stylistic demands of the format. But whereas they might have been able to pass themselves off as some kind of new act elsewhere in the country, in those regions where their past glories had long since evaporated from the local consciousness, this was Los Angeles. In Los Angeles, people knew who Sparks were...

It turned out not to be a problem - some people in Los Angeles might have known who Sparks were, but they also recognised music that would slip effortlessly onto the K-ROQ airwaves. Joseph Fleury recalled, 'I was in Los Angeles at the time, and there were all these people phoning into the station to ask them who this great new band Sparks was. So I asked Ron and Russell to play a special one-off gig at the Whisky-A-Go-Go. They really weren't keen. To go from not playing in six years to headlining their hometown was a big move! In the end I got them to agree, though. We advertised the gig and it sold out immediately. It was amazing. We added another two nights, which was all they had time for before they went to France, and the same thing happened. The gigs went off so well, there was an incredible amount of press – pages in the *Los Angeles Times*, things like that.'

'Suddenly, K-ROQ decided they were going to champion Sparks,' an astonished Russell confirmed. 'As a result, we played live and girls were screaming at us again, although nobody reacted to "This Town Ain't Big Enough..." or "The No. 1 Song In Heaven".'

The Whisky shows were phenomenal, and there could have been no better return to the road for the Maels. Sparks left for France almost regretting that they had ever agreed to go. After so many years of cultish obscurity, at last they were stars in their hometown. They just hoped they still would be when they got back.

Kendrick found their time in France a strange experience. '"When I'm With You" is very atypical of Sparks and it was Number 1, a very big record, so obviously we played that, but we played older songs as well. There was a certain number of older fans... in Marseille and Strasbourg and the big cities, they knew us, but we did a lot of shows in smaller places, where they only knew that one song.'

They quickly discovered that American audiences, too, were very much in the dark where it came to anything they'd not heard on the radio recently. 'Tips For Teens' and 'Funny Face' were joined on the K-ROQ playlist by 'Upstairs' and 'I Married A Martian', and when the radio station published their year-end countdown of the top 106.7 songs of 1981 (106.7 being the frequency on which the station broadcast), all four were on the list, with 'Funny Face' best-placed at Number 15. Of the other 'veteran' groups that the station favoured, only the Rolling Stones (whose 'Start Me Up' was everywhere that year, K-ROQ included) were ranked higher than Sparks.

Work on Sparks' next album began in Germany while 'Whomp That Sucker' was still working its magic in Los Angeles, and beginning to make headway elsewhere. 'There were four tracks from "Whomp That Sucker" getting played all over the country,' Joseph Fleury recalled, 'MTV had picked

---

Trouser Press clipping:

...imers.
We found we had a ...swing, 'cause all ...came out, wanting ...ks. Eventually we ...ew band [with gui-...Fisher, bassist ...lon and drummer ...ond].
f Winwood was the ...and who had signed ...d about who would One idea was Roy ...nen something hap-...e couldn't do it, so ...ed the album him-...nd of '73.
There we were in ...ording with a label ...ed. Then they re-...le and it became a ...song in most of ...is Town Ain't Big ...Both of Us" was a ...1 the album was ...ur. We did a tour, ...ere girls screaming ...y up on stage, claw-...pulling your hair. ...y like the fantasy ...about those types of ...it was happening to
...got into trouble, ...use we never ...urselves as a pop ...teenybop follow-...ces became 95 per-...ing girls, and we . ...hese songs with ...rds in them. ...could stick with us ...dn't because they' ...girls and assumed ...enybop band. The ...appened with the ...were no longer able ...r following. We ...grabbed onstage, ...away a lot of ...ordinarily would ...o our shows. ...We decided on an ...oook pride in the fact ...ould come up with ...parts to add to ...threw in every-...ole. We stuck gun ...his Town Ain't Big ...here were lots and ...s and notes in a ...space. ...ere was a lot of over-...was all done in an ...ifs way. I would sit ...igure out what could ...it. I've never had ...training but if I ...ning I can figure out

something else that will go with it. We just kept going, with no restriction as to how much to put on.
Just when we started record-ing the album England had an energy crisis and there was the strong possibility there wouldn't be enough vinyl to press records.
The strongest possibility for a single were "This Town Ain't Big Enough" and "Amateur Hour." One faction thought it should be the simpler "Ama-teur Hour," and one faction thought it should be something weird. I was pulling for "Ama-teur Hour"; I thought "This Town" was too weird to get played anywhere. But I was wrong.

under the microscope. Any-thing we did was going to be judged. We went into the studio with a lot of songs, but a bit scared. We kept thinking about the Beatles and their constant rise. We tried to make Propa-ganda a little more complex than *Kimono My House*.
One of the elements we thought could make it more grandiose was the singing. The song "Propaganda" was originally an acoustic guitar thing; we just kept recording voices. It was a lot easier to do things with the vocals than to figure out extra guitar parts. I think that vocal style was really influential to some big English bands that have since done pre-tentious albums.

format and wanted to elaborate on that more, which isn't neces-sarily a good idea. We had a lot of songs, but I don't recall the recording taking that long. We never took a lot of time in the studio because we always went in with the songs. The ones that sound complicated, like "Get in the Swing" or "Looks Looks Looks," were just Tony writing out charts.
Russell: Visconti is one of the real musician/producers. He's not only a technician who knows how to work the board, he's a real musician as well. He's a well-rounded producer, whereas Muff Winwood is a good coordinator.
Ron: The album was record-ed at Tony's house. He had a studio downstairs the size of a phone booth. There was no room for a bass amp, so bass speakers had to be built into the walls. It was incredibly tight, but it gave you the feeling you could concentrate without anyone knowing what you were doing.
We were sure the English store chain W.H. Smith's would ban "Tits"; they would ban something with the word "drat" in the title. So we called it "T*ts"—real hard to figure out.
We recorded 15 songs for this album; the two left-overs appeared later.
Russell: Mary Hopkin, who was married to Tony Visconti at the time, did a version of "Nev-er Turn Your Back on Mother Earth." We have a demo. Un-fortunately she never properly recorded or released it.

PROPAGANDA (1974)

INDISCREET (1975)

BIG BEAT (1976)

Ron: This album was incredibly hard [to do] because there was a lot of pressure. *Kimono* was incredibly popu-lar in England, and we were

Ron: We wanted to get more outside instrumentation. Tony Visconti [the LP's producer] knew about scoring. We had done two albums with the band

Ron: We got sick of En-gland. The weather was dis-gusting and we tired of the pro-vincial atmosphere. What at first is quaint later becomes

Robert Matheu

TROUSER PRESS 27

...million ...constantly ...s play in ...in't it be ...e instead ...a stuff. It
. They ...erred than ...e with, and ...idea of ...These ...crafted ...no feeling ...hing ...60 minutes ...ly said, "I ...ause of the

an eccentric rock band would turn out. This was the only al-bum we've ever gone into with almost no material; only "Bear the Clock" and "Academy Award Performance" were written beforehand. Giorgio wrote the music for at least half the other songs. I think the album has been shown to be incredibly influential for the whole English synthesizer pop movement.
We tried to get as much out of us as we could on No. 1, but at the same time we wanted an outside influence; obviously, we got it.

LOS ANGELES — A few minutes before the scheduled interview with Ron and Russell Mael, the brothers behind Sparks, I happen to meet Ron on the ground floor of the RCA building. Instead of proceeding upstairs however, we are detained by a bumbling security guard who thinks that Ron and I are a journalistic team there to interview an RCA publicist. He insists on calling the publicity department upstairs, and, getting no answer, tells us that we'll have to come back another day. Ron rolls his eyes, then quietly tries to explain the situation to the guard, who, still uncomprehending, starts to call upstairs again. At this point, the normally soft-spoken Ron declares quite firmly, "Look, my name is Ron Mael and I'm in a band called Sparks." Pause. "I'm a rock and roll star, goddamit!"

We proceed upstairs.

The episode with the security guard serves as a nice bit of symbolism for Sparks' frustration with their lack of recognition domestically. In Europe, they're bona fide stars, having had gold albums, Top Ten singles, numerous TV appearances, hoardes of screaming girls — the whole bit. In the U.S. however, despite the fact that it's their homeland (they're from Los Angeles), and despite the fact that they've just released their tenth album (*Whomp That Sucker*), they are still largely unknown.

"I think there's a big difference between the U.S. and Europe in their acceptance of things that are a little bit oddball," says Ron, back to his usual soft-spoken self. "Here, things that are eccentric are seen as kind of counter-cultural somehow. But in Europe, the same things are real show-biz, real middle-of-the-road."

Sparks may not be middle-of-the-road exactly, but neither do they deserve to be relegated to the status of a cult band; Ron may not look like a typical rock star, and Russell's flirtation with falsetto may be a little unusual, but Sparks is actually a very accessible group. The songs from their new album are upbeat, catchy numbers, mostly in an energetic, new wavish vein. Hooks abound, and more than half of the songs have instant sing-along choruses (even if you can't always sing high enough). And, as always, the songs feature Ron's marvelously inventive lyrics (with occasional help from Russell).

Even more than Russell's voice or Ron's mustache, it is the lyrics which are the true Sparks trademark. Sparks lyrics are immediately recognizable due to their offbeat subject matter, their non-stop wit, and Ron's truly original (and hilarious) means of expression. If Patti Smith is the high priestess of rock poetry, then Ron Mael is an equally talented clown prince — the Ogden Nash of rock and roll.

Over the course of Sparks' nine-year career, Ron has written so many memorable songs that any Sparks fan worth his weight in import 45s could rattle off a dozen candidates for his personal favorite, reciting the lyrics verbatim. The titles alone give a rough idea of Ron's lyrical eccentricity ("Everybody's Stupid," "Thank God It's Not Christmas," "Tits," "Tryouts For the Human Race," "Falling In Love With Myself Again," etc.), but to more fully appreciate his humor, a few songs should be examined more closely. Three representative samples would be "Amateur Hour," a primer on puberty ("Our voices change at a rapid pace/I could start a song a tenor and then end as bass") and sexual prowess ("It's a lot like playing the violin/You cannot start off and be Yehudi Menuhin"); "Beat The Clock," a hyperbolic tale of life in the fast lane ("Entered school when I was two/Ph.D'd that afternoon/Never looked too good in shorts/Never entered any sports/Got divorced when I was four"); and "White Women," a tongue-in-cheek look at racial preference ("I've tried most every package from Peking to Berdoo/I'm sticking with a brand name/I'm sticking with you").

The songs on *Whomp That Sucker* carry on the grand Sparks tradition of novel lyrics. Standouts include "I Married a Martian," "Wacky Women," "Funny Face," and most notably "Tips For Teens," which concerns a young adolescent girl who is given valuable advice, including the classic rhyme "Keep your mystique up/And wear a 'D' cup/No matter what."

Although Ron obviously enjoys writing funny songs, there are occasional traces of seriousness that indicate a deep side to him, perhaps waiting to

Russell (L) and Ron Mael. Photo: Gary Pearlson.

SPAR

A RETURN FRO

By David Gillerman

surface. One wonders if he will ever write a serious song.

"No, I don't think so," he says. "When I attempt to write a serious song, it comes out funnier than a funny one because the sentiments are really phony. I'm able to be a lot more serious within the framework of what we do now than I could if I were writing serious songs."

Adds Russell, "I think there's something really not funny about a lot of our humor. Sometimes it's bittersweet and sometimes it's just plain bitter, but I think there are serious issues in a lot of our songs — regardless of the fact that they might be told in a humorous manner."

Ron reconsiders the question: "I just think everything is funny," he confesses, prompting both brothers to begin laughing.

"...And that's serious!" says Russell without missing a beat.

Although the humor in Sparks songs has remained a constant element throughout their career, the music itself has gone through several phases. The first album (produced by Todd Rundgren) had a light, sparse sound to it — real art-rock stuff. By the third album, the artsiness had given way to frantic rock and roll, with Russell often spewing out more syllables per second than anyone had ever heard before. (It was during this period that Sparks were at the top of the British charts with a long string of hits from *Kimono My House*, *Propaganda* and *Indiscreet*. In 1976, the boys released *Big Beat*, trying their hand at a more gutsy, guitar-dominated sound. That sound was abandoned with the release of the ironically titled *Introducing Sparks* in 1977, a relatively weak album, after which they were dropped from Columbia.

After being silent for nearly two years, they surprised many people by teaming up with Giorgio Moroder (synthesizer wizard of Donna Summer and *Midnight Express* fame). The result was *Number One In Heaven*, a disco album ahead of its time, featuring only synthesizers and drums (and of course, Sparks lyrics). *Number One In Heaven* was followed up by *Terminal Jive* (never released in the U.S.) a similar but weaker album, and Sparks' disco era was over.

Wanting to return to a livelier rock and roll sound, Ron and Russell selected three members of LA group Bates Motel (Les Bohem on bass, Bob Haag on guitar and David Kendrick on drums) as their backing band, and took them to Munich to record *Whomp That Sucker*. With these players, Sparks is now able to tour — something the band hasn't done in over five years. Presently, they are touring France, Switzerland and Belgium. Before they left however, they decided to play three nights for their hometown fans.

Sparks may not be appreciated throughout the US as a whole, but in Los Angeles they're treated like mini-gods. The reaction was the same all three nights at the Whisky; the crowd went wild during the opening film of Ron shaving off his mustache (it had grown back by show-time), and never let up. The Sparkophiles watched, enraptured, as pretty-boy Russel, in gold lamé dinner jacket and pants, bounded all over the stage with five years worth of stored-up energy, while stodgy old Ron, in droopy pants, white shirt and narrow tie, absent-mindedly played his synthesizer, frequently staring into space and looking as disinterested as possible.

Any action by Ron, however slight, brought howls of delight from the audience — when he merely lip-synched a few words to a song, or when he tried to shoo Russell away as Russell danced around him and gestured him. Imagine, then, the crowd's euphoric disbelief the third night when Ron came back onstage for the final encore with his hair dripping wet, clad only in a towel. The place exploded.

The overwhelming success of the LA shows, especially the strong reception given the new material, was quite reassuring for Ron and Russell. Despite their carefree image, they put a lot of effort into what they do, and are as concerned as any other group about their acceptance.

"We're incredibly conscious about everything," explains Russell. "We're conscious about the way we look; about our songs; about our lyrics; about how we present ourselves onstage — we really care about

Ron Mael. Photo: Dave Patrick

everything we do."

"Sort of like Ronald Reagan," offers Ron.

One place where the Maels' conscientiousness has paid off is France. The single "When I'm With You," from *Terminal Jive*, became their biggest seller ever, going to Number One on the French charts and selling some 650,000 copies. As a result, Ron and Russell became huge celebrities in that country, making 20 or 25 appearances on talk shows within six months. (Russell is fluent in French; Ron can communicate.) In addition, they became involved in two musical projects there. The first was to write lyrics for Lio, an 18-year-old beauty and *the* biggest female singer in France, according to Russell — three songs from her first (and only) album sold over a million copies each. Hoping to expand Lio's popularity to English-speaking countries, her producers (a band called Telex) brought in Ron and Russell to write English lyrics for existing songs. So pleased with the results, Telex commissioned the brothers to write lyrics for their own album, as well.

Ron and Russell also have two film projects in the works. They are doing the music for a re-make of a film called *Peeping Tom*, which will star Peter Fonda. They are also working on their own "wacky comedy." It's still in the development stage, but a French film company has expressed interest, so the boys are hopeful.

The outside projects are a fun diversion, but Ron and Russell make it clear that Sparks is their number one concern. The day after they finish their European tour, the whole band is going back to Munich, where they will begin recording the next Sparks album. And they're already talking about more touring — planning to return to Los Angeles in February and promising the fans that "we're gonna be more visible next time around." There was even some talk about a possible U.S. tour.

But the Brothers Mael have been through it all before. Sure, they'd like to make it in America but that's not their primary goal. Regardless of the reaction in the U.S., they'll continue making Sparks music for whomever wants to hear it.

Says Ron: "We don't really think about a goal in terms of popularity; we just try to put as much personality into the music as we can, and know that there will always be a small following for that sort of thing. There's always going to be some place where our music will gain enough commercial success to be able to finance it for the rest of the world." □

up on the videos for "Tips For Teens" and "Funny Face". Yet, when Sparks got back from France and went off to record their next LP, RCA said they weren't going to take up the option on their contract. It didn't seem to matter how big they were becoming. RCA just weren't interested. Then Atlantic came in and picked up the band within three days.'

Mack was back as producer, and Jim Goodwin had been given full band status as well. It was a confident, comfortable team that returned to Musicland to record, and the new album – already titled 'Angst In My Pants', after one of the first songs written for it – would reflect the band's newfound status. Like 'Propaganda' eight years before, the Maels went into the sessions with a very good idea of what people expected from them. Unlike 'Propaganda', they had every intention of delivering it.

The newly expanded band made its public debut on German television on 9th December 1981, appearing on the national public broadcasting channel Bayerischen Rundfunk as part of a so-called Rock and Pop Festival being staged at the Circus Krone in Munich. There, a four-song set was performed on a stage crawling with TV crew and littered with other bands' equipment and highlighted by a unique version of 'This Town Ain't Big Enough...', extended to gargantuan proportions by Russell insisting on singing the same verse three times, and by the sight of Ron making his way to the conductors' podium at the front of the stage and conducting his band-mates from there.

It was a great show, and ended with all the performers – Sparks, Tangerine Dream and Peter Hammill among them – joining together for a percussive jam through 'Give Peace A Chance', a tribute to John Lennon who had been murdered the previous day

178

With so many other keyboard players on stage, Ron chose to forgo his instrument of choice and play a banana instead. 'It was pretty awesome,' remembered Kendrick.

Preparing to return to the studio, the band followed the same procedure as before. 'We learned the songs here and went to Musicland again with Mack, and I just remember the sessions going really well,' said Kendrick. Indeed, the recordings were completed very quickly, but Atlantic were even quicker. 'Angst In My Pants' was in the stores by May 1982, the swiftest follow-up album Sparks had released since 'Propaganda' was unleashed to capitalise on the success of 'Kimono My House'.

But there all the comparisons with the past end. Described by Russell as being 'based around some really good songs', and by Paul Tickell of the *New Musical Express* as 'not the greatest thing they have ever done', 'Angst In My Pants' would spawn a succession of radio hits. '"Whomp That Sucker" had four on the radio at one time,' Joseph Fleury said, 'but with "Angst In My Pants", more than half the LP was on the radio.' 'Mickey Mouse', 'Angst In My Pants', 'Eaten By The Monster Of Love', 'Moustache', 'Sextown USA'... the hits just flew off that album, and there could probably have been even more.

'To me, that was the highlight,' Kendrick later enthused. 'That record, I think, is fantastic. A lot of great songs, I love a lot of those songs.'

'I don't think there's any filler on it,' Russell confirmed shortly after the album's release. 'It's just doing what we should be doing. As an after-effect, it turns out the album's been played on the radio infinitely more than any other Sparks record in America. So we *can* do something that maintains the essence of what Sparks is, retaining personality and character, and still get airplay.

'It's much more pleasant to listen to than any of our other records,' he continued. 'I'm trying to get as much variety out of my voice as possible, whereas in the past it's always been limited to that high falsetto'. If sales figures are anything to go by this was exactly what the American public had been waiting for. 'More fun than a case of domestic champagne... positively effervescent with Europop fizz and California folly,' announced *Rolling Stone*'s Parke Puterbaugh.

The sleeve, showing the Maels as a happily married couple with Ron the blushingly moustachioed bride, drew laughter and amazement. More than a decade later, it was still being talked about, as *Details* magazine proved when it polled five of the day's leading transvestites for their opinion on the outfit. Hedda Lettuce summed it up best, though. 'With the runaway success of *Schindler's List* this bride's choice of the Hitler moustache makes a bold fashion statement. The combination of her hair and the eggshell wedding gown produces a successful marriage between grotesque and gorgeous. I do!'

Near-saturation of the airwaves gave the Maels only their second-ever Top 100 album. But everything paled beside 'I Predict', a strident shopping list of increasingly absurd claims and predictions that ended with Russell insisting that the song was going to fade out – at which point it stopped dead. 'I Predict' was all over the radio that spring. Nobody could have been the least bit surprised when it finally provided Sparks with a long-overdue return to the singles listings. What *did* come as a shock, however, was the discovery that the 'I Predict' video had been banned by MTV.

Directed by David Lynch, the video showed Ron in corset and stockings, performing a striptease on a nightclub stage. Yet it was not the sight of a skinny transvestite mincing across the stage that so outraged the powers of MTV, for they too had been entranced by the latest album cover. It was the belief that Ron was portraying Adolf Hitler, and that the nightclub was something straight out of pre-war Berlin's cabaret world. Without the ban, 'I Predict' would certainly have risen far higher than its eventual roost at Number 60, but Sparks were too busy to complain.

On 15th May 1982 the band, and Russell's absolutely outlandish wardrobe of newly acquired, garishly sequinned outsized suits, came to television's *Saturday Night Live* to perform 'I Predict' and 'Mickey Mouse'. Host Danny DeVito introduced them, standing dwarfed beside Ron as the deadpan organist regaled the audience with a bizarre monologue about, indeed, mice – creatures that he insisted do not spend all their time 'scaring women, eating saltine crackers… or ingesting huge amounts of saccharine in laboratory experiments.'

David Kendrick: '*Saturday Night Live* was a very enjoyable experience, because you go and spend part of the week there and rehearse chunks of the show, so it was interesting to see how skits progressed or got dropped.' Of course, they were also taking part in a television show that had been part of the national landscape since the mid-Seventies, but even that thrill paled beside the band's next major broadcast engagement, their return to *American Bandstand* on 28th August.

Dick Clark was still hosting the show and, whether he remembered the Maels from past appearances or not, it was clear that he enjoyed their company. 'Dick Clark was a very nice man,' said Kendrick, 'and he really liked Sparks. He appreciated the weird visual obscurity of them; he genuinely liked having us on.' Making their third of an eventual total of six appearances on the programme, Sparks' showing this time was definitely one of the most memorable, as Ron invaded the audience to explain how excited he was to be on the show while Clark was actually introducing the band, and then joined his brother in some light-hearted teasing of their genial host.

'How long has the band been going?' Clark asked.

'Too long,' they replied.

'And who is the older?'

'You are,' flashed Ron.

Later in the interview (which was bracketed with performances of 'I Predict' and 'Eaten By The Monster Of Love'), Russell, resplendent in his gold sequinned suit, defined the word 'angst' to Clark as 'a German word which means fear, but in English it means anxiety, problems, stress, but in this case, in the pants region.'

Meanwhile, a summer 1982 return to the American live circuit maintained Sparks' profile. Before they set off, there was talk of augmenting the line-up even further, with Joseph Fleury pushing especially hard for the Maels to recruit Alison East of the Swinging Madisons (and later Minors Aloud). Ultimately, however, the idea was rejected. The band sounded good enough as it was.

Neither was there any discussion as to which songs they should perform. 'Live, from "Whomp That Sucker" and "Angst In My Pants", there were ten songs that audiences wanted to hear,' David Kendrick laughed. 'On the first tour, there was always the lone voice shouting out for "Equator" – I know, because I was one of those guys. And this time around, there were nights when we knew we were playing to people who hadn't seen the group in quite some time, the real fans, and that was very cool to do because we were doing some songs from the two new records and then selected oldies. But later, no. It was all the new material.'

The Sparks show was a riot of colour. 'During that period, for each record, we did a different look,' Kendrick continued, 'so we had Elvis glitter suits – a couple of different versions of that. There were the black sequinned suits for one tour, the bright red ones, the grey shimmering, pimpy-looking suits….'

And there was mayhem. Around the country they went, playing clubs in cities that they had consciously avoided on every tour in the past, and being greeted everywhere by audiences that matched the old 'Kimono My House' crowds scream for scream in terms of intensity and excitement.

'That band live was pretty energetic,' said Kendrick. 'I'd love to see something from that period come out, a lot of the live shows were filmed. The song "Upstairs" was the one that would really take a musical journey! It was a pretty new scene, even in Los Angeles, but Sparks were really a popular band. In New York, we'd play the Ritz, in other places it was mostly club-sized venues, but there were pockets. Chicago was popular; in Texas, oddly, we did okay, but we played Kansas City, and places you'd never imagine, on that tour!'

Everywhere, however, audiences were rewarded with a performance that wasn't only capable of stretching out to as many as six encores, it also included a clutch of set pieces that are still talked about today; Ron lip-synching through the *Grease* standard 'You're The One That I Want' with a stuffed dog, stripping down to his underwear to the frantic throb of 'Upstairs' or doing a quick turn in the wedding dress immortalised on the 'Angst In My Pants' album cover.

He took to dancing onstage, explaining to the Sparks fan club, 'I began to feel that not enough was going on visually for Sparks. I thought a couple of brief moments of movement on my part would spice things up. I wanted to move in a way that was not considered a part of the pop music repertoire, and being a fan of old musicals, I tried to copy the way those old geezers moved. I couldn't quite get the movements right, but something else evolved. Recently, I became bored with the old shuffle and now do another sort of misquoted dance step.'

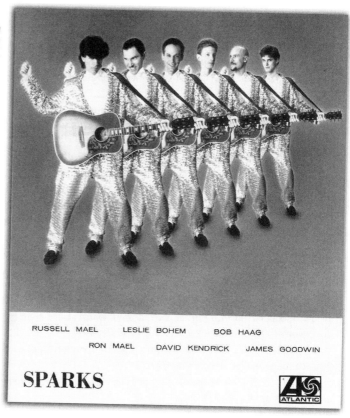

RUSSELL MAEL   LESLIE BOHEM   BOB HAAG

RON MAEL   DAVID KENDRICK   JAMES GOODWIN

SPARKS

ATLANTIC

The highlight of the itinerary was a triumphant return to Magic Mountain, the scene, of course, of the *Rollercoaster* disaster five years earlier. Sparks played there twice in 1982, and would be back on many more occasions – 'We probably played there twenty times altogether,' Kendrick recalled, 'and it was great, because it was always a super Sparks crowd. Kids would come specifically to see us. They had a pretty decent open air stage, and we'd do two sets, two shows.'

Los Angeles was especially hot, of course. At the Greek Theatre, they were supported by the young Red Hot Chili Peppers, then at the height of their 'cocks in socks' notoriety – if a gig went well, the band would strip off their clothes for the encore, then appear on stage naked except for a tube sock slipped over the genitals. That night, they kept their clothes on.

The Gun Club were support at the Santa Monica Civic Centre, as unbalanced a billing as Sparks had played since the bad old days with the Patti Smith Group. 'The really neat shows were at the Whisky, where we got to choose our support act ourselves,' said Kendrick. One evening saw the show opened by 'a really messy performance artist named Joanna Landt; there was an art-damaged band called the Fibonaccis; there was the Latino Roxy Music, Wild Kingdom. They were a great band! We played shows with Josie Cotton....'

Amidst so much craziness, it was sometimes very easy to forget that Sparks had a history, and an older audience that would still like to hear it. Or, at least, to continue complaining that the band seemed to have rejected it.

'The people who have the most trouble dealing with what we've been doing are the ones who analyze so much,' Russell told *BAM* magazine in 1983, 'the "older" rock fans. They tend to outguess our motives, and there are no ulterior motives. They think we're aiming at a special audience when we're not. At our concerts now, you see these really, really young kids, and they get it for what it is, get the essence of the lyrics. It's really amazing to realise we have the same age group following us now that followed us ten years ago. We get older and the audiences stay the same age. Our music has the same appeal, and seemingly for the same reasons. There's really no competition for that, we're always re-convincing people over and over again, not like the Rolling Stones or Grateful Dead, who hang on to their fans forever, regardless of how their music changes.'

K-ROQ published its traditional year-end round-up in December 1982. Once again, four Sparks songs were featured in the listing, but this year they'd broken into the Top 10. 'I Predict' was Number 7.

Hollywood came calling, relegating the *Rollercoaster* debacle to a painful memory and turning Sparks into one of those bands whose music seems to appear on every movie soundtrack of the era. They were approached to write the soundtrack for a proposed remake of *Peeping Tom*, starring Peter Fonda. It didn't happen, but there was no time for regret; even in Hollywood, the only film Sparks fans were talking about was the one which opened their live show, a two-minute sequence during which Ron shaved off his moustache, and then broke into a wild, clean-shaven grin at the end of it. The 'tache had grown back by the time of the tour, of course, but audiences never tired of the joke.

A little facetiously, one suspected, Russell outlined for the Popmatters.com website the process that allowed two of their songs, 'Angst In My Pants' and 'Eaten By The Monster Of Love', to be incorporated into the soundtrack of what would soon be regarded as the crucial celluloid documentary of the entire K-ROQ era, *Valley Girl*.

'February 21, 1982, Universal's legal department hinted that they may want to include some Sparks songs in the film, *Valley Girl*.

'February 22, we received a provisional deal memo from them with copies to our attorney and management.

'February 23, neither Ron nor I were available to discuss the pros and cons of using the songs in the film as we were out of town.

'February 25, we are back in town and can focus on the deal memo.

'February 26, we meet with cast and crew members to see if there is a genuine connection. That goes well.

'February 27, our attorney sees if there is any more money that can be squeezed out of Universal. Later that afternoon, Universal does cave and the initial low-ball offer was raised.

'February 28, a courier comes to my place with cash for the advance. While the courier waits, I count all the bills to make sure the designated amount is correct. After recounting the stacks of hundreds, the figures finally check out okay. I tip the courier a twenty for his extra waiting time. The deal is concluded.'

That one was comparatively plain sailing. More problematic was the invitation to write the theme music for a new American TV show, the ABC network's *Modesty Plays*, based on the vintage comic series *Modesty Blaise*. A song of that title was demoed and was, for a time, approved by the programme's producers. 'Then they changed their minds and went with some awful, typical Hollywood instrumental,' complained Fleury, although he certainly took some satisfaction once it became apparent that the show, which starred Ann Turkel and Lewis van Bergen, would get no further than its one-hour pilot episode before the plug was pulled. 'We'd almost forgotten about the song, then one day we got a call from Underdog, the French company, saying they really liked the song and could they release it in France? Of course we said yes, even though it really was only a demo. Actually I think that, of its type, it's a really good song.'

CHAPTER SEVENTEEN

CHART POSITION, BUBBLING UNDER, DROWNING

By summer 1982, reports of growing interest in the band in Japan had given rise to hopes that Sparks might undertake their first ever tour of the country, but in the event, nothing materialised. Instead, the group continued to gig sporadically for the remainder of the year, then started 1983 with a trip to Belgium to record material for their 12th album, 'Sparks In Outer Space', a set that the media insisted was especially notable for seeing the line-up temporarily augmented with a female vocalist, Jane Wiedlin of the Go-Gos.

'The president of the Go-Gos fan club wrote us a charming letter explaining that Jane was a great admirer of Sparks, and that she wanted to marry me,' Russell told the French *Rock* magazine. His response to the letter depended upon who was asking him about it. He told *Rock*, 'I found the letter so funny that I wrote back saying that I was all for it, Jane called me the next day', but the US TV magazine program *Live At Five* received a slightly saltier response; 'She said she wanted to marry me – I said I'd be willing to have an affair.'

When Dick Clark asked how the partnership came about during Sparks' next appearance on *American Bandstand* on 26th March 1983, wedding bells weren't even mentioned. Russell attributed it to 'Mutual admiration of each other's groups, and for each other's bodies,' while Wiedlin giggled beside him.

Wiedlin joined Russell on two songs on the LP – 'Lucky Me Lucky You', a sweet ballad that remains one of Ron's most overtly romantic songs, despite its protagonist's obvious lack of self-esteem ('we were the ones they voted most likely to fail'), and the manic 'Cool Places', the most obvious choice for a single and destined to become the biggest American hit Sparks have ever had.

Two weeks after *American Bandstand*, on 16th April, 'Cool Places' entered the US chart and, by the time it became a rare highlight on the lightweight, pop-oriented TV show *Solid Gold* on May 28th, it was halfway through a 12-week chart run that would see the single peak at Number 49. It wasn't quite the Top 40 smash that everybody had been predicting, but an 11-place improvement on 'I Predict' and surely the precursor of greater things to come, especially after MTV lifted the ban on the earlier single and launched it into rotation alongside 'Cool Places'.

A new cable television show, the K-ROQ-inspired *Rock Of The Eighties*, invited Sparks to appear. On a show that also featured JoBoxers and Oingo Boingo, Sparks performed four songs on a set decked out to resemble a highly stylised mock nightclub. There, Ron doubled as an unsmiling barman on the *faux* bar, while Russell sprinted from one end of the studio to another as the cameras cut back and forth between the concert and footage of Boy George apparently arriving at the venue and promptly disappearing downstairs. 'We have been elected the official band of the 1984 Olympics,' Ron informed the crowd, but it was 'Cool Places' that earned the biggest roar of approval.

'Sparks In Outer Space' followed in the hit single's footsteps, housed in an eye-catching sleeve that carried a portrait of the Maels posing side by side, while Ron stands steadfast in the face of what appears to be a hail of cream pies. But he was only hit by a few, Russell assured Dick Clark. 'Because he said they were heavy and they hurt.'

Later, Russell told the Sparks fan club newsletter, 'we only had seven pies to work with, so

Sept. 1984
No. 61

RECORD COLLECTOR

For all serious collec...
RARE RECORDS, PO
MEMORABILIA, ETC.

The ROLLING STO at De

Great Produc PHIL SPECT

Lavern Bak

SPARKS

★ ★ ★ ★ ★ ★

SPARKS

BIZARRE AMERICAN HITMAKERS
OF THE MID-SEVENTIES WHOSE
CAREER UNDERWENT A DECLINE
UNTIL THEIR RE-EMERGENCE
UNDER THE GUIDANCE OF
GIORGIO MORODER DURING
THE RECENT DISCO BOOM

BY JOHN MERRILL

★ ★ ★ ★ ★ ★

*Russell and Ron Mael of Sparks pictured at the time of the release
in 1974. The band survived early disappointment on Bearsville Records*

The year of 1974 has gone down into rock history as one of the least memorable to date. The sudden rush of new faces which had begun in the summer of 1972 was starting to wear thin, with only a handful of that year's big names maintaining any semblance of their former popularity. Bolan's reign was over, and in his place the Wombles had emerged to become the year's best selling-singles 'artists'. Elsewhere it was left to the power of television (via the Eurovision Song Contest, Opportunity Knocks and a sudden obsession with the martial arts) to challenge the chart supremacy of French balladeers and "Y Viva Espana".

Into this climate, Island Records plunged two totally dissimilar Californian brothers: one boyishly good-looking, all curls and ethereal falsetto; the other an undernourished cross between Charlie Chaplin and Adolf Hitler, with slicked back hair and gonky eyes. Their greatest joint ambition was to be "as big as General Motors". Ron and Russell Mael, former Los Angeles child models, formed Halfnelson late in 1969 after an earlier band,

Urban Renewal Project, had succeeded in little more than estranging them from even Los Angeles credibility.

The new line up consisted of Ron (keyboards), Russell (vocals and bass), Earle Mankey (guitar) and rock critic John Mendelsohn (drums), with Ralph Oswald later coming in to relieve Russell of the bass playing duties midway through the recording of Halfnelson's first demos. The steady diet of English psychedelia which the band had been taking in was regurgitated onto a twelve-track album, "A Woofer In Tweeter's Clothing", of which 100 copies were pressed and sent out to every conceivable record company mogul in the state. They were immediately returned, with terse little notes describing Halfnelson as a bunch of acid drenched freaks.

Unperturbed, Ron and Russell sacked their Rhythm section, recorded a more conventional four-song demo tape as a trio, and tried to solicit support from further afield.

One of the people on the latest mailing list was Todd Rundgren, who received the tape with delight. Assured that the band had been brought back up to full strength (by the addition of Earle Mankey's bass-playing Brother Jim, the drummer Harley Fernstein), Rundgren flew down to Hollywood to meet the Maels, and hear Halfnelson going through their paces. Still impressed, he then led the band into the studio to record what was to become their eponymous debut album.

MINIMAL

Released only in America, sales of the album were minimal, and eventually Albert Grossman, head of Halfnelson's record label Bearsville, called the group in to tell them where they were going wrong. He asked them to change their name to the Sparks Brothers, a suggestion which, initially, fell on deaf ears. However, rather than ruin what was otherwise a very happy working situation, Halfnelson agreed to become Sparks, and the first album was instantly reissued under the new band name.

"Wonder Girl" was pulled off as a single, and the band very suddenly found themselves

with a nu
County, Ala
the lower r
and Sparks
on America
East Coast
Max's Kans
jetted over
their spiritu

Represe
by former
Hewlett, S
ing in and
well atten
(supported
Queen), a
Whistle T
them as t
band retu
that eve
inspired
ations, w

Spar
their se
Clothing
inal den
widespr
soon a
swiftly
as to w
breakin
'73 An
the fir
total

it had to be gotten right in that amount of tosses. The pies had been frozen to keep their shape, but that made for a harder cream that Ron was forced to withstand. The best-looking toss unfortunately had some residual cream landing on me. So pre-Photoshop, the excess cream was retouched off of me.' This same messy scenario was repeated during the video shoot for 'All You Ever Think

184

live favourite, the studio version was never deemed satisfactory enough for inclusion. The song was revived again in 1974, but once more the Maels' perfectionism denied it a place on "Kimono". "I Like Girls" eventually appeared on "Big Beat", Sparks' sixth album, and Martin Gordon — who did the arrangements for the "Kimono" session — remains convinced that beneath the overdubs and remixes lies the version recorded in 1974.

SACKED

"Big Beat" was recorded in Los Angeles

...like arguing. How wrong

...'e brilliance as great as "Kimono", the Maels ...ct German disco-sup- ...and ask him to pro- Moroder agreed, and One In Heaven" (on Virgin) was directly ...fresh new life into ...had looked like be- ...pirth of "Saturday ...s were culled from ...mber One Song In ...k", and "Try-Outs ...all backed with ...ons of the A-side, ...rm as well. All ...the first time this ...on a Sparks single ...: Mother Earth", ...o cover was off- ...stimulate initial

...'n Heaven" and Top 20, and in ...at suspiciously ...een, in Sparks' ...he thing that ...(be it new or ...very e week that ...d to Top Of The ...100, two more ...ance 'Pop Musik") ...their while behind ...ce at red to their ...then

...k at arks to the ...aunt the limited ...John rent yellow ...play- Maels' for- ...two :least. The ...quee continuing ...nown , was very ...Grey single of ...cribed dominate ...The No. 1 in ...eemed untry. ...had r by the ...aspir- ths later, ...xtended ...wo cuts ...seemed before, ...to see nost as ...e orig- ived in ...ased to ...ing so r, and ...Girl", d by ...minds they ...oable of label. ...summer l for- ...en was piece ...nths of this ...d John S

...arp ...ased ...ing

form they returned to Moroder's Musicland studio to record "Whomp That Sucker". Following the brilliance of the two Virgin albums, "Whomp That Sucker" was somewhat disappointing, although Ron Mael's lyrics were as good as ever. Two singles were lifted from the album, "Funny Face" and "Tips For Teens" — the latter appeared as a 12" as well — but the label was to remain hit-less throughout Sparks' sojourn with them, and the two singles since become as elusive as the flops which preceeded them.

PATCHY

Since 1981, Sparks have released two further albums, with one single lifted from each. "Angst In My Pants" was a very patchy affair, whose best track — "I Predict" — gave the band a long overdue return to the American Top 100 singles, while last year saw the release of "Sparks In Outer Space", undoubtedly their finest overall collection since "Indiscreet". It was recorded in Belgium at the studio owned by Belgian band Telex, and the Maels repaid the favour by composing the English texts for that band's most recent album.

"Outer Space" is, perhaps, most notable for the long overdue fulfillment of the Maels'

intention to augment the band line-up with a girl vocalist. Jane Weidlin of the Go-Go's joined Russell on two tracks, "Lucky Me, Lucky You" and "Cool Places". The latter was taken as the single and, backed by a non-album track, "Sports", made further inroads into the American chart, although its UK counterpart remained fervently ignored by the British record buying public, and is sure to pick up in value over the next few years by virtue of that otherwise unobtainable flip.

Today Sparks remain as firmly independent as they have ever been. With the exception of the "Big Beat"/"Introducing Sparks" brace of turkeys in the mid-70s, they have remained unswayed by public opinion and demands, and continue along the neurotic and idiosyncratic paths which they first began charting almost fifteen years ago. Their music is constantly original, and often brilliant, and even if England should continue to remain impervious to their charms, Sparks are sufficiently succesful elsewhere around the world for that to be the least of their worries. And while their name is only now just beginning to make an impact in the record collecting world, the sheer overall quality of their back catalogue makes a serious investigation all the more worthwhile.

About Is Sex', Ron waiting stoically as a hail of cream pies rained down upon his face and keyboard and his bandmates slipped about in the resultant goo.

'Sparks In Outer Space' was very much a creature of its time. 'Less guitars, more synthesisers,' Russell explained. 'It's a much lighter album than 'Angst…', more danceable, more electronic.' He was surprised, he said, to hear 'a lot of people' describe 'Angst In My Pants' as 'too much of a rock'n'roll album,' although he took solace from the knowledge that Sparks have seldom been the critics' darlings.

In France, he reminded *Rock*, 'they said we'd gone too commercial with "When I'm With You". The newspapers have criticised Sparks ever since we started. These days they go on about how good the old stuff was, but they forget that we're only here today because we start each album trying to write things that make us come alive, and that are interesting. That's why we're still quite fresh. The fans don't pass everything under a microscope anyway.'

Ron, meanwhile, allowed the release of the album to continue the age-old debate of just how seriously the band's opponents should take his lyrics. In 'Dance, Godammit', for example, he insisted 'I like clubs, I like girls, I like music and that's it', and he admitted to *BAM* magazine, 'that's the way I'd like to be, if I only cared about girls, clubs and music. In my lyrics, I

talk about real things but in a fantasy kind of way. To be honest, I don't always know what my relationship is to the character in the song. I have strong opinions about what we do and what I want in music, but I assume my opinions are the way things actually are. I've been in the world of

185

these songs so long now, I re-write my own past, write from an adolescent's point of view, making it a real groovy world out there. One reason we've had success among young people is it comes out genuine. I'm not writing down to them. When you say I'm a satirist, that works against that feeling.

'Songs like "All You Ever Think About Is Sex" or "Praying For A Party" are not put-downs,' Ron insisted. 'If you're that kind of person, then love of sex and parties is a good thing. You see, I don't consider what we do satire – maybe I'm missing my own joke. It can get a little weird when I'm writing the words that have to go in Russell's mouth, so it looks like they're his opinions.

'But I'm not trying to set priorities for anyone, say they should get more interested in Central American relief. I'm not using reverse psychology. And I don't target the songs. Once you do that, and someone says, 'Oh! I see the point of that song,' then you've kind of finished with the value of the tune. That lyric approach is just too limiting, even if the music stands up.

'My songs just pop up – I don't decide what to write about. Sometimes it's not standard song fare, like "Mickey Mouse" or "I Predict" on "Angst In My Pants". Unfortunately, I'm not methodical enough to pick and choose, and just have to wait for things to come by. With "Popularity", one of the better songs on the new album [and which was performed alongside 'Cool Places' on *American Bandstand*], the song had different lyrics until the last day of studio work in Brussels, and I was forced to re-write it in twenty minutes so I could go with the rest of the guys to our favourite restaurant.'

Thoughts turned to a follow-up single: 'I Wish I Looked A Little Better' was certainly given a kick in the pants by another appearance on *Solid Gold*, but somehow it failed to take off. So, incredibly, did 'All You Ever Think About Is Sex,' and that despite a glamorous picture sleeve depicting Chynna (daughter of Michelle) Phillips and, on the vinyl, the marriage of a thunderous song to an even more thunderous dance remix.

Joking with the Sparks fan club newsletter, Ron outlined the birth of the remix; 'In the beginning, there was the seven-inch. But lo, the people said, prithee, why so short and so light on the bass drum? The Lord responded, "I shall satisfy your earthly desire. I shall extend the hymn by several minutes and unleash the full power of the rhythm section. Now get off my back."

'The people cheered and knew that not only was their Lord a good Lord, but that he could also get recording studio time at a very low rate. When the new twelve-inch creations arrived, the people sensed the dawning of a new era in all things carnal. They rejoiced and rejoiced and rejoiced a little more to the new sounds. Then went to an after-hours club. Unfortunately, on Sunday the people were too tired to properly thank the Lord for what he had given them, but instead remained in bed and read the Sunday papers.'

'All You Ever Think About Is Sex' was indeed a dance-floor hit, and elsewhere too, away from the regular singles market, Sparks continued to be in demand on the movie-score circuit.

In short order, Sparks' music appeared in the soundtracks for *Where The Boys Are* (with a re-recording of a 'Sparks In Outer Space' out-take, 'Mini-Skirted'), *Fright Night* ('Armies Of The Night'), *Heavenly Bodies* ('Breaking Out Of Prison') and the seldom-seen, straight-to-video *Bad Manners* (the entire soundtrack), although Fleury admitted that few of the songs ranked among the band's finest. 'They are all songs we'd never do on a Sparks album. It's just that the money is so good.' The sole exceptions to this rule were 'Minnie Mouse,' commissioned directly by the Walt Disney empire for *Mickey Mouse's Splash Dance* after Disney chiefs heard 'Mickey Mouse' from 'Angst In My Pants', and one of the songs included in *Bad Manners*, 'It's Kinda Like The Movies', performed by Gleaming Spires, Sparks without the Maels.

The brothers' own movie ambitions, too, were flying. They had plans for a film of their own, featuring two brothers fighting for the control of a large amusement park, while Ron auditioned for the role of the mad bomber in the comedy *Airplane II*. 'But I lost out to Sonny Bono, so that doesn't bode too well for my future career as an actor, to be beat out by Sonny Bono!'

Russell, meanwhile, tasted his first piece of serious acting when he was recruited to the cast of *Get Crazy*, a rock'n'roll comedy being made by Embassy Studios, to play the grotesque parody of an English superstar, Reggie Wanker (a name, incidentally, that means nothing to the average American).

Russell recalled, 'Originally Malcolm McDowell was the lead character. Troubles over his contract dragged on until they were forced to start shooting without him, and to seek a replacement. I was given the role.' After several weeks of shooting, however, the studio 'came to an agreement with McDowell and replaced me with the person that they originally sought for the role.'

There were no regrets, however. 'I was up for the role of the lead character in the film, but after seeing the movie I was quite happy that they gave the part to Malcolm McDowell. It was no *Clockwork Orange*.' Besides, Sparks did not leave empty-handed, as 'Get Crazy', another of those songs that Joseph Fleury didn't think too much of, was adopted as the movie's title theme.

Back on the road in the wake of 'Sparks In Outer Space', the band landed the opening spot on the American leg of teen idol Rick Springfield's latest outing, a massive affair that took them to the biggest American venues they'd ever played in – places like Madison Square Garden in New York City, Meadowlands in New Jersey, the Spectrum in Philadelphia and so on. Occasionally, Jane Wiedlin would fly out to join the tour, 'usually when we'd play somewhere fun like Hawaii,' laughed Kendrick.

And there were a lot of fun dates on that tour, as Sparks took the stage to a roar that was almost as loud as that which awaited the headliner, and then turned in a performance that completely dwarfed Springfield's own. Not quite the one-or-two hit wonder that history tends to suggest (in fact, he was touring in the wake of his eleventh hit, in a career that stretched back a decade), Springfield, who played Doctor Noah Drake in the daytime soap *General Hospital*, was nevertheless still better regarded for his television work, and his live show wasn't going to alter that. Sparks, on the other hand, had 15 years of experience behind them. They *knew* how to entertain, and the experience left Sparks in no doubt that, next time around, it would be they who headlined these cavernous arenas.

Sparks were flying. One more push, one more monster hit, one more step into the national consciousness. Comparisons with the past, even their most glorious British past, were redundant. In 1974, Sparks burst into view with 'Kimono My House', and then spent the rest of their stay in London trying to maintain that original momentum. This time around, their fame had grown organically, each album developing out of the success of its predecessor and paving the way intuitively for its successor. In a musical landscape that was dominated by the flash electro-pop of Duran Duran, Men Without Hats and the emergent Tears For Fears (their 'Mad World' was a huge K-ROQ hit that year), where Boy George was positively milking America's love affair with a tea-drinking transvestite, and even David Bowie had abandoned his past musical meanderings in order to strike out at the golden apple with the commercially measured *Let's Dance*, Sparks surely needed only to keep on doing what they'd already done, and they would be as huge as they'd ever dreamed of...

So why did Joseph Fleury feel so uncomfortable? 'Ron and Russell have never wanted to do things the easy way,' he sighed with perhaps just a hint of exasperation. 'That was why I loved them, because no matter what was expected of them by other people, they expected something else, and that's what they would do.' As the band went into the studio to begin work on their next album, 'Pulling Rabbits Out Of A Hat', Fleury knew...perhaps before the Maels themselves...that the group's direction was changing once again. The question was, would their American fans change course with them?

The first signs of a shift came as the band as a whole discussed their immediate plans. Shortly before the Rick Springfield tour, considerable thought was once again given to augmenting the line-up with a second guitarist. An audition or two was held, but nobody seemed to fit the bill, so the idea was shelved. Now, guitars themselves were shelved. Not altogether; there would still be room for the instrument on the record, but 'they started to shy away from guitars', as David Kendrick put it, looking instead towards Ron's growing bank of electronics to first supplement, then replace them.

It was not all down to the Maels, and certainly not simply the latest sideways step in the long and tangled dance with success that seemed so much a part of the Sparks story. Record-company politics, too, came into play as Atlantic Records demanded a suitably stellar follow-up to 'Cool Places', demands that left Fleury wondering whether Atlantic even deserved to have Sparks on their roster.

'"Sparks In Outer Space" had done really well, yet Atlantic still weren't happy,' Fleury complained. 'They told us that if we wanted to have a real hit, we'd have to get in some big-league producer. Well, someone had told us that Ian Little, who co-produced Duran Duran with Alex Sadkin, was actually responsible for that great sound the band got. So we called him in, but quite frankly, it didn't work out. After about a week, Ron and Russell were back to producing themselves and, while they are quite capable of doing that, the circumstances surrounding the sessions weren't too happy. The album has some great songs on it, but it's all a little too one-dimensional.'

Russell, too, admitted that it was Little's recent track record that had appealed. 'He was a guy who had programmed some Duran Duran albums – that was on his calling card, programmer for Duran Duran, sequencer, so we were "wow, we'll have one of those".'

Unfortunately, the programming and sequencing took over, as David Kendrick recalled. 'There's a lot of sequenced stuff, because Ian, the producer, was totally geared that way. I have to say, in that period, the sequencing was kinda new, the synth stuff, drum machines and all that were getting to be all the rage, and he was just geared that way. But at some point Ron and Russell were trying to be... not like Duran Duran, but get a little more sheen and polish, which I didn't think was really the way to go.

'To me, the best records were the ones where there's the most playing. By the time of 'Pulling Rabbits Out Of A Hat', it was studio. And the single from that, 'With All My Might', wasn't great.'

A gentle ballad, and a song that required rather more serious listening than most audiences would be prepared to give it, 'With All My Might' was quite possibly released without the band even being consulted, but if they were, it was certainly issued without their feelings being taken on board. Kendrick continued, 'the single was sappy and un-Sparks-like. Even to the people who really liked Sparks, it just wasn't happening and, once that happened, the big hit-making wheels were... I dunno, there's other groups who will play the game better. I don't know whose choice that single was, it definitely wasn't mine. We, the band, were saying "This isn't right".'

There were far better choices lurking on the LP. 'Pretending To Be Drunk' and 'Progress' were both released as 12-inch singles for the club and dance market, and when *American Bandstand* welcomed Sparks back into its studios on 6th October 1984, it was to perform 'Pretending To Be Drunk' and the album's title track, as well as indulging in some more of their now traditional banter with Dick Clark.

'He's a little scary,' Clark said of Ron, and Russell laughed, 'They only let him out of his room once a week to appear on television.' A little later, Ron took possession of Clark's own mike and took over the show, mimicking Clark's usual showbiz banter. Clark later wrote a letter to Ron that said, 'Dear Mr Mael, Thank you so much. I enjoyed being on your show. Sincerely, Dick Clark.'

The following week, Sparks were back in the *Solid Gold* studios, while they also filmed a performance for a Japanese show whose name, Russell insisted, translated as *Funky Tomato*. But record sales were sluggish and airplay sporadic, with even the normally loyal K-ROQ appearing to back away. At the end of 1983, 'Cool Places' had barely snuck into the Top 40 of the stations yearly countdown, while 'All You Ever Think About Is Sex' (the band's only other entry) made an appearance at Number 88. This year, 'Pretending To Be Drunk' reached Number 52, and 'Pulling Rabbits Out Of A Hat' made Number 71. And that, after the band's spectacular showing in 1981 and 1982, was it.

Russell reflected on this period with mixed feelings. 'I really liked those records a lot, by and large. Especially "Angst In My Pants" and "Whomp That Sucker".' Suggestions that he and Ron were growing bored with any kind of formula were certainly wide of the mark. 'We don't usually get tired, we're pretty resilient, so... it's hard to know exactly what was going through our minds because now we tend to work in a different way to then, and we have a different kind of mindset about how we approach what we're doing than we did during that time period.

'So we really are more methodical in what we do, and we make sure, at least from our perspective, that we are doing something that's hopefully really compelling and trying to push things. But when we did the twenty-one albums in London in 2008, we went back and rediscovered the K-ROQ albums, and we were pleasantly surprised there weren't the real lows, the albums you just wanted to forget about. You could see them in a fresh light when they were forced to be played again. It levelled out albums where maybe the recording wasn't as good as it could be, or the songs were stronger than how you did them on the album.'

'Pulling Rabbits Out Of A Hat' became the first Sparks' LP not to be granted a British release, at Joseph Fleury's instigation. 'I knew it would be our last album for Atlantic, and I had a good idea of what we wanted to do next, so I asked the company not to release it in Britain. The reasoning was that the two albums before it had done absolutely nothing in that country, and Atlantic had just put them out quietly and not advertised them or anything. And I knew that too many flop albums would work against us eventually. And I think I was proved right; "...Rabbits..." sold as many on import as "Angst..." and "...Outer Space" had on domestic release!'

David Kendrick didn't necessarily agree with Fleury's methodology. '"Cool Places" was the biggest commercial period, we went on a tour playing ten- to twenty- thousand-seater places, the record was in the chart and, at that point, all the mechanics of becoming a bigger band were there. It was all in position, but I don't think Sparks were quite up to it... Joseph certainly wasn't. He was absolutely lovely; you wish all managers were like that, so into the music. But you couldn't imagine him trying to get tough with the record company, or being the hard guy. He was great at making sure the lyric sheets were right, but yelling at people, he couldn't do that.'

Russell agreed. 'We had respect for Joseph because he was not enamoured with the whole business side of music. He was a true fan of music, Sparks obviously in particular, but a real fan of music, and you respect anybody who still had ideals about the music side of things, as opposed to selling any records. Maybe to his detriment, he was more concerned with the creative side of things.'

It wasn't only in the record stores that Sparks seemed to have peaked. Live, too, the group were pulling back. They remained a fairly regular draw in ever-loyal Los Angeles, but the musical complexities of the new album, and those inherent in the machinery that created it, rendered it difficult to present the songs live to the standard Sparks demanded. Kendrick continued, 'There would sometimes be a sequenced line, and to me those didn't hold up as well. There'd be a certain level of pulse, but we never played much from that record. We played "Pulling Rabbits Out Of A Hat" and "Pretending To Be Drunk", and we just played as a band.'

Yet all was not well. Guitarist Bob Haag and bassist Les Bohem were on their way out of the group, gently eased aside by the Maels' all-electronic plans for the future and, as 'Pulling Rabbits Out Of A Hat' stubbornly continued not to sell, those plans moved ahead faster than ever.

The problems that ensnared 'Pulling Rabbits Out Of A Hat' were not unique to Sparks. A number of the other bands that broke through in America during the early Eighties, including the much-lauded Duran Duran, were going through their own identity crisis at the time, either struggling to acquaint their audience with the natural changes in their music, or else simply falling out of favour as new bands came along to displace them. That, of course, was the normal sequence of events. No musical fashion, as the K-ROQ movement ultimately must be seen, has ever outlasted the three or four years it takes for the core audience to grow up and out of its early predilections and, if one considers that the 12-year-old who bought into 'Mickey Mouse' was now pushing 15 or 16 years of age, then the chances of Sparks' own musical shifts perfectly echoing those of an entire audience were minimal to say the least.

Whereas other bands might (and, indeed, did) simply give up or break up, however, Sparks had been in this position before, watching the 'Kimono My House' crowd turn away from 'Indiscreet' a decade earlier. The change did not hinder them then, and it wouldn't do so now. Sparks would simply carry on as they always had, and sooner or later an audience would catch up with them again.

The Maels knew, however, that they could not necessarily rely upon America any longer. Away from their own peregrinations, a major part of Sparks' current challenge was the fact that the music industry had finally got a handle on the video revolution.

When it first made its presence felt, five years earlier in the hands of the then-upstart MTV, video was a completely new medium. Many labels actively resisted it, incredulous that people would even want to watch their favourite songs on their television, and outraged, too, that MTV expected them to serve up the videos for free. Only as the first wave of unknown bands began to make an impact, breaking into the mainstream on the back of MTV's patronage, did the tide begin turning; and then, it was simply a matter of streamlining the medium to slot into the comfort zone that is the industry's own preferred way of doing things.

'Anything that has any sort of personality and eccentricity to it is completely out,' Russell complained to the British magazine *Record Mirror* in 1985. 'We were able to break through via video because MTV featured us. Now, though, the people in charge of choosing the videos are becoming the same as the radio stations. Everything is Billy Joel, which is sad.

'In America, there is a real corporate kind of thing that seeps through to the bands, even though they would never admit it. You can sense it, though. When you see Hall and Oates, they're really confident and they're really good, but there's something, this American corporate package that's thrown around, that isn't there for most English bands. There's a lot more of a naïve approach to what's done in England, which is why a lot of things can't get launched in the States.'

And that was why the Maels themselves continued returning to the UK.

CHAPTER EIGHTEEN

WHEN I TRY JUST TO KISS YOU, YOU SAY 'BETTER WAIT'

With the benefit of hindsight, Russell Mael later admitted that it was a mistake for Sparks not to have revisited the UK during the early Eighties; 'That's a really curious period for us, how it's perceived, especially from a British point of view because, that whole period, to this day we get interviews when we do stuff in England, "so where did you guys go? What happened to you in the Eighties?"

'Its weird how the two places at that time could have been so far off each other's radar as far as Sparks were concerned, because we had a really healthy situation, especially on the west coast of America, but also in New York, and then with the single "Cool Places", we played in the middle of the country as well. So, for us, that period is as significant in a way, not speaking from an artistic point of view or a qualitative point of view, but for visibility and commerciality, Sparks was having one of the biggest periods it ever had. And it's totally off the radar from a UK and European perspective, where we had had such big success before.'

He admitted that their record company, Atlantic, 'had no personal enthusiasm to champion Sparks in the UK,' but acknowledged, 'looking back, it was a real pity that we hadn't been able, for whatever reasons, to come to the UK during that time... Well, there was no reason we couldn't have, it was just one of those things. Things were going so well for us here, the profile was so high in Los Angeles, you kind of see the whole world from where you are. It becomes the centre of the universe. Were we to do it over again, we'd have tried to have this exposure in the UK, but it just didn't happen. So that's why. We had so much going on in America that we inadvertently overlooked our UK friends.'

'There was a lot of momentum here,' David Kendrick agreed. 'There's something about being big where you live.' And there's something else about knowing when to get out again...

Sparks returned to London in July 1985, for the first time in five years, bringing with them their best record of the decade so far. 'Change' was an epic single, a multi-faceted monster that spun through an almost bewildering succession of, well, changes, as it swept the musical taste of the past five years out of the window and presented the duo, once again, as a brand new creation. '[It's] probably more extreme than anything else we've done,' said Russell at the time, 'but we have really high hopes that it will strike some chord here – and maybe, who knows, creep in through some backdoor in the States.'

'Change' was recorded at Sin Sounds Studios in

r e v i e w e d   b y
j i m   r e i d

● **SINGLES OF THE WEEK**

SPARKS 'Change' (London) Giant studio panarama from one of the precursors of electro-pop. Simply trashes the other rockish releases this week with a rare impudence and a desire to go for those massive, massive instrumental statements. Thundered synths, thunder clapped drums, jagged guitars, moments of quiet menace and yes, those thoroughly distinctive vocals.

Brussels, and David Kendrick recalled, 'There's almost no real drums on that record, just a little bit. A lot of sampled stuff.' He is convinced that 'that song, the epic scope of it,' contributed much to the future sound of Sparks. 'That grand symphonic thing which they started doing with the vocal stuff later on, "Change" was the harbinger of that. But it's weird, from my years in the band, that was the last time the songs started from scratch in a band format, and since then... Now they have their own studio, they're more insular and they do it all their own way.'

At the time, however, 'Change' affected the listener in a way that perhaps no Sparks song since 'Equator', as it brought 'Kimono My House' to a stuttering conclusion, had been able to, utterly stripping back all the rules and regulations of conventional song structure to leave your ears wondering what on earth might happen next. Indeed, Peter Knego, writing in the Sparks fan club magazine when the single was still new, described 'Change' as completely unprecedented – 'much the same as the pioneering "Kimono..." and "No. 1 In Heaven" material. You will be shocked and delighted.' And he was right.

The song itself, Ron insisted, was 'the old, old story. The girl has left the guy, but there's still a glimmer of hope that the guy will get her back. What we wanted was to take a really clichéd situation like that, and picture it in a way that was incredibly fresh.'

DAILY MAEL

Ah! How time flies in the world of pop. Stephen 'Tin Tin' Duffy dusts off his Sparks fan club card and confronts Ron and Russ Mael. Andy Hurt takes notes, spots the changes and discovers this town ain't big enough for all of them

It was the accompanying bombast that really marked the song out, however. 'I like real jagged sound,' Ron admitted as the record crashed and thrashed through the firmament, 'and it's gonna get more and more jagged...' Unless, of course, you flipped the single over, and discovered the acoustic version of 'This Town Ain't Big Enough For Both Of Us' that they placed on the B-side. Ron explained, 'In America, people seem to think we're a new band, they're not aware of anything we did before "Whomp That Sucker". In England, the complete opposite is true, so we thought we'd give people something they could identify with.'

'It will be interesting,' added Russell. 'For the three or four people who might care.'

London Records, the division of PolyGram with whom Sparks were now (perhaps appropriately) signed, pulled out all the stops for the band, lining up a string of television appearances during their UK visit including, Ron laughed, the opportunity to make 'the world's cheapest ever video for "Change".'

On 29th July 1985, Sparks appeared at the unearthly hour of 9.20am on breakfast television, 'in this slot where bands got to show their new videos,' Russell recalled. 'We didn't have a video, so we just brought a cardboard cut-out of a TV screen and I mimed to the song while Ron held the screen over my face. It was our subtle way of telling the record company something.'

'London Records gave us half a million pounds to record the single and do the video,' Ron told Julie Brown, the show's incredulous host, and fellow guest Thomas Dolby. 'Unfortunately we spent the half million on the single, so I had to do the video on 50p.... You probably don't want to comment on the production values.'

Russell still adores 'Change'. 'It was one of those songs... you try to do stuff and you hope

every time you sit down to come up with a new song, that you're going to do something special. And that's one of those times where there's something that really clicked, and when it clicks with us it does it both lyrically and musically. The lyrics are really strong, and then having the seventy-five different sections musically going on, it just really works in that particular song.'

London Records certainly seemed to think so. Joking about Sparks' career-long habit of label-hopping – London was the group's seventh UK label in 14 years – Russell explained, 'we like to share the beauty of our music with all the labels. They need to be enlightened, so we like to not let one label hog it all. These bands like the Beatles, they stick with one label and it's kind of greedy. We're patrons of the entire music business community.' In reality, they genuinely felt they had landed with a company that would appreciate what Sparks already had, as opposed to what they could be moulded into, and at first that's how it seemed to be.

Russell continued, 'London did the single and I think they thought it really had something to it. But even an enlightened label like they were at that time…to their credit, they picked up on the song…but immediately they wanted an edited version of it to fit in with the radio in the UK, and they had us chop it down. But when you have a song like that, part of its strength is that you're in for a long ride. You're going along with the saga.

'There's ways of chopping things down without losing too much of the scope of something, but in that case we were obliged to chop it down to such an extent that they made the song even more confusing! It was hard to figure out what was going on because it was so hacked up, so their efforts to exploit it for radio actually made it more difficult to understand the song. Seventy-five changes in three minutes made it really bitty, and it lost a lot of the scope.

'We were really saddened that a song like that had to be hacked up. It was kind of obliterated in our eyes. In any case, it's one of those songs that should have been left alone and it could either have been one of the ones that makes it by its length, or it dies. But at least it could have been what it was.'

For once, the single was released well ahead of any new album. Three new songs were already in the can, and a handful of others were gestating healthily. But, as Russell puts it, there was no rush.

'After "Change" failed to chart, London wanted us to submit another track from the next

record

JULY 27, 1985 45p

tears for fears
untouchables
sparks
harold faltermeyer
luther vandross
denise lasalle

2 X | Funk

TOM DOLBY

ORDER

SPARKS' MUSICAL career has experienced plenty of highs — but its share of lows have crept in too. It was at one of those times that Sparks appeared in the disaster movie 'Rollercoaster'. Russel explains that he'd thought of film as a career while studying English at UCLA and had joined the film-making course. He doesn't view 'Rollercoaster' as the kind of thing he'd intended though. At the mention of the film, Ron coughs embarrassed and Russel explains:
"That was just being in a film...

how can you m

sunset

7" + 4 TRACK 12"

A6446

GUN

album. They suggested that we give them something more danceable. The idea was that if they liked it, they would put the album out. As it happens, we had written quite a lot of dancy new tunes, including a song called "Music That You Can Dance To".'

The joke, if that is what it was, backfired spectacularly. Convinced that they were the victims of a slice of the legendary Mael wit, London passed on the song and passed on the band's contract as well. In the event, it would be over a year before they completed the album that took its name from the song that London rejected, and when it appeared, it was on Curb, a label set up through MCA by the legendary producer Mike Curb, but one that was seemingly blighted with very little muscle in the marketing department. Sparks' willing embrace and, to a lesser extent, pre-empting of the Hi NRG-

e Brothers
n with their
ectro pop,
of its time
n the sub-
Ain't Big

r, Ron the
yboards —
moustache,
t into you,
annies and

turned to
at least —
Romantic-
aven'. As
e with a
anging.
ong hair,
eir ener-
e of the
ency of
ho had

for the
ow and
estra-
a half-
h with
s That

"The
mmer
What
situa-
was

with
it's

tish
en-
wn

country. It's not been an easy business.
"Anything that has any sort of personality
and eccentricity to it is completely out," says
Ron.
"We were able to break through via video
because MTV featured us. Now though, the
people in charge of choosing videos are becoming the same as the radio stations — everything is Billy Joel, which is sad."
"In America, there is a real corporate kind of
thing that seeps through to the bands — even
though they would never admit to it," continues Russel. "You can sense it though. When
you see Hall And Oates, they're really confident and they're really good but there's something — this American corporate package
that's thrown around — that isn't there for
most English bands. There's a lot more of a
naive approach to what's done in England —
which is why a lot of things can't get launched
in the States."

YOU GET the impression that Ron and
Russel are not particularly enamoured
with their fellow US recording artists.
"Not at all," agrees Russel. "I don't think
our music was a conscious reaction to anything though. It was just the type of music we
like — what amuses us. It just happens that
that isn't what is happening in the States.
"Los Angeles, where we're from, is unique
and plays lots of English things which are
obscure in other parts of the States. They
championed Sparks as well, so we've become
really successful there, but less so in the rest
of the country.
"But we've come this far," he continues, "so
we don't want to make concessions. 'Change'
is probably more extreme than anything else
we've done, but we have really high hopes
that it will strike some chord here — and
maybe, who knows, creep in through some
back door in the States."
"We don't take any pride in being esoteric,"
adds Ron.

style electronic dance music that would be sweeping the clubs as the decade neared its end deserved a great deal more attention than it received when 'Music That You Can Dance To' hit the racks with a hollow thud.

The album artwork continued Sparks' tradition of pairing up with great photographers, on this occasion, the Los Angeles-based Rocky Schenck. According to Ron, however, things did not go as Schenck planned. 'Much to his dismay, the cover photo that was the most appealing to us was the one where the floor light inadvertently fell over, and we were only lit from behind. So out of about 500 shots taken, all perfectly lit, we selected the one black sheep.'

Not that Sparks themselves seemed overly anxious to promote the record, although the now seemingly inevitable appearance on *American Bandstand* was a definite fillip as they unveiled the latest line-up of the band, with only David Kendrick surviving from the old Bates Motel era.

A new guitarist, Hamburg-born Hans Reunscheussel, arrived from the Los Angeles band What Is This? (a group otherwise best remembered for the early membership of Red Hot Chili Peppers Jack Irons and Flea). He was joined onstage by keyboard-player John Thomas, and the jazz singer Pamela Stonebrook, and there is no denying that it was an exhilarating performance.

Indeed, in keeping with the pulsating electronic backbeat, their final *Bandstand* appearance ranks among Sparks' most explosive television gigs of the Eighties, a storming rendition of the album's title track being supplemented by a highly distinctive rearrangement of Stevie Wonder's 'Fingertips,' making the song their first recorded cover version since 'Do Re Mi,' back in 1972. Or was it? When Dick Clark asked why Sparks recorded the song, Ron straight-facedly denied ever having even heard of 'this Steve Wonder' person. 'It's my song.'

A video was shot, a predominantly black-and-white romp through 'Music That You Can Dance To', and for the first time, Sparks retained control over every aspect of it. Russell Mael: 'As we were both real interested in films, the logical step was to make our own video. We took everything into our own hands. We financed it ourselves. We went and got the lighting. We're never in the same scene together because I shot the scenes that Ron's in and he shot the ones I'm in. It was all done on a low budget, but we managed to get the look we wanted. I guess it was down to our good taste.'

But the video was scarcely aired, and the brothers received far more exposure when they appeared, as two faces among many, in the video for the Ramones' 'Something To Believe In' single, raising funds for the utterly spurious but very convincing charity, Ramones-Aid.

Not even a promotional visit to the UK, Germany and France could drum up any enthusiasm, either for Sparks or, it seemed, by them. The Maels, Kendrick and Fleury made the trip together, but media interest was confined to just a handful of interviews.

Writer Edwin J Bernard described 'Music That You Can Dance To' as one of the 'freshest' albums he'd heard 'all year. It's punk disco, but with melody. There's an underlying horror beneath the deadpan seriousness of it all.' But he was a lone voice in the wilderness, and Russell sounded only half in earnest as he mused aloud on British television's *Music Box* about the possibility of a longer visit.

'If all goes well with the album,' he told the watching public, they would be over to tour. But the key words were 'if all goes well'. It was important, he insisted, to re-establish Sparks as a live touring entity again, but they needed a new hit record before that could happen. They had no intention of simply dragging a fossilised 'tribute band' around the provinces, playing the oldies to the fan club. Sparks could not and would not exist like that.

Live work was confined to a smattering of dates on the American west coast, then, and Kendrick admitted that his heart was no longer in it. 'Again, there was no guitar live, and a lot of sequencing. I dunno, for my taste, I missed having guitar on some of the songs.' Even Kendrick's drums seemed disposable – his happiest memory, at least of the newer material, revolves around performances of 'Change,' bolstered as it was by a dynamic timpani sound. 'There was talk again of going to Japan,' he continued, 'but, by that time, the live thing for them wasn't getting the results any more. And after that point, they stopped using a band altogether.'

It was a gentle break. Kendrick, who had now outlasted any previous member of Sparks in any of their incarnations, recalled, 'Did I know it was the end? Not in so many words. There was a little bad feeling with Bob when the guitars went away, and just from my personal taste, I didn't think those last couple of records were as good as the ones we did before them. But Ron and Russell were definitely moving towards the two of them working together.'

The only survivor was keyboard player John Thomas, who was called in to the Maels' newly completed home studio to work as an engineer. Asked to predict the brothers' next move, however, Kendrick would have drawn a blank. The Maels had recently fallen in love with a Japanese animation project, *Mai The Psychic Girl*, and they were also deep in discussions with director Tim Burton, at that time best known for *Pee Wee Herman's Big Adventure*, about a movie version of the play *Nightclub Confidential*.

'The original music is sort of Manhattan Transfer-style,' Russell said, 'so he wants us to write a totally new score.' Sadly the project never came to fruition, but still, said Kendrick, 'they liked the idea of doing something outside the record industry. So they were trying other things and purposefully pulling away.' Sparks would cut one more LP during the Eighties and then, for all intents and purposes, cut the strings on their musical career.

Away from their own music, Sparks remained capable of surprise. Having met the French band Les Rita Mitsouko at a television studio, the Maels threw themselves enthusiastically into a collaboration which ultimately reunited them with Tony Visconti, as he produced the band's 'Marc Et Robert' set, and spun off a major French hit single, 'Singing In The Shower'.

But Sparks' final LP of the Eighties, 'Interior Design', came and went with scarcely any fanfare whatsoever. The first album to be recorded in the home studio that sprawled across Russell's canyon home, it was also distinguished by the Maels taking over all the performing and production duties for the first time ever – which, they insisted, was something they should maybe have been doing all along.

As Russell reasoned, 'We're kind of very strongly opinionated about what it is we should be doing and if there was someone we could trust our output with, we'd be more than happy, because it's easier that way. I guess what we do now on our own is a lot more extreme because of that. So we tackle the production ourselves, rather than use someone from the outside to produce it, and I guess it gives the music a kind of reckless edge.

'It's a blessing to have a place you can work in, and not have to look at the clock. You just like to have independence, to have a place where you can try things and not have to worry about racking up a studio bill, especially the way we work. There's no other way we can do it. To be constantly at the mercy of a record company, especially if it's something you want to try and it's not related to an album of yours... Maybe at certain points you're almost forced to take that on, but in the end if you hadn't made that move to have your own studio, you'd be kind of foolish, I think. Also, at the time, the technology was getting cheaper and you were able to do stuff at your home with a decent quality and all. So it wasn't like saying in a pejorative way, "Oh you have a home studio", meaning it would have an inferior sound.'

Nevertheless, what emerged as 'Interior Design' proved to be a minor release on a minor record label, by a band that finally seemed to have reached its sell-by date. True, the cover recaptured the brothers' oldest values, returning to the Halfnelson notion of retouching a vintage Fifties-era photograph ('every 14 albums or so, it's a good idea to re-state your theme,' Russell laughed). The sleeve credits included the first-ever mention on a Sparks record of Christi Haydon, the photographer on this occasion but destined to become an integral part of the band itself.

And the video accompanying the 'So Important' single raised a few smiles with its depiction of Ron playing a mean lead guitar (for the first time since the early- Eighties live performances of 'Wacky Women'). But the song scarcely lived up to its title and it was easy to begin writing Sparks' epitaph. Indeed, as the years of silence began mounting up, it seemed less and less likely that Sparks would ever return.

'Not getting through becomes frustrating,' Ron admitted. 'You wonder how many times you can keep coming up with good songs. It was driving us nuts.'

A new supporter appeared on the horizon, bringing with him a rare ray of enthusiasm. Russell recalled receiving a letter from Morrissey 'saying that if it wasn't for 'Kimono My House', he'd never have gotten into music. We thought there might be collaboration there. He said it would be wonderful.'

Excitedly, the brothers scooped up six songs that they thought might fit the bill and sent them off. Morrissey's response was immediate; 'All he said was,

"Russell, your singing is better than ever".' But there was, the Maels quickly noticed, a certain 'vagueness' about whether or not he actually wanted to work with them; as a songwriter, after all, Morrissey had never needed to look beyond his own notebook for material, and as a solo performer, he was finally beginning to get into his stride after so many years either in, or escaping from, the Smiths.

His third solo album, 'Your Arsenal', would soon be taking shape under the supervision of another of his Seventies idols, Mick Ronson and his new band was more than a match for any he had ever performed with before. Morrissey really didn't need to collaborate with anybody at that time.

But he was a devoted Sparks fan and he wanted them to know that, at a time when they themselves were still questioning whether there was still any room in the world for their vision. So it was with a certain wry humour that Ron pointed out that, even here, there was a sting in the tail. When Morrissey toured the US in February 1991, the brothers were invited down to the Los Angeles show. 'We got free tickets and met David Bowie, who got on stage to duet with him. Someone else, Morrissey's biggest influence, wasn't invited onstage, of course, but we're just being bitchy now.'

Continuing in a similar vein a few years later, Ron told Q magazine, 'it's always Bowie, Ferry, and don't forget Eno. I don't mind getting left off the list for Bowie or Ferry, but when Suede start mentioning Cockney Rebel, it's a little disconcerting. It leaves you with a very paranoid feeling.'

As so often when he spoke his mind, Ron sounded as though he was joking – which of course was his intention. There was an undercurrent of genuine, and justified, grievance there, though, especially when the brothers looked back on the past decade and took stock of their own most lasting achievements, most of which seemed now to revolve around gifting other people with careers of their own.

Indeed, they were by no means the only people who looked askance at the activities of the Pet Shop Boys, the longest-lived of the synthipop duos that grew up during the first half of the Eighties, and mused aloud on just how deeply they must have supped on vintage Sparks when they were younger... all the way down to the flamboyant front man and his sombre, musicianly sidekick. Russell saw a lot of other comparisons, too.

'Our major strength lies with our songs. With Giorgio Moroder, we combined electronics and a dance feel with our style and our lyrical slant. I think maybe that's what we have brought into the pop music scene, the idea of a band working with dance rhythms and songs at the same time. I think that whole area's been explored by other bands like the Pet Shop Boys, [but] we kind of opened up that dialogue.'

And they weren't afraid to let people know it. 'We're supposed to be flattered,' Ron grumbled. 'You repeat "We Are Flattered" as a mantra, but you're in a band and therefore you're an egotist, so when you see people taking our surface element and, because they're not so stylised, selling more records, you get pissed off. You don't want to come across as bitchy, but I think we've written a lot of Pet Shop Boys tunes.'

There again, he also confessed that '"Bohemian Rhapsody" really pissed me off because we'd had "Get In The Swing". [And] look at Cheap Trick – two wacky guys, two pretty guys...'

Some of the bands who took their cue from Sparks had owned up by now. In 1989, Depeche Mode songwriter Martin Gore included a fragile version of 'Never Turn Your Back On Mother Earth' on his covers EP, 'Counterfeit', and declared 'Propaganda' to be one of his all-time favourite albums. Ron responded by numbering Gore among the 'very few writers who can compose electronic pop songs. It's an increasingly rare art form, as synthesiser music is usually dance tracks. But Martin does it so that you can't see the join between traditional elements and the electronic parts.'

MY TALE begins one day in the summer of 1974, the setting platform two, Beckenham Junction station. My two heroes de-train in my very presence. A *Beezer/Beano/Spectator* thought bubble materialises above my embarrassingly hirsute bonce. "Gosh! Cripes! Lumme!" As I caught the Maels by the buffers, I thrust a Roy Wood single under their four nostrils. "Sign here, lads, and this anecdote will return to haunt you in a decade," chortled the thought bubble. . .

Meanwhile in Birmingham, a gaunt youth by the name of Duffy was coming to terms with adolescence and Sparks. Little did young Stephen realise that a mere 11 years later he would come face to face with his idols. Had he known, he would probably have exclaimed "Crikey! Blimey!", etc etc. . .

Summer, 1985. The two fans and their youthful box-brownie operator accomplice are on time, in awe, and in Fortnum And Mason's St James' restaurant awaiting the arrival of Ron and Russell. Fifteen minutes elapse, and the interviewees are led into the arena by a press officer. Tea, four cakes, a coffee, and your starter for ten. . .

Duffy: "Why did you come here originally, after the two Bearsville albums?"

"It was pretty much desperation," admits Russell. "Nothing was happening for us in LA – we'd play the Whisky A Go Go, and apart from the four waitresses and three 12-year-old groupies, we were playing to nobody. We took up an offer to come to England, did the *Whistle Test*, and a buzz started on a small scale, but it was a buzz! Then 'This Town' came out of nowhere and gave us a large following."

"Where did that get to?" inquires young Stephen.

"Number two – goddam Rubettes!"

Duffy: "Why did you leave after that period of success? Did it begin to tail off?"

"It did begin to tail off, and also there were certain creature comforts we'd become used to back home and really missed." Such as, Ron? "We were used to sun – we kinda got conned that summer, because it was really hot, and we thought, 'this isn't so different!' – but we were here for three years, and I was getting chilblains."

Of course, some people had been saying much the same things about 'No. 1 In Heaven' and 'Terminal Jive' for over a decade at that point, but a new generation of rock writers, those who were maybe too young to remember precisely what they were talking about but for whom the Pet Shop Boys were a vital part of the soundtrack to their teenage years, took swift umbrage at the accusation. But the Maels were right to be pissed off. And while they insisted, 'heh heh, we will have our revenge,' it was difficult to see precisely how they might do so.

As the Nineties got up a head of steam, and a host of brand new musical diversions came along to amuse the youth of the day, Sparks were little more than a memory, something that would be dragged out for a 'remember the Seventies' radio spot in Britain, or a new wave nostalgia jam in America. 'I Predict' and 'Cool Places' might turn up occasionally on MTV, lumped in with old Billy Idol and B-52s videos, but that was it.

A slice of vintage *Top Of The Pops* footage for 'This Town Ain't Big Enough For Both Of Us' turned up on a glam-rock video collection, and that prompted a few more nostalgic wonderings. But Sparks themselves were gone.

'We really felt the next best project for Sparks to undertake would be something new,' Russell said. 'It was one of those reassessment moments, where we wanted to do something new

THE RETURN
OF THE
ODD
COUPLE

Sparks have had at least two careers already. First as early Seventies glamsters, second as late Seventies disco weirdos. Now they're back again... with a song about dancing
Story: **Edwin J Bernard**

that wasn't a part of our past normal release thing – "Oh, there's a new Sparks album", and you reach the point where it doesn't matter what the album is, it's just "Oh, it's another Sparks album". So we thought doing a movie musical would be the next best thing for Sparks, even though it wasn't a Sparks project *per se*; it wasn't a Sparks movie.'

When the Maels first became involved in Hollywood screenwriter and producer Larry Wilson's vision of bringing *Mai, The Psychic Girl* to the big screen, they could never have imagined that the project would consume the next five or six years of their lives. According to Russell, 'Larry's been a fan of Sparks for a long time. He wanted to figure out a way of using our music in some kind of film context. He optioned the rights to this comic book, and asked if we'd like to try and do a cutting-edge musical for the Nineties that hopefully didn't have all the clichés of musicals that have been made more recently. It's a pretty intricate project.'

So intricate that the time literally slipped away. 'We had been that whole period working on the movie musical, so that whole period was spent devoting all our time to it, because it was, and it still is, and we have our hopes up that it will be, something we really believe in.

'We're so happy that we spent six years of our lives in obscurity as far as Sparks people were concerned. What were we doing, off on an island in the sun, we were working on this thing really diligently. It was a special and unique project, and we were going through various directors and different companies, most of whom were really significant, and various rewrites of it because there's the whole Hollywood thing of rewriting everything, development hell and all that kind of stuff. So we were put through that whole process, because the music to the project is really integrated with the dialogue and the film.

'It's not just a film that has a separate screenplay and then there's a musical score; the music is really integral to the storytelling, so we were a big part of the whole development of that, and just for various reasons – everybody's heard every Hollywood story – it gets shuffled around between various film studios and various directors, and the one constant were ourselves and the screenwriter, as we were the guiding forces behind it in a creative way.'

Francis Ford Coppola and *Nightclub Confidential* dreamer Tim Burton (with whom Larry Wilson co-wrote and co-produced *Beetlejuice*) were among the Hollywood heavy-hitters who passed through the planning phase, but as time passed so the proposals and responses that came through seemed ever less impressive, and ever more infrequent. Finally whatever money had been available for the project ran out, although Russell is adamant that *Mai* lives on.

'There wasn't a starting or ending moment. Things drifted in and out, and even when we started working on our own next project, which was the 'Gratuitous Sax...' album, it wasn't like *Mai* was deceased. It was still lingering and, to this day, there's hope.'

At the same time, however, he acknowledged that 'At a certain point when you're working on a project like that, it becomes this masochistic thing. You have faith in it, you have quality people attached to the project, so you know there's something there, and that it's not just you being wrong. There were all these amazing people involved, directors who'd done great things being attracted to the film, so you cling on to the hope that, despite the odds, it'll work. So that's why we clung to it.

'But the years are going by with this project and, at a certain point, you wonder how long are you going to wait? We just said "well, the project's either going to work or not work"; it was done, we had done everything we could, so it didn't seem like it would matter if we sat there babysitting it that closely any more. It was either going to happen or not happen, no matter what we did, so we said "Well, let's do another Sparks album."'

Mai, The Psychic Girl was not the sole reason why Sparks did not record, however. Tragedy also played its part, as the brothers lost the one solid bedrock that they had always been able to rely upon for opinion and maybe even a little guidance; an ear to the streets that they themselves might not have visited, a quality-control monitor who would happily tell them if an idea or inclination was going nowhere. After a long battle with AIDS, Joseph Fleury passed away on 2nd March 1991 in Los Angeles, a little over a month before his 38th birthday.

Derek Paice, Fleury's friend back in London in the Seventies, had not heard from Joseph in years at that point, their friendship having been put on hold when Fleury returned to the United States in 1975. 'I was so sad and angry to read that he had died,' said Paice. 'I didn't know he was ill, and I only heard about it a couple of years after the event. I don't know what he was like as a manager, but the Joseph I knew was warm, kind and gentle, the most loyal of fans, and a friend I shall always be proud to have known.'

Russell: 'That was a very sad occurrence for us, because he'd been the guy that was really totally supportive of Sparks from the very beginning, from 1972 at Max's. He came to the show as a fan and from 1972 until the time he died, he went from at first just being a fan and a friend, and then taking on more as time went by. He was a really good guy.'

Fleury's humour, enthusiasm and knowledge would all be greatly missed, but, more than that, his death robbed him of the opportunity to see Sparks scramble out of the critical and commercial abyss into which the past few albums had deposited them and to finally, publicly, don the creative crown that he, paramount among all their admirers, had always insisted was theirs by default.

'That's the thing that people never understand about Ron and Russell,' Fleury said during that 1985 visit to London. 'Fans get it, but the critics and the public, they hear the records and they say "Oh, it's Sparks being quirky, or wacky, or taking the piss out of something", but that is never what they are doing. Sparks' whole reason for existing is to push the barriers of pop music and take it into new areas. They don't always succeed, and occasionally you could say they've sat back and simply done what they think will sell. But put their backs against the wall and tell them they're finished, and they will always come back and astonish you.'

He was talking about the then newly released 'Change' at that time, but fast-forward eight or nine years and he might easily have been discussing the brothers' latest activities as they prepared to end their five years of self-imposed silence. In terms of public awareness, their backs were indeed up against the wall – and maybe that was exactly how they planned it.

As Russell later reflected, 'It always seems to work that when you're under the most duress and desperate, things often tend to spur you on to do something that is creative in a way you might not have done had you been in a more comfortable situation.'

CHAPTER NINETEEN

A FEELING IS A-BREWING THAT WE DON'T NEED ANY MASTERS

By 1994, Sparks had been in existence for 25 years. That was how long it was since Urban Renewal Project curled up their collective toes and the Maels envisioned Halfnelson instead; that was how long it was since the brothers first began alternately infuriating and engrossing audiences with their sly encapsulations of life in all of its absurd and irreverent glory. And that was how long it was since Ron and Russell were asked for the first, but by no means the last time, how could they possibly devote their entire lives to hanging out with their brother?

It was a question whose answer they had long since grown accustomed to couching in humour and further irreverence, and those were the answers that would become set in stone, no matter how brutally they might contradict one another. It was time, finally, to lay the beast to rest. With one new song, 'When Do I Get To Sing "My Way"?', Ron bared his teeth at the Frankenstein he'd created and let his kid brother have it with both barrels.

It is a song of despair and dismay, the bitter lament of a singular talent watching as lesser beings clamber over him to stardom; and, in case the lyric was too subtle for most people, the video that would accompany 'When Do I Get To Sing "My Way"?' into the public domain left nobody in any doubt. There they are, the infant Maels, Ron still scowling beneath slicked-down hair and a tiny moustache, Russell all cherubic, the apple of his mother's eye, and it doesn't matter what work of genius Ron may write at the living room piano, it's Russell's performance that will win the hugs and kisses.

And so it goes on through life. Ron writes the songs, but he's seated in the shadows. Russell merely sings them and his life is lived out in the spotlight. When will Ron get to sing 'My Way'? When Russell is finally out of the way, of course.

And if you believe that, laughed Tammy Glover – who, by 2009, had outlasted even David Kendrick in the ranks of Sparks' longest serving musicians – you'll believe anything. She had yet to join Sparks when the song was released; was still touring the American west coast with one garage band or another, eating Fritos in the back of the van on their way to another grimy club gig. Since then, however, she has spent 10 years with the Maels, and she knows the truth about their relationship; the truth about 'My Way'.

'He's messing around with that visual image, that's all. Ron loves his brother, he appreciates the fact that Russell is the matinée idol and he's not. You have to understand that they're really like that; Russell is very fun and light and loves sugar and fashion and he'd rather spend money on a pair of shoes than a heavy meal, that's quite true about him. And Ron is his big brother.'

If there is a subtext to the song, hidden or otherwise, it is aimed at far more distant targets than his sibling. 'The sentiment of the song is Ronnie at his essence,' said Glover. 'It's a bad comparison, but somebody like Bruce Springsteen gets a lot of respect as a confessional songwriter, somebody who's speaking the truth, and Ron recognises that he's doing the same thing. But, because he uses irony and humour, and the things in his songs are considered to be funny, and he creates characters, people think that the truth isn't there in those songs.

'People haven't looked deeply enough to see that he's writing about as much of a truth as any "conventional" confessional songwriter, and again, if you think of a guy like Dylan, who has created a character and has lived his life through that character, Ron has done the same thing. He is as much of a character as Dylan. But he doesn't get that same respect because people are too busy finding it funny.'

They'd been finding it funny for 25 years... But things were set to change. In 1989, Ron and Russell stepped back from the brink because they did not want people ever to think their latest LP was 'just another Sparks album'. Starting again five years later, there would never be such a thing as 'just another Sparks album' ever again.

Work on the 'new' Sparks album began slowly, without the Maels themselves ever thinking in those terms. Neither did they see it as a comeback record. They had been writing and recording songs throughout the gestation of *Mai The Psychic Girl*, some that were intended for use in the movie, others that simply slipped out and were put to one side to be examined more closely later on. Now it was time to begin that examination process.

They worked slowly, just the two brothers and percussionist Christi Haydon, the woman whose photography had graced the sleeve to 'Interior Design' and who, according to Haydon herself, was discovered by the Maels while working in a perfume shop in Los Angeles. Since that time, she had been appearing among the background characters in television's *Star Trek: The Next Generation* as one of the show's regular extras across two seasons in the early Nineties.

There, Haydon was most frequently positioned in the aft stations of the bridge in roles that included a Command Division Ensign, a flight engineer and even a Romulan civilian. (The costume she wore as a Romulan in the episodes *Unification I* and *II* was later sold at the on-going It's A Wrap auction of *Star Trek* memorabilia. Eleven bids saw the outfit, which consisted of a pair of cropped green trousers with long mustard-coloured socks and a square-shouldered long-sleeve top, sell for $157.50).

There was never any sense of urgency as these latest recordings took shape. The sessions spun out over some two years, but Russell shrugged, 'There were no deadlines to adhere to, because we weren't signed at the time.' They simply recorded as and when they felt like it.

Finally, however, in November 1993, a new Sparks

single was released – their first since barely visible 'So Important' in 1989. Opening on a string crescendo that echoed the shower scene in Alfred Hitchcock's *Psycho*, 'National Crime Awareness Week' united Sparks with Finitribe, a semi-industrial dance-pop band from Scotland.

The introduction had been made by Sparks' music publisher of the time who also handled Finitribe's output, and the first contact was simply a tentative remark, as Russell puts it, that 'These guys in Scotland were real fans of ours, and would like to work with us. We'd already recorded "National Crime Awareness Week", and he suggested that we give it to them to remix. We thought what they did was fantastic. It wasn't just a remix in a dance sense, they reshaped and restructured our original song, and made it a much stronger single than we were able to do. We became really good friends with them, and they ended up shooting the video for "National Crime Awareness Week" in Edinburgh.'

It was a key collaboration. In the years since the Maels last recorded in earnest, the technique and technology of the remix had shifted light years ahead of where they'd left it. In 1989, after all, a remix necessitated nothing more than adding a few extra instrumental passages and maybe turning up the percussion a little. Four years later, however, the art of the remix had changed drastically, and now songs would routinely be reshaped and re-crafted to create visions far, far removed from the original but without losing either its essence or intent.

The Maels, by absenting themselves for so long, had missed that period of development, and missed, too, the frightful missteps that many other veteran artists would make as they attempted to keep 'up to date' with a constantly changing technology. They returned, therefore, to discover all the elements in place; elements that they themselves had believed were crucial years before they were possible. This serendipity would shape the musical future of Sparks as much as any other single element in their long musical career.

There was talk at the time of the collaboration extending even further, and Q magazine mentioned the possibility of a new Sparks album, 'due soonish, involving Scots dance collective Finitribe'. Russell pondered a joint version of 'When I'm With You' being recorded for inclusion on the Scottish trio's next album, 'Sheigrai'. In the event, neither happened, at least partially because Sparks' own career was suddenly taking off again.

Without exception, the songs that the brothers were stockpiling for the new album, which itself had already taken shape by the time 'National Crime Awareness Week' was released, were recognisably Sparks, but sounded unlike anything Sparks had produced before.

Like the earlier Sparks albums cited as examples of the Maels rewriting the rules of rock, 'Gratuitous Sax And Senseless Violins' owed little, if anything, to what was going on around it. In 1994, after all, America was still labouring beneath the colossus of grunge, while in Britain, it was BritPop, with Suede and Blur paving the way for a surge of similarly-themed new bands. And into this melee, Sparks dropped an album that married classical themes with pop-culture references, a disc-full of dance songs that demanded you sit down, and a series of such grandiose lyrical excesses that even the song titles extended their metier: 'Now That I Own The BBC', 'I Thought I Told You To Wait In The Car', 'When Do I Get To Sing "My Way"?', 'The Ghost of Liberace' and, best of all, 'When I Kiss You (I Hear Charlie Parker Playing)', a song that packed such a perfect Pet Shop Boys vibe that it is sometimes difficult to remember exactly who should be complaining about whose light fingers!

Going into the sessions, Russell declared, 'We just said that we were going to do something that lyrically is as uncompromising and interesting as we can make it – and as extreme – and that isn't timid musically. The real knack for us is finding areas that are accessible but extreme.' The result wasn't simply one of the best albums of the year, but one of the best albums Sparks had ever made.

A record deal fell into place. 'On someone's recommendation,' Russell recalled, 'we sent "When Do I Get To Sing 'My Way'?" over to a guy named Mark Stag in England for a remix.' Stag played the track to a friend of his at the Logic label in Germany; 'They liked the song, and asked to hear what else we were working on. Then they offered us a worldwide deal.' In November 1994, 'Gratuitous Sax and Senseless Violins' was released to what had suddenly revealed itself as the most avid European audience Sparks had enjoyed since 'Propaganda'. Russell laughed, 'Even compared with the others, we think this a really extreme Sparks album. And it's funny, but our most commercially successful periods seem to be when we make our most extreme music.'

And, as for those artists who they continued slyly sniping at in interviews? Suddenly the Maels found a lot of people agreeing with them.

SPARKS

It's at dinner that it really hits you. The figure to your left speaks, you turn to reply and - fuck me! It's Ron Mael!

Ah, you remember Ron Mael. Looks like Hitler, seldom smiles, scarcely speaks, is one half of the most inventive pop duo this country has ever produced, and he's sitting next to me, celebrating Sparks' first British hit single since before you were even born (15 years, that's about right, innit?). Then someone else speaks and you turn, doubletake, and in bug-eyed amazement you hope they wipe the seat down when you've gone. Russell Mael, Ron's brother, ethereal curls and bug-eyed falsetto, and the other half of, etc. Yep, Sparks are back.

Stop that head scratching, I'm about to explain. Straddling the '70s like a Californian colossus, Sparks knocked out a string of utterly compulsive British hits between '74 and '79. The two biggest, "This Town Ain't Big Enough For Both of Us" and "Never Turn Your Back on Mother Earth," have won cover versions from Siouxsie & the Banshees and Martin Gore respectively.

The hits dried up with the decade, and Sparks finally turned their back on Mother England around 1980, returning to California and pioneering instead the whole west coast American New Wave quirky-pop trick.

Dig out Rhino's recent *Just Can't Get Enough* collections, and Sparks dominate the buggers, in person (cuts on volumes six and nine) and in spirit. Arguably, without Sparks, you wouldn't be sitting there listening to whatever it is you're listening to right now.

Ah, but this ain't no retro-party. "It bothered us for a long time," admits Russell, "the things we'd been doing through the late 1970s, the whole electronic synth thing which started with 'Number One Song in Heaven' - it was obviously very influential, but whenever people talked about that music, it was always other people who got the credit."

Still, Russell speaks without bitterness - after 25 years and 16 albums, Sparks have long since accustomed themselves to rock'n'roll's habit of overlooking the innovators.

This time, though, karma came through. It's six years since Sparks' last album, the stopgap Interior Design, six years during which the world spun off onto a dance-relateds tangent which was tailor-made for their return. And the moment they came back, "people were calling us, saying how great they thought we were, and how much they'd like to work with us."

Now, everyone reckons Sparks were an influence, and the way things are building, that influence is ubiquitous. You can see kids in another 25 years, dancing to "(When I Kiss You) I Hear Charlie Parker Playing" and "The Ghost of Liberace," and Sparks will be on their umpteenth comeback, and the whole thing - basically, Sparks are unstoppable, aren't they?

Ron speaks. "Actually, we keep stopping. Then we start again, and each time we think we're a new band." The day after our interview, Sparks are off to Germany to appear on a show called New Faces. "And we still don't know whether we're the token old fogeys, or whether, too, think that we're new."

"Every time we reappear," Russell continues, "our audience breaks in half. It's approximately - 50% people who remember us from before, and 50% who think we're a brand new band." Throughout Sparks' early '80s US renaissance, the brothers actually gave up signing new-found fans who asked them to autograph copies of Sparks' first album. "People would turn out to be their tenth or eleventh. 'We recorded our first album in 1971 with Todd Rundgren,' Ron smiles, 'and had a number one single in Montgomery County, Alabama' - it sounded pedantic to keep telling people that."

"In America, we'll probably bring in more of the later songs that people there remember." He reveals that again during the mid-1980s Sparks had to ask American audiences not to play material from their seventies heyday as it confused people so much. "Over there, it was a different Sparks completely," Ron adds.

Which is as much a testament to Sparks' sheer versatility as it is a comment on America's cultural inversion - it didn't happen here, so it didn't happen at all. From "This Town" to "Beat The Clock," from "Angst in my Pants" to "Change," Sparks' sound has been characterized by a refusal to do anything by the rulebooks - their own included.

"When we started this album," Ron says, "we went into the studio thinking..."

The Mael brothers are back: older, better and ballsier

FIRST NIGHT

SPARKS
SHEPHERDS BUSH
EMPIRE
LONDON

...was an ...ities, ...s we ...e bal-...nt of ...gain ...tion ...Ron ...ther ...er of ...hit ...ugh ...ese ...us-...to ...of their four-on-the-floor version of "Doe A Deer" (I kid you not) was a camped-up triumph.

Perhaps because some parts of the arrangements emanated from a DAT player, the PA sound was superbly detailed. The gunshot in "This Town..." ricocheted from sneaker to speaker. "Never..." ...was spectacular. What really cemented this performance, though, was the obvious strength of the new material. Rhythmically, the title track of the forthcoming album *Balls* tipped the hat to The Prodigy's "Firestarter", and found Russell exhorting us to be courageous: to show some... well, balls.

Elsewhere, "More Than A Sex Machine" tagged an anthemic, electronica chorus to a quietly contemplative lyric, the singer now grappling with the downside of being perceived as a shag and nothing ...w ap-...might ...y con-...crowd ...then, ...n Mael ...f pop-...ongues ...rks are ...' forth-...album ...best in

...CNAIR

IT WAS their first London show in 17 years, but Sparks carried it off. They didn't so much dress the stage as address it, combining Hollywood Babylon kitsch with gay disco lasers and suburban garden furniture.

Generations of kitsch, camp followers mingled quite contendedly in Ron and Russell Mael's wake. For there was Russell, falsetto as ever, and there was Ron, he of the pencil-thin Gable 'tash and wild staring eyes, bossing the programmes that built up to an immediate reminder of why Sparks predated post-modernism.

Sparks arrived in the early Seventies as a welcome alternative to the grinding conservatism of American rock, and if some of what they now offered seemed mainstream, that was only because they had helped change the rules way back when.

Sparks
Shepherd's Bush Empire

MAX BELL

Switching from cocktail surf muzak to techno absurdity, Ron and Russ always kept the crowd on their toes. Long before ex-Suede guitarist Bernard Butler guested for the latter segments, which included faithful old friends like This Town Ain't Big Enough for the Both of Us and Amateur Hour, the Mael bros had made their ironic point. The exquisite (When I Kiss You) I Hear Charlie Parker Playing was proof enough.

207

'Erasure and the Pet Shop Boys should have the decency to blush,' insisted *Q* magazine's Tom Doyle as he considered Sparks' rebirth. 'Sparks, in more ways than one, invented the Pet Shop Boys,' agreed *The Face*'s Simon Williams. And so it went... But *What's On In London* magazine told the story's happy ending. 'Both Vince Clark [Erasure] and Dave Ball [Soft Cell] have remixed Sparks' [new] single, and a recent chance meeting with Neil

Tennant led to much shaking of hands and mutual appreciation.' Finally, the brothers' influence was being acknowledged...

On 12th November 1994, in a warm-up gig at Leicester University, Sparks played their first British concert in almost exactly 19 years – the final night of the 'Indiscreet' tour, at the Fairfield Halls, Croydon on 9th November 1975, had been the last time they had set foot on a British stage. Five days later, they would repeat the exercise in far more auspicious surroundings, the

Shepherds Bush Empire in West London. It sold out weeks in advance and, ahead of the shows, the handful of people who'd attended the warm-up were mercilessly quizzed for their recollections of the evening, as the crowd wondered exactly what to expect.

Pre-taped music filled the air, the opening moments of 'No. 1 Song In Heaven'. Then the brothers appeared, the performance began and it was goose-pimple time. Maybe the song had dramatically divided Sparks' audience down the middle when it was still on the chart, but a decade-and-a-half later it was welcomed back like an old friend When it swirled into a lush 'Never Turn Your Back On Mother Earth', Sparks could have probably left the stage there and then and the audience would have been satisfied. Of course they didn't; there were too many other old favourites to play through first, all the way back to 'Do-Re-Mi'.

But the night wasn't about the past. A decade earlier, when Russell told *Music Box* that Sparks would only consider touring if they had a new album whose sales backed up their decision, he

was not kidding. 'Gratuitous Sax And Senseless Violins' was still far too fresh on the shelves for it to have done much more than rack up a few reviews, but that night there was a surge of excitement in the audience that didn't waver for a moment as the attention shifted to the new songs, and went into overdrive for the most quintessentially anthemic of them – 'Let's Go Surfing'' a song that so exquisitely summed up all that Sparks had ever cared about that, even today, it is unmistakeable.

As Tammy Glover reflected, 'Ron and Russell revere pop culture. They're all about girls and fast cars and sunshine, and they're citizens of the world. They're uniquely qualified to talk about that.' And when Bernard Butler, still newly departed from Suede, stepped out to join them for the final encore, Sparks had achieved the next-to-impossible. They had wholly merged their past with our future to create a new age in which they would never fear stepping out on a limb again. The band was a quarter of a century old, but it had finally found its place. Butler, incidentally, later appeared alongside Sparks on the UK television show *The White Room*, as well as creating an ambient 'Fashionable World Of Fashion' remix of 'When I Kiss You (I Hear Charlie Parker Playing)'. Sparks moved on to Europe following the London gig, but they would be back in the UK in March 1995 for a further six concerts, all as avidly attended and enthusiastically received as the first. But, if Britain was fascinated by Sparks' renaissance, Germany was absolutely enthralled.

Although there had never been any doubt as to their popularity there in the past, Sparks had never toured the country before, something of a surprise when one considers how many albums they recorded in Munich. Now they set about remedying that situation, then watched as the single 'When Do I Get To Sing "My Way"?' achieved sales in the region of 500,000 copies. In December 1994, German television even devoted an hour-long *Rock Archiv* show to the reborn Sparks, interspersing interviews and vintage footage with live performances of half a dozen of the new album's finest moments.

Back in the UK, 'When Do I Get To Sing "My Way"?' climbed to Number 38, Sparks' first British hit since 'Tryouts For The Human Race' in 1979, and the cue for a welter of television appearances – including a notable slot alongside MTV Europe puppets Zig and Zag, highlighted by Zag's own inimitable impression of Ron, stock still at his keyboard, his woollen face turned to the camera to reveal a crudely drawn-on moustache.

A single of 'When I Kiss You (I Hear Charlie Parker Playing)' was next out of the box, a Number 36 hit to coincide with the live shows in March 1995, and two months later 'When Do I Get To Sing "My Way"?' returned to the charts, climbing this time to Number 32. A Christmas show at the London Forum marked the end of the year, but 'Gratuitous Sax And Senseless Violins' produced one more UK chart single when 'Now That I Own The BBC' made it to Number 60 the following March.

The Maels kept themselves busy. Plans were afoot for a Christi Haydon solo album. Haydon was a prominent member of the band now, both as percussionist and backing vocalist, and the Maels had even written her a showcase song, 'Katherine Hepburn', to accompany her other in-concert excursion, the old Bee Gees ballad 'Holiday'. An appearance on British TV's breakfast-time *It's Bizarre* gave 'Katherine Hepburn' its first (and so far only) broadcast airing, while a couple of other song titles circulated among the fan club members, 'Titanic' and a cover of the Who's 'Boris The Spider'. In the event, the project faded from view, but another was soon in the pipeline.

As far back as the 1994 Shepherds Bush Empire show, Ron and Russell had been considering what their next album might be, and were already acknowledging that it would probably be a hits package. But not any old compilation. Recent years had seen the music industry become obsessed with the notion of the tribute album, a hit-and-miss concept that involved an album's worth of disparate artists paying 'tribute' to a past act that had somehow influenced their career. Sparks, in a variation on the theme, were going to orchestrate and perform a tribute to themselves.

The idea originated at the Logic label headquarters in Germany and was not, initially, received with particular enthusiasm by the Maels; indeed, according to Russell, he and Ron were 'really opposed' to it. They wanted to move on from where 'Gratuitous Sax And Senseless Violins' had taken them, to push their own ideas forward, not sit back and let the old ones take precedence again.

Logic, however, had logic on their side. An entirely new audience had grown up around 'Gratuitous Sax And Senseless Violins', especially in Germany, and though the Maels were content to allow that audience to discover their past in its own time, it was also worth remembering that, in doing so, they would be wholly at the mercy of whatever repackaging any of Sparks' nine former record labels considered appropriate.

The band had been late arrivals in the CD market; a French 'Best Of' in 1985 and 'Music That You Can Dance To' and 'Interior Design' over the next couple of years were the first of their albums released in the new format, and since that time both had been reissued time and time again, under increasingly bizarre and often entirely inappropriate titles. 'Music That You Can Dance To', for example, had already been repackaged as 'The Best Of Sparks', but whether anybody was lured into purchasing either of them under the impression that they were picking up something further-reaching is debatable.

A handful of compilations had done a better job of introducing fans to at least one facet of the band, notably 'Mael Intuition' with its wide-ranging round-up of the Island-era material and 'Profile', which offered a broader sampling of their Seventies and Eighties work. But Ron and Russell had already raided their archive once, when they compiled the 'Heaven' and 'Hell' collections of, respectively, hits and rarities for their French label in 1993. They had little interest in returning to the vault.

Their German friends, however, had other ideas and, although the Maels remained uncomfortable 'with the general direction', they agreed to do it, particularly after producer Tony Visconti was brought on board to work with them for the first time since the Les Rita Mitsouko sessions in 1988.

Publicly, of course, the brothers never made anything less than the best of the situation. 'People might know us for our better-known songs,' said Russell, 'but for example when we had a hit in Germany with "When Do I Get To Sing 'My Way'?", we suddenly realised that a lot of the younger fans had no idea about our previous recordings. So we thought that it would be a good idea to introduce some of our older stuff to a younger audience. And we wanted to do it in a creative way, and come up with new arrangement of those songs.'

Visconti was especially delighted to be involved. The string arrangements he wrote for what would very pointedly be titled 'Plagiarism', he told the Sparks fan club newsletter, were filled with 'unexpected turns of phrases and chords that make me wriggle with painful delight. I'd like to be a fly on the wall twenty years from now, and watch a kid's face when he finds his granddad's CD of 'Kimono My House' in the attic, dusts off the archaic boom box and hears Sparks for the first time.'

Other 'names' came into the frame – singer Jimmy Somerville, whose falsetto-powered Bronski Beat were among the bands that arose in the UK while the Maels were breaking America; Vince Clark's Erasure, one of those two-man synth and vocal bands that the Maels had once glared so menacingly towards; and Faith No More, an American rock act whose own love of Sparks would probably have surprised their fans as much as it did Sparks' own. There was also a collaboration with Bernard Butler for what the guitarist described as a 'very Nirvana-ish' assault on 'Beat The Clock'. That, sadly, remained in the can, but still there could be no complaints.

Together, this unlikeliest of teams pulled off a minor miracle, taking songs that Ron and Russell had previously considered more-or-less perfect in their original form and transporting them down whole new avenues.

'Plagiarism' was designed as the career-spanning hits collection that no other label could ever have mustered, even in those years of corporate take-overs and multinational conglomerations. Almost every song on the album had been a hit, or at least a well-aired single, somewhere in the world, from the old K-ROQ semi-favourite 'Pulling Rabbits Out Of A Hat' to the smash that started it all, 'This Town Ain't Big Enough For Both Of Us', presented here in two distinctly different versions – one fired by Visconti's orchestra, the other by the full frontal assault of Faith No More.

'Plagiarism' might not have qualified strictly as a greatest hits collection – there was no 'Cool Places', no 'Looks Looks Looks' and no 'Wonder Girl' either – but it was a remarkably successful attempt to condense the story of Sparks into just 16 songs, ranging from the earliest hits all the way through to the 'Interior Design'-era 'Big Brass Ring', and when the band toured in the album's wake the fresh takes on the old songs breathed new life into each of them. Before the end of 1997, the 'Plagiarism' versions of both 'No. 1 Song In Heaven' and 'This

Town Ain't Big Enough For Both Of Us' had made it on to the UK chart, the former reaching Number 70 and the latter, 23 years after its first appearance, Number 40.

It was Sparks' guest slot at the Europride '97 Festival in Paris on 28th June that perhaps climaxed the period, an orchestral version of 'This Town Ain't Big Enough For Both Of Us' ringing out over the packed and darkened Place de la République, before Jimmy Somerville cavorted out for an exuberant and, in places, almost slapstick 'No. 1 Song In Heaven'. Most significantly, it was the biggest audience Sparks had appeared before since they commenced their latest

run, but it also marked the concert debut of the latest member of the band, with drummer Tamera 'Tammy' Glover taking over from Christi Haydon.

Glover had been a Sparks fan since the K-ROQ period - 'I have photos of me at one of their Eighties Disneyland performances, I'm beaming, my braces reflecting the camera flash. I was a child of the Eighties, so my first exposure to the band was as a fan during the 'Angst...' period, and stuff like 'I Wish I Looked A Little Better' and 'All You Ever Think About Is Sex'... the Valley Girl movie was a big touch point for me, because I was a teenager. I was just a fan, I went to some of the Magic Mountain dates... punk had happened, and new wave was all about kids in High School, and that was very much my scene, listening to the Cure, the Smiths, the Police, Pat Benatar, Chrissie Hynde, the Go-Gos; it was another time in

pop music when people were highly stylised, and that always works for Sparks.'
Amazingly, and quite coincidentally, Sparks even played her High School graduation party at Rancho Alamitos in 1984. Glover explained, 'When they were a K-ROQ band and K-ROQ sponsored all

those Magic Mountain gigs, it was a big thing to play those grad nights. I have a photo somewhere of me with Meg Ryan-style permed bangs, and the band is on stage in the background wearing their sequinned suits.'

Thirteen years later, however, such things were far from her mind as she ground her way around the independent club circuit, while simultaneously making her way up the executive ladder of American television. She was fortunate enough to be able to juggle the two careers, something she's still managing to achieve.

Having spent much of the Nineties 'being in bands that were summarily signed and dropped', Glover was drumming with former Wondermints front man Brian Kassan's Chewy Marble when a friend recommended her to the Maels.

'When I got the call to audition and went to their studio, I'd sort of lost touch with Sparks,' she admitted. 'I didn't even know about 'Gratuitous Sax...'. A friend who knew they needed a drummer recommended me to them. I auditioned, but didn't hear anything back right away so I thought maybe I didn't get the gig. Then their manager Eric called and said "You've got the gig, do you have a passport?"

'Well, Chewy Marble played with different bands around Los Angeles; Baby Lemonade, the Brown Eyed Susans... we were contemporaries with guys who are doing interesting things now, a tight-knit group of people, and my very first gig with Sparks was the Paris show. I went from playing club dates like the Troubadour and the Whisky and the Roxy, all the normal club things in Los Angeles, to suddenly playing this huge event in front of thousands of people. So I flew over, played that gig. I was very, very green, super excited, I flew in for the weekend, and it was a thrill.'

Glover would go on to become a stalwart of the Sparks set-up for the next decade.

CHAPTER TWENTY

FOR AFFAIRS WITH STAYING POWER, I GO AFTER LIMOUSINES

Having dedicated a song to Japanese director Tsui Hark, the Hong Kong-based action movie maker, on 'Gratuitous Sax And Senseless Violins', Sparks were now to work with him on their next project, as they were invited to contribute the soundtrack to *Knock Off*, a Jean-Claude van Damme thriller set on the eve of the handover of Hong Kong from Britain to China. It was Hark's second film with Van Damme (following 1997's *Double Team*), and also his second since relocating to Hollywood to try his luck on the American movie scene.

Tapping into one of consumer society's greatest fears, the piracy of designer brand clothing and accessories, *Knock Off* was as wild a ride as any of Hark's earlier Hong Kong efforts, with Van Damme and co-star Rob Schneider proving as unlikely a successful double act as Hollywood itself could ever have imagined. Sparks' contributions to the film, a clutch of incidental instrumentals and a luscious title song, were exemplary. It was, Russell said, 'exciting to make a musical contribution to what was anticipated to be a high-profile film', and 'Knock Off' evidenced that, conjuring one of Ron's most straightforward lyrics ever into a piece of absurdist joy in which the narrator's clothing is only the first of the blatant forgeries he purchased in Hong Kong. The song he sings, too, is a 'knock off'!

But critics who relished the absolute mayhem of Hark's past work were disappointed by the wham-bam chaos of *Knock Off* and, following their lead, audiences stayed away in droves. And while Russell confirmed Sparks' own admiration for the project when he described the experience as 'an honour... Tsui Hark is one of the Hong Kong greats, and it was an honour to be working with him,' the projected soundtrack album was cancelled.

'Knock Off' itself, however, would live on, as it was added to the slowly growing stockpile of songs intended for the next Sparks album. Working, of course, at their own studio, and at their own pace, the sessions were, according to Glover, 'a natural progression of them recording and continuing to make relevant records.' Her own presence added to this process; her drive home from work took her directly past Russell's house, so she would simply drop in on the way to see if there was anything they needed her to do; a casual set-up to be sure, but one that brought an entire new dimension to the music.

'Once I came into the mix, they had a drummer that was local, instead of working with the synthesised stuff they had been doing. Even though there's a lot of electronic drums on [what would become the 'Balls' album], if you listen to how that stuff was put together I played a lot on top, so there's an organic quality. You hear the loops, but you can also hear the live fills that happened in 'Bullet Train', for instance, or the cymbal stuff in 'The Angels'. They demoed a song, and then I'd come in and play. Russ would record sections of songs, and whatever sounded better was kept. Because they were unlimited in their studio time, they could play around as much as they wanted.'

Not everything they recorded during this period was intended for 'Balls'. Having worked with the French animators Olivier Kuntzel and Florence Deygas on the video for the 'Plagiarism' version of 'No. 1 Song In Heaven' (and planning to do so again for 'The Calm Before The Storm'), Ron and Russell now wrote and performed a five-song soundtrack to the Kuntzel and Deygas short

A *Cute Candidate*, the tale of an animated character who becomes so popular that 'he' is persuaded to run for political office, with devastating consequences.

Still, the album was the main attraction, as the movie soundtrack would be available only as a limited edition single the next time the band played live. Arriving in 2000 with a range of alternate cover designs that put one in mind of the multi-coloured vinyl options that Virgin Records offered Sparks fans years before, 'Balls' was a powerful and very immediate collection. Nobody could deny that it overwhelmed the senses on the first few hearings, but somehow it didn't retain that same power across repeated listens. Not for the first time in their career there were suggestions that Sparks were cruising for a moment, considering their next move and simply releasing an album out of habit.

The single 'Calm Before The Storm' won a German Internet 'Favourite Video of the Summer' poll and reignited enthusiasm with one of the most audacious remixes Sparks (or anybody else) had ever released, one which eschewed the traditional pattern of eliminating the vocals by taking the opposite approach entirely.

'We didn't want to have the traditional club remixes,' Russell explained, '[because] we are pretty bored with that whole convention. We preferred to do an alternate version of the song with Sparks' sensibility rather than some faceless club mix.'

A second single, 'The Angels' inspired a masterful remix from Tony Visconti, but 'Balls' itself just didn't seem to bounce, at least not as a studio recording. In concert, it became an altogether different proposition, as if Sparks had deliberately set out to make a record they *could* perform live as opposed to the usual dilemma of trying to make the music fit into a stage production.

Laughing, Glover contrasts the Sparks touring experience with her previous bands, and admits there is no comparison. 'They're such a pleasure to work with. As a drummer, I don't have aspirations to be a composer or a singer, so this is the perfect gig for me because there's a lot of overlap in our sensibilities. Ron and Russell drinking chamomile tea and reading the *New Yorker* backstage, it's a pleasure to play with people who love good food, stay in great hotels and are civilised!

Sparks

David Hemingway meet:
perennial pop maverick:

A pair of former child actors and catalogue n Sparks are a pop phenomenon. Releasing the album in 1971, they pre-empted Queen's crea melodramatic, neo-operatic pop. After collaborati legendary Donna Summer producer Giorgio Morode end of the same decade, they served as the bluep pretty much every 80s synth-duo with a flamboyant and an enigmatic keyboard player including, most Soft Cell, the Associates and Pet Shop Boys.

In the 90s, they've collaborated with the likes of Butler and Faith No More, and luminaries such as Bjö Order, Depeche Mode, Pulp and Saint Etienne have be as fans. They've written songs name-checking dead pur 50s crooners, ostentatious homosexual pianists, the auth *Street Car Named Desire* and the American architect ac for the interior of the Guggenheim Museum. Better still, t album contained a song based on the chilling, childhood riposte, "I Thought I Told You To Wait In The Car".

But there's only one secret I want the Mael brothers to Ron and Russell, I've been wondering, what moisturiser use?

"Good question," agrees Russell Mael.

It's an important one. You appear to be defying the ageing "Well, it may be more than moisturiser."

Oh. Face packs as well?

"Not face packs, no. It's the lifestyle. We abstain from a that's fun. We abstain from drinking, smoking and eating th you'd really like to but you shouldn't because it's not good fc good moisturiser always helps, but abstaining from anythin able for your entire life is worth as much as any beauty produ

"I", announces Ron without any embarrassment whatsoever, "use L'Oreal Line Eraser."

With a piercing stare that could stun small mammals, Ron Mael is the most iconic of keyboard players. Impeccably dressed in a well-cut suit, his perfect knot, his hair slicked back just so, he has, for 25 years or so, stood inert and deadpan behind his inst only occasionally venturing into the spotlight to te audiences with the kind of frankly disturbing danci comes from hours spent in front of a full-length mirror pre to speed-skate.

The first time I saw you dance was a shock to the system "I can imagine it was. I apologise for that."

Does this stage persona come naturally?

"It does. People ask whether it's an act. It doesn't feel act at all. It's just what I do. It's completely natural and have an alternative to it."

*"Abstaining from an
enjoyable for your
life is worth as mu
any beauty prod*

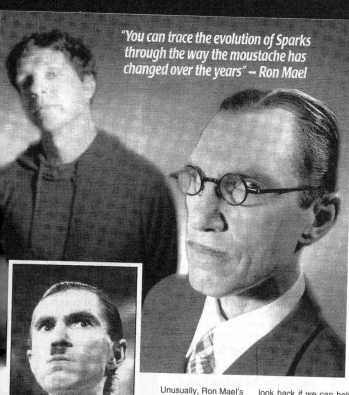

"You can trace the evolution of Sparks through the way the moustache has changed over the years" – Ron Mael

Unusually, Ron Mael's moustache also seems to have acquired a legendary status in the World of Sparks.

"It's important," claims Ron, running his finger along the neat, thin line e his top lip. "To me, the moustache was always like a logo. can trace the evolution of Sparks through the way the stache has changed over the years. It continues, but it ges. The other thing, just as an aside, is that I look horrible ut the moustache so it's going to stay.

rly on, I misinterpreted the way the moustache would be " he admits now of his original face furniture, and it was wrong- umed to have been inspired by Hitler and, subsequently, led to ncellation of shows in France. "I never thought of it as some f right-wing political statement. That was dumb on my part."

alising that the moustache had become so legendary, the ade a video of it being shaved off to the theme from *Dragnet*. resented the video before one of their LA shows. e reaction was horror," the brothers state in unison.

 odd couple have just released their eighteenth album, the atively titled "Balls" (Recognition CD REC 510). Accentuating udevillian, post-80s pop of 1994's "Gratuitous Sax And ess Violins", the new album reveals the duo to be growing aying young?) disgracefully: "We're really opposed to the eat at a certain point in your career, you're supposed to things down," they rage, quietly. "For us, it's almost the e." Sparks are — delightfully — sounding beefier.

"More Than A Sex Machine" laments the loss of identity felt by an imagined pop star who feels emotionally castrated by his reputation as a red-hot lover ("Is it autobiographical? No, not really.") "Irreplacable" bemoans the deliberate, built-in obsolescence of late 20th- and early 21st-century consumer durables with the observation, "They're designed to break/They're designed to fail". "Bullet Train" celebrates the aesthetically pleasing Japanese locomotive that revolutionised the country's rail system and, more than this, was symbolic of all that was enviably modern about the country in the 70s and 80s: "It's a testament, a testament to science and art," sings Russell Mael, poignantly. "It's a testament, a testament to who that we are."

Such modernity, claim the duo, is paramount to Sparks' existence.

"The incorporation of contemporary elements is essential to what we do," asserts Russell Mael. "We're always aware of what is going on."

"Just the fact that they're not songs about traditional subjects makes it 'modern'," agrees Ron. "We're always searching for topics that haven't been covered."

Likeably, given that they've been creating music together since 1970, Ron and Russell Mael claim to detest nostalgia. They're more than happy *not* to talk about their past.

"We've had 18 albums and we don't look back if we can help it," claims the latter. "We're proud of our past, but we like focusing on the future."

For Sparks then, in the year 2000, rock has to find new ways of being provocative.

"These days, whenever there's something provocative," they despair, "it seems to be done in a calculated way. White rap-metal groups are supposedly as provocative as it gets, but they just seem really contrived. Those bands are all really formulaic. They're not provocative, they're maintaining the status quo. Even a lot of black rap acts seem intense and mean, then you see them on a Sarasota beach on MTV's *Dance Party* showing that they're just as willing to sell their souls to get coverage as anyone else."

So how can someone be provocative?

"In a way, what we're doing *is* provocative. It's puzzling to a lot of people. Doing the sort of music we're doing and having the sort of career we've had is subversive in its own sort of way. It's going against the grain of what people are doing. It's on the outside of different trends or styles."

"The Prodigy seemed to be provocative in a certain way," asserts Russell, citing one of his favourite bands, "but it's becoming a little bit of a caricature, the more it seems they're attempting to tackle America. They're trying to be more like a rock band."

Though they once imagined themselves to be comparable to the Who or the Rolling Stones, the Mael brothers get rock/pop just wrong enough to mark them out as icons to be cherished.

Some people will never get it.

> *"The incorporation of contemporary elements is essential to what we do"*

119

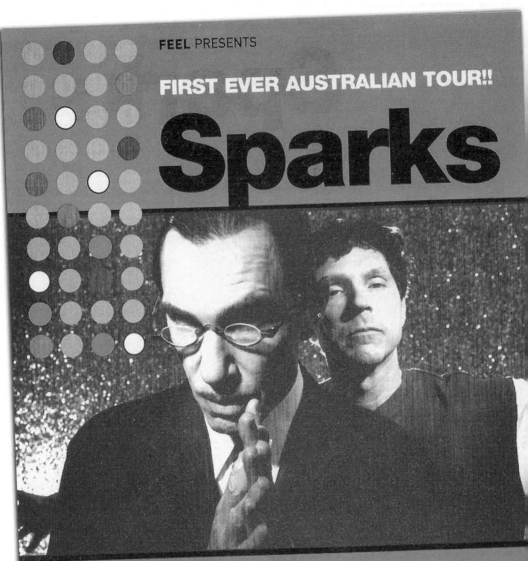

FEEL PRESENTS

FIRST EVER AUSTRALIAN TOUR!!

Sparks

Fri. 12th Jan ● The Metro
WITH SPECIAL GUESTS GERLING + PURE POP DJS
TICKETS ON SALE NOV. 29TH FROM THE METRO PH: 9264 2666 & RED EYE

Sat. 13th Jan ● Corner Htl
WITH SPECIAL GUESTS GERLING + TRIPLE R DJS
TICKETS ON SALE NOV. 29TH FROM GASLIGHT, GREVILLE, POLYESTER & THE CORNER PH: 9427 9198

NEW SPARKS CD 'BALLS' OUT NOW THROUGH FMR   FEEL RRR

'They have a different schedule when they're touring, compared to other musicians. They live like normal people. We get up and eat breakfast, they go and do any press that's needed. Then we might go to a gallery or take a walk, go shopping, do something fun. We soundcheck, and play the show, and the guys are so focused. When everyone else is running around, Ron and Russell take things really seriously, focusing on giving the people who came to see them their very best. Then, after the show, when other bands would typically just be getting started, we're headed back to the hotel to sleep.'

It was thrilling, too, for her to discover the vast network of fans, spread out across the world, for whom a Sparks show was more than a concert, more than a night out. She had already witnessed how excited Ron and Russell became as they looked at each day's itinerary and speculated over who might be waiting for them when they got into each new city: people like the French journalist who interviewed them back in 1974, the German passer-by who befriended them in Munich in 1979, long ago promoters and hotel valets, an address book stuffed full of names and faces that they might barely have thought of since the last time they met, but whose memory could be recalled with barely a moment's hesitation.

Now, however, Glover was meeting the friends and fans themselves, and learning exactly what made them – and, by an indefinable process of osmosis, Sparks themselves – tick.

'Sparks are always struggling against this cliché about a singer-songwriter, and I think that a lot of people don't understand that Ron's music is as sincere and heartfelt and romantic as anybody's, because on the surface it might not feel that way to them. And that's unfortunate because it's every bit as crafted and, if you actually look at what's going on in those songs, there's a very deep emotional content. But you have to be able to connect with it and understand it, and that's why Sparks fans are so special.

'I love the fact that, wherever you go in the world, you meet these people who think they're members of a secret club. Whether we're in Tokyo, Sydney, Berlin...you will find guys in thin ties and slicked-back hair, thinking they've found their partner in crime. Obviously now, with social networking and the web, they're all finding each other, but 10 years ago they weren't doing that, and they didn't know the others even existed.

'Part of why I love playing shows is to see Ron and Russell so happy, and it just fills my heart with joy to see them getting the respect and the adoration that they deserve.'

Sparks' touring itinerary this time around took them further afield than they had ever been before. August 2000 brought shows in Los Angeles and Anaheim; a return to London saw the band re-conquer the Shepherds Bush Empire on 1st September before they marched through Germany (they played the New Year's Eve party by the Brandenburg Gate), Japan and even Australia, a continent they first talked of visiting in September 1975 but which they had somehow managed to avoid ever since. And the entire experience was bound up in a live show (captured on the 'Live In London' DVD) that effortlessly eclipsed the album's disappointing reception.

The show opened with a new song, a massed choir of 20 separate voices ('a Tabernacle Choir of Russells,' the singer joked) leading the fanfare 'It's A Sparks Show Tonight'. From the Formula One falsetto of 'Something For The Girl With Everything' to the nagging self-torment of 'When Do I Get to Sing "My Way"?', and from the second-album indecision of 'Girl From Germany' to the most recent album's sultry 'Scheherazade', an outsider might have concluded that Sparks remained as much an acquired taste as they ever were. But the 2,000-plus souls packed into the Empire to witness the brothers' first London concert in six years wouldn't've had it any other way.

The 19 songs they performed were, of course, just the tip of the Sparks iceberg, and the inclusion of six tracks from 'Balls' squeezed the greatest-hits quotient even harder. But they hit all the right spots regardless, until it was difficult to believe that three people were even capable of making so much noise, or that a simple bit of back projection and a handful of novelty routines for Ron could translate into such an enthralling visual spectacle.

True, it was over an hour before they played the song with which they so majestically opened on the 1994 tour, and a positively spectral, stunningly beautiful 'No. 1 Song in Heaven' graced the encore section of the performance. But they had already hit so many highlights by that time that it didn't really matter.

'It's a joy to play with them,' said Glover. 'We've gone through phases of working out together, jogging, spinning, weight training together and we'll be in the middle of a show and Russell is still as fresh as he was at the beginning, when I'm tiring. I'm amazed that Russell's voice still sounds like that, and that he can do that for two and a half hours. When we play 'This Town...' it's such a thrill to hear him hit that high note at the end of the song, and I wait for it. As a drummer and as a fan, I wait for it.'

'I do lots of cardiovascular exercise which seems to increase my ability to breathe better while singing, increasing my lung capacity,' Russell told the Sparks fan club, 'and Tony Bennett said his trick on tour was to drink tons of water. I took his advice and it seems to work...

'Our image is important,' he continued. 'Our live presentation is very visual now. They are all important elements of packaging the album. Obviously, the music is the most important thing, but those visual elements are part of what a pop band should be taking care of, so we treat them seriously. We have a fairly elaborate live presentation. It's highly visual and complementary to what we're doing musically right now.'

But what were they doing musically? Returning from what amounted to almost eight months of promotional and live work (albeit at a more leisurely pace than many seasoned road warriors), Sparks' thoughts were already turning towards a new album, wondering just what form it should take. A new LP's worth of songs, very much a continuation from all that 'Balls' had offered, was demoed, but neither Ron nor Russell could shake a nagging feeling that they had been down this road before.

'We were seeing what other people were doing; we don't work in a complete vacuum, we are aware of the general pop- music context, and it seemed that nothing was going on,' Ron told *Record Collector* magazine. And what Russell described as a 'natural evolution' from 'Balls' seemed increasingly to be falling into that same void.

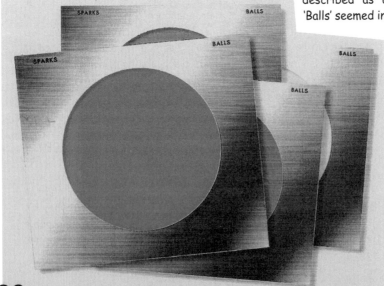

'We got back from doing all the "Balls" promo and touring,' Glover recalled, 'and it was clear that that album was not going to have the long life that 'Gratuitous Sax And Senseless Violins' did. I enjoyed making that album, and we definitely enjoyed playing it live; some of those songs are still my favourites to play, because they're so energetic and there's so much to do on drums. But "Balls" wasn't as organic, and it's sometimes hard for people to connect with those things.'

One day she arrived at the studio to discover that a radical decision had been made. 'Ronnie was still writing, and he threw almost a whole album away. The songs they had were more straight-up. They realised that they had to completely rework what they were doing, and come to things with a completely fresh approach.'

Of course it wasn't the first time that Sparks had made such a decision, nor the first time that it had caused them such soul-searching beforehand; as Ron put it, 'it's hard as a songwriter to scrap songs you have written, because each one is a precious gem.' In the past, however, they had allowed the process to take shape in and around their awareness of what was happening in the outside world – 'No. 1 In Heaven' building on the possibilities inherent in that Donna Summer single, the so-called K-ROQ years expanding from a musical base that permeated the airwaves. Even 'Kimono My House' was at least partly informed by the sounds and sensations that had already been thrown up by the glam-rock movement.

This time, however, they were looking to create something that had absolutely no bearing on anything else that was out there; whose sole frame of reference would be their own internal yearnings, and which would sink or swim entirely on its own merit. It was an act of absolute courage, but also of absolute selfishness – after all, any halfway-decent experimental composer can fashion *something* that nobody else could imagine, but Sparks had a belief that not only could they create something new and 'impossible to pigeonhole', but it could have mass appeal as well, a new form of *pop* music.

Glover: 'I think maybe part of it was coming off "Gratuitous Sax...", which is such a lush record. The stuff on "Balls" that worked... if you think about "When Do I Get To Sing 'My Way'?", that is an incredible melody and it's really big, and some of the songs on "Balls", like "Irreplaceable" and "Calm Before The Storm", have more of a melody, and a hook, so they're similar...

'But then you think of "Bullet Train" or "Aeroflot" or "Balls", they're really an attempt to be very big and bombastic and more extreme, which is what Sparks tend to do, and when that didn't connect they thought they'd exhausted that way of doing things. They had to completely change that and do something entirely different. To them, there were songs on "Balls" that were more extreme than anything on "Gratuitous Sax...", and if that wasn't going to shake people up, then they had to do something else.'

The very nature of Sparks' working environment changed. In the past, said Glover, 'the process for recording was that Ron demoed all the songs, and then brought them in like you normally do in any band. He writes everything, demos everything, and he brings it into the context of working in the studio.

'That way completely shifted. They were in the studio together the whole time, with Russ engineering and Ron writing in real time, so they never had any preconceived notion of what they were doing, what it would be, where it would go. And they would just write for fourteen or fifteen hours a day. It was torture. They would just sit there and it didn't matter how obscure a reference was, or where it was going, they would follow it through.'

Still, Russell acknowledged that the first track that they attempted, 'The Rhythm Thief', left them hanging on the edge of a self-imposed musical precipice. 'We thought "Have we shot ourselves in the foot doing something like this? Is anybody going to respond to this?"'

There were no demos. The music was pieced together slowly as it was recorded. 'I loved "The Rhythm Thief", but I heard it in different pieces,' says Glover. The first song she heard in its entirety was 'My Baby's Taking Me Home', 'and that was the moment I knew they were doing something completely different. None of the other songs were finished, but they played me that and I was sitting on the couch listening to it as a whole piece of music, and the first time I heard it, I got it. To hear that phrase repeating over and over again, and understanding that the meaning of the phrase changed from the first time it was said to the end.

'It blew me away. I'm the most enthusiastic person in the world about their music, and I practically leapt off the couch. "This is amazing!" It blew my mind how the whole meaning of that song changed, although the words didn't. Hearing that phrase, understanding the journey of the character in the song, I was then able to start applying that to "The Rhythm Thief" and all the other things that were coming together in bits and pieces, and I knew it was going to be genre-breaking. It was incredible.'

But it was also hard work, and the task grew even more daunting as the sessions continued. As the Maels worked painstakingly on, they began to appreciate the enormity of the task they'd set themselves; the need to make the music throughout the disc feel consistent, at the same time as avoiding any sense of repetition; the problem of producing an album's worth of songs that fitted together seamlessly yet, at the same time, were as different from one another as they were from anything else that was happening in the wider world. A full disc's worth of songs that sounded like 'The Rhythm Thief' was never a possibility; but neither, at times, was the possibility of a full disc of songs that were equally arresting.

And so, for a year, they beavered away on what *Rolling Stone* magazine would ultimately, and accurately, declare to be 'nine songs of lethal grandeur built from Ron's swollen waves of strings and fistfuls of piano, and Russell's one-man operatic chords.'

At last it was complete; at last they could emerge from isolation and talk about what they had tried to achieve. 'The sensibility,' Russell assured the world, 'is the same as it's always been. But the new album is drastically different from its predecessors. It's doing away with a lot of rock and pop conventions and trying to have an album that's not relying on a lot of things that have become clichés in pop music. Trying to do something that's really adventuresome. This album, even for us, is more idiosyncratic. My singing character, and Ron's lyrical slant. It wasn't based on songs in the traditional way, the way our past albums have been. It's something else and, in that way, it's really different from what we've done.

'We had to go to different areas to absorb influences. If anything, there are more classical-sounding elements. Anything from the pop world would be treatment of the vocals, repetitive phrases, in a hip-hop sort of way. But the combining of those elements... is something that is not that related to either. Fewer elements have been absorbed specifically from other types of music.'

SPARKS
Biography

Brothers Ron and Russell Mael, also known as **Sparks**, are most recognized here in the States for their Eighties' Top 40 hit *"Cool Places,"* (duet with Go-Go's Jane Weidlin) and their influence on new-wave music. However, the brothers Mael have been critically praised as extraordinary innovators in the world of international pop music for over two decades.

With the much-anticipated release of their 18th album, *"Balls"* (Oglio Records), **Sparks** is poised to gain a new popularity amongst today's music fans. Initially, **Sparks** will perform two Los Angeles area concerts to promote the release of the CD. The first, which is sure to be a sell-out performance, will be at West Hollywood's Key Club on Friday, August 25th; followed by a show at Orange County's much acclaimed The Sun Theatre on Saturday, August 26th.

Additionally, the band has recently completed production on the first ever **Sparks** concert film, *"Sparks Live in London,"* set for release later this year. Unbeknownst to many, this is not **Sparks'** first foray into filmmaking. The Maels have flirted with film throughout their entire career.

The band provided soundtrack contributions for a slew of youth-oriented feature films, including the hit **"Valley Girl."** The Maels also wrote the score for Tri-Star's action film **"Knock Off"** and, most recently, they collaborated with Gallic animation team Kuntzel + Deygas on the short film **"The Cute Candidate,"** a project with a Roger Rabbit type concept. More notably, the brothers developed a live-action musical version of the Japanese Manga comic, Mai the Psychic Girl.

Anticipating the music video explosion of the Eighties, **Sparks** produced eight conceptually based music promos (or videos) during the Seventies and amassed a career total of 21 never-less-than-intriguing mini-films.

First garnering attention in 1972 with their Todd Rundgren produced debut album, **Sparks** went on to rack up five Top 40 hits in the U.K. The Eighties saw their popularity soar in the U.S. with the single "Cool Places," a guest host appearance on Saturday Night Live and heavy rotation on alternative rock/new-wave radio stations such as Los Angeles' influential KROQ. The Nineties saw the band make a triumphant return to British charts with four Top 40 singles and a series of concerts hailed as the "Best Ever U.K. Gigs."

Sparks have been acknowledged as primary influences on such well-known artists as Morrissey, Bjork, Pet Shop Boys, Duran Duran, Erasure, Ramones, Siouxsie and The Banshees and Cheap Trick; have worked with muso luminaries William Orbit, Tony Viconti, Mick Ronson and Muff Winwood. They also blueprinted the synth-pop and electronica revolutions in their landmark late-Seventies collaborations with Academy Award-winner Giorgio Moroder and were among the first artists to self-produce their albums incorporating the new digital technology.

The Mael's collaboration with accomplished artists in numerous fields, along with the outstanding efforts of a consistently fascinating career, will promise to make the next decade of **Sparks'** music offer more classic songs, more exciting shows and more well-earned opportunities for the brothers.

"Balls" has a street date of August 22nd. For more information, check out the official **Sparks** website at SparksOfficialWebsite.com. Tickets are available for both shows by calling Ticketmaster at 213-480-3232 or by visiting Tickmaster.com.

#

Ron continued, 'We wanted to get away from working within song structures, to go into the studio and see what happens. Sometimes you could be working on something for three months, and you don't even know where it's going. I guess the obsessive-compulsive part is not knowing where to stop. "Well, it's been seven months, maybe we should move onto something else". But we try not to put what we're doing in any kind of context, because if you stand back from it a little bit then the whole thing is kind of ridiculous. Not necessarily the song, but the process. Especially as the kind of music we're making is not neo-classical. It's pop music.'

Tammy Glover: 'It was torture for them. There was nothing I could contribute musically, and I didn't. They knew what they wanted, and they're very insular.'

The Maels did not operate a completely closed shop. 'The freedom is there that if they hear something or there's something they want to do, we can explore it,' Glover continued. 'Ron's on the couch, Russell's behind the console, and they just audition the part and see if it's going to work. Sometimes I'll do parts with Russell and they know what I want to do, sometimes I'll do harmonies and round it out just to give it character.'

Occasionally engineer John Thomas would drop by and join Russell in mixing the finished takes. And Glover continued, 'there are people who have continuity; there are engineers they work with on a regular basis. Brian, who engineered 'The Angels', the closing track on 'Balls', goes back to the Seventies with them and so does Tony Visconti'. Her husband, Dave Park, would make the final sketch of Lil' Beethoven himself, from a cartoon that Ron provided, 'so there are people along the way who are all able to jump in, who know the material and understand the sensibility.'

But the only other truly significant addition to the studio set-up was guitarist Dean Menta, who was a member of Faith No More when he first met the Maels as a result of that band guesting on the 'Plagiarism' versions of 'This Town Ain't Big Enough For Both Of Us' and 'Something For The Girl With Everything'.

Like so many young Americans, Menta first encountered Sparks in the early Eighties. 'I was a pretty big fan of the album "Angst In My Pants" when that came out. I loved every single song on it (and still do today). I also have distinct memories of seeing them perform on *Midnight Special* in the Seventies. I was intrigued but I was an ignorant Kiss fan at the time.'

He first met Ron and Russell, he says, while he was playing guitar on tour with Faith No More in the mid-Nineties. 'Ron and Russell proposed the collaboration for the "Plagiarism" album which was an amazing experience for me. Then we kept in touch loosely over the years after that until they asked me to be involved with the recording and touring of "Lil' Beethoven".'

The introduction of his savage guitar to the album, Menta said, stemmed from 'Ron and Russell's desire to have guitars return as an element of what they were trying to achieve, which was quite idiosyncratic in that was not in a typical rock or pop vein. It was a somewhat unusual approach for me to take, but exciting and challenging in a very good way. Knowing that Ron and Russell approved of what I came up with for the album was extremely gratifying.'

His time in the studio was short. 'The actual recording sessions for me usually don't take very long. My parts get hashed out ahead of time. They give me demos of songs well in advance of the recording sessions, and I try to devote a lot of time to coming up with options to give them. I will record my own demos on top of their demos to give to them to check out, before I come in to record parts at Russell's studio.'

'The only other people who would come in,' Glover continued, 'were the people who were mastering the tapes. Apart from that, Ron and Russell did everything on their own, very insularly, and it was...it was torture.

'They are brothers and people think they get on really well, but they're also very reasonable people, and they understand that, on some level, they're tied to one another and they have to make it work. They've been doing this for forty years, and that's what makes them so very special, because it creates this hermetically-sealed environment which is only the two of them, and nobody can really penetrate that. But it's not very pleasant in that studio!'

But 'Lil' Beethoven' was worth it. Anybody looking for Sparks to return to the timeless lushness of 'Under the Table With Her', the sonic indiscretions of 'Change', the disconcerting dynamics of 'Equator' or the pulsing repetition of 'No. 1 Song in Heaven' was going to recognise those qualities in 'Lil' Beethoven' almost immediately. But anybody holding any of those ideals too dear was going to be left in disarray. 'Lil' Beethoven' was a summation of everything Sparks had been promising for the past 30 years, but it was also quite unlike anything they had ever delivered before.

The classical pretensions of the title were mirrored in the music. Strings, acoustics, piano, and chorales were the album's primary assets, layered with such guile that their essential simplicity was almost completely disguised. Lyrically, 'Lil' Beethoven' was sharper than Sparks had sounded in a while – at least since the best bits of 'Gratuitous Sax…', with the closing 'Suburban Homeboy' a brilliant summary of every rich kid blasting out rap from his mother's SUV.

One song, though, was constructed almost wholly around a joke that is older than dirt ('How Do I Get to Carnegie Hall? – practice, man, practice'), while another took the bulk of its lyric from a stubborn voice-mail system ('Your Call Is Very Important to Us – Please Hold'). But, while the repetition itself could grow…well, repetitive, on an album that staked out its parameters by introducing 'The Rhythm Thief' ('Oh no, where did the groove go?'), then letting him steal every beat off the record, the mantras themselves became a pulse of sorts around which the orchestrations took the wildest flights.

There were breaks. The exquisite 'I Married Myself' was a lush, loving ballad that wore its Beatles influences proudly on its sleeve, the entire song stretching out over the kind of prelude that other people might have reserved for a pretty prelude alone. Later, 'Ugly Guys With Beautiful Girls' was less a lyric, more a son-of-'Change'-style diatribe, but the greatest shock came when you realise just how easily conditioned you had been by the rest of the album. A thumping beat and Menta's wired guitar leapt out with such resolute energy that it felt like you were listening to another record entirely – every time you played it. And that was the magic of 'Lil' Beethoven'. It took a few plays to understand and a few more to appreciate. But how many times can you listen to it all the way through and still be discovering new things to admire? That's a question that time alone will answer.

The reviews were ecstatic, the response out of this world, and then another example of their past hurtling forward to embrace their present was delivered by a call from Chris Blackwell, offering them an American deal for the album's release – the one major territory they had barely imagined reaching out to.

The former Island Records boss was now masterminding a new label, Palm Pictures, but it wasn't mere hyperbole at work when he declared 'I think [Sparks] will now be recognised as the geniuses they really are. To me, ['Lil' Beethoven'] sounds incredibly fresh and theatrical, almost like an original cast album for a theatrical production.'

He admitted that he'd not spoken to, or even listened to Sparks in almost 28 years, since he played his advance tape of what would later become 'Big Beat'. 'Then someone said I ought to listen to "Lil' Beethoven" and I realised it sounded like tomorrow's record, y'know? If "The Rhythm Thief" can be heard on the radio, it'll be a traffic-stopper.'

'"The Rhythm Thief" was when we knew we were doing something special,' Russell responds. 'We really liked that song, and it was kind of heart-warming when we had the blessing of Chris Blackwell again, and particularly about that song. We didn't yet have any American distribution for "Lil' Beethoven", and Chris was made aware of the album; we'd had no contact with him since the Island period.

'Just out of the blue, he surfaced and he'd got a copy of the pre-release thing from the UK, he heard it and he absolutely flipped over it, especially over "The Rhythm Thief", and it was just a heart-warming thing for us because we had a lot of respect for Island during the Seventies; it meant a lot to us that they took a chance on the band and it worked, and thirty-odd years later, to have the guy who was responsible for that whole label really responding to a song of yours, and an album, and to be responding on a musical level, not a nostalgic level because of fond memories of Sparks... He said "This is an amazing thing you've done, can we work together again?" It was as simple as that, and we were really excited about that, because in our own minds it made us realise we were *doing* something.'

It was untrue, as the brothers told the American satirical magazine *The Onion*, that a young California fan of theirs survived getting lost in Yosemite 'on nothing but an import CD of "Lil' Beethoven" and a large bottle of Perrier, eating two pages per day of what she had previously considered an overly wordy lyric booklet.' Nor was there any accuracy to their claim, in the same organ, that failure to buy the album would force them to 'cut short our holidays in Mexico, thus depriving a living wage to many of our neighbours to the south.'

But they may not have been quite so sarcastic when Ron dismissed the value of creating a masterpiece. 'The appeal of masterpieces and their makers is a fleeting thing. When's the last time you saw Igor Stravinsky on *Larry King Live*?' They knew that 'Lil' Beethoven' was a very special accomplishment. The challenge for them in the future would be to maintain its uniqueness across everything else they did.

CHAPTER TWENTY-ONE

THERE IS BEAUTY IN PAIN, HELP IS COMING

It was never going to be easy translating the 'Lil' Beethoven' experience to the live arena, but the Maels knew from the outset that they wanted to. They also knew that the show, like the music, needed to be utterly unlike anything they, or anybody else, had ever attempted. Shot in one of the bedrooms at Glover's house, a series of photographs was taken initially for an online presentation, but also, once they realised how effectively they could be enlarged, for the stage as well. Glover recalled, 'For part of the "Balls" tour, we used a short film where Ron and Russell pretended to get into a fight backstage. It was really effective.

'Ron has always had quirky things in the show like the tap dance and, even though it seemed like it's always been a multi-media presentation, it was very basic and a lot of that grew out of the fact that it was just the three of us, and we had to work very hard to keep it fresh and not come out like a power trio and pretend we were Cream.

Sparks: Ron (left) and Russell Mael, Kensington, London, July 5, 2006.

'So things like the tap dance and Baby Leroy were all sequences that were worked out as a way to pace the show, and we were trying to think of something else that was special, which is where all the photographs and images came in. We weren't doing video at that time, it was all stills, but it looked really good.'

As in the studio, the Maels and Glover were joined by guitarist Dean Menta for the live presentation, and he recalled, 'being able to be part of the process from planning and developing the stage show to seeing the whole thing come to life was thrilling. We were travelling in uncharted territory for a lot of the staging stuff. We implemented a lot of technology that ended up being the basis for how Sparks shows operate now.' Menta himself contributed many of the animations that eventually become an integral part of the performance. Plus, he laughed, simply getting ready for the show made him feel like Diana Ross.

Nevertheless, it was a challenge. Preparing to perform the new album in its entirety, and then follow through with a densely packaged greatest hits set was not the same, after all, as simply formulating a set list and then going out to play it. The 'Lil' Beethoven' material, in particular, needed to be refined to at least the same level of sonic perfection as its album counterpart; the Maels would not countenance the possibility of improvisation or compromise.

Despite all the rehearsal that was required, initially there was just one performance of 'Lil' Beethoven' scheduled, at the Royal Festival Hall in London on 19th October 2002, just five days after the album hit the stores. There they delivered a dynamic performance, one that fulfilled both band's and the audience's expectations of a body of music that made no concessions whatsoever to anything beyond the album's immediate frame of reference, and the applause was still echoing through the building as the musicians looked at one another and realised there was no way this could be the end of the show.

Glover: 'Ron and Russell are uniquely passionate about playing live and, once they go out and they're touring, they love it. They look at that as the reward for all the pain in the studio. They love it, absolutely love it. That's the reward, getting out and getting to meet their fans, and the adoration. You can see it in the shows. They absolutely love that. For me, the initial show for "Lil' Beethoven" was a particular challenge. My son was born in July, so I only had a few weeks to get into rehearsal mode and then acclimatise a baby to the time difference in London once we performed the show, and then travel with him to Portugal and Sweden.'

Sparks went on to perform 'Lil' Beethoven' across Europe... bracketed by shows in Lisbon, Portugal, and back in London, two gigs at Stockholm's Sodra Teatern on 23rd and 24th March 2003 were their first Scandinavian appearances since 1975. But it was their subsequent return to the United States that truly confirmed Sparks' resurgence.

Their performance at New York's Central Park SummerStage Festival on 3rd August was their first show in the city in almost 15 years. Russell admitted, 'We didn't know what to expect. This was the first time we played in New York in...years, and the first time playing our new album live in America. We presented the album in its entirety, in order, and it was a phenomenal reaction, a phenomenal crowd, one that was really willing to embrace our approach. We were ecstatic about the reaction.

'We didn't really have any clue how it might be taken. A lot of times in London, the reactions have been strong and fervent. Sometimes, people check it out and want to hear more before they're willing to commit. [In New York] right from the beginning, people were really willing to embrace what we're doing. It was a really moving evening for us.'

To kick off their New York weekend, on the evening of Friday 1st August, Ron and Russell signed autographs for a crowd of ardent fans at Tower Records in Greenwich Village, as copies of 'Lil' Beethoven' flew off the shelves. Ron treated the audience to a complete reading of the album's lyrics, and Russell sat on a chair beside Ron's podium and applauded right along with the audience. It was obvious, Madeline Bocaro observed, 'that Russell is his brother's most avid fan!'

'Li'l Beethoven' continued to work his magic, gigs in San Francisco and Los Angeles in April 2004 extending the experience even further as the baby maestro continued to demonstrate that an album that was almost all studio trickery could easily translate to the stage.

'It was a very structured show,' Glover acknowledged, 'but it had its own beauty because whenever you have a set form, then you know that form is stable, and you can play in and out of those boundaries. Spontaneous things happen all the time within that structure.'

Certainly no two nights were ever exactly the same, an extra reward from the band to the fans who, not content with simply remaining loyal for years after they might have abandoned them, eschewed attending one show in favour of making it to as many as they could.

Sharon Hotell was still living in Alabama, but when she heard Sparks were playing the California shows, she dropped everything to be there. 'I really can say that experiencing them live was

well worth the wait. They were incredible! To hear and see them perform right in front of me was the best part, but it was also fantastic to glance back at a sea of people singing along. I remembered my friends in high school and thought, "Obviously some people, besides me, understand the words he is saying".'

Perhaps the most important, and certainly the most prestigious of all 'Lil' Beethoven' live presentations arrived when Sparks were invited to appear at the 2004 Meltdown Festival in London. A staple of the city's cultural calendar since 1993, when it was a strictly classical affair, the nine day festival of music, art, performance and film was staged across a complex of London's most famous venues, including the South Bank Centre, the Royal Festival Hall and the Queen Elizabeth Hall. Equally significantly, each year's line-up would be selected by a specially appointed curator – Elvis Costello had been the first rock artist to take the post in 1995, since when, talents as disparate as DJ John Peel, reggae icon Lee 'Scratch' Perry, David Bowie and Nick Cave had overseen affairs. This year it was Morrissey's turn.

The bill he chose was typically eclectic. Comedian Alan Bennett, punk legends Ari Up, the Cockney Rejects and the New York Dolls, Sixties darlings Jane Birkin and Nancy Sinatra and modern heroes the Libertines were all lined up to appear. And so were Sparks, booked into the Royal Festival Hall on 12th June. There, they announced, they would showcase two albums in their

'From punk to glam to techno, their son been witty, quirky and clever'

NUMBER ONE IN HEAVEN

Sparks – Lil' Beethoven LIVE I

Cert: E ■ Year: 2004-07-29 ■ Price: £17.99 ■ Supplier: demonVISION ■ Starring: Russell Mael, Ro

In the guise of Sparks, brothers Ron and Russell Mael have been quietly subverting the music industry since 1971. You might remember them mainly for chart hits *This Town Ain't Big Enough For the Both Of Us*, *The Number One Song in Heaven* and *When I'm Near You*, but their body of work includes nineteen albums,

some of the earliest pop videos, and collaborations with Giorgio Moroder and Orbital. Their style has veered from punk to glam to rock to techno, but their songs have always been witty, quirky and clever.

Singer Russell's falsetto voice and keyboard player Ron's child-scaring deadpan mug are as much to the fore as

SPA

Sparks :

Tracklisting: 1.T
Important To Us
14.Nothing To D
To Sing My Way

ⓘ **MOVIE INFO**
Release Date:

Director:
Distributor: D
Original Release:
Audio: Dolby Digital 2.0, Dolb
Visuals: 16:9 Anamorphic
Running Time:
Price:
Film supplied by: Brazen PR

The brothers grim.

entirety: 'Lil' Beethoven', of course, and as a special gift to Morrissey, 'Kimono My House'. Now all they had to do was find musicians who could do it with them.

'We had mixed feelings about doing "Kimono My House",' Russell confessed. 'We were really flattered to be asked, but we've re-established our group as a current creative force. We didn't know how we could justify doing it to ourselves. [But] doing "Kimono My House" and "Lil' Beethoven" will make it an interesting and conceptual show.' In his eyes, as well as those of the critics, 'Lil' Beethoven' was 'a modern equivalent of what "Kimono My House" represented.'

Tammy Glover was a given, of course. So was Dean Menta. Steve McDonald, bassist with the long-running Los Angeles punk band Redd Kross, was a friend and fan who leapt at the opportunity. But they needed a rhythm guitarist, and it so happened that Russell had the vaguest notion that he might know of one.

Jim Wilson was a Sparks fanatic... in his own words, 'a Sparks geek'. Born in Delaware, but now based in Los Angeles, he discovered the band in his early teens, when 'I Predict' was doing the radio rounds. 'That was when I first heard Sparks, and soon after I went to Jeremiah's Record Exchange in Wilmington, and I found "Kimono My House", and that was like nothing I'd ever heard. I listened to the album and I was so blown away, I wanted to hear it again, but my parents were

home so I put my headphones on, so they didn't go "what on earth are you listening to?"' He even joined the band's fan club and recalled, 'If you look through the old newsletters from the early Eighties, I won a contest in one of those.'

Since that time, Wilson and his best friend, fellow Sparks fan Marcus Blake, had formed Mother Superior, their own supercharged power-pop band, and made their way into various other artists' touring bands as well. But Sparks were seldom far from Wilson's mind. Touring Europe and elsewhere, first with the Henry Rollins Band, and then with

IL' BEETHOVEN – LIVE IN STOCKHOLM

ing to fly.

t To Carnegie Hall? 3.What Are All These Bands So Angry About? 4.I Married Myself 5.Ride 'Em Cowboy 6.My Baby's Taking Me Home 7.Your Call's Very
Beautiful Girls 9.Suburban Homeboy 10.It's A Sparks Show 11.National Crime Awareness Week 12.Here In Heaven 13.Number One Song In Heaven
16.The Ghost Of Liberace 17.Talent Is An Asset 18.Hospitality On Parade 19.Charlie Parker 20.This Town Ain't Big Enough For Both Of Us 21.When Do I Get

a curtain on the music menu slip into the twisted pop-orld of psychedelic glam Sparks, who have been rhythm and making merry lodies since the early 70s. Californian bred band who you 'This Town Ain't Big or Both of Us' have a new , by all accounts, a pretty Swedish fan base. dience in the Södra Teatern olm begin a slow and clap. The stage erupts and but still perfectly polished pear like creatures from a

Where there's sparks...

ECIAL FEATURES

Hammer House of Horror fancy dress party. Lights twirl, video effects wow and sound tramples down your eardrums and refuses to give you one second's peace. Despite over 30 years in pop, brothers Ron and

imaginative featurettes. You even get the two hidden songs 'Something For The Girl With Everything' and 'This Town Ain't Big Enough For Both Of Us'. *Sparks* is an incredibly well

231

Daniel Lanois, he stopped by every record store he came across to pick up whatever local varieties of Sparks vinyl might be to hand. And while working with Tony Visconti on string arrangements for the track 'Four Walls' on Mother Superior's own '13 Violets' album, and chatting about the producer's work with Bowie, Bolan and so many more, Wilson naturally mentioned his love of Sparks.

'Tony went "Oh you've never met those guys? You should know those guys, they're really cool." And he had a birthday party coming up, so he sent us an e-mail and invited us, and Ron and Russell were there. I had to sit right next to Russell, too, and slowly I started talking to them.'

They parted; then, a couple of months later, Wilson walked into a Mexican restaurant and there sat Russell and Tammy Glover. They recognised one another, spent some time talking, and Wilson mentioned one of his greatest treasures, a piece of original artwork depicting the brothers that Marcus had picked up for him at a comic-book convention.

He offered to send it along for Russell's own collection of Sparks memorabilia, addresses were exchanged, 'and we kept in touch by e-mail for the next year. Then one day, Russell wrote saying "We're going to London for the Meltdown show that Morrissey's putting together, we're going to do 'Kimono' in its entirety, we're gonna have a full band, we're gonna have a bass player and everything..."'

Wilson took the bait. 'I asked my girlfriend, "Hey, should I be really bold and say if you need bass, I can play and I know the album by heart?" So I did and he e-mailed back and said "Actually we have a bassist, Steve McDonald, what we need is another guitarist." And I was, like...that's what I play!'

Wilson 'auditioned' for Sparks by inviting them to come to an upcoming Daniel Lanois gig; weeks later, he was in London at the Meltdown Festival.

'Nothing tops [that show],' Glover enthused. 'It was a surreal privilege. I loved the way my drums sounded that night, and it felt like every song was a little celebration. I thought people's heads were going to explode the moment Russell played the first castanets hit in "Hasta Mañana, Monsieur". It was incredible fun to watch grown adults giggle and then turn to the person sitting next to them, as if to say "Can you believe this? Even the castanets!"

He just looked so cheeky picking them up; he knew he was going to get that response and the whole crowd responded because they couldn't believe he had them. And they just fed off it, because he did it three times. That just killed me.'

There was at least one moment of unscripted drama. To recreate the authentic ending of 'Thank God It's Not Christmas', Glover equipped herself with a huge Chinese gong, which toppled forward towards her just after she hit the final note. Leaping from his keyboard, Ron ran over to rescue her from certain concussion, catching the gong even as its dramatic crash resonated through the venue.

Unforgettable, too, was the evening's performance of 'Equator' (up there with 'Change' and 'Those Mysteries' among her all-time favourite Sparks songs) 'for a couple of reasons,' she explained. 'Number one, it's the only Sparks song that, when you play it live, it has a jazzy ending that you don't have to play the same way every single time, which is unusual in Sparks songs, because they have a beginning, a middle and an end, and you have to play that. But "Equator" changes every time. And the lyric about "all the gifts are now melted and dead"; just the image of all the gifts, every time Russ sings that line, it makes me laugh. And then at the end, being able to do the call and response thing between the drums, the sax and the guitar. That's really a lot of fun.'

Touring finally at an end, it took Sparks almost two years to follow up an album that was still winning them new converts long after any other record would have disappeared from the shelves.

The geeks shall inherit the Earth: brothers Russell and (below) Ron

Mael bonding

Anoraks of the world, unite! Ron and Russell return to the capital

Sparks
ROYAL FESTIVAL HALL, LONDON
FRIDAY MARCH 21, 2003

IF GEEKS HAD THEIR OWN political party, they'd probably be able to organise their conferences around the same time and place as the next Sparks gig, thus ensuring a 100 per cent attendance. That's how London's Festival Hall feels tonight, anyway. Sparks fans make your average Trekkie look like Elvis – that's young Elvis, of course: although even old, fat, shit Elvis wouldn't look so bad beside a myopic thirtysomething in a lurid "Lights Out Ibiza" T-shirt. They're the geekiest of geeks, bless 'em, but this – Salvador Dali goes pop – is their rock'n'roll.

It's only been six months since the brothers Mael were last here in this same venue. Back then, in October 2002, their latest album – *Lil' Beethoven* – wasn't yet in the shops, so their decision to premiere it in its entirety with an accompanying visual feast of slide projections and minor costume changes, was bold to say the least. Consequently, that performance had a nervous, audacious energy about it that tonight's virtual repeat can't quite match, even if it's a similarly wacky spectacle; Ron's entry with 10-foot arm extensions for "How Do I Get To Carnegie Hall?", Russell's leapfrogging between four different microphones during "My Baby's Taking Me Home", and those same vivid projections.

Yet for all *Lil' Beethoven's* cleverness, it's the second half of the show – when Sparks play The Hits and the geeks get to dance their pants off – that counts. From the first throb of "The Number One Song In Heaven", bodies and bad hair-dos of all shapes and sizes are a-bouncing, hands clapping above their heads "Radio Ga-Ga"-style to every metronomic beat. You could almost forget Sparks were ever a 'rock' band since this, ducky, is pure 21st-century gay disco. Even the once sombre "Never Turn Your Back On Mother Earth" gets a hi-energy megamix makeover. Ron is doing his old 'don't look at me, I'm just a stuffed Hitler' routine of deadpan nonchalance. Russell is running on the spot like the happiest man on the planet. Just a pity it sounds horrible.

The geeks don't care, though. They're going bananas anyway so – ach! – when in Rome, eh? Here comes the opening cartoon gunshot of their ever magnificent glam-operetta 'This Town Ain't Big Enough For The Both Of Us'. And it's fantastic. Who but a real geek wouldn't be cool enough to be going bananas with them?
SIMON GODDARD

> You could almost forget that Sparks were ever a 'rock' band since this, ducky, is pure 21st-century gay disco

In 1985, Ron and Russell had been justifiably proud when they were informed that a British club band, Fatal Charm, had taken to encoring with 'This Town Ain't Big Enough For Both Of Us'. A couple of years later, Siouxsie and the Banshees applied their own distinctive branding to the same song. Now it was back again, only this time it was as big a hit as it had been the first time around in the hands of British Whale, a pseudonym for the solo activities of Justin Hawkins, vocalist with the Darkness. His cover of 'This Town Ain't Big Enough For Both Of Us' soared to Number 2.

In truth, the record itself was less impressive than the statistics. Emphasising the elements that the original record's detractors would have singled out as

THE DREAM POLICE

Coming from LA to London in 1973, **Sparks** changed the laws of pop – filling the UK charts with piano-led mini-symphonies of wit, bombast and madness. **Jay Babcock** speaks to the band's revolutionary brothers, Ron and Russell Mael.

MAY 1975. ONCE AGAIN, THE MANAGEMENT OF Hollywood's Hyatt House hotel are being confronted with a rock band behaving badly. Usually this means noise, nudity, fire alarms and firearms... The subject of tonight's complaint is Sparks. Fronted by two local brothers – the Maels – the band are fresh from making it big in England and are celebrating their homecoming gig at the Santa Monica Civic. They're a little weird, even for a rock band.

"Our party consisted of milk and cereal in these little individual cardboard boxes," remembers Sparks singer Russell Mael, chuckling. "We didn't want the traditional trappings of an after-gig party. That's more like who we are: we enjoy having cereal. There were bagels too, and somebody chucked a piece of bagel out the window, and it hit somebody in the street.

"So we got permanently banned from the Hyatt. Keith Moon gets banned for motorcycles in the hallway, and for us it's innocent bagel tossing."

In 1975, Sparks were doing that all the time: finding their own way to fulfil pop's many requirements. They wrote stomping guitar riffs... on piano. Their vocalist was a counter-tenor – if not rock's first, then certainly its finest and most divisive. Their songs were danceable, dizzying three-minute pop arias, catchy without being T.Rex/Gary Glitter-simple; cleverly composed and technically demanding, but free of prog's pretension and bloat. Amid the lowbrow semi-literacy of glam, boogie and metal, their lyrics sparkled with wit and erudition; in a time of outrageous hair, theirs was keyboardist Ron Mael's controversial Chaplin-Hitler moustache.

Somehow, though, all these idiosyncratic gambits clicked. Starting with 1974's landmark over-the-top single This Town Ain't Big Enough For Both Of Us and ending not long after the release of the Tony Visconti-produced *Indiscreet* in '75, Sparks temporarily reversed the Anglo-American cultural exchange, conquering the UK pop charts with a sensational sound-vision that seemed to arrive fully-formed. This is the story of how Sparks got there – and why they left. ➤

THE MAEL BRO[...]
quite recognisab[...]
fans still excitedly[...]
mall, about how Ron[...]
Russell is still so... Ru[...]
home, sitting in the liv[...]
ing studio. They wor[...]
never really stopped [...]
back three decades, [...]
disco, new wave, tech[...]
temporaries – and the[...]
But these are the rec[...]
dilettantes. That rest[...]
finish this interview s[...]

"We don't like loo[...]
paralyses you. You sta[...]
worse, we just plough[...]

Ron Mael was bo[...]
later. The brothers gr[...]
newspaper, died of a[...]
were raised by their s[...]
concerts and got them[...]
alogues. Ron took pi[...]
Russell was the quart[...]
the time both were st[...]
ic design, Russell the[...]
ous – and infectious.[...]

"Talk about being[...]
a fellow UCLA stude[...]
delic shop, in the Pali[...]
full of stuff from the[...]
with bobbing heads.[...]

"I'd never stopp[...]
anything pop. Our fa[...]
although our mother[...]
in a visceral way. It w[...]
interested in."

cally broke up. I got a job with a recordi[...]
tually got me in with The Beach Boys, an[...]
er were going to school. We were just do[...]

Meanwhile, back in England, indust[...]
d made a quic[...]
d, older brothe[...]
, had see[...]
image, t[...]
ely differ[...]
y often,[...]
g them.[...]
ed to I[...]
d recen[...]
d for the[...]

e with [...]
Ron. "[...]
ng wha[...]
lisaster[...]
w versa[...]

Kenne[...]
ing a b[...]
er. The[...]
cially fa[...]
e Mae[...]
nage[...]
body[...]
isicia[...]
wha[...]
v wel[...]
ok a[...]
and[...]
n the[...]
uc[...]

most obnoxious, layering on harmonies that simply served to remind the world how much Queen had borrowed from Sparks, it struck many older fans as little more than a pastiche... but it then begged forgiveness from the faithful by recruiting Ron and Russell to appear in the video, as hosts of a darts game.

At the same time as British Whale was pondering cannibals, showers and airline stewardesses, 23rd June 2005 saw Sparks return to the Meltdown Festival as guests of that year's curator Patti Smith, for *Stand Bravely Brothers*, a tribute to Bertolt Brecht. Alongside a host of other artists, all of whom were given one song to perform in tandem with the London Sinfonietta, Ron and Russell treated the crowd to a wonderfully stylised version of 'The Mandalay Song', and

waving vaguely from the distance, as though he was in a sort of Dunhill cigarette advert, and there was Ron, looking as though he'd escaped from some mad school for budding Hitlers. Absolutely wonderful."

Twenty-year-old Russell had always slotted perfectly into th[e] [tradi]tional pop singer role on-stage, but keyboardist Ron, now 25, se[emed to] have created a unique stage persona in order to feel comfortable[.]

"From the very start, playing live, I never knew what [...]

Souls of indiscretion: Sparks '75 (from left) Trevor White, Ron Mael, Russell Mael, Dinky Diamond, Ian Hampton in out-take from Gered Mankowitz's 1975 Indiscreet shoot.

◄ left off. Screaming teenage girls accompanied the band's TV and concert appearances, while the press flipped for the absurdly quotable and photogenic Mael brothers. Fellow musicians were open with their [...]

[...] I did like the [...] while smugly [...]te-'74 to quit [...] 'round, the [...] are washed [...]vant.' I said, [...] says Russell, [...] weren't in

NUMBER [O]NE SONGS [IN] HEAVEN
[The B]est of Sparks on CD.
[M]artin Aston.

[W]oofer In Tweeter's [Cloth]ing ★★★★ (BEARSVILLE, 1972)
In songs, performance and concept, *Woofer*, their second album, brings home the prototype promise of their debut. It ticks to its own pop logic – a Eurocentric, proto-glam world the Maels' LA peers. Even now, it [fan]tastically off-the-wall, especially the [m]usic cover Do-Re-Mi. Daft, unique.

[Kim]ono My House ★ (ISLAND, 1974)
Doubtless encouraged by their A&R man Muff Winwood's production and a new line-up, the Maels shook out the musical kinks, and buffed up. As [...] streamlined, hyperactive [...] ed on Spectorish grandeur, [ab]out pure pop hooks, bordering [...]tic. Ron's lyrics follow suit, cover[ing] cruelty, child misfits and miscon[duct]s of love. Their masterpiece.

[Indiscr]eet ★★★☆ (ISLAND, 1975)
After the *Kimono* sequel that was *Propaganda*, *Indiscreet* returned to the first two albums' eclectic mania, albeit in a big-budget, widescreen manner. Flushed with success, [puns] run rife, and the result (musi[c]) is only just the right side of opu[lenc]e, with numerous period paro[dies,] Broadway and country barn [dance] entertainment.

[Number One Songs In] Heaven ★★★ (VIRGIN, 1979)
Sparks' post-peak slide into caricature was halted by an advance into electronic dance – the blueprint for most later Sparks releases. Their leap into the dark was made easy by the [pro]d Giorgio Moroder, the first [an]d co-writer with the boys. Late [dis]co suited them well.

were treated to an unbelievable Sparks spectacle. "Ron never smiles, he'd just sit there," remembers Visconti, still amused. "So, for Looks Looks Looks he wore blackface, and he had a smile glued from ear to ear! He'd studied Count Basie and he did the same exact thing, even tickled the piano ivories sparsely, like Basie. It was *sooo* daring. It was fabulous."

BUT THE DREAM DIDN'T LAST MUCH LONGER. AFTER two years of living in London, the Maels began to tire of the damp and the cold. They were Southern Californians after all. So, in late '75, Ron and Russell split the band and came home to Los Angeles to give America another shot. "It's never really been a goal to conquer America, because we've always had some success somewhere or other," says Ron. "Obviously, even from a dollar-and-cents standpoint, you want to become incredibly popular in America, but it wasn't like we were devastated at not having success at that time. We were so successful all over Europe, not just in England, that in a snobbish kind of way, we could say [about Americans], They just don't get it, it's fine."

They still live there today, making brilliant records that occasionally catch the public's fancy. Their latest album, 2002's *Lil' Beethoven*, just re-released in the UK on the band's own Lil' Beethoven label, is a startling concept piece that foregoes guitar, drums and bass (well... almost) but remains elementally wedded to the pop, dance and rock genres that Sparks have explored for three decades. You'd call it an experiment if it didn't so obviously succeed.

Ironically, or fittingly, or both, *Lil' Beethoven* was released in America by Palm Pictures, a label founded by Chris Blackwell – the same man who founded Island, which gave Sparks their biggest break.

"That whole period at Island, he was so involved in it," says Russell. "So we were so pleasantly surprised that after almost 30 years, he was made aware of our new album, contacted us, and said, 'I love this thing, I wanna put it out.' It was so heartwarming for us that someone who was involved in this rich period in the '70s, could, in 2003, just respond *musically* to what we were doing."

On record and in business, Sparks' many distinct eras have begun to collapse together. The same thing happens when they perform live.

"Now when we perform, when we do stuff from any of the eras, it all kind of blends together in a good way," says Russell. "It doesn't sound dated. It's all kind of seamless."

Perhaps that's because Sparks songs are timeless. Although definitely pop, the Maels' compositions are less commentaries on a specific moment than observations on the peculiarities and absurdities of human behaviour. As the narrator in one song on *Lil' Beethoven* wonders, "Beautiful girls with ugly guys/What do they take us for, anyway?" In 2004, Sparks are still talking about the unspoken things that have always happened, and always will.

"Eternal truths," laughs Ron, "that's what we deal in." **Ⓜ**

Thanks to Freddy Crisp, Fred Dellar, Susan Montford, Matt Devine and John Payne. Sparks play The Ocean, Hackney, London on March 20-21. The Deluxe Edition of Lil' Beethoven *is out now on Lil' Beethoven Records.*

WHOMP THAT SUCKER (1981)

The synth duo stick around at Giorgio's place in Munich but acquire a band. Highlights include I Married A Martian, about the pitfalls of life with an extraterrestrial spouse.

This is a favourite because we felt liberated after the constraints of *Terminal Jive*. It didn't feel like a step back for us, even though it was working with a band again. We really felt free to work within what for us are traditional frameworks but with other ꞁꞁꞁꞁꞁ support system ꞁꞁꞁꞁꞁꞁ

PULLING RABBITS OUT OF A HAT

Sparks play it (relatively) straight o ꞁꞁ and A Song That Sings Itself, ꞁꞁꞁ controls his outrageous falsetto so ꞁꞁ

We were living the pop star ꞁ after Cool Places became a hit. W ꞁ big venues like the Greek T ꞁꞁ Angeles, and we ꞁꞁꞁꞁꞁ

2020 ꞁ

Ron and R ꞁ back at th ꞁ be 21) a ꞁ Intervi ꞁ

F ew b ꞁ
fewe ꞁ
back ꞁ
no ꞁ
& Geor ꞁ
turned- ꞁ
rock c ꞁ
descri ꞁ
serie ꞁ
enti ꞁ
Ac ꞁ
d ꞁ

for the ꞁ
The Bolloc ꞁ
of all time.

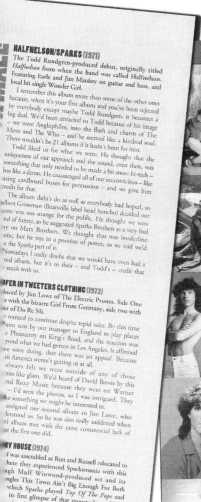

then returned to the stage at the end for an ensemble rendition of 'The Solidarity Song'. They were back in London in October to attend the *Q* magazine music awards, and rounded off a remarkable year by making a totally unexpected appearance in author Gary Roberts' *Only Human*, the latest in the long-running series of novels spun off from television's *Doctor Who*.

'People here have no idea what's going to last from their culture,' writes the character Captain Jack Harkness. 'You come back and expect them to be grooving along to Van Der Graaf Generator and reading Shena Mackay novels but no, it's all U2 and *The Da Vinci Code*, whatever they are. I spoke to a girl the other day who'd never even heard of Sparks. *Wake up people!*'

The rest of the time, though, the shutters were down and the blinds were drawn, as the Maels pieced together 'Hello Young Lovers' over an 18-month period during which they cut themselves off from the outside music scene altogether, except to use it as the inspiration for not being inspired by it. 'It's not for the timid,' Russell cautioned as they wrapped up the mixing. 'It's elaborate, excessive, adventurous, more extreme with lots of vocals. And there is much more diversified instrumentation. We've attempted to push the parameters for those who thought "Lil' Beethoven" was about as far as things could get pushed.'

Once again, the album was largely created in isolation. Tammy Glover explained, 'You can hear in "As I Sit Down to Play The Organ At The Notre Dame Cathedral", that there's things that go from one extreme to another, and that's because they were sitting there in real time, just trying to be as explosive and genre-bending and extreme as they could possibly be. They didn't have the filter of other musicians there, or frameworks for a song.'

The word 'torture' again sprang to mind as she searched for a simple summary of the recording sessions. 'If you can imagine how frustrating and volatile that situation had to get; they worked real hard...they've *always* worked real hard, but being there in that studio space with just each other, and Russell's air conditioning wasn't working at the height of a Los Angeles summer; you'd get over there and they'd be a hot sweaty mess by seven or eight at night.

'It was painful, really painful, being around them at that time. I didn't fit in in a musical sense at all, it was all them; the way I fit in was a similar way to John [Thomas]; there for when they would need things like the little bit in "...Notre Dame" that's like a jazz intro, that kind of stuff.'

Recording '(Baby Baby) Can I Invade Your Country', Sparks' first overtly political song ever, she was invited to cut loose with both an acoustic guitar *and* a drum cadence that she wrote for her High School marching band; 'Russ would play me what they were working on, and say "Can you do something with that?" and I'd sit there and mess around and we'd see what would work. But it wasn't like a band situation where people sit around with the guitar player until they come up with a riff, and then the singer comes up with a chorus; they've never worked like that. It's Ronnie sitting there racking his brain, it's all on him. I watched *Amazing Journey – The Story of The Who* and there's a shot of Pete Townshend with his back toward the camera playing to his amp. I see the similarity between Ron and Townshend – that sort of "Behind Blue Eyes" sensitivity. Russ is engineering, but there isn't anybody besides the two of them there to take up the weight. The band members get to do the fun stuff. I even get to play the acoustic guitar on "My Baby's Taking Me Home" when we play it live.'

Echoing the gestation of 'Lil' Beethoven', the pair shunned even the most basic attempt at demoing or setting themselves any kind of framework in which to operate. 'And any time there aren't demos, it's extremely difficult,' confirms Glover. 'To sit down and just work in real time and create from scratch, it's really hard. The way they're approaching these albums is very hard to do. And they're always trying to push themselves, and be over the top with whatever they attempt. They're very bored with pop music and are constantly trying to redefine it and come up with something no-one's ever done before. Yet, at the same time, they're the biggest fans of pop; they love it as an art form, they immerse themselves in it. And they still believe that you can make a three-minute pop song that will change people. There's a lot of people who used to feel that way, and they've given up. Sparks haven't.'

Slowly, painstakingly, the music came together. 'Here Kitty', 'Rock Rock Rock', 'Perfume'....

No less than during the 'Lil' Beethoven' sessions, Glover would arrive at the studio after work, never knowing whether she was going to be asked to contribute a vocal here or there – 'Waterproof' became a true *tour de force* that way – or just listen to a finished piece of music, and marvel once again at Ron's lyrics. Long before the album was complete, Glover was convinced that Sparks had pulled off a minor miracle. They had followed the sheer unpredictability of 'Lil' Beethoven' with an album that matched it blow for unexpected blow.

Larry Hardy, head of the In The Red label, first heard Sparks via a stolen 8-track cartridge of 'Kimono My House'. He would listen to it in a friend's parent's Cadillac, sitting out on the driveway with the music blaring. 'It sounded positively otherworldly. I fell in love with them almost immediately.' The moment he received, and played, an advance tape of 'Hello Young Lovers', he knew that Sparks had consummated that love. In early 2006, In The Red would become Sparks' new home, and find themselves confronted with an album that even its creators admitted was difficult to describe.

Even an attempt to suggest a lineage rendered Russell happily nonplussed. 'Well, I can see that it's kind of hard to pigeonhole what it is, but really we are more concerned with creating something that is less specific and maybe harder to figure out where it's coming from. It's something we are proud of, the fact of being able to create music that doesn't really fit neatly into any specific genre. We do produce music that can be really complex, and the album has got some really thought-out arrangements and there are some kinds of jarring elements that occur. We like to be innovative and provocative through our music.'

Thoughts were turning towards the live presentation

239

even before the individual songs were complete. No longer restricting themselves to still photography alone, Sparks embraced the concept of a full multi-media extravaganza, but whereas so many other artists would view that as an opportunity to vanish up their own egos, the Maels were determined to remain as light-hearted as they could. And when video director Shaw Petronio sent them a sequence of animated cat heads, they knew they had found what they were looking for. Glover recalled, 'We were figuring out what to do for the live show and the idea of having the cat heads came up, Shaw had sent that to us and we looked at them on the computer and we doubled over laughing. It just looked so creepy and fantastic, so they decided to use it – it made us laugh so hard.'

With each cat head painstakingly grafted onto a human body, the imagery would dominate the live show; it would also become the theme for the video for the album's first single, 'Dick Around' – a glorious song extolling the virtues, as did 'Goofing Off' in 1977, of not really doing anything of any particular import. Transplanted into the life of a fat-cat corporate executive, however, the song's indolent message took on even greater relevance as America began eyeing the slow development of the worst economic recession since the Thirties, so it seemed all the more incredible when Sparks discovered that, far from being embraced by radio, the song had actually been banned!

It was all a storm in a teacup, of course, brewed up after BBC Radio London DJ Jono Coleman appeared to snub the song for fear that some sensitive ears might misconstrue its title. Ron dashed off an official statement immediately. 'That a piece of music can be condemned purely by its title without the decision-makers even having the decency to open the CD case is a travesty and an insult to both us, as the creators of the music, and to the listeners of the BBC,' he snarled. The BBC were swift to respond with the conciliatory assurance that the single had not been banned, merely that 'the breakfast team hadn't heard the track and decided to err on the side of caution because of the title.'

They did in fact spin 'Perfume,' 'the other side of the single,' the BBC reminded anybody who cared, but the scandal did its job regardless. 'Dick Around' picked up a good deal more airplay and newspaper

arthur *a review of life, arts & thought*

MAY '08 FREE in the US and Canada

#1 band in heaven
SPARKS
A VISIT TO THE POP MAVERICKS' BUNKER!
with complete 20 album discography!

THE GOVERNMENT TOOK MY TV AWAY
by Erik Davis
Rushkoff on the FAKE ECONOMY
A NEW MANIFESTO
by Peter Lamborn Wilson
How to Make DANDELION WINE
SKATEBOARDING
as a mind-body practice
PLUS Comics, Record Reviews, Spring Fashion, Rudy Wurlitzer & Ralph Bakshi
Talking With Plants!

240

coverage, at the same time as Ron was telling *Billboard.com*, 'If the public were only allowed to hear one song from the new album, I have no doubt that "Dick Around" would be the one selected to best encapsulate the spirit and scope of our new work.

'It's bold, audacious and non-formulaic. Though the album version is over six minutes long, we found a way to edit the piece to single length so that it could take on its own life and not be glossed over by radio simply because of its length. We like the fact that if someone only hears the single edit, they will be surprised to hear the numerous other sections which are on the album version.'

Sparks toured throughout the summer of 2006, another two-hour-plus extravaganza that this time married the new album in its entirety to another romp through the band's earlier repertoire. Menta and McDonald were joined this time by Josh Klinghoffer, a guitar-playing multi-instrumentalist whose résumé looks a little like a *Who's Who* of twenty-first century rock talent – PJ Harvey, Beck, Nine Inch Nails, the Red Hot Chili Peppers and the Butthole Surfers have all employed him in the past. Tammy Glover, too, was on board, but only for the first half of the tour – festivals as far afield as St Petersburg, Barcelona, Madrid, Dublin and Paris before moving indoors for gigs across the UK and, for the first time since 2001, Japan. 'They had a lot of live stuff scheduled and I knew I couldn't commit to it all,' the vice-president of production at Comedy Central admitted; and, on 16th July, she took her leave of the tour following the Guilfest gig in England.

Her replacement was already waiting in the wings; Detroit-born, Los Angeles-based drummer Steve Nistor, who was promptly relieved of his Christian name when he joined the band. There was already one Steve in the rhythm section, so the new arrival became known simply as Nistor, and Glover was swift to bestow her blessings upon him.

'Nistor is a great replacement for whatever shows I can't do live. He's a great guy' – so great that she even left her Roland V drums at Russell's studio for Nistor to borrow.

Sparks' 2006 World Tour rolled on without a break, and the Maels relished every moment of it. All too soon, they knew, they would be back in Russell's studio, stabbing figurative pencils into each other's eyes. They just hoped that this year, the air conditioning would keep running.

In September 2007, Russell alone was invited to take part in a project designed to mark the fortieth anniversary of the release of the Beatles' 'Sgt Pepper's Lonely Hearts Club Band' album. Led by the London Sinfonietta, with whom he and Ron had performed at the 2005 Meltdown Festival, the event was largely inspired by a handful of other recent full recreations of legendary LPs, including Arthur Lee's onstage resurrection of Love's 'Forever Changes' at the Royal Festival Hall in 2003, and Brian Wilson's reassembling of the legendary lost Beach Boys album 'Smile' at the same venue the following year. And, of course, Sparks themselves had accomplished similar feats with both 'Lil' Beethoven' and 'Hello Young Lovers', and would doubtless be doing again for their next album.

This concert was to take place at the Fiero Milano exhibition centre on the outskirts of Milan, Italy, on 21st September, and featured appearances from Jarvis Cocker, Marianne Faithfull, the Residents and Robyn Hitchcock, each performing one or two songs with the orchestra and the Los Angeles band Baby Lemonade. Fifty-nine year old Russell looked ahead five years with a plaintive 'When I'm 64', before returning to the stage later in the evening for 'It's All Too Much', a song not included on the original 'Sgt Pepper…', but recorded at the same sessions. It was a stunning evening, but more than that, it planted a seed in Russell's mind that would blossom a lot sooner than even he expected.

Then it was back into the studio where, this time, their plans were already crystallising. 'Exotic Creatures Of The Deep' would be Sparks' 21st album. That in itself was a headline-worthy milestone. But the Maels wanted to do something more than simply grab a few news stories and maybe blow out birthday candles on live television.

'Exotic Creatures Of The Deep' itself certainly deserved fanfare. Another exercise in the laborious piecing together of ideas and themes, with Glover and Menta again in attendance, it was undeniably the child of its predecessors, extravagant minimalism setting sparse soundscapes beneath Russell's multi-layered vocals, while angry guitars punctuated the empty spaces.

But the harmonies inhabited pure Beach Boy territory, while the accompaniment swooped along melodic passages that flirted with some of Sparks' most electrifying past moments. 'Good Morning' was especially majestic, while ultra-memorable titles like 'Lighten Up, Morrissey' and 'I Can't Believe That You Would Fall For All The Crap In This Song' were affixed to other stunning creations.

'It's the two of us working in a room,' Russell reiterated for the third successive album. 'We worked exactly one year in this room without any sort of outside stimuli. Our mindset has been that we want to make what we're doing to be as extreme as possible – still being accessible, but to make it not conform. You know the pop music world just seems sort of bland; it feeds off itself. There isn't enough... adventure and, with the last three albums, we wanted to make them as uncompromising as we can.'

And how did they accomplish that?

'We just find new ways to impress ourselves.'

And others too, it seems, although it was no surprise that the song that received the most attention (and which would be belatedly released as Sparks' new single in April 2009) was the one

with most eyebrow-raising title, 'Lighten Up, Morrissey' – not a plea for the band's arch-supporter to abandon his customarily lachrymose musical ways, but rather an open letter from a fan who was finding it impossible to live up to his girlfriend's demands that he, too, live a Morrissey-like life – celibacy and vegetarianism included.

'We gave [the song] to Morrissey about two weeks ago and he's in love with it,' Russell told *The Times*. 'We wanted him to hear it before it got out there.' But Ron acknowledged that 'it could have gone either way! There is some humour in telling Morrissey to lighten up, but I would hate it if he ever did, because then he wouldn't be Morrissey. He would just be . . . one of us.' A lot like Ron and Russell would be, perhaps, if somebody wrote a song called 'Play It Straight, Maels.'

There was no danger of that occurring, of course. And if anybody did suspect that Sparks might have settled upon a formula...albeit one whose parameters were established by the fact that there is no formula...and were now sticking to it, their plans for the album's public presentation would swiftly sweep any such misconceptions aside.

'We're really proud of the new album,' Russell mused. 'We think it's really good and we didn't want to run the risk of it trickling out and only a couple [of] people hearing it. We really want people to hear what we're doing now.'

According to Ron, they had two all-pervading notions as to how they could celebrate the milestone that 'Exotic Creatures Of The Deep' represented. They could either kill themselves, or they could book a venue and play all 21 albums in their entirety – a concept, Russell cautioned, that was 'only slightly more of a pleasant experience.'

An idea that had been buzzing around his mind since they'd visited Italy, but which may even have been lurking there before that, when they reinvented 'Kimono My House' for Meltdown, had finally come to fruition. 'How do we best unveil our new album?' Ron asked. 'How about playing in concert every single song off of every album that preceded it, all twenty albums on twenty consecutive nights, culminating in the premiere of our latest? That's approximately 250 songs, or for you musicians, 4,825,273 notes. Come celebrate each and every one of those notes with us!'

'The tendency can be there with a band that has had twenty-one albums to rely on the fact that you have a fan base of a certain size, and you can just keep doing the same thing. But I think the reason we've survived this long is that we kind of inspire ourselves,' Russell explained. The inspiration now was to delve back into those 21 albums and explore what made them come alive, with all the hindsight that the subsequent years and recordings allowed.

In the past, after all, the Maels tended to regard each album as the end of one particular school of musical thought and creativity. Stylistically, there might be links between two or three consecutive discs: 'Kimono My House' and 'Propaganda', 'Whomp That Sucker' and 'Angst In My Pants' or 'Music That You Can Dance To' and 'Interior Design'. But those links are forged as much by the technology and instrumentation at the band's current disposal, or the requirements of the market that they were then courting, as by any deliberate policy of recording a straightforward 'follow-up'.

No two Sparks albums could ever be described as peas in a pod, then, but band member Steve McDonald was not the only person who acknowledged 'all Sparks records play well with one another. The songs weave a continuum that makes the music undeniably Sparks. All good bands are insular. Sparks are definitely not to be excluded from that tradition. They have their own set of values and interests that are unique to Sparks and Sparks fans alike. All my friends that have been deep Sparks enthusiasts from the get-go are all truly unique freak-flag fliers, my favourite kind of people!' And Russell, as he and his brother began the process of actually listening to all 21 records with a view to transferring them to the stage, acknowledged another of the band's hidden strengths.

'That was a major part of the task, to re-listen and reassess. We went through a lot of the albums that we had thought in our own minds were...you place certain albums lower down in your hierarchy, how you rate them in your own mind, but when we listened to them it was a good exercise because, by and large, we liked a bit more than we had thought we would. There are certain albums that you cast aside in your own head, just as there are certain albums that stick out because they had better commercial success, or you were in a certain country at a certain time, they have a sentimental value that doesn't resonate with anybody else. They have a certain place in your heart, so we went back to reassess and relearn, and even the ones we had placed a

WHAT GOES ON!

Sparks

THE EVERGREEN BROTHERS MAEL, IN THEIR OWN WORDS AND BY THEIR OWN HAND.

We look like this...

SELF PORTRAIT HALF EMPTY

Ron: I received the same degree, in graphic design.

WORD OF MOUTH

People we like and the things they like

Sparks
Inscrutable brothers of out-there art-pop

MUSIC: Russell Mael: I'd recommend the **Richard Galliano Septet's** *Piazzolla Forever*, an album of traditional accordion music in tribute to Astor Piazzolla, a great Argentinian tango artist. He mixed tango with symphonic music in a very exciting new way and these versions push the boundaries too. It's got all the aggression and excitement of pop but it's complex, satisfying music.
Ron Mael: Like most of the world I'm obsessed with **Miles Davis** but I feel like I've got it all. But I just went to Japan and found a fantastic live recording, *Miles Davis And John Coltrane Live In Stockholm 1960*. It's unbelievably exciting – worth going to Japan for. Also the soundtrack to the animated movie *Belleville Rendezvous*. It's extremely clever. There's just one song which, when the movie begins in the '30s, is in the music hall style. As the film moves through the years it's constantly updated, it mutates into the style of the day. There's like 75 versions of it. Russell and I tend not to talk much about music, strangely enough.
Russell: Music's overrated.
MOVIES: Russell: Lars Von Trier's **Dogville**. It's all shot on one soundstage which presents one small town, very little goes on – Nicole Kidman's on the run from the mob, and a small town agrees to shelter her – but it's

gripping and it's very brave, both of Von Trier to shoot a movie this way and Nicole Kidman to appear in a low-budget, oddball picture like this. I loved it.
Ron: I have about six VHS copies of Jean Renoir just come out on double DVD so I had to get tha from Renoir. It was so controversial when it cam newspapers on fire and threw them at the screen still watch it over and over. And Beat Takeshi's re series *Zatōichi* about a blind swordsman: very hy women in kimonos playing giant drums... very Sp
BOOKS: Ron: More Japan, I'm afraid. **The Compl Conversational Japanese** helped me understand why the Japanese speak English in such an economical fashion. And I'd recommend **The Complete James Thurber** which is so subtle and beautifully written and also might persuade a few of your readers that American humour can be sophisticated.
Russell: I like Bill Bryson. We do a lot of travelling so you feel kinship with him. It stops you thinking "Am I the only person who thinks this place is really strange?" Funny, very biting insights but never cruel. I think he got the Brits right in **Notes From A Small Island.**

Sparks release a deluxe version of their acclaimed album LIL' BEETHOVEN *on March 15 and play the Hackney Ocean, London, on March 20-21.*

little lower in our estimation, when we started to work them up live, we discovered we liked them.'

Three of the albums, of course, required little readjustment: 'Kimono My House', 'Lil' Beethoven' and 'Hello Young Lovers'. Others, however, might not have been looked at since they were released. All of the albums up to and including 'Big Beat' had been toured relentlessly, but there were songs on all six that had never been played live, while 'Introducing Sparks' and 'Interior Design' were virgin territory from start to finish. Swathes of 'No. 1 In Heaven', 'Terminal Jive', 'Pulling Rabbits...' and 'Music That You Can Dance To', also required relearning from scratch, while there was also a bevy of B-sides, soundtrack numbers and other fan favourites that would need to be examined carefully.

'It's like going back to school,' Ron confirmed. 'We haven't even heard most of the songs for twenty or thirty years, and most of them we never played live anyway, so part of the process was figuring out how to do that. We couldn't cut any corners, we're doing everything, including a lot of the B-sides as well.'

New arrangements were often necessary. 'Think of songs on albums that fade out. You have to have an ending for that song now.' And with somewhere in the region of 250 songs to learn, 'to figure things like that out times 250 is *so* time-consuming. Just the sheer volume you have to digest.'

'I never thought it would happen,' Jim Wilson admitted. 'Russell called me with the idea, and I said it sounded incredible, "Count me in!" Being a Sparks geek gave me a little bit of an advantage, because I knew the songs. But I'd never played them, so it was work.'

Initial hopes that they might be able to stage the event in Los Angeles were quickly set aside. 'We would have loved to have done twenty-one nights [there],' said Russell, 'but logistically it's such a hard thing to do – block out a venue for a month-and-a-half, and to make that demand on your audience to rearrange their life.' Besides, Ron admitted, 'we have a larger following in London. It's so expensive to put this on that the only viable way was to do it in London.'

For 20 consecutive nights, beginning 16th May 2008, Sparks would all but live at the Islington Academy in London; for the 21st album, 13th June would see them shift operations back to the Shepherds Bush Empire, to premiere 'Exotic Creatures Of The Deep'. A few months earlier, in February 2008, Eighties goth band the Mission took over that same west London venue to play through their first *four* albums on consecutive evenings. It was an

245

impressive undertaking... Sparks, however, would be playing five times that many.

A potential problem arose. Steve McDonald would only be available for the first few shows, before his Redd Kross duties took him elsewhere. That proved to be okay, because Marcus Blake, Wilson's best friend and band-mate in Mother Superior, would be happy to take over. There would be another change over later in the run, as Steve Nistor stood aside for Tammy Glover to return for 'Balls', 'Lil' Beethoven' and 'Hello Young Lovers'.

'I first heard of Sparks through Jim,' Blake said. 'I remember seeing Sparks on *American*

Bandstand and *Saturday Night Live* around then too. I'd keep up on the music they were doing over the years with interest.' He didn't catch the band in concert, however, until 2006, by which time Wilson was well ensconced in the group and already looking for ways to introduce his friend to the line-up. Now he had his chance.

'Russell asked me if I would like to play bass for the nights Steve couldn't,' Blake continued. 'Of course, I said "Yes!" During rehearsals, though, some of the songs on the albums that I wasn't scheduled to play on needed additional rhythm guitar and background vocals. So, gradually, I added more and more guitar and vocal bits and eventually, I ended up playing on most of the songs on all twenty-one nights!'

Four months of rehearsal for the band – Jim Wilson, Marcus Blake and drummer Steven Nistor – commenced in January 2008. 'We did it everyday,' Wilson shuddered. 'We went over to their place every day at twelve o'clock, and took it one album at a time. And after you get through one, there's another to go. It seemed like it would never end, but eventually it came together.'

The band was not expected to commit everything to memory; even Ron would occasionally stop mid-rehearsal and demand to know whether something was in A flat or A minor, while the others looked on in amazement. 'You wrote the song, why don't you know?'

'Everybody had notes,' Wilson continued. 'It was pretty much impossible to do it without them, because everything was happening so fast. It's not like you go on tour and do it every night, and learn the songs that way. We had one chance to do it right.'

Blake, meanwhile, was having difficulties of his own. 'I am a bass player by trade so it was challenging to play guitar on a lot of stuff. I also do the high harmonies and, as you know, Russell can sing pretty high. "Biology 2" was super-duper high to sing. In fact, the background was sped up on the original recording! But we rehearsed our butts off for the event and I hope we did the songs justice.'

Exactly as the Maels warned them, not every song was going to sound familiar, even to people who owned, or had at least heard, every record. 'I knew most of the albums pretty well from being exposed to them since I was very young,' said Blake. 'Some of them, I hadn't heard in years, though. There were some favourites that I knew better than the others, but upon digging into each album to learn them, there would be gems that I discovered like "A Song That Sings Itself".' And if the band were bemused by some of what they discovered they'd forgotten, then audiences were in for an even greater surprise.

'That's the thing, yeah,' agreed Ron, 'some of those albums may have slipped through the cracks, and some of those albums, people may already have an opinion about. So when people see them in a live context, it's a kind of new reassessment in a different way. So I hope some albums might shine in a different way from the perception people already have of them. That's particularly so with some of our Eighties albums, as there are a lot of gaps, especially in the UK.'

In the event, however, performances of the unknown albums would be as well-attended, and well-received, as the popular ones. Wilson: 'All the albums that everyone thought were going to flop, like "Interior Design", the audience was great. There wasn't a bad night, there wasn't anything that went wrong. You can't even remember "Terminal Jive" night, for example, because it all happened so fast, but every show was great, and you'd meet a different group of people each night, who were into different albums, the "Angst..." fans, and the "In Outer Space" fans... and then there were some people who stuck it out and came to every night, and that was weird because when you're touring, every night it's a different town, different fans. We got to know some of these people really well!'

The rehearsals did not end even after the shows started. 'Every day,' Wilson continued, 'we'd get to the venue at two, run through that night's album, take a break, go on stage, play the album, go to bed, and then the next day, in at two, play the album.... Every day you'd wake up and have to think about a different set of songs.'

'Soundchecks got to be quite long, but I'm glad we did it,' laughed Blake, 'except for "Terminal Jive" night, because it's the shortest album! We did "Dancing Is Dangerous" as an encore, so that lengthened the night out.'

Some albums presented more problems than others. 'Sparks In Outer Space', for example, was recorded almost wholly with sequencers, keyboards and drum machines. 'So it was up to us to translate that to our current line-up,' said drummer Nistor. 'Real guitars and bass were added, and I used plenty of electronics and added a lot of processing to my drums. Hello gated reverb!'

'Plagiarism', too, was awkward, not because it required them to learn new material, but because it demanded they *unlearn* old. 'Eighteen songs, and all different to how we'd already played them,' Wilson recalled. 'With strings and everything. It wasn't that we were dreading it musically, but how was it gonna work?' Afterwards, however, Blake admitted that 'Plagiarism' turned out to be his favourite night. 'Funnily enough! That album has a fine selection of songs and we had the kitchen sink live with us that night. We had a string section, a brass section, and Jimmy Somerville play with us that night!

'We also worked really hard on the *a capella* stuff on the long version of "Propaganda". Everybody pulled together to make this a very special night.'

'Indiscreet', another album that is layered with outside instrumentation, produced challenges of its own, but it also afforded Wilson a rare opportunity to witness history in the making. 'We were doing "Under The Table With Her", and I wasn't playing anything because we had the strings, so I walked off stage and watched from the front of the stage. And that was pretty heavy. I realised when I got back up for the next song that I should never have left the stage, because I was like – "Well, this is an event!" I had to separate my Sparks fandom from my musicianship!' And afterwards?

'It was really exciting, just because so many people came to a lot of the shows,' Ron said. 'That kind of fanaticism was both encouraging and kind of frightening in a way, that people could give up their lives for almost a month to come see what were basically rock shows.' The true devotees who made it to every show were rewarded with a CD single recorded exclusively for them, 'Islington N1' – home to the immortal verse:

> Hey, it's only 20 nights
> We'll return to former heights
> Pianissimo again
> Even this we will transcend
> Then you'll see those open arms
> And again the lovely charms
> Of Islington N1'

'We're proud that we got through it because we think that no other band will ever do that,' Russell said. 'Most people that have twenty-one albums maybe aren't as hungry in a general way as we are. You really have to be driven in a certain way, and I just can't see Mick and Keith sitting there for four months saying, "What were the chords to 'Satisfaction' again?" It won't happen... We're quite certain it will be a one and only.'

It certainly was for Sparks. Following the final night of the sequence, at the Shepherds Bush Empire, they then took 'Exotic Creatures Of The Deep' on the road, with shows at far-flung festivals in Estonia, Lithuania and Finland. But a new round of live activity in March 2009 would bring about at least a pair of minor reprises.

First, 'Kimono My House' breathed again before a packed UCLA Royce Hall in Los Angeles

on 14th February, and again in London on 20th March. The following evening, the same city hosted 'No. 1 In Heaven' in its entirety, before Sparks moved on to Tokyo on 23rd April to start their latest Japanese tour. 'Three great shows, and totally appreciative and freaked-out crowds,' rejoices Jim Wilson.

But lest there be anybody who may have witnessed an earlier performance of Sparks' 1974 masterpiece, and thought that perhaps the band ought to be moving on once again, 'Kimono My House' was still capable of delivering a shock, a full 35 years after it was originally released.

Russell: 'We've been re-examining "Equator" quite a bit. When we played UCLA, that was the big one that evening. We did it extra long on the end, it was really good.' All these decades later, that bizarre saga of loss and bemusement retains its appeal, for audiences and performers alike. 'It's one of those songs that's kind of hard to place where it's coming from, and that's always a positive thing... where something is in its own universe, and it doesn't have any relation to the outside world – the outside music world – or the outside world in a bigger context.

'Sometimes you pick up that something's really special while you're doing it, and sometimes you're told that it's special by the outside world, and you don't realise it *while* you're doing it. There's always certain songs that fall into that category. When we were doing "Dick Around", we felt that was something really special, but then there's others that other people highlight, and we go "Well, why that one?" and they say "That one's more special..."' 'Equator', he admitted proudly, epitomises that quality.

Sparks are unique. Their canon echoes with special songs, because that is what the Maels set out to achieve in the first place, way back in 1967 when Urban Renewal Project first stepped out of the garage and asked a room full of Los Angeles design students to dance to 'Computer Girl'; and that is what they have striven to achieve across every record they've made since then.

'Creating a body of work that's eternal, and that means something to people,' said Tammy Glover. 'That's what keeps them going.'

It's what keeps their audience going, too. Forty years of unbridled creativity have passed since the Mael brothers first stepped out onto the public stage, 40 years characterised not only by music and art, but also by a determined insularity that has allowed them to create a private world into which nothing of which they do not approve, nothing that does not make its own indelible contribution to their vision, has been allowed to intrude.

The brothers do not live together, but they are rarely out of one another's sight. Neither has ever married, and any personal relationships that they might have enjoyed remain such a closely-guarded secret that they may as well not exist – at least so far as the outside world is concerned. They have friends and friendships, but they, too, exist far outside the bubble that is Sparks. If and when the Maels themselves sit down to tell the story of their lives and their career, it will doubtless be a very different book to any that a mere writer or historian could ever create, depicting a world of fable and fantasy, of vivid colour and scintillating drama, a Disneyland fairytale that will draw the visitor in and never allow mundanity to intrude upon the realities of life as they have lived it.

Because that, at the end of the day and the end of this book, is what Sparks are all about. Magic and mystery, sun, sea and sand, girls and cars and Beach Boys records, the eternal adolescence of an American Dream that they are willing to share with the rest of the world.

The presumed highs and lows of their musical career and commercial stock have little, if anything, to do with all of that; from the outside, we may view their partnership as a series of records and concert dates, but that is simply the most obvious outward manifestation of the universe they have created. What Sparks really are, and all they have ever wanted to be, is the way those records and concerts make you feel inside, beyond the evidence of your eyes and ears, the tapping of toes or the dancing of feet. And that is such a personal, individual, experience that even they could never truly describe it.

So they just keep on creating it instead.

Acknowledgements

Special thanks to everybody I talked with during the creation of this book – a process that dates back to 1981, when my researches for another book entirely, the story of John's Children, Jook, Jet and Radio Stars, first brought me into direct contact with the world of Sparks. The project dipped in and out of focus over the years that followed, but I never forgot about it, or missed the opportunity to add to it as I built up the storehouse of original interviews that are the backbone of this biography.

Thanks, then, to everybody I spoke to, whose words and thoughts are now published here: Danny Benair, Marcus Blake, Dinky Diamond, Larry Dupont, Harley Feinstein, Joseph Fleury, Adrian Fisher, Tammy Glover, Martin Gordon, Ian Hampton, John Hewlett, David Kendrick, Ivan Kral, James Lowe, Sal Maida, Dean Menta, Hilly Michaels, Mick Ronson, Greg Shaw, Cherry Vanilla, Tony Visconti, Trevor White, Jim Wilson, and Ron and Russell Mael for interviews that spanned the years 1985-2009 – although the publishers wish to make it clear that this book is not authorised by Sparks and neither Ron Mael or Russell Mael took part in or contributed to interviews conducted specifically for the book.

Thanks also to Madeline Bocaro of the Sparks International Official Fan Club Newsletter, TV Smith, Siouxsie Sioux, Mike Sharman, Sharon Hottell, Theresa K, Derek Paice, Neil McBride and Merral Wyer for their own recollections and thoughts, and to Mark Johnston for his 2009 interviews with John Hewlett and Ian Kimmett.

Photographs and other illustrative material used in this volume have come from the author's own collection, and the collections of Madeline Bocaro and the Sparks International Official Fan Club, Harley Feinstein, Martin Gordon, Sharon Hottell, Ivan Kral, Neil McBride, Hilly Michaels, Mike Sharman and Merral Wyer. Many thanks to all of the above for making this material available.

In and around my own researches, I am also indebted to a small library's worth of past witnesses to the Sparks story, including interviews, articles and reviews in the following publications: *BAM*, *The Beat*, *Bravo*, *Creem*, *The Daily Mirror*, *Disc*, *Filter*, *Hit*, *Hit Parader*, *The Independent*, *LA Weekly*, *Look-In*, *Melody Maker*, *Mirabelle*, *Mojo*, *Music Scene*, *New Musical Express*, *New York Rocker*, *Q*, *Record Collector*, *Record Mirror*, *The Record Producers* by John Tobler and Stuart Grundy (BBC Books), *Rock*, *Rolling Stone*, *Smash Hits*, *Sounds*, *Spiral Scratch*, *The Sun*, *The Times*, *Trouser Press* (most notably an exhaustive 1982 account of their complete history), *Uncut*, *The Word* and also to my own writings on the band in *Goldmine*, *Record Collector* (as John Merrill), *Pandemonium*, *Focus* and elsewhere.

And, of course, to everybody at Cherry Red for allowing me to finally cross Sparks biography off my to-do list.

Finally, to everybody who lived through the writing of this book, while I remained oblivious to their screams for mercy: Amy Hanson, Jo-Ann Greene, Jen, Jenny, Linda and Larry, Phil and Paula, Sue and Tim, Deb and Roger, Dave and Sue, Oliver, Toby and Trevor, Karen and Todd, Anchorite Man, Bateerz and family, Chrissie Bentley, Blind Pew, Mrs B East, Gef the Talking Mongoose, the Gremlins who live in the heat pump, Geoff Monmouth, Naughty Miranda, Nutkin, a lot of Thompsons and Neville Viking.

SPARKS DISCOGRAPHY
& COLLECTORS GUIDE

PART ONE: 7-INCH SINGLES

UNITED KINGDOM

Nov 1972 **Wondergirl/(No More) Mr. Nice Guys** (Bearsville K15505)

Apr 1974 **This Town Ain't Big Enough For Both Of Us/Barbecutie**
(Island WIP 6193)

Jul 1974 **Girl From Germany/Beaver O'Lindy** (Bearsville K15516)

Jul 1974 **Amateur Hour/Lost And Found** (Island WIP 6203)

Oct 1974 **Never Turn Your Back On Mother Earth/Alabamy Right**
(Island WIP 6211)
Limited edition in picture sleeve

Jan 1975 **Something For The Girl With Everything/Marry Me**
(Island WIP 6221)

Jun 1975 **Get In The Swing/Profile** (Island WIP 6236)

Sep 1975 **Looks Looks Looks/Pineapple** (Island WIP 6249)

Mar 1976 **I Want To Hold Your Hand/England** (Island WIP 6282)
Withdrawn

Mar 1976 **I Want To Hold Your Hand/Under The Table With Her** (Island
WIP 6282)
DJ Promo only

Oct 1976 **Big Boy/Fill 'Er Up** (Island WIP 6337)

Nov 1976 **I Like Girls/England** (Island WIP 6357)

Sep 1977 **A Big Surprise/Forever Young** (CBS S 5593)

Mar 1979 **The No. 1 Song In Heaven/The No. 1 Song In Heaven**
(Virgin VS 244)
Picture sleeve. Limited edition in green vinyl

Jul 1979 **Beat The Clock/Beat The Clock (alternative)** (Virgin VS 270)
Picture sleeve.

Sep 1979 **This Town Ain't Big Enough For Both Of Us/Looks Looks
Looks**(Island WIP 6532)

Oct 1979 **Tryouts For The Human Race/Tryouts For The Human Race
(alternative)** (Virgin VS 289)
Picture sleeve.

Jan 1980 **When I'm With You/When I'm With You (instrumental)** (Virgin VS 319)
Picture sleeve.

May 1980 **Young Girls/Just Because You Love Me** (Virgin VS 343)
Picture sleeve.

May 1980 **Young Girls/Just Because You Love Me/When I'm With You/When I'm With You (instrumental)** (double pack) (Virgin VS 343/319)

May 1981 **Tips For Teens/Don't Shoot Me** (Why-Fi WHY 1)
Picture sleeve.

Sep 1981 **Funny Face/The Willys** (Why-Fi WHY 4)
Picture sleeve.

May 1982 **I Predict/Moustache** (Atlantic K11740)

—- 1985 **other artist/Armies Of The Night** (Epic A 6671)
Picture sleeve.

Jul 1985 **Change/This Town Ain't Big Enough For Both Of Us (acoustic)** (London LON 69)
Picture sleeve.

Nov 1986 **Music That You Can Dance To/Fingertips** (Consolidated TOON 2)
Picture sleeve.

Jan 1987 **Rosebud/Theme For Rosebud** (Consolidated TOON 4)
Picture sleeve.

Jul 1988 **So Important/The Big Brass Ring** (Carrere CAR 427)
Picture sleeve.

—- 1989 **So Important/Just Got Back From Heaven** (Carrere CAR 431)
Picture sleeve.

Mar 2009 **Lighten Up, Morrissey/Brenda's Always In The Way** (Lil' Beethoven)
Picture sleeve.

ARGENTINA

1980 **When I'm With You/Just Because You Love Me** (RCA S-0094)

AUSTRALIA

1974 **This Town Ain't Big Enough For Both Of Us/Barbecutie** (Island K 5530)

1974 **Amateur Hour/Lost And Found** (Island K 5636)

1975 **Never Turn Your Back On Mother Earth/Alabamy Right** (Island K 5702)

1975 **Something For The Girl With Everything/Marry Me** (Island K 5883)

1975 **Looks Looks Looks/Pineapple** (Island K 6137)

1976 **I Want To Hold Your Hand/England** (Island K 6338)

1976 **I Like Girls/England** (Island K 6641)

1979 **La Dolce Vita/My Other Voice** (Virgin VS 906)

1979 **The No. 1 Song In Heaven/The No. 1 Song In Heaven** (Virgin VS 244)

1979 **Beat The Clock (alternative)/Beat The Clock (edit)** (Virgin K 7587)

1979 **When I'm With You (edit)/When I'm With You (instrumental)** (Virgin K-7793)

1982 **I Predict/Moustache** (Atlantic 45 4030)

1983 **Cool Places/Sports** (CDG/Oasis 104474)

1985 **Change/This Town Ain't Big Enough For Both Of Us (acoustic)** (London 6837862)

1986 **Music That You Can Dance To/Shopping Mall Of Love** (Festival K 5702)

BELGIUM

1973 **Girl From Germany/Beaver O'Lindy** (Bearsville K 15516)

1986 **Music That You Can Dance To/Shopping Mall Of Love** (Magix S 7710)

BRAZIL

1976 **Big Boy/Fill 'Er Up** (Island 110.033)

1983 **Cool Places/Sports** (Atlantic 10170)

CANADA

1974 **This Town Ain't Big Enough For Both Of Us/Barbecutie** (Island IS 001X)

1977 **Over The Summer/Forever Young** (CBS 3-10579)

1979 **Beat The Clock/Tryouts For The Human Race** (Elektra E 46045)

1980 **When I'm With You/When I'm With You (instrumental)** (Polydor 2065 431)

1982 **I Predict/Moustache** (Atlantic KAT 4030)

1983 **Cool Places/Sports** (Atlantic 7-898667)

1983 **Get Crazy/other artist** (Morocco M 1692 X)

FRANCE

1973 **Girl From Germany/Beaver O'Lindy** (Bearsville 15516)

1974 **This Town Ain't Big Enough For Both Of Us/Barbecutie** (Island 6138044)

1974 **Never Turn Your Back On Mother Earth/Alabamy Right** (Island N6138054)

1975 **Propaganda/At Home, At Work, At Play/Marry Me** (Island 6138061)

1975 **Get In The Swing/Profile** (Island 6138069)

1975 **Looks Looks Looks/Pineapple** (Island 6837.296)

1976 **I Want To Hold Your Hand/England** (Island 6138088)

1976 **Big Boy/Fill 'Er Up** (Island 6138098)

1976 **This Town Ain't Big Enough For Both Of Us/Amateur Hour** (Island 6837723)

1976 **Confusion/I Bought The Mississippi River** (Island 6837862)

1979 **La Dolce Vita/Tryouts For The Human Race** (WEA PRO 124)

1980 **When I'm With You/Just Because You Love Me** (Underdog 49652)

1980 **Young Girls/Rock'n'Roll People In A Disco World** (Underdog 49705)

1981 **Funny Face/Tips For Teens** (Underdog 497526)

1982 **I Predict/Moustache** (Underdog 49949)

1982 **This Town Ain't Big Enough For Both Of Us/Amateur Hour** (Island 6837723)

1982 **Modesty Plays/Modesty Plays (long)** (Carrere 13001)

1983 **Cool Places/Sports** (Underdog 13157)

1983 **Please Baby Please/Rockin' Girls** (Underdog 13287)

1983 **Get Crazy/other artist** (Morocco 101 816)

1984 **With All My Might/Sparks In The Dark** (Carrere 13573)

1985 **Change/This Town Ain't Big Enough For Both Of Us (acoustic)** (London 8820667)

1986 **Music That You Can Dance To/Shopping Mall Of Love** (Curb 102175)

1988 **So Important/The Big Brass Ring** (Carrere 14406)

1988 **Madonna/So Important** (Carrere 14594)

GERMANY

1974 **Girl From Germany/Beaver O'Lindy** (Bearsville BEA 15516)

1974 **This Town Ain't Big Enough For Both Of Us/Barbecutie** (Island/Ariola 13263 AT)

1974 **Amateur Hour/Lost And Found** (Island/Ariola 13488)

1974 **Never Turn Your Back On Mother Earth/Alabamy Right** (Island/Ariola S 13634A)

1975 **Something For The Girl With Everything/Marry Me** (Island/Ariola 13825 AT)

1975 **Get In The Swing/Profile** (Island/Ariola 16153 AT)

1975 **Looks Looks Looks/Pineapple** (Island/Ariola 16153 AT)

1976 **Big Boy/Fill 'Er Up** (Island/Ariola 117380AT)

1977 **A Big Surprise/Forever Young** (CBS S 5593)

1979 **La Dolce Vita/My Other Voice** (Ariola 1002 9410)

1979 **The No. 1 Song In Heaven/The No. 1 Song In Heaven**
(Ariola 1006 7810)

1979 **Beat The Clock/Beat The Clock (alternative)** (Ariola 1008 7310)

1980 **When I'm With You/When I'm With You (instrumental)** (Ariola 101 230)

1980 **Young Girls/Just Because You Love Me** (Ariola 101 999)

1981 **Tips For Teens/Wacky Women** (Ariola 103 279)

1981 **Funny Face/Don't Shoot Me** (Ariola 102 744)

1982 **Angst In My Pants/Moustache** (Metronome 0030479)

1982 **This Town Ain't Big Enough For Both Of Us/Amateur Hour**
(Island 103 937)

1982 **Modesty Plays/Nicotina** (Oasis 0030564)

1983 **Cool Places/Sports** (Oasis 613809)

1983 **Get Crazy/other artist** (Morocco 10015 099)

1985 **Change/This Town Ain't Big Enough For Both Of Us (acoustic)** (London 614439AC)

1986 **Music That You Can Dance To/Shopping Mall Of Love** (Curb INT112726)

1995 **(When I Kiss You) I Hear Charlie Parker Playing/(When I Kiss You) I Hear Charlie Parker Playing**
(Logic 1267727)

IRELAND

1974 **This Town Ain't Big Enough For Both Of Us/Barbecutie** (Island WIP 6193)

1975 **Something For The Girl With Everything/Marry Me** (Island WIP 6221)

1975 **Get In The Swing/Profile** (Island WIP 6236)

1976 **Looks Looks Looks/Pineapple** (Island WIP 6249)
A Sparks curiosity - the label on the B-side read 'The Wedding of Jacqueline Kennedy to Russell Mael', but the record actually played 'Pineapple'

ITALY

1974 **This Town Ain't Big Enough For Both Of Us/Barbecutie** (Island/Dischi WIP 2619)

1974 **Amateur Hour/Lost And Found** (Island/Dischi 26203)

1974 **Never Turn Your Back On Mother Earth/Alabamy Right** (Island/Dischi WIP26211)

1975 **Something For The Girl With Everything/Marry Me** (Island/Dischi WIP26221)

1975 **Get In The Swing/Profile** (Island/Dischi WIP26236)

1979 **La Dolce Vita/My Other Voice** (Durium DE 3052)

1979 **The No. 1 Song In Heaven/My Other Voice** (Durium DE 3077)

1980 **When I'm With You/When I'm With You (instrumental)** (Durium DE 3117)

1980 **Young Girls/Just Because You Love Me** (Durium DE 3142)

1981 **Funny Face/Don't Shoot Me** (Durium DE 3167)

1983 **Cool Places/Sports** (CGD 104474)

JAPAN

1974 **Amateur Hour/Lost And Found** (Island IRL10657)

1974 **Never Turn Your Back On Mother Earth/Alabamy Right** (Island IRL10674)

1975 **Something For The Girl With Everything/Marry Me** (Island ILR10724)

1975 **Get In The Swing/Profile** (Island ILR10835)

1975 **Looks Looks Looks/Pineapple** (Island ILR10868)

1976 **I Want To Hold Your Hand/England** (Island ILR20008)

1976 **Big Boy/Fill 'Er Up** (Island ILR20131)

1983 **Cool Places/Sports** (Atlantic P 1760)

MEXICO

1981 **When I'm With You/When I'm With You (instrumental)** (Peerl 11688)

NETHERLANDS

1972 **Wondergirl/(No More) Mr. Nice Guys** (Bearsville (WEA BEA 15505)

1973 **Girl From Germany/Beaver O'Lindy** (Bearsville —-)

1974 **This Town Ain't Big Enough For Both Of Us/Barbecutie** (Island/Ariola 13263 AT)

1974 **Amateur Hour/Lost And Found** (Island/Ariola 13488 AT)

1974 **Never Turn Your Back On Mother Earth/Alabamy Right** (Island/Ariola 13634 AT)

1977 **A Big Surprise/Forever Young** (CBS CBS 5593)

1979 **Beat The Clock/Beat The Clock (alternative)** (Ariola 1008 7310)

1980 **When I'm With You/When I'm With You (instrumental)** (Oasis/Ariola 101 230)

1981 **Funny Face/Don't Shoot Me** (Ariola 102 744)

1985 **Change/This Town Ain't Big Enough For Both Of Us (acoustic)** (London 8820667)

NEW ZEALAND

1974 **This Town Ain't Big Enough For Both Of Us/Barbecutie** (Island K 5530)

1974 **Amateur Hour/Lost And Found** (Island K 5636)

1974 **Girl From Germany/Beaver O'Lindy** (Warner Bros WB 15516)

1974 **Talent Is An Asset/Lost And Found** (Island K 5798)

1974 **Never Turn Your Back On Mother Earth/Alabamy Right** (Island/Festival K5702)

1975 **Something For The Girl With Everything/Marry Me** (Island/Festival K5883)

1975 **Get In The Swing/Profile** (Island/Festival K6059)

1975 **Looks Looks Looks/Pineapple** (Island K 6137)

1976 **I Want To Hold Your Hand/England** (Island K 6338)

1979 **La Dolce Vita/My Other Voice** (Virgin VS 906)

1979 **The No. 1 Song In Heaven/The No. 1 Song In Heaven** (Virgin VS 244)

PERU

1983 **Cool Places/Sports** (Atlantic 0089866.0)

1984 **With All My Might/Sparks In The Dark** (Atlantic 0789645.3)

PORTUGAL

1974 **Amateur Hour/Lost And Found** (Island/Ariola 13488)

1974 **Never Turn Your Back On Mother Earth/Alabamy Right** (Island WIP 6211)

1985 **Change/This Town Ain't Big Enough For Both Of Us (acoustic)** (London 8820667)

SINGAPORE

1974 **This Town Ain't Big Enough For Both Of Us/Hasta Mañana Monsieur/Amateur Hour/Talent Is An Asset** (Island ILE 4005)

SOUTH AFRICA

1974 **This Town Ain't Big Enough For Both Of Us/Barbecutie** (Island TOS 991)

SPAIN

1974 **This Town Ain't Big Enough For Both Of Us/Barbecutie** (Island/Ariola 13263 A)

1974 **Amateur Hour/Lost And Found** (Island/Ariola 13488 A)

1975 **Something For The Girl With Everything/Marry Me** (Island 13825 A)

1975 **Get In The Swing/Profile** (Island 16153 A)

1979 **La Dolce Vita/My Other Voice** (Ariola 1002 9410)

1981 **Tips For Teens/Don't Shoot Me** (Why-Fi WHY 1)

THAILAND

1974 **Never Turn Your Back On Mother Earth/+ 3 other artists** (4 Track FT 191)

1975 **Get In The Swing/+ 3 other artists** (4 track FT 247)

UNITED STATES

1972 **Wondergirl/(No More) Mr. Nice Guys** (Bearsville BSV 0006)

1974 **This Town Ain't Big Enough For Both Of Us/Barbecutie** (Island IS 001)

1974 **Talent Is An Asset/Lost And Found** (Island IS 009)

1974 **Girl From Germany/Beaver O'Lindy** (Warner Bros BEA15516)

1974 **Achoo/Something For The Girl With Everything** (Island IS 023)

1976 **Looks Looks Looks/The Wedding Of Jacqueline Kennedy To Russell Mael** (Island IS 043)

1977 **Over The Summer/Forever Young** (CBS 3-10579)

1979 **Beat The Clock/Tryouts For The Human Race** (Elektra EF 90157)

1979 **Tryouts For The Human Race/The No. 1 Song In Heaven** (Elektra E 46045)

1982 **I Predict/Moustache** (Atlantic 4030)

1982 **Eaten By The Monster Of Love/Mickey Mouse** (Atlantic 4065)

1983 **Cool Places/Sports** (Atlantic 7-89866)

1983 **All You Ever Think About Is Sex/I Wish I Looked A Little Better** (Atlantic 7-89797)

1983 **All You Ever Think About Is Sex/Dance Godammit** (Atlantic 7-86990)

1983 **I Wish I Looked A Little Better/I Wish I Looked A Little Better** (Atlantic 7-89797)

1983 **Get Crazy/other artist** (Morocco 66842)

1984 **Pretending To Be Drunk/Kiss Me Quick** (Atlantic 7-89616)

1984 **With All My Might/Sparks In The Dark** (Atlantic 7-89645)

1985 **Armies Of The Night/other artist** (Private 1 2405627)

1986 **Music That You Can Dance To/Shopping Mall Of Love**
(Curb MCA 52879)

1994 **When Do I Get To Sing 'My Way'?/When Do I Get To Sing 'My Way'?** (Logic LGJD59007)

2006 **Dick Around/Hospitality On Parade (live)** (In The Red ITR 137)

YUGOSLAVIA

1974 **This Town Ain't Big Enough For Both Of Us/Barbecutie** (Yugoton S 188767)

1974 **Never Turn Your Back On Mother Earth/Alabamy Right** (Yugoton S 188813)

1977 **A Big Surprise/Forever Young** (CBS CBS 5593)

PART TWO: 12-INCH SINGLES

UNITED KINGDOM

Mar 1979 **The No. 1 Song In Heaven/The No. 1 Song In Heaven (version)** (Virgin VS24412)
Picture sleeve.
Limited edition in red vinyl
Limited edition in blue vinyl.

Jul 1979 **Beat The Clock/Beat The Clock (alternate version)** (Virgin VS27012)
Picture sleeve.
Limited edition in blue vinyl
Limited edition in yellow vinyl
Limited edition in pink vinyl
Limited edition in orange vinyl.
Limited edition in red vinyl.
Limited edition in green vinyl.

Oct 1979 **Tryouts For The Human Race/Tryouts For The Human Race (long version)** (Virgin VS28912)
Die-cut picture sleeve.
Limited edition in green vinyl.
Limited edition in yellow vinyl
Limited edition in blue vinyl
Limited edition in orange vinyl.

May 1979 **Young Girls/Young Girls (long version)/Just Because You Love Me** (Virgin VS34312)
Picture sleeve.

May 1981 **Tips For Teens/Don't Shoot Me** (Why-Fi WHYT1)
Picture sleeve.

May 1983 **The No. 1 Song In Heaven/Beat The Clock/When I'm With You/Young Girls** (Virgin VS59012)
Picture sleeve.

Jul 1985 **Change/This Town Ain't Big Enough For Both Of Us (acoustic)**
(London LONX69)
Picture sleeve.

—- 1985 **other artist/Armies Of The Night** (Epic TA6671)
Picture sleeve.

Nov 1986 **Music That You Can Dance To (UK Extended Club
Version)/Fingertips (Extended Club Version)** (Consolidated TOON T2)
Picture sleeve.

Jan 1987 **Rosebud (Extended Club Mix)/Theme For Rosebud (Cinematic
Mix)/Rosebud (FM Mix)** (Consolidated TOON T4)
Picture sleeve.

Jul 1988 **So Important (Extremely Important Mix)/So Important
(Incredibly Important Mix)/So Important (single version)**
(Carrere CART427)
Picture sleeve.

—- 1989 **So Important (Extremely Important Version)/So Important
(single version)/Just Got Back From Heaven (Heaven Can Wait mix)**
(Carrere CART431)
Picture sleeve.

Nov 1993 **National Crime Awareness Week (Thirteen Minutes In Heaven
Mix)/National Crime Awareness Week (Perkins Playtime)** (Finiflex FF1004)
Picture sleeve.

Oct 1994 **When Do I Get To Sing 'My Way'? (Rapino Brothers Extended
Sola Mix)/When Do I Get To Sing 'My Way'? (The Pro-Gress Mix
v.10.3)/When Do I Get To Sing 'My Way'? (The Grid's Ron and Nancy
Mix)/When Do I Get To Sing 'My Way'? (Microbots Club Mix)/National
Crime Awareness Week** (Logic WAY 2)
Picture sleeve.

Oct 1994 **When Do I Get To Sing 'My Way'? (Rapino Brothers Extended
Sola Mix)/When Do I Get To Sing 'My Way'? (The Pro-Gress Mix v.10.3)/When
Do I Get To Sing 'My Way'? (The Grid's Ron and Nancy Mix)/When Do I Get To Sing
'My Way'? (Microbots Club Mix)** (Logic 7432134461)
Picture sleeve.

Feb 1995 **Now That I Own The BBC (Motiv 8 Radio Edit)/Now That I Own The BBC (Motiv 8 Dub)/Now That
I Own The BBC (Tony Catania and Ingo Keys Mix)** (Logic 7432 134461)
Picture sleeve.

Mar 1995 **(When I Kiss You) I Hear Charlie Parker Playing (Bernard
Butler's Fashionable World of Fashion Remix)/(When I Kiss You) I Hear
Charlie Parker Playing (When I Dub You Remix)/(When I Kiss You) I
Hear Charlie Parker Playing (The Beatmaster's Full Blown Dub)/(When
I Kiss You) I Hear Charlie Parker Playing (Red Jerry Remix)/(When I
Kiss You) I Hear Charlie Parker Playing (Oliver Leib Mix)**
(Logic 74321264261)
Picture sleeve.

Oct 1997 **The No. 1 Song In Heaven (Plagiarism version – Tin Tin Out Mix)/The
No. 1 Song In Heaven Part Two (Heavenly Dub)** (Roadrunner RR 22626)
Die-cut picture sleeve.

AUSTRALIA

1979 **The No. 1 Song In Heaven/The No. 1 Song In Heaven** (Virgin X-13.32)

1986 **Music That You Can Dance To/Music That You Can Dance To/Music That You Can Dance To**
(RCA Victor TDS353)

CANADA

1986 **Fingertips/The Scene/Fingertips** (Curb MCA23684)

FRANCE

1982 **I Predict/Moustache** (Underdog/Carrere 8.159)

1983 **Modesty Plays/Angst In My Pants** (Underdog/Carrere 8.226)

1983 **Cool Places/Sports** (Underdog/Carrere 8245)

1983 **All You Ever Think About Is Sex/Dance Godammit** (Underdog/Carrere 8291)

1984 **Progress/Sparks In The Dark/With All My Might** (Underdog/Carrere 8429)

1985 **Change/This Town Ain't Big Enough For Both Of Us (acoustic)** (Polygram 882066-1)

1986 **Music That You Can Dance To/Music That You Can Dance To/Music That You Can Dance To**
(Curb 312057)

1988 **So Important/So Important/So Important** (Carrere 8864)

1993 **National Crime Awareness Week/When I'm With You** (Sony COL658972)

GERMANY

1979 **La Dolce Vita/My Other Voice** (Ariola/Oasis 600011)

1979 **The No. 1 Song In Heaven/The No. 1 Song In Heaven** (Ariola/Oasis 600056)

1979 **Beat The Clock/Tryouts For The Human Race** (Ariola 01502113)

1979 **When I'm With You/When I'm With You** (Ariola/Oasis 600175)

1985 **Change/This Town Ain't Big Enough For Both Of Us (acoustic)** (London 6.20478)

1986 **Music That You Can Dance To/Music That You Can Dance To/Music That You Can Dance To**
(Curb INT.127.726)

1993 **National Crime Awareness Week (4 mixes)** (Zyx Music ZYX6923)

1995 **(When I Kiss You) I Hear Charlie Parker Playing (10 mixes) (3 x 12")** (Logic 74321267691)

1999 **More Than A Sex Machine (album version)/More Than A Sex Machine (Whirlpool Sex Dub Mix)/More Than A Sex Machine (Two Phunky People Full Vocal Disco Fever Mix)/More Than A Sex Machine (Two Phunky People More Than A Sex Mix)** (WEA LC 04281)

ITALY

1979 **Beat The Clock/Tryouts For The Human Race** (Durium DEX13010)

NETHERLANDS

1985 **Change/This Town Ain't Big Enough For Both Of Us (acoustic)** (London LONDX69)

1993 **National Crime Awareness Week/When I'm With You** (Columbia 17546)

UNITED STATES

1979 **Tryouts For The Human Race/Beat The Clock** (Elektra/Asylum AS11412)

1982 **I Predict/I Predict** (Atlantic DMD325)

1983 **Modesty Plays (mix by Cardinal and Pallares)/other artist** (Disconet MWDN511)

1983 **Cool Places/Sports** (Atlantic 089863)

1983 **All You Ever Think About Is Sex/Dance Godammit** (Atlantic 086990)

1983 *Sparks On Tour*: **All You Ever Think About Is Sex (live)/Cool Places (live)/Popularity/Praying For A Party** (Atlantic EPPR516)

1984 **Progress/Sparks In The Dark/With All My Might** (Atlantic 086939)

1984 **With All My Might/With All My Might** (Atlantic PR617)

1984 **With All My Might (mix by Gary Otto)/other artist**
(Disconet MWDN702A)

1984 **Pretending To Be Drunk/Kiss Me Quick** (Atlantic 86917)

1986 **Music That You Can Dance To/Music That You Can Dance To/Music That You Can Dance To** (MCA/Curb MCA23640)

1986 **Music That You Can Dance To/Shopping Mall Of Love**
(Curb MC23640)

1986 **Fingertips/The Scene/Fingertips** (Curb MCA23684)

1988 **So Important/So Important/So Important**
(Fine Art/Rhino RNTW70410)

1988 **So Important (dance edit by Mr. E.)/other artist** (Art Of Mix Vol. 2)

1989 **Just Got Back From Heaven (5 mixes)** (Fine Art/Rhino RNTW70412)

1989 **Just Got Back From Heaven (reincarnation mix M. Marshall)/other artist** (Art Of Mix Vol. 8)

1993 **National Crime Awareness Week (4 mixes)** (Finiflex 8187628271)

1994 **When Do I Get To Sing 'My Way'? (4 mixes)** (Logic LUS010)

1995 **(When I Kiss You) I Hear Charlie Parker Playing (5 mixes)** (Logic 79591590231)

1998 **The No. 1 Song In Heaven (Dave Aude's Heavenly Vocal)/The No. 1 Song In Heaven (Tin Tin Out Remix)/The No. 1 Song In Heaven (Dave's Rubber Dub)** (Oglio 5003-1A/1B)

1999 **Beat The Clock (Wide Mix)/Beat The Clock/other artist** (Columbia CAS 42328)

PART THREE: CD SINGLES

UNITED KINGDOM

Nov 1993 **National Crime Awareness Week (Psycho Cut)/National Crime Awareness Week (Thirteen Minutes In Heaven Mix)/National Crime Awareness Week (Highly Strung Hoedown)/National Crime Awareness Week (Complete Psycho)** (Finiflex FFCD1004)

Oct 1994 **When Do I Get To Sing 'My Way'? (Sparks Radio Edit)/When Do I Get To Sing 'My Way'? (The Grid Radio Edit)/When Do I Get To Sing 'My Way'? (The Rapino Brothers Extended Sola Mix)/When Do I Get To Sing 'My Way'? (The Grid's Ron and Nancy Mix)/When Do I Get To Sing 'My Way'? (The Grid's Frank and Kitty Mix)/When Do I Get To Sing 'My Way'? (Men Behind Club Mix)** (Logic 4321234462)

Oct 1994 **When Do I Get To Sing 'My Way'? (Vince Clarke Remix)/When Do I Get To Sing 'My Way'? (Vince Clark Extended Mix)/When Do I Get To Sing 'My Way'? (Pro-Gress Mix)/When Do I Get To Sing 'My Way'? (Microbots Remix)** (Logic 4321234472)

Feb 1995 **When Do I Get To Sing 'My Way'? (3 mixes)/Now That I Own The BBC (BBC session – acoustic)** (Logic 74321274012)

Feb 1995 **Now That I Own The BBC (Motiv 8 Extended Vocal Mix)/Now That I Own The BBC (Motiv 8 Dub Mix)/Now That I Own The BBC (Tony Catania and Ingo Kays Mix)/Now That I Own The BBC (Legend B Remix)** (Logic BBC2)

Feb 1995 **Now That I Own The BBC (Motiv 8 Radio Edit)/Now That I Own The BBC (BBC Underworld Mix)/Now That I Own The BBC (acoustic BBC session)/When Do I Get To Sing 'My Way'? (acoustic BBC session)** (Logic)

Feb 1995 **Now That I Own The BBC (mixes)/She's An Anchorman** (Logic 74321348662)

Mar 1995 **(When I Kiss You) I Hear Charlie Parker Playing (Bernard Butler's Fashionable World Of Fashion Remix)/(When I Kiss You) I Hear Charlie Parker Playing (When I Dub You Remix)/(When I Kiss You) I Hear Charlie Parker Playing (The Beatmaster's Full Blown Dub)** (Logic 74321264262)

Mar 1995 **(When I Kiss You) I Hear Charlie Parker Playing (Red Jerry Remix)/(When I Kiss You) I Hear Charlie Parker Playing (Oliver Leib Mix)/This Town Ain't Big Enough For Both Of Us (BBC session – acoustic piano)** (Logic 74321264272)

May 1995 **When Do I Get To Sing 'My Way'? (3 mixes)/Beat The Clock (live)** (Logic 74321348672)

Oct 1997 **The No. 1 Song In Heaven (3 mixes)** (Virgin/Roadrunner RR22623)

Oct 1997 **The No. 1 Song In Heaven (4 mixes)** (Virgin/Roadrunner RR22629)

Dec 1997 **This Town Ain't Big Enough For Both Of Us (w/Faith No More)/This Town Ain't Big Enough For Both Of Us – *Plagiarism* orchestral album version/Something For The Girl With Everything (w/Faith No More)/The Great Leap Forward** (Virgin/Roadrunner RR22513)

Dec 1997 **This Town Ain't Big Enough For Both Of Us (w/Faith No More)/This Town Ain't Big Enough For Both Of Us (*Plagiarism* orchestral album version)/This Town Ain't Big Enough For Both Of Us (*Plagiarism* orchestral album version – instrumental)/Pink Panda** (Virgin/Roadrunner RR22519)

—- 1999 **Music from the Motion Picture *A Cute Candidate*: A Cute Candidate Opening Theme/This Town Ain't Big Enough For Both Of Us (1920 archival recording)/The Winney Empire/The Cute Candidate On TV/The Race For President/Winney and Loosey cartoon (Quicktime movie)** (Winney CD IFPI LAE 1)

—- 2000 **The Calm Before The Storm (Radio Edit)/The Calm Before The Opera/It's Educational** (Recognition Records/Universal CDREC14)

Mar 2003 **Suburban Homeboy (single edit)/Suburban Homeboy (Ron Speaks Version)/Wunderbar (Concerto in Koch Minor)** (Artful LILBCD 2)

—- 2006 **Perfume (Radio Edit)/Baby, Baby, Can I Invade Your Country (alternate lyrics)/Perfume (Clor's Eau De Perfume remix)** (Gut Records)

Sep 2006 **Dick Around/Waterproof/Change (live)/videos** (Gut Records CDGUT 79)

May 2008 **Islington N1** ("Golden Ticket" holder's bonus)

AUSTRALIA

1994 **When Do I Get To Sing 'My Way'? (6 mixes)** (Logic 74321232652)

1995 **(When I Kiss You) I Hear Charlie Parker Playing (6 mixes)** (Logic —-)

FRANCE

1993 **National Crime Awareness Week (4 mixes)** (Columbia CO 6589721)

1994 **When Do I Get To Sing "My Way" (2 mixes)** (Logic 74321233012)

1995 **Let's Go Surfing (Radio Edit)/Let's Go Surfing (Catch A Wave Remix)/She's An Anchorman** (BMG unreleased)

GERMANY

1993 **National Crime Awareness Week (4 mixes)** (ZYX Music ZYX69238)

1994 **When Do I Get To Sing 'My Way'? (4 mixes)** (Logic 74321232652)

1994 **When Do I Get To Sing 'My Way'? (6 mixes)** (Logic 74321235062)

1995 **(When I Kiss You) I Hear Charlie Parker Playing (5 mixes)** (Logic 74321254822)

1995 **(When I Kiss You) I Hear Charlie Parker Playing (6 mixes)** (Logic 74321267722)

1995 **Now That I Own The BBC (4 mixes)** (Logic 74321313392)

1995 **Beat The Clock/No. 1 Song In Heaven/With All My Might/Cool Places** (Bud Music CMA61002)

1995 **Now That I Own The BBC (3 mixes)/When Do I Get To Sing 'My Way'? (live)** (Logic 74321313392)

1997 **The No. 1 Song In Heaven (3 mixes)** (Virgin GmbH 724389428421)

1999 **This Town Ain't Big Enough For Both Of Us (Sparks '99 Edit (Rover Ad w/extra gunfire))/This Town Ain't Big Enough For Both Of Us (With Faith No More)/Never Turn Your Back On Mother Earth (Sparks '99 Edit)/This Town Ain't Big Enough For Both Of Us (Instrumental)** (Virgin Schallplatten GmbH 7243 895730 2 2)

1999 **More Than A Sex Machine (Sparks album version)/More Than A Sex Machine (radio version)/More Than A Sex Machine (Two Phunky People Full Vocal Disco Fever Mix)/More Than A Sex Machine (Two Phunky People More Than A Sex Mix)/More Than A Sex Machine (Whirlpool Sex Dub Mix)** (WEA 3984 29145-2)

1999 More Than A Sex Machine (Radio version)/More Than A Sex Machine (Sparks definitive version)/More Than A Sex Machine (Radio Edit)/More Than A Sex Machine (Disco Fever Radio Edit)/Aeroflot (WEA 3984 29149-2)

2000 The Calm Before The Storm (Single Version)/Full Instrumental Version/The Calm Before The Opera/It's Educational (Strange Ways Way 179, Indigo 9523-2)

2000 The Angels (remix by Sparks and Brian Reeves)/The Angels (remix by Tony and Morgan Visconti)/More Than A Sex Machine (album version)/The Angels (album version) (Strange Ways Way 188 – Indigo 9769-2)

JAPAN

1994 When Do I Get To Sing 'My Way'? (3 mixes) (Logic —-)

1994 When Do I Get To Sing 'My Way'? (2 mixes) (Logic BVDP-119)

UNITED STATES

1986 Music That You Can Dance To (Razor Maid)

1988 So Important/So Important (Fine Art/Rhino PRO2 90006)

1989 Just Got Back From Heaven/Just Got Back From Heaven (Fine Art/Rhino R2 70413)

1989 Just Got Back From Heaven (Art Of Mix)

1995 When Do I Get To Sing 'My Way'? (6 mixes) (Logic 79591-590072)

1995 (When I Kiss You) I Hear Charlie Parker Playing (6 mixes) (Logic 9591-590232)

1999 The No. 1 Song In Heaven (Plagiarism version)/The No. 1 Song In Heaven (Dave Aude's Heavenly Vocal)/The No. 1 Song In Heaven (Dave's Rubber Dub)/Hey Skinny/The No. 1 Song In Heaven (video) (Oglio CD5)

1999 *Plagiarism* Radio Sampler: Angst In My Pants/Funny Face/This Town Ain't Big Enough For Both Of Us (with Faith No More)/The No. 1 Song In Heaven (radio edit)/Full Length Video of The No. 1 Song In Heaven (Oglio —-)

1999 Beat The Clock (Plagiarism Version Radio Edit)/other artist (Columbia CSK42303)

1999 Music from the Motion Picture *A Cute Candidate*: A Cute Candidate Opening Theme/This Town Ain't Big Enough For Both Of Us (1920 archival recording)/The Winney Empire/The Cute Candidate On TV/The Race For President/Winney and Loosey cartoon (Quicktime movie) (Lift-Off Productions Inc WIN-07b)

2006 Dick Around/Baby, Baby, Can I Invade Your Country (alternate lyric)/Happy Hunting Ground (live Hollywood May 20, 2006)/Bon Voyage (live Hollywood May 20, 2006)/In The Future (live Hollywood May 20, 2006)/interview/video content (In The Red 51372)

PART FOUR: ALBUMS

'HALFNELSON'
LP 1971 as 'Halfnelson' (Bearsville BV 2048) (USA)
LP 1972 as 'Sparks' (Bearsville BV 2048) (USA)
LP 1974 as 'Sparks' (Bearsville/WEA K45511) (UK)
LP 1981 as 'Wonder Girl' (Underdog/Carrere 67772) (France)
CD 1988 as 'Halfnelson' (Victor VDP28044) (Japan)

Russell Mael – vocals
Ron Mael – keyboards
Earle Mankey – guitar
Harley Feinstein – drums
Jim Mankey – bass
Produced by Todd Rundgren

Wonder Girl /Fa La Fa Lee/Roger/High C/Fletcher Honorama/Simple Ballet/Slowboat/Biology 2/Saccharin And The War/Big Bands/(No More) Mr. Nice Guys

'A WOOFER IN TWEETER'S CLOTHING'
LP 1972 (Bearsville 45510) (USA)
LP 1973 (Bearsville K45510) (UK)
LP 1973 (Bearsville/WEA BEA45510) (Germany)
LP 1973 (Bearsville 45510) (France)
CD 1990 (Repertoire RR4051-C) (Germany)

Russell Mael – vocals
Ron Mael – keyboards
Earle Mankey – guitar
Harley Feinstein – drums
Jim Mankey – bass
Produced by Thaddeus James Lowe

Girl From Germany/Beaver O'Lindy/Nothing Is Sacred/Here Comes Bob/Moon Over Kentucky/Do Re Mi/Angus Desire/Underground/The Louvre/Batteries Not Included/Whippings And Apologies

'KIMONO MY HOUSE'
LP 1974 (Island ILPS9272) (UK)
LP 1974 (Island/Antilles AN7044) (USA)
LP 1974 (Island/Ariola 87818IT) (Netherlands)
LP 1974 (Island/Phonogram 9101632) (France)
LP 1974 (Island/Ariola 89227XAT) (Germany)
LP 1974 (Island/Trutone ILPS9272) South Africa
CD 1993 (Island PHCR6717) (Japan)
CD 1994 (Island IMCD198) (UK)
CD 1994 (Island 74321224262) (Germany)
CD 1994 (Island IMCD198) (France)

Russell Mael – vocals
Ron Mael – keyboards
Adrian Fisher – guitar
Dinky Diamond – drums
Martin Gordon – bass
Produced by Muff Winwood

This Town Ain't Big Enough For Both Of Us/Amateur Hour/Falling In Love With Myself Again/Here In Heaven/Thank God It's Not Christmas/Hasta Mañana Monsieur/Talent Is An Asset/Complaints/In My Family/Equator

CD 1997 (Island)
As above plus bonus tracks: **Barbecutie/Lost And Found**

CD 2006 (21st Century Edition) (Universal 984317)
As above plus bonus tracks: **Barbecutie/Lost And Found/Amateur Hour (live 1975)**

'PROPAGANDA'

LP 1974 (Island ILPS9312) (UK)
LP 1974 (Island/Phonogram 6396036) (France)
LP 1974 (Island ILPS9312) (USA)
LP 1974 (Island/Ariola 88379IT) (Netherlands)
LP 1974 (Island/Ariola 88426XOT) (Germany)
LP 1974 (Island ILPS 9312) (Sweden)
LP 1974 (Island 9312) (Brazil)
LP 1974 (Island ILS90071) (Japan)
CD 1993 (Island PCR6718) (Japan)
CD 1994 (Island IMCD199) (UK)
CD 1994 (Island 74321224262) (Germany)

Russell Mael – vocals
Ron Mael – keyboards
Adrian Fisher – guitar
Dinky Diamond – drums
Ian Hampton – bass
Trevor White – guitar
Produced by Muff Winwood

Propaganda/At Home, At Work, At Play/Reinforcements/B.C./Thanks But No Thanks/Don't Leave Me Alone With Her/Never Turn Your Back On Mother Earth/Something For The Girl With Everything/Achoo/Who Don't Like Kids/Bon Voyage

CD 1997 (Island 5240352)
As above plus bonus tracks: **Alabamy Right/Marry Me**

CD 2006 (21st Century Edition) (Universal 9843410)
As above plus bonus tracks: **Alabamy Right/Marry Me/*Saturday Scene* interview**

'INDISCREET'

LP 1975 (Island ILPS9345) (UK)
LP 1975 (Island ILPS9345) (USA)
LP 1975 (Island/Ariola 89434XOT) (Netherlands)
LP 1975 (Island/Phonogram 9101650) (France)
LP 1975 (Island/Ariola 89434XOT) (Germany)
LP 1975 (Island/Trutone ILPS9345) (South Africa)
LP 1975 (Island ILPS 9345) (Sweden)
LP 1975 (Island 9345) (Brazil)
CD 1993 (Island PHCR6719) (Japan)
CD 1994 (Island IMCD200) (UK)
CD 1994 (Island 74321224252) (Germany)

Russell Mael – vocals
Ron Mael – keyboards
Dinky Diamond- drums

Ian Hampton – bass
Trevor White – guitar
Produced by Tony Visconti

Hospitality On Parade/Happy Hunting Ground/Without Using Hands/Get In The Swing/Under The Table With Her/How Are You Getting Home/Pineapple/Tits/It Ain't 1918/The Lady Is Lingering/In The Future/Looks Looks Looks/Miss The Start, Miss The End

CD 1997 (Island 5240322)
As above plus bonus tracks: **Profile/I Wanna Hold Your Hand/England**

CD 2006 (21st Century Edition) (Universal 9843411)
As above plus bonus tracks: **Profile/The Wedding Of Jacqueline Kennedy To Russell Mael/Looks Looks Looks (live)**

'BIG BEAT'
LP 1976 (Island ILPS9445) (UK)
LP 1976 (CBS PC34359) (USA)
LP 1976 (Island/Ariola 28142XOT) (Netherlands)
LP 1976 (Island/Dischi ILPS19445) (Italy)
LP 1976 (Island/Phonogram —-) (France)
LP 1976 (Island 9445) (Sweden)
LP 1976 (Island/Festival L36050) (Australia)
CD 1993 (Island PHCR6720) (Japan)
CD 1994 (Island IMCD201) (UK)
CD 1994 (Island 74321224242) (Germany)

Russell Mael – vocals
Ron Mael – keyboards
Hilly Boy Michaels – drums
Jeffrey Salen – guitar
Sal Maida – bass
Produced by Rupert Holmes

Big Boy/I Want To Be Like Everybody Else/Nothing To Do/I Bought The Mississippi River/Fill 'Er Up/Everybody's Stupid/Throw Her Away (And Get A New One)/Confusion/Screwed Up/White Women/I Like Girls

CD 1995 (Island 201)
As above plus bonus tracks: **Tearing The Place Apart/Gone With The Wind**

CD 2006 (21st Century Edition) (Universal 9843412)
As above plus bonus tracks: **I Want To Hold Your Hand/England/Gone With The Wind/Looks Aren't Everything/Intrusion – Confusion**

'INTRODUCING'
LP 1977 (CBS CBS82284) (UK)
LP 1977 (CBS PC34901) (USA)
LP 1977 (CBS CBS82284) (Netherlands)
LP 1977 (CBS CBS82284) (Germany)
LP 1977 (CBS 82284) (Sweden)
LP 1977 (CBS/Sony 25AP856) (Japan)
CD 2008 (Lil Beethoven)

Russell Mael – vocals
Ron Mael – keyboards
Ben Benay - guitar

Alan Broadbent - piano
David Foster - keyboards
Ed Greene - drums
David Paich - keyboards
Mike Porcaro - bass
Reinie Press - bass/saxophone
Lee Ritenour - guitar
Thom Rotella - guitar
Tom Bahler – backing vocals
Al Capps – backing vocals
Stan Farber – backing vocals
Jimmy Haas – backing vocals
Ron Hicklin – backing vocals
Mark Piscitelli – backing vocals
Nick Uhrig – backing vocals

Produced by Terry Powell, Ron Mael and Russell Mael
Engineered by Lenny Roberts

A Big Surprise/Occupation/Ladies/I'm Not/Forever Young/Goofing Off/Girls On The Brain/Over The Summer/Those Mysteries

CD 2009 (Imperial Records TECI-26546X) (Japan)
As above plus bonus tracks: **Breathe, Fact or Fiction, Those Mysteries (demo version)**

'NO. 1 IN HEAVEN'
LP 1979 (Virgin V2115) (UK)
Limited edition in yellow vinyl
LP 1979 (Elektra/Asylum 6E186) (USA)
LP 1979 (Elektra/Asylum 6E-186) (Canada)
LP 1979 (Ariola/Oasis 200353) (Germany)
LP 1979 (Ariola ARI 200353) (Sweden)
LP 1979 (Warners Brothers 56619) (France)
CD 1995 (Bud Music CMP62004C) (Germany)

Russell Mael – vocals
Ron Mael – keyboards
Keith Forsey – drums
Produced by Giorgio Moroder

Tryouts For The Human Race/Academy Award Performance/La Dolce Vita/Beat The Clock/My Other Voice/The No. 1 Song In Heaven

CD 2009 (Imperial Records TECI-26547X) (Japan)
As above plus bonus tracks: **Dancing is Dangerous, Is There More To Life Than Dancing, Beat The Clock (Meat Beat Manifesto remix 'Double Bass Remix')**

Sparks.
Terminal Jive.

'TERMINAL JIVE'
LP 1980 (Virgin V2137) (UK)
LP 1980 (Ariola/Oasis 201289) (Germany)
LP 1980 (Underdog/Carrere 67597) (France)
LP 1980 (Polydor 2424213) (Canada)
LP 1980 (Durium DAI30346) (Italy)
CD 1995 (Bud Music CCMP62005) (Germany)
CD 1998 (Oglio Records OGL 81600-2) (USA)

Russell Mael – vocals
Ron Mael – keyboards
(Other performers uncredited)
Produced by Giorgio Moroder and Harold Faltermeyer

When I'm With You/Just Because You Love Me/Rock'n'Roll People In A Disco World/When I'm With You (instrumental)/Young Girls/Noisy Boys/Stereo/The Greatest Show On Earth

CD 2009 (Imperial Records TECI-26548) (Japan)
As above plus bonus tracks: **The Farmer's Daughter, After Dark, Modesty Plays (instrumental)**

'WHOMP THAT SUCKER'
LP 1981 (Why-Fi WHO1) (UK)
LP 1981 (RCA/Why-Fi AFLI-4091) (USA)
LP 1981 (Why-Fi/RCA/Victor AFLI-4091) (Canada)
LP 1981 (Ariola/Oasis 203355) (Germany)
LP 1981 (Underdog/Carrere 67677) (France)
LP 1981 (RCA RPL8080) (Japan)
LP 1981 (Durium DAI30374) (Italy)
CD 1995 (Bud Music CMP62006) (Germany)
CD 1998 (Remastered) (Oglio Records OGL 81601-2) (USA)

Russell Mael – vocals
Ron Mael – keyboards
Bob Haag – guitar
David Kendrick – drums
Leslie Bohem – bass
Produced by Mack

Tips For Teens/Funny Face/Where's My Girl/Upstairs/I Married A Martian/The Willys/Don't Shoot Me/Suzie Safety/That's Not Nastassia/Wacky Women

CD 2009 (Imperial Records TECI-26549X) (Japan)
As above plus bonus tracks: **Love Can Conquer All (clang version), The Oblongs, Love Can Conquer All (smooth version)**

'ANGST IN MY PANTS'
LP 1982 (Atlantic K50888) (UK)
LP 1982 (Atlantic ATLKS50888) (Germany)
LP 1982 (Atlantic SD19347) (USA)
LP 1982 (Atlantic/WEA XSD19347) (Canada)
LP 1982 (Atlantic SD19347) (Australia)
LP 1982 (Underdog/Carrere 67856) (France)
LP 1982 (Underdog/Carrere 606105) (Portugal)
LP 1982 (Atlantic P11215) (Japan)
CD 1995 (Bud Music CMP62007) (Germany)
CD 1998 (Remastered) (Oglio Records OGL 81602-2) (USA)

Russell Mael – vocals
Ron Mael – keyboards
Bob Haag – guitar
David Kendrick – drums
James Goodwin – keyboards
Leslie Bohem – bass
Produced by Mack

Angst In My Pants/I Predict/Sextown USA/Sherlock Holmes/Nicotina/Mickey Mouse/Moustache/Instant Weight Loss/Tarzan And Jane/The Decline And Fall Of Me/Eaten By The Monster Of Love

CD 2009 (Imperial Records TECI-26550X) (Japan)
As above plus bonus tracks: **Angst in My Pants (radio promo advert), Kidnap, A Trying Day, Dancing is Dangerous (I Ought To Know)**

'IN OUTER SPACE'
LP 1983 (Atlantic 7800551) (UK)
LP 1983 (Atlantic 80055-1) (USA)
LP 1983 (Atlantic 7800551) (Canada)
LP 1983 (Underdog/Carrere 67981) (France)
LP 1983 (CDG/Oasis INT20354) (Italy)
LP 1983 (Atlantic P11360) (Japan)
LP 1983 (Teldec/Oasis 625520) (Germany)
CD 1995 (Bud Music CMP62008) (Germany)
CD 1998 (Oglio Records OGL 81603-2) (USA)

Russell Mael – vocals
Ron Mael – keyboards
Bob Haag – guitar
David Kendrick – drums
James Goodwin – keyboards
Leslie Bohem – bass
Jane Wiedlin – vocals (tracks 1,8)
Produced by Ron Mael and Russell Mael

Cool Places/Popularity/Prayin' for A Party/All You Ever Think About Is Sex/Please Baby Please/Rockin' Girls/I Wish I Looked A Little Better/Lucky Me, Lucky You/A Fun Bunch Of Guys From Outer Space/ Dance Godammit

LP 1983 (Underdog/Carrere 67981) (France)
As above plus bonus track: **Modesty Plays**

CD 2009 (Imperial records TECI-26551X) (Japan)
As above plus bonus tracks: **Miniskirted, All You Ever Think About Is Sex, Sports**

'PULLING RABBITS OUT OF A HAT'
LP 1984 (Atlantic 801601) (USA)
LP 1984 (Underdog/Carrere 66160) (France)
LP 1984 (Teldec/Oasis 625952) (Germany)
CD 1995 (Bud Music CMP62009) (Germany)
CD 1998 (Remastered) (Oglio Records OGL 81604-2) (USA)

Russell Mael – vocals
Ron Mael – keyboards
Bob Haag – guitar
David Kendrick – drums
John Thomas – keyboards
Leslie Bohem – bass
Produced by Ian Little

Pulling Rabbits Out Of A Hat/Love Scenes/Pretending To Be Drunk/With All My Might/Sparks In The Dark (Part One)/Everybody Move/A Song That Sings Itself/Sisters/Kiss Me Quick/Sparks In The Dark (Part Two)

'MUSIC THAT YOU CAN DANCE TO'

LP 1986 (Curb INT147724) (Germany)
LP 1986 (MCA/Curb MCA5780) (USA)
LP 1986 (Magic 99177) (Brazil)
LP 1986 (Curb/Vogue 540138) (France)
LP 1986 (Consolidated Allied TOONLP2) (UK)
CD 1986 (Curb/Intercord 847724) (Germany)

Russell Mael – vocals
Ron Mael – keyboards
Bob Haag – guitar
David Kendrick – drums
John Thomas – keyboards
Leslie Bohem – bass
Robert Mache – guitar on 'Fingertips'
Produced by Ron Mael and Russell Mael

Music That You Can Dance To/Rosebud/Fingertips/Armies Of The Night/The Scene/Shopping Mall Of Love/Modesty Plays (New Version)/Let's Get Funky

LP 1986 (MCA/RCA/Victor VLP1 6729) (Australia)
CD 1990 as *The Best Of Sparks* (Curb D277335) (USA)
CD 1990 as *The Best Of Sparks* (Curb/Redhot 4686173) (UK)

Music That You Can Dance To/Rosebud/Fingertips/Change/The Scene/Shopping Mall Of Love/Modesty Plays (New Version)/Let's Get Funky

'INTERIOR DESIGN'

LP 1988 (Fine Art/Rhino R270841) (UK)
LP 1988 (Fine Art/Rhino R170841) (USA)
LP 1988 (Underdog/Carrere 66526) (France)
LP 1988 (Underdog/Carrere 66526) (Israel)
CD 1988 (Fine Art/Rhino R270841) (USA)
CD 1988 (Victor VDP1346) (Japan)
CD 1991 as *Just Got Back From Heaven* (Success 22505CD) (EEC)
CD 1992 as *Just Got Back From Heaven* (Soundwings 11011152) (Czech)
CD 1992 (Magnum CDTB 141) (UK)
CD 1993 as *The World Of The Sparks – Madonna* (Trace 0401102) (Netherlands)
CD 1994 as *The Magic Collection* (ARC MEC949034) (Netherlands)
CD 1995 as *Gold* (Gold 106) (Netherlands)
CD 1995 as *So Important* (LaserLight 12571) (Germany)
CD 1995 as *Heaven And Beyond* (WZ WZ90159) (Germany)

Russell Mael – vocals
Ron Mael – keyboards
John Thomas – keyboards
Spencer Sircombe – guitars
Pamela Stonebrook – backing vocals on Just Got Back From Heaven

So Important/Just Got Back From Heaven/Lots Of Reasons/You've Got A Hold Of My Heart/Love-O-Rama/The Toughest Girl In Town/Let's Make Love/Stop Me If You've Heard This Before/Walk Down Memory Lane/Madonna

CD 2008 (Lil Beethoven LBR CD 014)
As above plus bonus tracks: **Madonna (French)/Madonna (German)/Madonna (Spanish)/The Big Brass Ring/So Important (Extremely Important Remix)**

'GRATUITOUS SAX AND SENSELESS VIOLINS'

LP 1994 (Logic/BMG 74321232671) (Germany)
LP 1994 (Logic/BMG 0802398320) (Netherlands)
LP 1994 (Logic/BMG 74321232671) (USA)
CD 1994 (Logic 74321232) (UK)
CD 1994 (Logic 7432123262) (USA)
CD 1994 (Logic BVCP-827) (Japan)
CD 1994 (Logic/BMG 74321232672) (Germany)
CD 2006 (Lil Beethoven 102)

Russell Mael – vocals
Ron Mael – keyboards
Special thanks to Christi Haydon
Produced by Ron Mael and Russell Mael

Gratuitous Sax/When Do I Get To Sing 'My Way'?/(When I Kiss
You) I Hear Charlie Parker Playing/Frankly, Scarlet, I Don't Give A Damn/I Thought I Told You To Wait In
The Car/Hear No Evil, See No Evil, Speak No Evil/Now That I Own The BBC/Tsui Hark/The Ghost Of
Liberace/Let's Go Surfing/Senseless Violins

'PLAGIARISM'

CD 1997 (Virgin GmbH 724384427528) (Germany)
CD 1998 (Oglio Records OGL 89109-2) (USA)
CD 1998 (Flavour of Sound TFCK-87606) (Japan)
CD 2000 (Roadrunner RR 8791-2) (UK)

Russell Mael – vocals
Ron Mael – keyboards
Dean Menta – guitar (track 4)
Eskimos and Egypt – bass, guitar, drums (track 6)
Faith No More (tracks 10, 16)
Erasure (track 13)
Jenny O'Grady – vocals (track 14)
David Porter-Thomas – vocals (track 14)
Jimmy Somerville – vocals (track 18)
Orchestral and choral arrangements by Tony Visconti
Produced by Tony Visconti, Ron Mael and Russell Mael

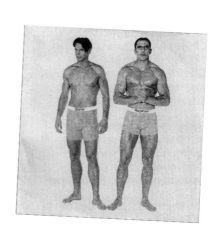

Pulling Rabbits Out Of A Hat (Orchestral Version)/This Town Ain't Big Enough For Both Of Us (Orchestral
Version)/The No. 1 Song In Heaven (Part 2)/Funny Face (New Version)/When Do I Get To Sing 'My Way'?
(Orchestral Version)/Angst In My Pants (New Version)/Change (Orchestral Version)/Popularity (New
Version)/Something For The Girl With Everything (Orchestral Version)/This Town Ain't Big Enough For
Both Of Us (w/Faith No More)/Beat The Clock (New Version)/Big Brass Ring (New Version)/Amateur
Hour (w/Erasure)/Propaganda (Orchestral Version)/When I'm
With You (New Version)/Something For The Girl With Everything
(w/Faith No More)/Orchestral Collage/The No. 1 Song In Heaven
(w/Jimmy Somerville) (Orch. Version)/Never Turn Your Back On
Mother Earth (Orchestral Version)

'BALLS'

CD 2000 (Strange Ways Way 180, Indigo 9523-2) (Germany)
CD 2000 (Oglio Records 89119-2) (USA)
CD 2000 (Recognition Records CDREC 510) (UK)
Red jewel case
Yellow jewel case
Blue jewel case
Green jewel case

Ron Mael
Russell Mael
Tamera Glover – drums
Aksinja Berger – Aeroflot hostess
Amelia Cone – narration on Scheherazade
Produced by Ron and Russell Mael

Balls/More Than A Sex Machine/Scheherazade/Aeroflot/The Calm Before The Storm/How To Get Your Ass Kicked/Bullet Train/It's A Knock-Off/Irreplaceable/It's Educational/The Angels

CD 2000 (Flavour Of Sound Records FVCK-80121) (Japan)
CD 2008 (Lil Beethoven LBRCD 103)
As above plus bonus tracks: **The Calm Before The Opera/The Calm Before The Storm – full length instrumental**

CD 2000 (Festival/Mushroom 333322) (Australia)
As above plus bonus tracks: **The Calm Before The Opera/The Calm Before The Storm – full length instrumental/CD-ROM material**

Limited edition also includes: **Now That I Own The ABC**

'LIL' BEETHOVEN'
LP 2004 (Lil Beethoven LBRV 001)
CD 2002 (Artful LILBCD 2) (UK)
CD 2002 (Palm Pictures 2126) (USA)
Released worldwide
Limited edition hardcover pack

Russell Mael – vocals
Ron Mael – keyboards
Tamera Glover – drums/vocals
Dean Menta – guitars
Produced by Ron and Russell Mael

The Rhythm Thief/How Do I Get To Carnegie Hall ?/What Are All These Bands So Angry About/I Married Myself/Ride 'em Cowboy/My Baby's Taking Me Home/Your Call Is Very Important To Us, Please Hold/Ugly Guys With Beautiful Girls/Suburban Homeboy

CD 2004 "deluxe edition" (Lil Beethoven)
As above plus bonus tracks: **The Legend Of Lil' Beethoven/Wunderbar/The Rhythm Thief (instrumental version)/CD-ROM material**

'HELLO YOUNG LOVERS'
LP 2006 (In The Red ITR 131) (USA)
CD 2006 (Gut GUTCD 53) (UK)
CD 2006 (In The Red 131) (USA)
CD 2006 (In The Red 131) (Canada)
CD 2006 (Bertus) (Benelux)
CD 2006 (Border Music) (Sweden)
CD 2006 (Rough Trade) (Germany)
CD 2006 (Everlasting) (Spain)
CD 2006 (Goodfellas) (Italy)
CD 2006 (Nocturne) (France)
CD 2006 (Tuba) (Norway)
CD 2006 (Kartel) (Poland

Russell Mael – vocals
Ron Mael – keyboards

Tamera Glover – drums/vocals
Dean Menta – guitars
Jim Wilson – guitar
Steve McDonald – bass
Produced by Ron and Russell Mael

Dick Around/Perfume/The Very Next Fight/(Baby Baby) Can I Invade Your Country/Rock Rock Rock/Metaphor/Waterproof/Here Kitty/There's No Such Thing as Aliens/As I Sit To Play The Organ At The Notre Dame Cathedral

'EXOTIC CREATURES OF THE DEEP'
2008 CD (Lil' Beethoven LBRCD 011) (UK)
2008 CD (Lil' Beethoven 11) (USA)
2008 CD (Lil' Beethoven 11) (Germany)
2008 CD (Border) (Scandinavia)
2008 CD (Bertus) (Benelux)
2008 CD (Soyuz Music) (Russia)
2008 CD (Edel) (Portugal)

Russell Mael – vocals
Ron Mael – keyboards
Tamera Glover – drums/vocals
Dean Menta – guitars
Produced by Ron and Russell Mael

Intro/Good Morning/Strange Animal/I Can't Believe That You Would Fall For All The Crap In This Song/Let The Monkey Drive/Intro Reprise/I've Never Been High/(She Got Me) Pregnant/Lighten Up, Morrissey/This Is The Renaissance/The Director Never Yelled 'Cut'/Photoshop/Likeable

2008 CD (Japan)
As above plus bonus track: **Brenda's Always In The Way + video/DVD**

PART FIVE: RARITIES, SOUNDTRACKS AND ODDITIES

UNTITLED ACETATE (AKA 'A WOOFER IN TWEETER'S CLOTHING')
Demo LP 1970
Unreleased

Russell Mael – vocals and bass
Ron Mael – keyboards
Earle Mankey – guitar (and lead vocals on Big Rock Candy Mountain)
John Mendelsohn – drums
Surly Ralph Oswald – bass
Produced by Halfnelson

Chile Farm Farney/Johnny's Adventure/Roger/Arts and Crafts Spectacular/Landlady/The Animals At Jason's Bar And Grill/Big Rock Candy Mountain/Millie/Saccharin And The War/Join The Firm/Jane Church/The Factory

'SPARKS SING FOLK SONGS FROM CALIFORNIA'
Demo cassette 1971
Unreleased

Fa La Fa Lee/High C/Slowboat/Wonder Girl

'ONE AND A HALFNELSON'
Bootleg recorded 1974
Unreleased

Russell Mael – vocals
Ron Mael – keyboards
Adrian Fisher – guitar
Dinky Diamond – drums
Ian Hampton – bass
Trevor White – guitar

Hasta Mañana Monsieur (live 1974)/Something For The Girl With Everything (live 1974)/Talent Is An Asset (live 1974)/Thank God It's Not Christmas (live 1974)/B.C. (live 1974)/Here In Heaven (live 1974)/This Town Ain't Big Enough For Both Of Us (live 1974)/Lost And Found/Barbecutie/Alabamy Right

'MUSIKLADEN'
German TV broadcast recorded 1975
CD 1995 as 'Amateur Hour' (CD and Video CD) (Master Tone MM5125) (Germany)

Russell Mael – vocals
Ron Mael – keyboards
Adrian Fisher – guitar
Dinky Diamond – drums
Ian Hampton – bass
Trevor White – guitar

This Town Ain't Big Enough For Both Of Us/Amateur Hour/B.C./Never Turn Your Back On Mother Earth/Something For The Girl With Everything

MICK RONSON DEMOS
Recorded 1976
Unreleased

Russell Mael – vocals
Ron Mael – keyboards
Mick Ronson – guitar
Sal Maida – bass
Hilly Michaels – drums

Big Boy/Everybody's Stupid/I Want To Be Like Everybody Else

'LIVE AT THE AGORA, CLEVELAND 1976'
Proposed live album
Unreleased

Russell Mael – vocals
Ron Mael – keyboards
Sal Maida – bass
Hilly Boy Michaels – drums
Jim McAllister – guitar
Luke Zamperini – guitar

Nothing To Do/I Want To Be Like Everybody Else/Something For The Girl With Everything/White Women/Talent Is An Asset/I Bought The Mississippi River/Everybody's Stupid/B.C./Equator/This Town Ain't Big Enough For Both Of Us /Amateur Hour/I Like Girls/Big Boy

'LIVE AT THE BOTTOM LINE 12/21/76'
Bootleg
Unreleased

Russell Mael – vocals
Ron Mael – keyboards
Sal Maida – bass
Hilly Boy Michaels – drums
Jim McAllister – guitar
Luke Zamperini – guitar

Nothing To Do/I Want To Be Like Everybody Else/Something For The Girl With Everything/White Women/Everybody's Stupid/B.C./Equator/This Town Ain't Big Enough For Both Of Us/Amateur Hour/I Like Girls/Big Boy

DEMOS
Recorded 1978
Unreleased

Russell Mael – vocals
Ron Mael – keyboards

After Dark/Biggest Party In The World/B.R.E.A.T.H.E./Get Laid/I Wish I Could Dance Like Black People/Trying Day

'BBC ROCK HOUR (LIVE CONCERT AT THE WHISKY 13.06.1982)'
LP 1982 (London Wavelength 324) (USA)

Russell Mael – vocals
Ron Mael – keyboards
Bob Haag – guitar
David Kendrick – drums
Leslie Bohem – bass

Sextown USA/Funny Face/Eaten By The Monster Of Love/Mickey Mouse/I Predict/Moustache/I Married A Martian/Tips For Teens/Angst In My Pants/Wacky Women/Upstairs

'KBFH LIVE CONCERT (LIVE CONCERT 11.07.1982)'
LP KBFH (USA)

Russell Mael – vocals
Ron Mael – keyboards
Bob Haag – guitar
David Kendrick – drums
Leslie Bohem – bass

'IN CONCERT ((LIVE CONCERT 18.07.1983)'
LP 1983

Russell Mael – vocals
Ron Mael – keyboards
Bob Haag – guitar
David Kendrick – drums
Leslie Bohem – bass

'WESTWOOD ONE IN CONCERT (LIVE CONCERT 22.07.1983)'
LP 1983 (Westwood One 83-15) (USA)

Russell Mael – vocals
Ron Mael – keyboards
Bob Haag – guitar
David Kendrick – drums
Leslie Bohem – bass

'BBC ROCK HOUR (LIVE CONCERT, 05.06.1983)'
LP 1983 (London Wavelength 423) (USA)

Russell Mael – vocals
Ron Mael – keyboards
Bob Haag – guitar
David Kendrick – drums
Leslie Bohem – bass

I Wish I Looked A Little Better/Angst In My Pants/All You Ever Think About Is Sex/Modesty Plays/Mickey Mouse/Eaten By The Monster Of Love/Moustache/I Predict/Cool Places

'GET CRAZY'
LP 1983 (Morocco/Motown 6065CL) (USA)

Various artists – includes **Get Crazy/Auld Lang Syne**

'SPLASH DANCE'
LP 1983 (Disneyland/Vista 62520) (USA)

Various artists includes **Minnie Mouse**

'WHERE THE BOYS ARE'
LP 1984 (RCA BL85039) (Germany)

Various artists – includes **Mini Skirted**

'HEAVENLY BODIES'
LP 1984 (Private/Vogue 540115) (France)

Various artists – includes **Armies Of The Night**

BAD MANNERS SOUNDTRACK
Recorded 1984
Unreleased

Bad Manners/Growing Pains/Motorcycle Midget/What You're Wearin * **(duet with Laurie Bell)** /Screaming a.k.a. Scared (Runnings)/Riot With Me * **(performed by Laurie Bell)** /Descended From The Apes (performed by Charlie Sexton) /Things Can Change Overnight * **(performed by Adele Bertei)** /It's Kinda Like The Movie * **(performed by** "Gleaming Spires")/Growing Pains (reprise)

MAI, THE PSYCHIC GIRL SOUNDTRACK
Recorded 1990-1992
Unreleased

The Dream/The Patchwork Symphony (The Wake-Up)/The Matchmakers/The Date/Wagner Metal/Bigger Than Me, Bigger Than You/The Wisdom Alliance/The Tribal Theme/Grandmother's Them/A Glimpse Of Mother/Up From A Dream/What Was That?/Too Bad/The Melancholy Patchwork Symphony/She Used To Be One Of Us/The Chosen Ones (Part 1: The Wisdom Alliance Tour)/That Looks Great On You/The Chosen Ones (Part 2: Turm/Mai Battle)

DEMOS RECORDED 1990-1992

The Farmer's Daughter
The Japanese Have Come…
National Crime Awareness Week
She's An Anchorman
Frankly Scarlett, I Don't Give A Damn
Where Did I Leave My Halo
Retro-Boy Retro-Girl
Love Can Conquer All
Singing In The Shower
This Angry Young Man Ain't Angry No More
Live In Las Vegas
Drawn By Picasso
She's Beautiful (So What!)
Can Can (vocals by 'Eleanor Roosevelt' aka Christi Haydon)

RADIO ONE LIVE – 1994 BBC SESSIONS
Promotional cassette

Russell Mael – vocals
Ron Mael – keyboards

When Do I Get To Sing 'My Way'? (from the Mark Goodyear Roadshow 20 Oct 1994)/Now That I Own The BBC/When Do I Get To Sing 'My Way'?/This Town Ain't Big Enough For Both Of Us/Frankly Scarlett, I Don't Give A Damn (from Simon Mayo Show, 21 Oct 1994)

KNOCK OFF SOUNDTRACK
Recorded 1998
Unreleased

Boat Chase/The Finale/Tong Market/Interrogation/Romance Theme/Night Market/Underwater/Sexy/Chase/V6 Jeans/Piano/Theme

'SPARKS MOVIE MUSIC SAMPLER'
CD 2000 DEF Ltd

Opera Intro/Boat Chase – from *Knock Off*/The Finale – from *Knock Off*/Tong Market – from *Knock Off*/Interrogation – from *Knock Off*/Romance Theme – from *Knock Off* /That Looks Great On You – from *Mai, The Psychic Girl*/The Big Brass Ring – alternate edit/The Patchwork Symphony – from *Mai, The Psychic Girl*/She Used To Be One Of Us – from *Mai, The Psychic Girl*/Night Market – from *Knock Off*/Hey Skinny – alternate edit/Underwater – from *Knock Off*/Sexy – from *Knock Off*/Chase – from *Knock Off*/V6 Jeans – from *Knock Off*/What Was That? – from *Mai, The Psychic Girl*/Piano Theme – from *Knock Off*/Opera/Balls – original version/This Town Ain't Big Enough For Both Of Us – Orchestral *Plagiarism* version/It's A Knock-Off – alternate edit/Looks Looks Looks– original version/When Do I Get To Sing My Way – alternate edit/Cool Places – original version/Change – original version/This Town Ain't Big Enough For Both Of Us – original version

281

'GÜNTER KOCH REVISITED'
CD 2001 (Intermedium 007/Indigo 2 CD 96832)

Various artists – includes **Concerto In Koch Minor**

'One Word One Sound'
CD 2002 (Intermedium rec. 005)

Various artists – includes **Kakadu**

'MORRISSEY – UNDER THE INFLUENCE'
CD 2003

Various artists – includes Halfnelson demo **Arts And Crafts Spectacular**

'MORRISSEY – SONGS TO SAVE YOUR LIFE'
CD 2003 (free with *New Musical Express*)

Various artists includes **Barbecutie**

UNCUT MAGAZINE CLASH TRIBUTE
CD 2003 (*Uncut* November 2003)

We Are The Clash

NORTH AMERICAN HALLOWEEN PREVENTION INITIATIVE: DO THEY KNOW IT'S

HALLOWEEN?
12-inch 2005 Vice Records

Do They Know It's Halloween?/Do They Know It's Halloween? (Radio Edit)/Do They Know It's Halloween? (Disco D Remix)/Do They Know It's Halloween? (Th' Corn Gangg Remix)

Russell Mael sings a few lines on the UNICEF charity single: "We're dying of fear, and they don't even know it!" and "Spell This!!!" Steve McDonald plays bass.

Other contributors include Beck, Thurston Moore and Malcolm McLaren.

PART SIX: DVDs

'SPARKS: LIVE IN LONDON' (SEPTEMBER 2000)
DVD 2000 (Lift Off 84001)

It's A Sparks Show Tonight/Aeroflot/Something For The Girl With Everything/Scheherazade/(When I Kiss You) I Hear Charlie Parker Playing/More Than A Sex Machine/Do-Re-Mi/Angst In My Pants/Ron Performs Waiting for Godot with Rex the Wonderdog/How to Get Your Ass Kicked/Talent Is An Asset/Girl From Germany/Balls/Ron Levitates Baby Leroy/Bullet Train/Beat The Clock/This Town Ain't Big Enough For Both Of Us/No. 1 In Heaven/Never Turn Your Back On Mother Earth/Amateur Hour/When Do I Get To Sing 'My Way'?

'LIL BEETHOVEN LIVE IN STOCKHOLM' (MARCH 2004)
DVD 2004 (Demon Vision DEMONDVD 001) (UK)

The Rhythm Thief/How Do I Get To Carnegie Hall?/What Are All These Bands So Angry About/I Married Myself/Ride 'em Cowboy/My Baby's Taking Me Home/Your Call Is Very Important To Us Please Hold/Ugly Guys With Beautiful Girls/Suburban Homeboy/It's A Sparks Show/National Crime Awareness Week/Here In Heaven/The No. 1 Song In Heaven/Nothing To Do/The Calm Before The Storm/The Ghost Of Liberace/Talent is An Asset/Hospitality On Parade/(When I Kiss You) I Hear Charlie Parker Playing/This Town Ain't Big Enough For Both Of Us/When Do I Get To Sing 'My Way'?/Amateur Hour

'DEEVEEDEE' (LONDON, SEPTEMBER 2006)
DVD 2006 (Liberation 6066)

Rock Rock Rock/Dick Around/Perfume/The Very Next Fight/(Baby Baby) Can I Invade Your Country/Metaphor/Waterproof/Here Kitty/There's No Such Thing as Aliens/As I Sit To Play The Organ At The Notre Dame Cathedral/It's A Sparks Show/Achoo/Something For The Girl With Everything/Tryouts For The Human Race/The Number 1 Song In Heaven/Pineapple/Never Turn Your Back On Mother earth/When Do I Get To Sing 'My Way'?/This Town Ain't Big Enough For Both Of Us/Amateur Hour/Happy Hunting Ground/Suburban Homeboy/Change/Dick Around (reprise)

PART SEVEN: COLLABORATIONS

BIJOU
'Pas Dormit'
LP 1979 (Philips 9120 430) (Canada)

Produced by Ron and Russell Mael

NOEL
'Is There More To Life Than Dancing'
LP 1979 (Virgin V2126) (UK)

Dancing Is Dangerous/Is There More To Life Than Dancing/The Night They Invented Love/Au Revoir/I Want A Man

7-inch 1979 **Dancing Is Dangerous/I Want A Man** (Virgin VS 258) (UK)
12-inch 1979 **Dancing Is Dangerous/I Want A Man** (Virgin VS 25812) (UK)
7-inch 1979 **Dancing Is Dangerous/Au Revoir** (Virgin) (France)
12-inch 1979 **Dancing Is Dangerous/The Night They Invented Love** (Virgin) (France)
7-inch 1979 **The Night They Invented Love/Au Revoir** (Virgin VS 286) (UK)

Written and produced by Ron and Russell Mael

ADRIAN MUNSEY
7-inch 1979 **C'est Sheep (part 1)/C'est Sheep (part 2)** (Virgin VS 226) (UK)
12-inch 1979 **C'est Sheep (part 1)/C'est Sheep (part 2)/C'est Sheep (Part 3)** (Virgin VS 22612) (UK)

Written and produced by Ron and Russell Mael

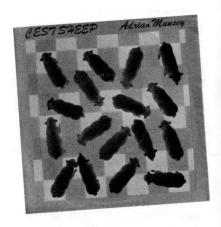

THE RAMONES
'Pleasant Dreams'
LP 1981 (Sire SRK 3571)

Backing vocals by Russell Mael

TELEX
'Sex (Birds And Bees)'
LP 1982 (Interdisc INTO 1)

Brainwash/Drama, Drama/Haven't We Met Somewhere Before?/Long Holiday/The Man With The Answer/Carbon Copy/Exercise Is Good For You/Dream-O-Mat/Sigmund Freud's Party/Mata Hari/Dummy/L'Amour Toujours/Loops/Cloches Et Sifflets/Don't Put All Your Dreams In One Basket/I Can't Turn You Loose/Brainwash (long version)/The Look Of Love/Basta

11 songs lyrics written by Ron and Russell Mael

'I (Still) Don't Like Music Volume 2' Remix Collection
CD 1999 (SSR 211CD)

Includes 'Brainwash (Julian Atkins Mix)', lyrics by Ron and Russell Mael

LIO
'Suite Sixtine'
LP 1982 (WEA WE 835) (France)

I'll Expose You/Marie Antoinette/My Top Twenty/Party For Two/Housewife Of The Year/Clothes

Lyrics by Ron and Russell Mael

THE GO-GOS
'Talk Show'
LP 1984 (IRS 7041)

Includes 'Yes Or No' (Wiedlin/Mael/Mael)

SALON MUSIC
'This Is'
CD 1987 (Japan)

'Special Guest" – Russell Mael

'O Boy'
CD 1988 (Moon 32XM-79) (Japan)

Ron 'African wood' on 'In My Life'
Russell backing vocals on 'Say Hello, Wave Goodbye'

LES RITA MITSOUKO
'Marc Et Robert'
CD 1988 (Virgin CDV 2572) (France)

Hip Kit/Singing In The Shower/Live In Las Vegas

Featuring Ron and Russell Mael

7-inch 1988 **Singing In The Shower/Smog** (Virgin 90489) (France)
12-inch 1988 **Singing In The Shower/Smog** (Virgin 611861-213)
(France)

A-side featuring Ron and Russell Mael

'Re'
CD 1990 (Virgin CDV 2637) (France)

Hip Kit (remix)/Singing In The Shower (remix)

7-inch 1992 **Hip Kit/Andy (live)** (Virgin VS 1296) (France)

A-side featuring Ron and Russell Mael

'Taratara'
CD 1995 (Barclay 529 509-2) (France)

Various artists collection that includes 'Singing In The Shower (live)'

CHEAP TRICK
'Busted'
CD 1990 (Epic 466 8761)

Russell Mael – background vocals on 'You Drive, I'll Steer'

GRAND POPO FOOTBALL CLUB
'Shampoo Victims'
CD 2000 (Atmospheriques 82876501)

Yo Quiero Mas Dinero/La Nuit Est La

Co-written with Ron and Russell, with Russell and Tamera Glover on backing vocals

PIZZICATO 5
'Ca Et La Du Japon'
CD 2001 (Nippon Columbia COCP 50460)

'Kimono' + spoken word (Ron) hidden track

MARC MOULIN (EX-TELEX)
'Top Secret'
CD 2002 (Blue Note 5360342)

Vocals on 'What?' by Ron Mael, engineered by Russell Mael

KRISTIAN HOFFMAN
'Kristian Hoffman And...'
CD (Eggbert ER 80032)

Russell duets on 'Devil May Care'

ORBITAL
'The Blue Album'
2004 CD (ATO 21527)

Sparks collaborate on 'Acid Pants'

PART EIGHT: SELECT COMPILATIONS

'TWO ORIGINALS OF SPARKS'
LP 1975 (Bearsville/WEA K85505) (UK)
CD 1993 as 'Sparks/A Woofer In Tweeter's Clothing' (Dojo LOMACD23) (UK)

Wonder Girl/Fa La Fa Lee/Roger/High C/Fletcher Honorama/Simple Ballet/Slowboat/Biology 2/Saccharin And The War/Big Bands/(No More) Mr. Nice Guys/Girl From Germany/Beaver O'Lindy/Nothing Is Sacred/Here Comes Bob/Moon Over Kentucky/Do Re Mi/Angus Desire/Underground/The Louvre/Batteries Not Included/Whippings And Apologies

'THE BEST OF SPARKS'
LP 1979 (Island/Ariola 25026ET) (Germany)
LP 1979 (Island/Ariola 25026XOT) (Netherlands)
LP 1979 (Island/EMI ILPS9493) (UK)
LP 1979 (Island ILPS9493) (USA)
LP 1981 (Island 9123 030) (France)

This Town Ain't Big Enough For Both Of Us/At Home, At Work, At Play/Hasta Mañana Monsieur/Tearing The Place Apart/Never Turn Your Back On Mother Earth/Get In The Swing/Looks Looks Looks/Amateur Hour/Thanks But No Thanks/Gone With The Wind/Something For The Girl With Everything/Thank God It's Not Christmas

'THE HISTORY OF SPARKS'
LP 1981 (Underdog/Carrere 67826) (France)

When I'm With You/Young Girls/Tips For Teens/Rock'n'Roll People In A Disco World/The No. 1 Song In Heaven/(No More) Mr. Nice Guys/Beat The Clock/Funny Face/Wonder Girl/Just Because You Love Me/Tryouts For The Human Race/Girl From Germany

'PROFILE – DISK 1'
CD 1990 (Rhino/Fine Art R270731) (USA)

Wonder Girl/(No More) Mr. Nice Guys/Girl From Germany/I Like Girls (original 1972 version)/This Town Ain't Big Enough For Both Of Us/Barbecutie/Amateur Hour/Talent Is An Asset/Lost And Found/Hasta Mañana Monsieur/Propaganda/At Home, At Work, At Play/Something For The Girl With Everything/Never Turn Your Back On Mother Earth/Achoo/Get In The Swing/Looks Looks Looks/Happy Hunting Ground/Big Boy/Nothing To Do/Over The Summer/A Big Surprise

'PROFILE – DISK 2'
CD 1990 (Rhino/Fine art R270732) (USA)

Beat The Clock/The No. 1 Song In Heaven/Tryouts For The Human Race/When I'm With You/Funny Face/Tips For Teens/Upstairs/Angst In My Pants/Sextown USA/I Predict/Moustache/Modesty Plays/Cool Places/All You Ever Think About Is Sex/With All My Might/Change/Music That You Can Dance To/So Important

'MAEL INTUITION'
CD 1990 (Island IMCD88) (UK)
CD 1990 (Island PSCD1042) (Japan)
CD 1992 (Island 260693) (Germany)
CD 1992 (Island PHCR18758) (Japan)

This Town Ain't Big Enough For Both Of Us/Amateur Hour/Here In Heaven/Thank God It's Not Christmas/Hasta Mañana Monsieur/Complaints/Never Turn Your Back On Mother Earth/Something For The Girl With Everything/Achoo/Propaganda/At Home, At Work, At Play/Reinforcements/B.C./Hospitality On Parade/Happy Hunting Ground/Without Using Hands/Get In The Swing/It Ain't 1918/In The Future/Looks Looks Looks

'IN THE SWING'
CD 1993 (Spectrum 5500652) (UK)
CD 1993 (Spectrum 5500652) (Germany)
CD 2000 as 'This Town Ain't Big Enough For Both Of Us'

This Town Ain't Big Enough For Both Of Us/Hasta Mañana Monsieur/Amateur Hour/Lost And Found/Never Turn Your Back On Mother Earth/I Like Girls (LP version)/I Wanna Hold Your Hand/Get In The Swing/Looks Looks Looks/England/Big Boy/Something For The Girl With Everything/Marry Me/Gone With The Wind

'THE HEAVEN COLLECTION'
CD 1993 (Columbia 4735152) (France)

This Town Ain't Big Enough For Both Of Us/The No. 1 Song In Heaven/Beat The Clock/Tryouts For The Human Race/When I'm With You/Young Girls/Funny Face/Tips For Teens/I Predict/Angst In My Pants/Modesty Plays/Cool Places/With All My Might/Change/Music That You Can Dance To/So Important/Singing In The Shower (w/Les Rita Mitsouko)/National Crime Awareness Week

'THE HELL COLLECTION'
CD 1993 (Columbia 4735162) (France)

Shout (Live at the Forest National, Brussels 1981)/All You Ever Think About Is Sex (Dance Mix)/Get Crazy (Alternate Recording)/Jingle For 'Brussels' Concert/Rosebud (Extended Dance Mix)/Je M'Appelle Russell/'Nissan' Commercial/Singing In The Shower (Original Demo Version)/Madonna (French Version)/The Japanese Have Come And They Bought My Number One/Jingle Announcing 'Magic Mountain' Concert/Just Got Back From Heaven (Heaven Can Wait Mix)/Dance Godammit (Dance Mix)/The Armies Of The Night (Alternate Version)/Breaking Out Of Prison (Alternate

Version)/Jingle Announcing 'Magic Mountain' Concert/I Predict (Live At The Palace, Hollywood, 1985)/Sextown USA/Achoo (Live At Fairfield Halls, Croydon UK, 1975)/This Town Ain't Big Enough For Both Of Us (Live At Fairfield Halls, Croydon UK, 1975)

'NO. 1 IN HEAVEN – THE ULTIMATE HITS OF SPARKS'
CD 1995 (Bud Music CHP61502) (Germany)

La Dolce Vita/Beat The Clock/The No. 1 Song In Heaven/Rock'n'Roll People In A Disco World/The Greatest Show On Earth/When I'm With You/Tips For Teens/Funny Face/Angst In My Pants/I Predict/Sextown USA/Cool Places/All You Ever Think About Is Sex/A Fun Bunch Of Guys From Outer Space/With All My Might/Pulling Rabbits Out Of A Hat/Modesty Plays

'THE 12 INCH MIXES'
CD 1996 (Bud Music CMP62010)

All You Ever Think About Is Sex (12-inch mix)/Beat The Clock (12-inch mix)/Cool Places (12-inch mix)/Dance Godammit (12-inch mix)I Predict (12-inch mix)/Modesty Plays (12-inch mix)/The No. 1 Song In Heaven (12-inch mix)/With All My Might (12-inch mix)/Young Girls (12-inch mix)

'THE 12-INCH COLLECTION'
CD 1999 (Oglio Records OGL 81605-2) (USA)

All You Ever Think About Is Sex (12-inch mix)/Beat The Clock (12-inch mix)/Young Girls (12-inch mix)/Cool Places (12-inch mix)/Dance Godammit (12-inch mix)/I Predict (12-inch mix)/Modesty Plays (12-inch mix)/Kiss Me Quick (12-inch mix)/Pretending To Be Drunk (12-inch mix)/The No. 1 Song In Heaven (12-inch mix)

'SPARKS OGLIO CATALOG SAMPLER'
CD 1998 (Oglio Records 03749-A) (USA)

Cool Places/All You Ever Think About Is Sex/Angst In My Pants/I Predict/Tips For Teens/Funny Face/When I'm With You/Young Girls/With All My Might/Pretending To Be Drunk

'HTV MUSIC HISTORY'
CD 2001 (HTV HAL 124) (Russia)

Thank God It's Not Christmas/Miss The Start, Miss The End/B.C./Amateur Hour/Looks Looks Looks/Bon Voyage/Here In Heaven/Pineapple/Achoo/Hasta Mañana Monsieur/Never Turn Your Back On Mother Earth/Under The Table With Her/Don't Leave Me Alone With Her/Falling In Love With Myself Again/It Ain't 1918/At Home, At Work, At Play/The Lady Is Lingering/Who Don't Like Kids/Get In The Swing/This Town Ain't Big Enough For Both Of Us/Propaganda/Without Using Hands/Something For The Girl With Everything/Tits/Reinforcements

'SPARKS GREATEST – MUSIC GALLERY'
CD 2001 (Lighthouse 8 290101) (Eastern Europe)

This Town Ain't Big Enough For Both Of Us/Barbecutie/Talent Is An Asset/Lost And Found/At Home, At Work, At Play/Never Turn Your Back On Mother Earth/Get In The Swing/Happy Hunting Ground/Beat The Clock/The No. 1 Song In Heaven/When I'm With You (instrumental version)/Funny Face/Tips For Teens/Upstairs/Cool Places/All You Ever Think About Is Sex/So Important/(When I Kiss You) I Hear Charlie Parker Playing/Balls/How To Get Your Ass Kicked

'THIS ALBUM'S BIG ENOUGH –THE BEST OF SPARKS'
CD 2002 (Music Club MUCB503.2) (UK)

This Town Ain't Big Enough For Both Of Us/Amateur Hour/The No. 1 Song In Heaven /Get In The Swing/Looks Looks Looks/Something For The Girl With Everything/Beat The Clock/Young Girls/Cool Places/La Dolce Vita/Fun Bunch Of Guys From Outer Space/Dance Godammit/Tryouts For The Human Race/Never Turn Your Back On Mother Earth

PART NINE – 21 X 21

Between 16th May and 13th June 2008, Sparks performed all 21 of their albums to date live at the Islington Academy (the first 20 shows) and at the Shepherd's Bush Empire, in London

Full set lists as follows:

'HALFNELSON/SPARKS'
Wonder Girl /Fa La Fa Lee/Roger/High C/Fletcher Honorama/Simple Ballet/Slowboat/Biology 2/Saccharin And The War/Big Bands/(No More) Mr. Nice Guys/England

'A WOOFER IN TWEETER'S CLOTHING'
Girl From Germany/Beaver O'Lindy/Nothing Is Sacred/Here Comes Bob/Moon Over Kentucky/Do Re Mi/Angus Desire/Underground/The Louvre/Batteries Not Included/Whippings And Apologies/Arts and Crafts Spectacular

'KIMONO MY HOUSE'
This Town Ain't Big Enough For Both Of Us/Amateur Hour/Falling In Love With Myself Again/Here In Heaven/Thank God It's Not Christmas/Hasta Mañana Monsieur/Talent Is An Asset/Complaints/In My Family/Equator/Barbecutie

'PROPAGANDA'
Propaganda/At Home, At Work, At Play/Reinforcements/B.C./Thanks But No Thanks/Don't Leave Me Alone With Her/Never Turn Your Back On Mother Earth/Something For The Girl With Everything/Achoo/Who Don't Like Kids/Bon Voyage/Lost And Found

'INDISCREET'
Hospitality On Parade/Happy Hunting Ground/Without Using Hands/Get In The Swing/Under The Table With Her/How Are You Getting Home/Pineapple/Tits/It Ain't 1918/The Lady Is Lingering/In The Future/Looks Looks Looks/Miss The Start, Miss The End/Gone With The Wind

'BIG BEAT'
Big Boy/I Want To Be Like Everybody Else/Nothing To Do/I Bought The Mississippi River/Fill 'Er Up/Everybody's Stupid/Throw Her Away (And Get A New One)/Confusion/Screwed Up/White Women/I Like Girls/Tearing The Place Apart

'INTRODUCING'
A Big Surprise/Occupation/Ladies/I'm Not/Forever Young/Goofing Off/Girls On The Brain/Over The Summer/Those Mysteries/Alabamy Right

'NO. 1 IN HEAVEN'
Tryouts For The Human Race/Academy Award Performance/La Dolce Vita/Beat The Clock/My Other Voice/The No. 1 Song In Heaven/Dancing Is Dangerous

'TERMINAL JIVE'
When I'm With You/Just Because You Love Me/Rock'n'Roll People In A Disco World/When I'm With You (instrumental)/Young Girls/Noisy Boys/Stereo/The Greatest Show On Earth/Singing In The Shower

'WHOMP THAT SUCKER'
Tips For Teens/Funny Face/Where's My Girl/Upstairs/I Married A Martian/The Willys/Don't Shoot Me/Suzie Safety/That's Not Nastassia/Wacky Women/Get Crazy

'ANGST IN MY PANTS'
Angst In My Pants/I Predict/Sextown USA/Sherlock Holmes/Nicotina/Mickey Mouse/Moustache/Instant Weight Loss/Tarzan And Jane/The Decline And Fall Of Me/Eaten By The Monster Of Love/Minnie Mouse

'IN OUTER SPACE'
Cool Places/Popularity/Prayin' for A Party/All You Ever Think About Is Sex/Please Baby Please/Rockin' Girls/I Wish I Looked A Little Better/Lucky Me, Lucky You/A Fun Bunch Of Guys From Outer Space/Dance Godammit/Sports

'PULLING RABBITS OUT OF A HAT'
Pulling Rabbits Out Of A Hat/Love Scenes/Pretending To Be Drunk/With All My Might/Sparks In The Dark (Part One)/Everybody Move/A Song That Sings Itself/Sisters/Kiss Me Quick/Sparks In The Dark (Part Two)/National Crime Awareness Week

'MUSIC THAT YOU CAN DANCE TO'
Music That You Can Dance To/Rosebud/Fingertips/Armies Of The Night/The Scene/Shopping Mall Of Love/Modesty Plays (New Version)/Let's Get Funky/Change

'INTERIOR DESIGN'
So Important/Just Got Back From Heaven/Lots Of Reasons/You've Got A Hold Of My Heart/Love-O-Rama/The Toughest Girl In Town/Let's Make Love/Stop Me If You've Heard This Before/Walk Down Memory Lane/Madonna/Big Brass Ring/It's Kinda Like The Movies

'GRATUITOUS SAX AND SENSELESS VIOLINS'
Gratuitous Sax/When Do I Get To Sing 'My Way'?/(When I Kiss You) I Hear Charlie Parker Playing/Frankly, Scarlett, I Don't Give A Damn/I Thought I Told You To Wait In The Car/Hear No Evil, See No Evil, Speak No Evil/Now That I Own The BBC/Tsui Hark/The Ghost Of Liberace/Let's Go Surfing/Senseless Violins/Marry Me

'PLAGIARISM'
Pulling Rabbits Out Of A Hat/This Town Ain't Big Enough For Both Of Us/The No. 1 Song In Heaven/Funny Face/When Do I Get To Sing 'My Way'?/Angst In My Pants/Change/Popularity/Something For The Girl With Everything/Beat The Clock/Big Brass Ring/Amateur Hour/Propaganda/When I'm With You/Something For The Girl With Everything/Orchestral Collage/Never Turn Your Back On Mother Earth/Looks Aren't Everything

'BALLS'
Balls/More Than A Sex Machine/Scheherazade/Aeroflot/The Calm Before The Storm/How To Get Your Ass Kicked/Bullet Train/It's A Knock-Off/Irreplaceable/It's Educational/The Angels/Katherine Hepburn

'LIL' BEETHOVEN'
The Rhythm Thief/How Do I Get To Carnegie Hall?/What Are All These Bands So Angry About/I Married Myself/Ride 'em Cowboy/My Baby's Taking Me Home/Your Call Is Very Important To Us, Please Hold/Ugly Guys With Beautiful Girls/Suburban Homeboy/Wunderbar

'HELLO YOUNG LOVERS'
Dick Around/Perfume/The Very Next Fight/(Baby Baby) Can I Invade Your Country/Rock Rock Rock/Metaphor/Waterproof/Here Kitty/There's No Such Thing as Aliens/As I Sit To Play The Organ At The Notre Dame Cathedral/Profile

'EXOTIC CREATURES OF THE DEEP'
Intro/Good Morning/Strange Animal/I Can't Believe That You Would Fall For All The Crap In This Song/Let The Monkey Drive/Intro Reprise/I've Never Been High/(She Got me) Pregnant/Lighten Up, Morrissey/This Is The Renaissance/The Director Never Yelled 'Cut'/Photoshop/Likeable/Moustache/Looks Aren't Everything/Big Boy/Goofing Off/Katherine Hepburn/Shopping Mall Of Love/Those Mysteries/Dick Around/Get In The Swing/Looks Looks Looks/Batteries Not Included/Whippings And Apologies/Change/This Town Ain't Big Enough For Both Of Us

ALL THE YOUNG DUDES

Mott The Hoople & Ian Hunter

Campbell Devine

This, the official biography of
Mott The Hoople, traces their
formation and their inevitable
rise to international stardom.
Author Campbell Devine has
successfully collaborated with
Ian Hunter and members of
'Mott' to create a biography
devoid of borrowed information
and recycled press clippings but instead new, sensational and
humorous inside stories, controversial quotes and an array of previously
unpublished views from the band. With first hand input from members
Hunter, Griffin, Watts, Allen and Ralphs, this book gives the complete
insight into the legend of Mott The Hoople. Queen, The Clash, Kiss, Def
Leppard, Primal Scream and Oasis have all cited Mott The Hoople as a
major influence.

Queen's Brian May and Def Leppard's Joe Elliott have provided their own
foreword to pay a long overdue tribute to a band who were simply one of
rock's most treasured.

Already described as the 'definitive tome' on their careers, this unique and
fascinating biography is by far the most scrupulously researched written
work ever produced on Mott The Hoople. This book is welcomed by both
the committed and casual rock reader as well as the ageing rocker and of
course all the young dudes.

Relaunched in 2009 to coincide with the band's re-formation tour after
more than 30 years.

 *Other must-read titles availab*

All The Young Dudes: Mott The Hoople & Ian Hunter
Campbell Devine

Bittersweet: The Clifford T Ward Story
David Cartwright

Burning Britain – A History Of Uk Punk 1980 To 1984
Ian Glasper

Cor Baby, That's Really Me !
John Otway

Deathrow: The Chronicles Of Psychobilly
Alan Wilson

Death To Trad Rock – The Post-Punk fanzine scene 1982-87
John Robb

Embryo – A Pink Floyd Chronology 1966-1971
Nick Hodges and Ian Priston

Goodnight Jim Bob – On The Road With Carter USM
Jim Bob

Good Times Bad Times – The Rolling Stones 1960-69
Terry Rawlings and Keith Badman

Hells Bent On Rockin: A History Of Psychobilly
Craig Brackenbridge

Independence Days – The Story Of UK Independent Record Labels
Alex Ogg

Indie Hits 1980 – 1989
Barry Lazell

Irish Folk, Trad And Blues: A Secret History
Colin Harper and Trevor Hodgett

Johnny Thunders – In Cold Blood
Nina Antonia

Music To Die For – The International Guide To Goth, Goth Metal, Horror Punk, Psychobilly Etc
Mick Mercer

No More Heroes: A Complete History Of UK Punk From 1976 To 1980
Alex Ogg

Our Music Is Red – With Purple Flashes: The Story Of The Creation
Sean Egan

Quite Naturally – The Small Faces
Keith Badman and Terry Rawlings

Random Precision – Recording The Music Of Syd Barrett 1965-1974
David Parker

Rockdetector: A To Z Of '80s Rock
Garry Sharpe-Young

Rockdetector: A To Z Of Black Metal
Garry Sharpe-Young

...om Cherry Red Books:

Rockdetector: A To Z Of Death Metal
Garry Sharpe-Young

Rockdetector: A To Z Of Doom, Gothic & Stoner Metal
Garry Sharpe-Young

Rockdetector: A To Z Of Power Metal
Garry Sharpe-Young

Rockdetector: A To Z Of Thrash Metal
Garry Sharpe-Young

Rockdetector: Black Sabbath – Never Say Die
Garry Sharpe-Young

Rockdetector: Ozzy Osbourne
Garry Sharpe-Young

Songs In The Key Of Z – the Curious Universe of Outsider Music
Irwin Chusid

Tamla Motown – The Stories Behind The Singles
Terry Wilson

The 101 Greatest Progressive Rock Albums
Mark Powell

The Day The Country Died: A History Of Anarcho Punk 1980 To 1984
Ian Glasper

The Legendary Joe Meek – The Telstar Man
John Repsch

The Rolling Stones: Complete Recording Sessions 1962-2002
Martin Elliott

The Secret Life Of A Teenage Punk Rocker: The Andy Blade Chronicles
Andy Blade

Those Were The Days – The Beatles' Apple Organization
Stefan Grenados

Trapped In A Scene – UK Hardcore 1985-89
Ian Glasper

Truth... Rod Stewart, Ron Wood And The Jeff Beck Group
Dave Thompson

You're Wondering Now – The Specials from Conception to Reunion
Paul Williams

Please visit www.cherryredbooks.co.uk for further information and mail order.

*For more information on the
Cherry Red family,
CDs, DVDs, mail order, contact,
merchandise and links to our
associated labels and channels,
please visit www.cherryred.co.uk*

CHERRYRED.TV

CHERRYRED.TV was launched as in Internet TV station in December 2007, with the intention of doing something a little different.

There are currently two sides to the channel. Firstly, the music section where there is some great concert footage to be found from over 100 artists including Alien Sex Fiend. Marc Almond, Exploited, The Fall, Felt, GBH, Hanoi Rocks, Robyn Hitchcock, Jim Bob, Meteors, Monochrome Set, Nico, Spizz, Thompson Twins and Toyah amongst others. This list is being constantly added to.

There is also an interview section where the cherryred.tv team has tracked down some fascinating characters for some great in-depth interviews, divided into three subsections: 'Artists,' 'Label Stories' and 'Business.'

Artists interviewed include Bid, John Fiddler, Morgan Fisher, Claire Hamill, Sonja Kristina, Simon Turner and others, whilst the label story interviews include Cooking Vinyl, El, Glass, Midnight Music, No Future, Nude, Oval and, of course, Cherry Red.

It's early days and we'll see where this particular Cherry Red adventure leads.
If you have any ideas or suggestions, please do contact:
iain@cherryred.co.uk

www.cherryred.tv

CHERRY RED BOOKS

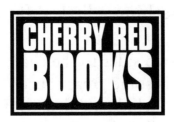

Here at Cherry Red Books we're always interested
to hear of interesting titles looking for a publisher.
Whether it's a new manuscript or an out of
print/deleted title, please feel free to get in touch if
you've written, or are aware of, a book you feel
might be suitable.

richard@cherryred.co.uk
iain@cherryred.co.uk

www.cherryredbooks.co.uk
www.cherryred.co.uk

CHERRY RED BOOKS
A division of Cherry Red Records Ltd.
3a, Long Island House,
Warple Way,
London W3 0RG.